Adobe®

Flash® CS3 Professional Video

STUDIO TECHNIQUES

Robert Reinhardt

Adobe

Adobe Flash CS3 Professional Video Studio Techniques

Robert Reinhardt

Copyright © 2008 Robert Reinhardt
This Adobe Press book is published by Peachpit. For information on Adobe Press books, contact:

Peachpit Press
1249 Eighth Street
Berkeley, CA 94710
510/524-2178
Fax: 510/524-2221

For the latest on Adobe Press books, go to www.adobepress.com

Find us on the Web at www.peachpit.com

To report errors, please send a note to errata@peachpit.com

Peachpit Press is a division of Pearson Education

Project Editor: Wendy Sharp
Developmental Editors: Carol Person, Wendy Katz
Technical Editor: Elliot Mebane
Production Editor: Tracey Croom
Copyeditor: Tiffany Taylor
Compositor: Jerry Ballew
Indexer: Rebecca Plunkett
Cover design: Aren Howell
Cover coordinator: Charlene Charles-Will
Cover illustration: Regina Cleveland

Notice of Rights

Notice of Liability

Trademarks

ISBN 13: 978-0-321-48037-8
ISBN 10:   0-321-48037-6

9 8 7 6 5 4 3 2 1

Printed and bound in the United States of America

Contents at a Glance

Introduction   ix

Section I Working Foundations   1

Chapter 1   Pre-production Primer   3

Chapter 2   Capturing and Processing Video   23

Chapter 3   Compression Primer   43

Chapter 4   Delivery and Deployment Primer   63

Section II Production Essentials   77

Chapter 5   Placing Flash Video on a Web Page   79

Chapter 6   Exploring the FLVPlayback Components   111

Chapter 7   Building Your Own Video Player   159

Chapter 8   Integrating Multiple Bitrates   179

Section III Creative Explorations   211

Chapter 9   Building a Video Index and Playlist   213

Chapter 10 Constructing Banner Ads and
              Captioned Videos   239

Chapter 11 Constructing an Interactive Video Host   257

Chapter 12 Delivering a Reliable Video Experience   291

Appendices

Appendix A Software Installation   329

Appendix B Flash Video Project Checklist   333

Appendix C Encoding Flash Video   337

Appendix D Troubleshooting Flash Video   345

Index   349

Contents

Introduction   ix

Section I   Working Foundations   1

Chapter 1   Pre-production Primer   3
 Designing the Video Experience   3
 Planning Your Video Shoot   7
 Selecting Equipment   9

Chapter 2   Capturing and Processing Video   23
 Capturing Video   23
 Processing Video with Adobe After Effects   31

Chapter 3   Compression Primer   43
 Distinguishing Source Files and Their Differences   43
 Understanding Video File Bitrates   47
 Learning About Player Versions and Codec Options   53
 Determining Your Video Compression Profiles   59

Chapter 4   Delivery and Deployment Primer   63
 File Formats: SWF, FLV, and HTML   63
 Protocols: HTTP vs. RTMP   65
 Delivery: Web Server, Flash Media Server, or CDN?   70
 Playback: Live Streaming vs. Prerecorded   72
 Budgets: Bandwidth and Transfer Rates   74

Section II   Production Essentials   77

Chapter 5   Placing Flash Video on a Web Page   79
 Integrating Flash Video with Dreamweaver   79
 Playing Video with Flash CS3 Components   87
 Gathering Files for Deployment   108

Chapter 6   Exploring the FLVPlayback Components   111
 Overview of the Components   111
 Configuring the Component   112
 Enhancing Playback with Cue Points   121
 Dynamically Placing Video on the Stage   144
 Modifying Skins   150
 Building a Player with Custom UI Components   156

Chapter 7   Building Your Own Video Player   159
 Making a Connection   159
 Building Basic Playback Controls   166
 Reading Metadata from a Flash Video   175

Chapter 8	Integrating Multiple Bitrates	179
	Knowing When to Offer More than One Bitrate	179
	Determining Which Bitrates to Offer	182
	Preparing SMIL Files	184
	Calculating Available Bandwidth	187
	Enabling Dynamic Buffering with a Real-time Stream	200
Section III	**Creative Explorations**	**211**
Chapter 9	Building a Video Index and Playlist	213
	Making a Marker Index for Video	213
	Building a Video Playlist	223
	Playing Video Ads during a Video Feature	231
Chapter 10	Constructing Banner Ads and Captioned Videos	239
	Coding a Video Banner Ad	239
	Controlling Captions with Timed Text XML	252
Chapter 11	Constructing an Interactive Video Host	257
	Planning the User Interface	258
	Producing the Video Footage	261
	Encoding the Flash Video	280
	Developing the ActionScript 3.0 Code Base	285
Chapter 12	Delivering a Reliable Video Experience	291
	Creating a Deployment Plan	292
	Encoding the Flash Video	295
	Developing the Video Player	313
	Customizing the Video Experience with HTML and JavaScript	324
Appendices		
Appendix A	Software Installation	329
Appendix B	Flash Video Project Checklist	333
Appendix C	Encoding Flash Video	337
Appendix D	Troubleshooting Flash Video	345
Index		**349**

About the Author

Robert Reinhardt, VP of the Multimedia Platforms Group for Schematic, is a highly respected authority on Flash and Flash Video. He has authored or co-authored numerous books on Flash, including the *Flash Bible* series and the *Flash ActionScript Bible*, and his blog and other online writings garner a wide audience. With his partner Snow Dowd at [*the*MAKERS], he has developed multimedia courses for educational facilities in Canada and the United States, and is an Adobe Certified Instructor for Flash courses at Portland State University. Robert is a frequent presenter at conferences such as Flashforward, FITC, Flashbelt, WebVisions, and SIGGRAPH. Robert is also a partner and writer at CommunityMX.com, a Web site dedicated to articles and tutorials covering many Adobe products. Robert studied film, video, and photography at Ryerson University in Toronto, Canada. You can find more information about Robert at www.linkedin.com/in/flashsupport.

Robert maintains forums and updates for this book at FlashSupport.com, where you can share questions and answers with other readers. You can contact Robert via e-mail at robert@theMakers.com.

About the Technical Editor

Elliot Mebane is the president of Roguish.com, specializing in Flash video application and game development. Recent projects include a virtual pinball machine, broadband video players, and online phonics software. Roguish clients include E! Networks, Tygirlz.com, Mars (Whiskas), TBWA\Chiat\Day, Yahoo!, Healtheon/Web MD, ClickN' Kids, and McGraw-Hill. Elliot is an Adobe Community Expert and an active member of many Los Angeles digital media user groups.

Acknowledgments

This book could not have been written without the year-long dedication of several individuals. I offer my deepest gratitude to everyone at Adobe Press and Peachpit Press who was involved with this book. Wendy Sharp, the acquisitions editor for this book, gave me the tough love necessary to see this book completed on time. She afforded me several extended schedules to properly research and test the examples I created for this book. My thanks go out to Tracey Croom, this book's production editor, who oversaw the many resources necessary to create this beautiful four-color book. Carol Person, the primary development editor, patiently worked with me on the text and figures to produce a picture-perfect book. Wendy Katz was invaluable as our second project editor while Carol moved across the country. Wendy, I appreciate the fact that you lived in the same time zone for my midnight emails and submissions. More importantly, you treated me like a friend and colleague. Tiffany Taylor carefully copyedited every word in this book. Thank you, Tiffany, for catching more grammatical errors than I'd care for my high school English teachers at Chaminade College Preparatory to see.

Over the last decade, I've written several computer books. While the technical accuracy of each book is largely up to me, the difference between a good computer book and a great computer book often boils down to step-by-step exercises free of errors and to chapters that include extra technical tidbits that help you in special cases. On both counts, this book's technical editor, Elliot Mebane, provided in-depth commentary for every chapter. Thank you, Elliot. I couldn't have asked for a better pair of fresh eyes to review my material.

This book was written across two versions of the Flash authoring tool, Macromedia Flash 8 and Adobe Flash CS3 Professional. I would like to express my appreciation to everyone on the Flash teams. Both the Macromedia and Adobe product teams provided round-the-clock advice and assistance. I owe special thanks to Mike Downey, Jen Taylor,

Richard Galvan, Kenneth Berger, Jeff Kamerer, Mike Chambers, Nivesh Rajbhandari, Jen deHaan, Peter deHaan, Erica Norton, and Hugh Silin.

I received only the best advice and support for Flash Video encoding vendors. I owe many thanks to Randon Morford at Sorenson Media for his time and email responses to my queries. John Luther at On2 gave me quick responses over instant messenger and email. Janet Swift at Telestream provided access to several tech resources on her staff for questions related to Episode Pro.

While writing a book, a computer book author quickly determines who's a good friend. I'd like to thank Richard Blakely and Jerry Chabolla at Influxis.com for providing the real-time streaming Flash Video hosting for this book's examples. One of the video samples I included in Chapter 8 features my father-in-law, Peter Bookmyer, performing a song on my acoustic guitar. Thank you, Peter, for allowing me to record your marvelous voice. I'd also like to thank Phillip Kerman, Geoff Stearns, Joey Lott, Danny Patterson, and Roger Braunstein for their opinions and advice during instant messenger chats.

Finally, and by far the most important thanks of all, I thank my wonderful partner, Snow Dowd, for enabling me to succeed with this book. Not many spouses allow their significant others to take over a home dining space or entire backyard for a video production and a 9 foot by 12 foot green screen. Snow, you're the best partner I could have imagined. During the final production phase of this book, Snow and I had our first child, Maia. What a wonderful gift to celebrate this book's first edition!

I

Introduction

Flash Video has taken the Internet by storm. There's no doubt that the de factor Web standard for video is Flash Video. From YouTube.com to Google Video to all the major broadcast TV Web sites, Flash Video is the video format of choice for content creators who want to offer their audiences a pain-free, high-quality video experience. Not only can Flash Player deliver video to the browser, but it can also integrate advanced interactivity with the video during loading and playback. No other Web video format can boast the wide range of capabilities offered by the Flash platform and ActionScript.

End-to-End Production Know-how

Unlike other Web video formats, Flash Video can require more pre-planning and production work to be successfully deployed on the Internet. Why? Most Web video players simply play their proprietary video file format directly. Simply create a video file, create the HTML code to embed the player plug-in, and you're done. With Flash Video, you always need to create a Flash movie (SWF file) that acts as a go-between for the Flash Video content and the Flash Player plug-in. The Flash movie controls all operations with the Flash Video content. Some Flash Video encoders provide these video-player SWF files with their products, but all are limited in their range of customization. With Adobe Flash CS3 Professional, you can create any video player you want—and this book shows you several approaches to building video solutions that work.

There are two sides to the Flash Video production coin—one side is the realm of encoding source video files to the Flash Video format, and the other side is the world of deploying Flash Video content. There's an art and a science to each side of production, and I've made every attempt to remove any guesswork from both encoding and deployment procedures.

Concepts such as bitrate, frame rate, and real-time streaming will no longer be foreign to you after you've read the content of this book.

Who Should Read This Book?

Adobe Flash CS3 Professional Video Studio Techniques serves as your guide to the world of Flash Video. Whether you're a video editor or video compressionist who's new to the Flash platform, a Web designer or Web developer just starting to learn Flash, or an experienced Flash user, this book can help you master Flash Video.

If you haven't worked with digital video in the past, the "Working Foundations" section will assist you with learning the groundwork of video capture, processing, compression, and delivery formats. Regardless of your video experience, I recommend that you read Chapters 3 and 4, which discuss Flash Video encoding and deployment concepts.

If you're looking for detailed step-by-step examples to practice and master your Flash Video skills, the "Production Essentials" and "Creative Explorations" sections provide over seventy Flash files that you can re-create or build from scratch. You can also skip to specific chapters to learn tasks that are most important to your Flash Video production work. For the last five years, I've been teaching Flash Video concepts in workshops around the world, and this book's lessons are derived from real-world solutions that I've implemented for a wide range of business clients. I've also included a large sampling of source video files that you can use in Flash Video encoding software to help develop your craft of creating high-quality Flash Video.

What's in This Book?

Adobe Flash CS3 Professional Video Studio Techniques is composed of three sections. Here's a quick overview of what you'll find where.

▶ **I: Working Foundations.** Before you can encode and deploy Flash Video, you may need to create, capture, and process the raw video footage that you or your clients have shot. The first chapter demonstrates a variety of Flash Video implementations on the Web and explains the nuts-and-bolts of video production equipment such as video cameras and microphones. I wrote this chapter because far too often I hear complaints that Flash Video produces low-quality video—usually, any low-quality Web video is the direct result of low-quality source material. The second chapter walks you through the process of working with Adobe Premiere and Adobe After Effects to capture and process video footage. Regardless of your Flash Video encoding software, well-processed video footage will always provide better quality Flash Video output. The last two chapters of this section provide an overview of compression and deployment processes. If you've ever felt that you were working blind with all of those encoding settings and server options, these chapters are a must-read.

▶ **II: Production Essentials.** After you've encoded a Flash Video file, you're ready to learn how to build a Flash movie (SWF file) that can play the content on a Web page. The chapters in this section teach you how to use the Flash Video object in Adobe Dreamweaver, the SWFObject JavaScript detection library, the FLVPlayback components in Adobe Flash CS3 Professional, and much more! The examples in these chapters show you how to effectively reuse the same Flash SWF file to play Flash Video content. You don't have to rebuild a Flash SWF file every time you want to put a piece of Flash Video content on the Web—you can pass a dynamic reference to a Flash Video (FLV) file with JavaScript and HTML. You also learn how to build your own Flash Video player with custom ActionScript 2.0 or 3.0 code, using the `NetConnection`, `NetStream`, and `Video` classes. The last chapter of this section shows you how to build a Flash SWF file that can play an appropriate Flash Video bitrate for each user's connection speed.

▶ **III: Creative Explorations.** Learning how to load and play a piece of Flash Video content is just the start of your road to mastery. In the last section, you learn how to build a variety of user interfaces that incorporate Flash

Video content. Want to learn how to build a playlist, or display a list of cue points? Do you need to build a Flash SWF that's less than 20 KB to play video in a banner ad? Maybe you need to create text captions to appear on top of your video content. Perhaps you want to create a video clip with a transparent background. Could you use a Flash solution that automatically updates or installs the Flash Player plug-in? If any of these scenarios sound like a task you need to learn, look no further. In the last section, you can find plenty of Flash files that help you understand the process of building these examples and more!

▶ **Appendices.** You can find several tips and tricks in each appendix located at the end of this book. From project guidelines to encoding-tool comparisons, you might just find the answer to a specific problem.

What's on the DVD?

You will find a nearly-9-GB repository of Flash files and source video clips on the DVD-ROM accompanying this book. Perhaps more importantly, many of the Flash examples discussed in this book can be accessed directly and conveniently via Flash Project (FLP) files that you can open in the Project panel of Adobe Flash CS3 Professional. Whenever feasible, I've also included many Flash documents (FLA files) that can be opened in Macromedia Flash Professional 8. Throughout the book, you will be directed to folder paths that can be found on the DVD-ROM.

In the source folder of the DVD-ROM, you can find all of the source video used in this book's examples. Standard Definition (SD) and High Definition (HD) source clips are included on the DVD-ROM. With High Definition video, you can encode very high-quality Flash Video content, even at resolutions below standard High Definition sizes. Many of the source video files are MPEG files that you can also find and download on www.archive.org, a site featuring many public-domain video clips.

Where Do I Go Beyond This Book?

If you want to continue learning more about Adobe Flash CS3 Professional or Flash Video beyond this book, consider reading other books that I've co-authored, such as the *Adobe Flash CS3 Professional Bible*. I also write articles and tutorials every two weeks for CommunityMX.com, a site dedicated to the mastery of Adobe and former Macromedia products, from Dreamweaver to Flash to After Effects. You can find a list of my most recent articles at www.flashsupport.com/cmx.

Check out this book's Web site at FlashSupport.com for forum threads created by me or other members of the site. Any corrections, updates, or bonus files for this edition of the book will be available on the threads located at www.flashsupport.com/fvst.

If you have a question that isn't answered in the book, I'd encourage you to post the question first on the FlashSupport.com forums, and then send me an email at robert@theMakers.com to follow up. While I make every attempt to personally answer your questions, I've built a membership of over 4,000 users on the site. If I'm not available to review your question, chances are that another experienced Flash designer or developer can.

PART I

Working Foundations

Chapter 1   Pre-production Primer   3

Chapter 2   Capturing and Processing Video   23

Chapter 3   Compression Primer   43

Chapter 4   Delivery and Deployment Primer   63

1

Pre-production Primer

Before you start any Flash Video project, carefully consider how the video will be presented to your audience. Don't fall into the practice of shooting first and planning later. In this chapter, you'll learn what questions you should ask before picking up a video camera or asking for video source files from your client.

Designing the Video Experience

Flash Video—and video viewing in general—can be experienced across a wide variety of form factors. For some projects, the user may click a Play button and watch the video. For other projects, the video augments the information presented to the user. No matter how the video is viewed, it can be displayed in various shapes and sizes in your Flash applications.

If you're creating unique or custom video content, visualize and design how the video will be displayed before you start the video. The way you display the video to the user can predetermine what kind of video works best for the environment. For example, a live stream of a breaking news story may work better in a sidebar adjacent to the other information being displayed. A preview trailer of a high-impact action film may be better displayed in a large central area of the layout or a floating window on top of the content providing details of the film. Regardless of the situation, you need to be familiar with the ways to display Flash Video to an audience.

Nonfloating rectangular video

Traditionally, video content presented to an online audience is displayed in a rectangular window positioned with layout elements such as text, branding graphics, and other elements (**Figure 1.1**).

Figure 1.1 Typical use of video on a Web page.

As you'll see in Chapter 6, "Exploring the FLVPlayback Components," you can easily use this component to add Flash Video to your Flash presentations and applications. As a nonfloating window, this video form has a fixed location in relation to the text and other graphic elements on the stage in your Flash layout.

You can use the FLVPlayback component when you want the user to have access to the video and its controls, or when the video is the primary objective of the presentation.

Floating rectangular video

Another form of Flash Video display is a floating window that overlaps the other content in your Flash layout (**Figure 1.2**). This type of presentation is useful when you want to play short clips (less than a few minutes) as secondary information related to existing text and graphics already visible on the stage. You might want the user to drag this video window to a new location on the stage. Or, you might want the video window to be modal—a *modal* window disables user interactions outside the video area, whereas a *nonmodal* window allows the user to interact with elements such as buttons that are outside the video-playback area.

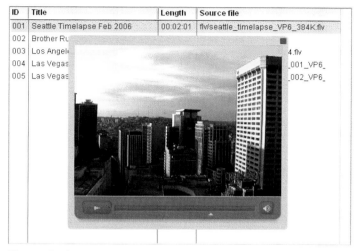

Figure 1.2 Video content that overlays other elements in your Flash movie.

Masked video

One unique aspect of Flash Video for online video experiences is the Flash Player's ability to mask the video frame with just about any vector or bitmap shape. For example, you can display your video content through a circular shape (**Figure 1.3**). By nesting an FLVPlayback component instance or Video object below a mask layer (or dynamically creating a mask shape in ActionScript), you can customize the look and feel of your Flash Video.

You could use an oval mask for video clips of a talking head, or an animated mask to reveal video content during a transition in your Flash presentation.

TIP

▶ You can even overlay transparent Flash Video with HTML elements. The <object> and <embed> HTML tags for the Flash Player feature a WMODE parameter (<object>) or attribute (<embed>). When this value is set to transparent, the Flash movie's background color disappears.

Figure 1.3 Video content playing through a circular mask.

Chroma-keyed video

As video content creators, we can selectively mask portions of the video frame to overlay the footage with other video content. One popular method of creating a transparent background effect is to shoot your subject on a green or blue backdrop (known as a *green* or *blue screen*) and use a video application such as Adobe Premiere Pro or Adobe After Effects to replace the green or blue areas with a transparent fill. The On2 VP6 codec available in Flash Player 8 or higher enables you to retain alpha channels created in your video clips, allowing you to seamlessly composite the video content on top of other Flash or HTML content (**Figure 1.4**).

Figure 1.4 Video content (the dog) with transparent areas reveals other background elements (the forest photo) of the Flash movie's stage.

To use an alpha channel with Flash Video, you should export the content as a QuickTime video file using the Animation codec. This codec supports three 8-bit color channels (RGB) and one 8-bit alpha channel.

Resizable video

A resizable video display enables the viewer to change the frame size of the video. This type of video control is also called *scalable* or *scaling* video. Using ActionScript, you can change the size of the video frame (**Figure 1.5**). You can add a resize button or video corner to any of the video frames discussed in this section. You can also change the video frame from one viewing size to another. For example, you could initially have your video content in a fixed rectangle on the Flash movie's stage. When the user clicked a resize button, the video would reappear in a larger, floating video window that could be moved.

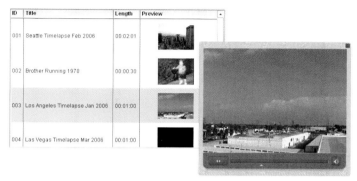

Figure 1.5 The data grid features a list of video thumbnails, which can play at a small size. When clicked, the video plays in a larger window.

Planning Your Video Shoot

When you're creating your video content, spend a little time developing a plan—you'll be amazed how much worry you can eliminate from the video shoot. In this section, I'll provide an overview of core objectives you should take into consideration. However, this is only an overview—several books have been written solely on the subject of planning film and video productions, so consider this section a layperson's quick guide.

Shot list and storyboards

A shot list is usually generated from a *storyboard*, which is a visualization of your video content. Storyboards can be rough or detailed; you don't need to be a skilled character animator or illustrator to produce a storyboard—stick figures are fine. After you have the storyboard outlining the scene(s) for your video content, you can generate a shot list, indicating the locations you need and how many camera angles you need to shoot at each location. A shot list

NOTES

▶ You don't need to encode your Flash Video file at the maximum size allowed by your resize controls. For example, you can change the X and Y scale of the video container with a lower-resolution video clip. Many users prefer to watch video at a large size even though the video's resolution doesn't match the viewing size.

CLOSE-UP

And Beyond...

One of the best reasons to use Flash Player for your rich multimedia experience on the Web is that you can customize just about anything in a Flash movie, especially with loaded multimedia assets. Flash Player lets you invent new ways to display video. For example, you might want a cartoon animation of a character with a Dick Tracy–style video watch and need to create masked video that follows a motion tween (or frame-by-frame animation) of the character's wrist while the video is playing. With Flash, your creative options for video playback are nearly endless.

NOTES

▶ If you typically don't produce your own video content, or your client provides the video content, jump to Chapter 2, "Capturing and Processing Video," for more information on the video formats you should request from your clients.

NOTES

► Shot lists don't need to include multiple shots. Especially for Web video, where content clips may be very short (less than a few minutes), you may shoot one camera angle without any cuts or transitions.

► You can find templates, storyboard samples, and shot lists in the Audio/Video Articles section of the links page at www.flashsupport.com/links.

itemizes every camera angle you want to take with you into the editing room.

Location scouting

After you've compiled a storyboard and a shot list, you need to determine where to record the video footage. The options will vary based on your budget and shooting schedule. Here's a quick list of things to do at each location you're considering:

► **Bring your camera(s).** If you have access to the camera(s) you'll be using on the shooting day, go through the motions of setting up the equipment at each location. This rehearsal is often referred to as a *camera test*. Don't be shy about shooting some footage; then, watch the footage back in your studio. Not only will you feel less stressed when you return for the shoot, but you'll also discover any problems that may be specific to the location, thus enabling you to bring additional equipment to correct the problem. For a more detailed explanation of a camera test, check out this book's resources at www.flashsupport.com/links, and go to Audio/Video Articles.

► **Observe natural light.** Often, a location will have ample ambient light, ranging from existing lighting fixtures to natural sunlight. Try to visit each location at the same time of the day that you'll be shooting on the production day.

► **Listen for noise.** Does the location have a loud heating or cooling system? Are you in the middle of a field with frequent wind gusts? Is there more or less noise at different times of the day or from one day of the week to the next? If you discover odd noises on the location site, come prepared with proper windscreens for your microphones.

► **Check the local city office for required permits.** If you're shooting on private property, you'll need to secure permission from the property owner to be on the location for shooting (and for scouting!). If you're shooting on private or public property, you'll likely need a permit for on-location shooting, especially if you need extensive parking arrangements for production vehicles.

Talent

A high-quality acting performance is very important in your content. (Not all video requires actors.) Don't settle for a quick volunteer as an actor (unless he or she happens to be talented!). You've likely seen TV commercials on your local station featuring the proprietor of a car dealership, carpet showroom, and so on; acting is one key feature that set these commercials apart from nationwide commercials.

To find actors, you can post listings in your local paper or weeklies, as well as online at sites such as craigslist.org. Don't be afraid to have a casting call to audition actors, even if you have little or no budget. Depending on your location, there may be a large community of unemployed actors looking for a chance to practice their craft.

Wardrobe, props, and other considerations

Other factors that influence the quality of your video include the costumes (or wardrobe) your actors wear, the objects your actors handle during the shoot (props), and surrounding elements such as parked cars, passers-by, and extras. The more time you (or someone you can hire) can spend carefully selecting and managing these tertiary elements, the more professional your content will be.

Selecting Equipment

The old adage, "garbage in, garbage out," applies to video content as well. The better your original footage, the less hassle, and the higher quality your final Flash Video will be. Many content creators mistakenly believe that Web-quality video doesn't require broadcast-quality video, and they use sub-par techniques for video production. Part of this belief lies in the fact that Web video frame sizes are usually 320 by 240 pixels, roughly a quarter of the resolution used for standard definition (SD) television broadcast. But resolution is just one aspect of the video experience;

other factors such as image sharpness, lighting aspect ratios, and audio clarity affect the overall quality of the video. In this section, you learn how to prepare for a video shoot to obtain the highest quality video source material for your Flash Video production.

Video formats

A new video format seems to spring up every year, and the task of keeping up with the latest and greatest video technology is almost impossible. Here's a broad overview of the video acquisition formats currently on the market, from highest to lowest quality.

High definition (HD) video

One of the most commonly used buzzwords in digital video today, high definition (HD) video has quickly become an affordable high-quality video format for both consumers and professionals. HD is a general term for video that is usually 1280 by 720 pixels (known as 720p) or 1920 by 1080 pixels (known as 1080i or 1080p) frame size. Both of these frame sizes have a 16:9 aspect ratio, commonly referred to as *widescreen*. You need a monitor or television capable of displaying HDTV signals in order to view the full resolution of HD video.

The frame rate of HD video can vary from 23.97 progressive frames per second (fps) to 60 interlaced fps, depending on the acquisition format. A *progressive* frame of video contains information for every pixel row. An *interlaced* frame breaks up the full video frame across two fields of video, each containing half the pixel rows for the frame. The terms progressive and interlaced are also referred to as *scan modes*, because they describe how each frame of video is captured by a camera and displayed on a TV or monitor The effects of interlacing can most easily be seen on subject matter that moves quickly across the camera's view—because the subject isn't in the same position across the two fields of a frame, jagged horizontal lines appear around the subject when the video is paused (**Figure 1.6**). When the camera's view or subject stays fixed in one position, the effects of interlacing are minimized (**Figure 1.7**).

Figure 1.6 An interlaced frame of video, shot while the camera was zooming on the subject.

Figure 1.7 An interlaced frame of video, shot while the camera was fixed on a slow-moving subject.

The frame rate and scan mode required for HD video depends on the subject matter. Several sports networks have adopted 720p as their HD format, with the preconception that sports fans love to pause their favorite moments or watch them in slow motion. A full progressive frame lends itself to this HD format because a single frame of 720p video contains the full vertical resolution, or 720 lines. However, with 1080i HD video, a paused frame only contains half the vertical resolution, or 540 lines.

If your video will be watched on television, an interlaced resolution is fine—you're not likely to watch sitcoms or dramas in slow-motion, and the perceived detail and sharpness of a 1080i image is higher than a 720p image.

What does all this mean for Flash Video, and online Web video in general? Thankfully, all computer monitors display progressive frame rates—you don't need to worry about your Web audience. Because computer monitors are progressive displays, it's best to de-interlace any footage acquired in 1080i or any interlaced format (more interlaced formats are discussed in the following section). *De-interlacing* is the process of combining interlaced frames into one frame. Most video production tools offer a de-interlacing filter or control.

Initially, each video camera manufacturer rolled out its own implementation of HD video, as outlined in the following

NOTES

▶ Some HDTV sets are capable of displaying 1080p, or full frame 1920 by 1080 pixels non-interlaced. Although this isn't the norm for the majority of HDTV units, presumably more 1080p content will become available over the next few years. Currently, most HD content broadcast in North America is 1080i. To date, no 1080p entry-level camcorders are on the market.

list. Luckily, since 2005, most manufacturers have rallied behind the HDV format:

▶ **Sony HDCAM and HDCAM SR:** One of the first commercial HD formats to hit the market, Sony's HDCAM equipment is targeted to high-end production facilities such as film and broadcast television studios. Equipment prices are in the $60,000 to $100,000 range. The Sony HDW-F900 CineAlta camera can be rented for about $1,100 a day at professional video stores. Most multimedia producers don't need this prohibitively expensive hardware.

▶ **Panasonic DVCPro-HD / DV100/ D7-HD:** Panasonic's high-end HD format, commonly referred to as DVCPro-HD, is available across a wide price range. The high end matches Sony's HDCAM line. On the low end, cameras such as the Panasonic AG-HVX200 (priced around $8,500 and usually available for rent at professional video stores for $250 a day) provide 720p or 1080i resolution at a variety of frame rates. The AG-HVX200 is one of the first cameras to use Panasonic's P2 card technology, which records HD video directly to digital media resembling PC cards (or PCMIA cards) for laptop computers. The DVCPro-HD format was designed for optimal recording of 720p resolution; although the format can support 1080i, only 1280 horizontal pixels (versus the maximum of 1920) are recorded, resulting in some resolution loss.

▶ **HDV:** In 2003, four key manufacturers—Canon, Sharp, Sony, and JVC—agreed to adopt the High Definition Video (HDV) standard. The most important factor in the agreement is the use of miniDV tapes. These tapes are widely adopted for SD digital video camcorders and can provide backward compatibility for SD formats on newer HD cameras. HDV camcorders are by far the most accessible cameras for multimedia producers (including you!) to purchase or rent. You can buy high-quality HDV camcorders for less than $3,000 or rent them for $200 a day or less. In order for HD video data rates to fit on miniDV tape, you can make some compromises with the native frame size. For example, Sony's

NOTES

▶ For more information about the HDV format, read the Adobe white paper "Understanding and Using High-Definition Video." You can find the link to this PDF document on the links page in the Audio/Video Articles section: www.flashsupport.com/links.

HDV camcorders use a 1440 by 1080 frame size instead of the full 1920 by 1080 frame size.

If you decide to shoot video in the HD format, you'll most likely use HDV. Another critical aspect of the HDV adoption is the ability to record HD video in the following resolutions and frame rates:

▶ 720 lines; 60, 50, 30, or 25 fps progressive (720p)

▶ 1080 lines; 30 (60i) fps, 25 (50i) interlaced (1080i)

Potentially, future HDV cameras may support the following specs:

▶ 720 lines; 24 fps progressive (720p)

▶ 1080 lines; 30, 25, or 24 fps progressive (1080p)

Not all HDV cameras support all these recording modes. JVC has generally adopted 720p modes, whereas Sony has adopted 1080i modes. Regardless of the mode, the maximum data transfer rate for HDV over FireWire (or IEEE1394) is the same as miniDV: 25 Mbps. As such, native HDV footage consumes about 250 MB per minute. Make sure you have enough space on your computer system to store the content. HDV footage is recorded with MPEG2 compression for video and MPEG1 Audio Layer 2 compression (384 Kbps) for sound.

Standard definition (SD) video

The vast majority of prosumer (aka professional + consumer) equipment available today records video at standard definition. The newer camcorders sold at popular retail outlets such as Best Buy and Circuit City are often DV camcorders that use miniDV tape. You can still find other video formats on older camcorders. SD video usually has a 4:3 aspect ratio, with a frame size of 720 by 480, 720 by 486, 640 by 480, or 640 by 486.

If you live in a country that uses the NTSC signal standard, such as the United States, Canada, or Japan, SD camcorders record at a frame rate of 29.97 fps (sometimes rounded up to 30 fps, or 60i) with interlaced frames. If you live in a country that uses the PAL standard, like the UK, SD camcorders record at a frame rate of 25 fps with progressive frames.

CLOSE-UP

1440 by 1080: How Does It Work?

Most if not all HDV camcorders use a 1440 by 1080 frame size but still display the video image at a 16:9 aspect ratio. If you do the math, 1440 by 1080 is technically a 4:3 aspect ratio. How can it be HD? HDV camcorders record the video image at 1440 by 1080, but the image is stretched to 1920 by 1080 during playback. If you capture HDV to your computer (as discussed later in this chapter), most video applications such as Adobe Premiere Pro or Apple Final Cut HD will properly display the video image. However, some applications (such as Ulead Movie Factory 5) can display the video at a 4:3 aspect ratio. Your best bet for proper display is to capture the video with the application you'll use to edit the footage.

► For more information on color-sampling space, see Adam Wilt's excellent articles "The DV, DVCAM, and DVCPro Formats," and "DV Pix: Sampling Methods." You'll find links to these articles in the Audio/Video Articles links page at www.flashsupport.com/links.

Introduced in 1996, the miniDV digital tape format and the DV system revolutionized desktop video and nonlinear editing systems. This tape format records a digital signal compressed in the DV codec. Using IEEE1394 or FireWire connections available on most computer systems, digital video can be easily captured from miniDV camcorders without any resolution loss. Prior to the advent of miniDV, most video footage was acquired from an analog (nondigital) signal with expensive capture cards installed on desktop systems. In addition, miniDV footage uses compression ratios that are much friendlier for storage on hard drives. Uncompressed SD footage can use as much as 30 MB of storage *per second*! If you do the math, that's about 1.75 GB of space per minute of footage. DV footage captured from miniDV tape consumes far less space—about 2 GB per 9 minutes of footage. All DV formats capture video with a 720 by 480 frame size and use a 4:1:1 color-sampling space.

SD video can be recorded on the following media:

► **Sony Digital BetaCam (or DigiBeta):** This digital tape format is considered the gold standard of SD digital video, with one of the highest quality color-sampling spaces available in digital video (4:2:2). This standard is at the highest end of commercial video production and isn't employed by most multimedia producers. DigiBeta uses its own compression codec and tape formats separate from DV and miniDV.

► **Sony DVCAM:** This digital tape format records the DV signal to standard miniDV cassettes, with a higher (that is, faster) track pitch than standard miniDV camcorders. DVCAM formats also record audio in locked sync with the video frame. Locking the audio track means there's little chance the audio track will be out of sync with the video track. Popular DVCAM camcorders include Sony's PD line, such as the Sony PD-170. The line resolution of DVCAM tape is the same as miniDV: approximately 525 lines.

► **Panasonic DVCPro 25 and 50:** Panasonic dubs its version of miniDV DVCPro 25, where the *25* stands for 25 Mbps. DVCPro 25 is similar to Sony's DVCAM in that a faster track pitch is used to reduce errors. However, DVCPro 50 is more on par with Sony's DigiBeta standard. The *50* in DVCPro 50 represents 50 Mbps, the bitrate used for recording. DVCPro 50 uses a vastly superior color-sampling space (4:2:2) and produces much higher quality images than Sony DVCAM, DVCPro 25, and miniDV.

▶ **DV and miniDV:** This is the most popular tape format for digital video and one of the most affordable. You can buy a 60-minute miniDV tape for less than $5, and compared to those clunky VHS tapes, a miniDV cassette is incredibly small—6.5 cm long by 5 cm wide by 1 cm high. A miniDV tape is capable of recording 525 lines of video resolution, exceeding the resolution used by the NTSC broadcast signal.

▶ **Digital 8:** Introduced by Sony to help Hi8 camcorder owners transition to digital video, the Digital 8 format uses standard Hi8 video tape to record DV signals. You can also play and record the older analog Hi8 (and Video 8) signal. The process for capturing video from a Digital 8 tape or miniDV tape is identical, using IEEE1394 (FireWire) to transfer the footage to your computer. Unless you have a collection of Hi8 (or Video 8) tapes, don't feel compelled to buy a camcorder that uses Digital 8 technology.

▶ **DVD format video recording:** In 2003, Sony introduced one of the first video camcorders to record digital video directly to a small DVD recordable disc. The recorded disc can be popped into most DVD players and played back instantly, cutting out the tedious process of capturing video to your computer and outputting to a recordable DVD disc. This format was introduced for consumers who don't want this capture hassle and don't edit their footage. This format automatically compresses a SD signal to the same MPEG2 codec used by DVD Video technology.

▶ **Super VHS (S-VHS) or Hi8:** Once the "high definition" of analog video, some camcorders could record high-quality SD video onto Super VHS tape (the same tape cassette as VHS) or 8 mm videotape. These tape formats capture up to 410 lines of horizontal resolution, 25 percent less than miniDV. More important, the captured signal with S-VHS and Hi8 is analog; during the capture process to your computer, resolution and detail in the video image are lost.

▶ **VHS, VHS-C, Video 8:** These tape formats were among the first consumer tape formats to be widely used. Although camcorders that used these tape formats were much more convenient than the Super 8 film cameras of the 1970s, the resolution recorded by these devices is less than half (roughly 250 lines) of the resolution of SD television sets. In other words, a VHS recording is equivalent to a 320 by 240 video image, with very high compression.

Which video is best for your needs? You should start with nothing less than a camcorder that can record onto miniDV tape. Anything less will result in low-quality video at the beginning of the production process—you won't be able to go back and enhance the video quality in post-production. The next question is which definition format to use: standard or high. If your budget can support the purchase or rental of an HDV camcorder, you'll reap more benefits through the Web video production process. You'll also be able to repurpose the video footage for other needs of your business clients, such as building a DVD Video (or HD DVD or Blu-Ray) disc.

Video cameras

In any class of video formats, you'll find a range of camcorders that produce widely varying results. Just because you have a miniDV or HDV camcorder doesn't mean your camera can produce great-looking video. Three primary categories define the quality of the video image produced by your camcorder: the imaging device in the camcorder, the quality of the optics, and exposure control.

Imaging device

One factor that distinguishes the high-end camcorders from the low-end is the type of imaging-capture device installed behind the lens of the camcorder. In other words, how well

Multifunction Digital Cameras

Today's market offers hundreds of reasonably priced digital cameras and camera phones that also function as digital video camcorders. Most of these multifunction devices record to removable disk media, such as a Secure Digital (SD) card, a Compact Flash (CF) card, or a Memory Stick card. All these cameras use built-in hardware compression to record video, usually MPEG2 or MPEG4. The quality of the video depends on several factors, including lens quality, frame size, and frame rate. Regardless of the video quality, though, most multifunction cameras record a mono (single channel) audio track with subpar microphone technology, resulting in low-quality audio.

does the camera capture the quality of light coming through the lens? There are three types of capture sensors:

▶ **Three CCD or three-chip:** Most camcorders use a charged coupled device (CCD) to convert visible light into electric impulses that can be converted into binary data stored on the camera's tape or storage card. High-end cameras have three CCD plates, one per color channel: Red (R), Green (G), and Blue (B). A prism behind the camera's lens diverts the appropriate color wavelengths to the corresponding chip. As such, the color fidelity captured by these cameras is much better than cheaper models with only one CCD. You'll spend $500 to $1,000 or more for a three-CCD camcorder, compared to its single-CCD counterpart.

▶ **CMOS:** Sony's newer HDV prosumer line of cameras use a Complementary Metal Oxide Semiconductor (CMOS) chip instead of one or more traditional CCDs. CMOS-based cameras require less power (and thus have a longer battery life) but don't necessarily perform better in low light conditions. Some research indicates that a single CMOS camera can yield better color fidelity than a three-chip camera.

▶ **Single CCD:** Most consumer-end miniDV camcorders use a single CCD to process image information. Although a single CCD uses less power than three CCDS, three CCDs can better process color information, yielding a higher quality image.

Bottom line: If you can get your hands on a three-chip camcorder (or a newer CMOS camcorder), you'll have a better video image when you head into post-production.

Lens quality

Another gap between inexpensive miniDV cameras and their more expensive counterparts is the type of lens used by the camera. Most inexpensive miniDV cameras (under $1,000) suffer from two problems: inferior lens elements and small apertures. A larger lens can gather more light than a small one. The more light, the less digital noise you'll see in your final video image. Also, be sure your camera has a suitable optical zoom for your video shooting needs. If you need telephoto capability, don't rely on digital zoom technology for a clean, sharp picture. Some cameras, such as Canon's XL-1 series, allow you to use interchangeable lenses. Most camcorders have a fixed lens and use a variety of lens adapters to change the effective focal length of the camera.

Another factor to consider with a camera's lens is the quality of image stabilization. Just about all camcorders have some degree of camera-shake correction, but you should compare the image stabilization quality of cameras in your price range. Inferior stabilizers noticeably soften the image quality, whereas other systems engage the stabilization only when excessive movement is detected.

Finally, be sure you're comfortable with the camera's focusing mechanism. Some cameras may not offer a manual focusing ring by the lens to control focus or zoom level. Even if your camera has such rings, check to see if the ring controls an electronic servo to control the lens, or if the ring is directly connected to manual mechanisms to alter the lens elements. Usually, the latter offers far greater control, precision, and responsiveness compared to electronic-driven parts.

Exposure control

You should be comfortable with the degree of control the camera offers for various aspects of exposure, from shutter speed to aperture to white balance. Perhaps more important, be sure these controls are easily accessible with the buttons on the exterior of the camera—some cameras hide critical controls deep within onscreen menus.

Microphones

It doesn't matter what kind of video image you can attain with your camera if the sound portion is filled with background noise or if you can barely hear your actors speaking. From home theaters to multimedia slideshows, budgets for audio quality and equipment are usually forgotten or overlooked until the last minute. Some experts recommend spending at least half your equipment budget on high-quality sound recording devices. Even the high-end camcorders have a less-than-ideal microphone, so don't assume your fancy camera's going to do the job of recording audio on its own.

When you're considering audio recording devices, there are two general types: balanced and unbalanced.

Balanced audio

A *balanced* audio signal separates the electric impulses on three separate wires: positive, negative, and ground (neutral). By adding a ground wire to a microphone cable, the source signal can be carried more faithfully to the recording device. Typically, microphone signals are weak and easily interfered with by other electromagnetic fields (EMFs) generated by power cables or radio equipment. The industry standard for balanced audio is an XLR connector (**Figure 1.8**). If your camera doesn't support XLR connectors (most high-end camcorders feature them), you can buy an XLR adapter box that converts the signal to a standard mini jack.

Figure 1.8 XLR connectors: male (left), female (right).

Most microphones that use XLR connections require *phantom power*, an electric current supplied to the microphone's elements. Most camcorders with XLR connections can supply phantom power. If your camera doesn't supply phantom power, make sure your microphone can accept an additional power source such as an AA battery.

Unbalanced audio

If your microphone has only two wires throughout its connecting cable (one for the positive current and another for the negative current), your microphone signal is labeled *unbalanced*. Although you can find quality microphones that use only two wires, most unbalanced microphones don't produce the same results as balanced microphones. Most mid- to low-end camcorders that accept external microphones use a standard unbalanced ⅛-inch mini jack for microphone plugs (**Figure 1.9**). If you must use an unbalanced microphone, make sure the length of the cable is as short as possible.

Figure 1.9 A standard mini jack.

NOTES

▶ The dvcreators.net site features an excellent "shotgun shootout" comparing several shotgun microphones. For more information, see the Audio/Video Articles section of links at www.flashsupport.com/links.

TIP

▶ Be sure to watch your combination of daylight and tungsten light sources. Tungsten (indoor) lighting usually has a yellow cast or quality, whereas daylight (outdoor) lighting has more of a blue cast. Most camcorders have a white balance setting. Don't rely on an automatic setting—set the white balance to the light source that is predominant in your scene. More advanced camcorders may have a custom white-balance setting: Frame a piece of white board (or wall) that receives light from your sources, and press the white balance button to customize the white level to the light in the scene.

NOTES

▶ For more information on lighting a professional video shoot, look at the DV Enlightenment DVD-Video disc sold by dvcreators.net. You'll find a link to this disc in the Audio/Video Articles section link page at www.flashsupport.com/links.

Regardless of the audio signal type, you can easily spend thousands of dollars on high-quality microphones; but for less than $500, you can buy an excellent shotgun microphone (with a balanced signal) for your camcorder. A *shotgun* microphone is considered unidirectional, designed to pick up the sound in the direction the microphone is pointed. Most built-in camera microphones are *omnidirectional*, enabling the microphone to pick up sound in all directions.

The type of microphone(s) you need on a video shoot will depend on your subject matter. If you can bring your microphones to a location while testing, you can test the noise picked up by each type. Often, you may want an omnidirectional mic to pick up crowd and street noises. However, if you want to narrow the recorded audio to your actors' voices only, be sure to position a shotgun-style microphone as close to your subject as possible. You can also use a lavalier mic that pins to your subject's clothing to pick up their voice. This type of microphone is best used with a wireless UHF microphone system connected to your camcorder.

Lighting

Another aspect of video shots that multimedia producers often overlook is lighting. Most amateur video uses available light, or the naturally occurring and existing light at a location. Available light can be from the sun, lighting fixtures in a room, or street lamps, to name a few examples. If you conducted a camera test at a location and determined the available light is adequate, you may not need to bring additional lighting equipment. More often than not, though, you'll find that adding your own light sources gives you greater creative control over the video's mood and overall picture quality.

You can rent lighting kits for as little as $50 per day from local pro photo or video stores, or purchase a comprehensive DV lighting kit for just under $2,000. You don't have to spend a lot of money to buy accessories that enable you to work with available light—having some white posterboard or foam core on hand can help you reflect (or bounce) light back onto your subject matter.

Tripods and stands

No video shoot is complete without a tripod for your camera. Unless you specifically want a "reality TV" or hand-held look to your video, always mount your camera on a sturdy tripod. Level the tripod's base below the head, so your camera's view doesn't appear tilted or skewed—some tripods include a built-in level, but you can purchase a small level at your local hardware store that you then place on the tripod head as you adjust the legs. If you're planning to keep the camera in a fixed position during the entire take of a scene, turn off any image-stabilization feature (like SteadyShot on Sony cameras). Image stabilization can often soften the image quality.

Also make sure you have stands for additional lights, bounce cards, microphones, and backdrops. It's usually a good idea to have sandbags (specifically designed for stands) draped over the base of a stand, on top of its legs, to keep the stand in place. Anything from wind movement to slight tugs on a light's cable can send an expensive piece of equipment barreling to the ground, potentially damaging the equipment or injuring someone on the site. You should also tape down any wires that run between the stands and your recording equipment. Some crews even use striped yellow-and-black-banded caution tape along the edges of stands and stand legs so they're visible to everyone on the site.

Hard drives and storage

Because storage media has become relatively inexpensive compared to other equipment costs, don't underestimate the amount of storage you'll need for your video footage. Remember that 9 minutes of captured DV footage requires 2 GB of file space. One project can easily eat up a 300 GB external hard drive. It takes only one 60-minute DV tape to occupy 13 GB of space on your system.

NOTES

▶ Native HDV format recorded on miniDV tape typically requires the same amount of space on your system.

You may opt to record directly to nonlinear media from your camera. Companies such as Focus Enhancements (www.focusinfo.com) have products like the FireStore FS-4 that hook directly to your DV or HDV camcorder to record content. After you've recorded the material, you connect

NOTES

▶ One of the best places to read about the latest in camera and video equipment reviews is DVmag.com. You may need to register (for free) on the site to access the articles, but it's well worth the effort. Also, you'll find information and forums at dvcreators.net. For a comprehensive list of video and audio resources, visit the links page for this book at www.flashsupport.com/links.

the unit (essentially a portable hard drive) to your computer. Each take is available as a separate file, eliminating the need to capture the video in real-time. Although these units are expensive, ranging from $800 to $2,000, you'll save hours of time in the edit room.

Backdrops

A *backdrop* is any material or surface that you place behind the subject matter you're shooting. You can create your own backdrop from large pieces of colored fabric mounted to stands or hooks, or purchase high-quality durable backdrops from pro photo and video stores. A backdrop can serve many purposes beyond the immediate aesthetic quality behind the subject matter. Backdrops can help reduce echo in an otherwise sparse studio or room. The textures of a backdrop can emphasize the quality of light behind the subject. Backdrops can also serve as chroma key backgrounds that are removed later in post-production with a tool such as Adobe After Effects. I talk more about chroma key removal in Chapter 11, "Creating an Interactive Video Host."

2

Capturing and Processing Video

After you've shot the video footage you want to use online or for your business, the next step is saving the video on your desktop computer. In this chapter, you'll learn the dos and don'ts of video capture. At the end of the chapter, you'll perform fundamental video effects on your footage in Adobe After Effects.

Capturing Video

Unless the video footage you've acquired was shot on an analog tape format such as VHS, Hi8, or high-resolution Betacam SP, the process of digitizing the video footage into an editable file on your desktop is simple and straightforward. *Digitizing* is a general term used to describe the process of converting media content into binary files. If you have DV or HDV content on a miniDV tape (or any comparable format), the camera has digitized the footage on the tape—the content is already binary. Unlike digital still-camera files, DV and HDV video aren't recorded as named files, so you can't copy a file from one hard drive to another. Most digital video footage is captured in real time, which means the footage must be played back at the same rate it was recorded. That's one of the primary drawbacks of recording to linear media such as a videotape—there's no random access to content. You can't instantly jump to the middle of the videotape to view the footage you recorded.

Guidelines for better video captures

Most nonlinear editors (NLEs) like Adobe Premiere Pro and Apple Final Cut Pro have a similar approach to capturing digital video. I describe the capture process in the following sections.

Connecting the video device to your computer

Most DV and HDV camcorders or videotape recorders (VTRs) connect to your desktop computer with an IEEE 1394 cable, commonly referred to as FireWire (Apple) or iLink (Sony). Most video cameras have a four-pin port, whereas most desktop computers have a six-pin port. The extra two pins are used to power certain FireWire devices, such as a small external hard drive. Most Windows-based laptops have a four-pin port. Make sure you have the correct cable configuration for your device and computer. You can find cables in four-pin to four-pin, four-pin to six-pin, or six-pin to six-pin variations. You can also purchase a six-pin to four-pin adapter to convert a six-pin cable.

Running your video capture program

Each video-editing application that supports video capture has its own way of entering the capture process. Usually, the capture option is in the File > Import menu, the Window menu, or the Tools menu.

Log the video clips you want to capture. The process of logging footage can be time consuming. Create in and out points as you watch all the footage, and then wait for the computer and camera (or video deck) to seek to the each segment and capture the video frames in real-time. Depending on your video-editing application, you can specify one or more video clips on your camcorder to capture. All video-capture programs have a preview window that displays the current footage playing (or paused) on the tape and have familiar playback controls (forward and back, for example). Specify an in point (the starting point) and an out point (the ending point) for the clip. If you want to combine multiple clips, be sure to cushion your in and out points with a few seconds of extra footage—some programs offer this option in the capture dialog.

Specifying a capture location

The video footage needs a home on your computer system. Make sure you have ample free space on an internal or external hard drive to store the video footage. As you learned in the last chapter, DV and HDV formats require roughly 250 MB of hard-drive space for each minute of footage. Here's a general rule: A 60-minute tape requires about 15 GB of free hard-drive space.

A fast hard drive lessens the chance of dropped frames during the capture process. A *dropped frame* is a video frame that wasn't successfully captured from the tape to the digital file on your computer. Any hard drive with a rotation speed of 7200 rpm or higher is fast enough for DV or HDV footage. If you're capturing high-resolution analog footage such as Betacam SP, you may need a Random Array of Inexpensive Drives (RAID) system to capture the footage. Laptops with slower hard drives (5400 rpm or lower) can capture DV or HDV footage, but if you have a faster external USB or FireWire drive, you should use it.

If your computer has only one internal hard drive, you should create a separate partition just for video files. A partition optimizes the capture process and reduces the likelihood of dropped frames.

If you're using a brand-new external USB or FireWire drive, the drive may be formatted as FAT32, which has a 4 GB file-size limitation. Any individual DV or HDV captured clip that exceeds nine minutes in length will be larger than 2 GB. If you don't want to worry about the FAT32 limitation, you can reformat your external drive with NTFS on Windows or HFS Plus (also known as Mac OS Extended) on Mac OS X.

Initiating the capture process

After you've logged the clip(s), you can start the capture process. Regardless of how much you like to multitask, don't switch to any other program while the NLE is capturing the footage. Even on the fastest computers, make sure the NLE application is the only application writing to the capture location (that is, your hard drive), to avoid dropped frames. Also, temporarily disable all screensavers, scheduled tasks, and instant messenger programs running on your system before you start the capture process, particularly for captures that take longer than a few minutes.

Saving the clip list

If your video application allows, be sure to save a list of the in and out points you specified for the captured clips. This list will make restoring the footage later easier if for some reason your capture footage is deleted. The clip-list file (or *scene list*, as some applications call it) is usually small and specific to the NLE program.

Backing up the capture files and source tape

If your capture file is small, it will fit onto a DVD+/-R disc (4 GB or 8 GB, depending on the disc size), and you can make a copy of the capture file on this quick, affordable backup media. Remember, DV and HDV capture from tape in real time; being able to restore an accidentally erased 4 GB clip from a disc can literally save you almost 20 minutes.

Video acquisition with Adobe Premiere Pro (Windows only)

Adobe Premiere Pro has come a long way toward becoming a professional video-editing tool. With Premiere, you can capture and edit DV and HDV footage. Although it's beyond the scope of this book to cover an entire Premiere workflow, I'll show you how to capture DV or HDV footage from your camcorder.

Preparing your video device

Before you launch Adobe Premiere Pro, make sure you've loaded the tape cassette with the desired footage into the video camera or videotape deck. I suggest you assign a project code to the tape and write it on the videotape label that ships with the videotape case—Adobe Premiere allows you to save information about the tape so you can more easily locate the tape, should you need to recapture footage. Connect the video device to your computer with a FireWire

NOTES

▶ To learn more about Premiere Pro 2.0, look at the book Adobe Premiere Pro 2.0 Studio Techniques by Jacob Rosenberg. You can find a link to this book at www.flashsupport.com/books.

cable, and turn on the video device. If the device is a camera, make sure it's in Play or Edit mode. If it's in Camera mode, Premiere may capture live video from your camcorder.

Use the power adapter for your camcorder for a capture session. Battery power can quickly deplete during the capture process. Also, be sure to lock the miniDV cassette's record tab to prevent accidentally erasing your video footage before starting the capture process

Creating a new project

You can create a new project or open an existing one with Adobe Premiere Pro. If you're starting a new project, click the New Project button on the Adobe Premiere Pro splash page. In the New Project dialog, choose one of the Available Presets. Generally, you should pick a preset that matches the video format for the majority of your source footage, or select the video format you want for your video content output. The DV–NTSC folder contains the four common North America DV formats (**Figure 2.1**). For the purpose of video capture, choose the format that matches your camcorder's format.

TIP

▸ If you have a HDV camcorder, make sure the video-output mode is set to the correct format. Most, if not all, HDV camcorders can also record in regular DV format. If you're capturing DV footage, make sure your HDV camcorder is set to the correct mode. You may need to reconnect the FireWire cable after you change this setting.

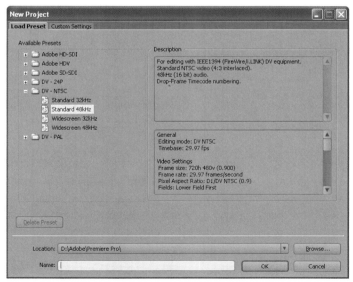

Figure 2.1 The presets of the New Project dialog in Adobe Premiere Pro.

NOTES

▶ Most DV camcorders, when set at the factory defaults, record audio at a sampling rate of 32 kHz. If you've changed the audio-sampling rate to 48 kHz on your camera, make sure you choose the respective preset in Adobe Premiere Pro.

In the New Project dialog, you can also choose a location for your video project files, which is the default location for files generated from video capture sessions in Premiere. You may want to change the location to an external hard drive or a separate partition from the system drive.

Starting a video capture

After you create a new project or open an existing one, you can start a capture session. Choose File > Capture (F5) to open the Capture window. Follow these steps to capture one clip from your tape:

1. Rewind or advance your tape to the start of the clip using the player controls below the preview area.

   Make sure your in point is just before the actual start of your scene.

2. Click the Set In Point button, labeled with a left curly brace ({). You can also press the I key to select the current frame as the in point.

3. Advance your tape to the end of your clip.

   To give yourself some wiggle room during editing, you should add a couple of seconds to the out point.

4. Click the Set Out Point button, labeled with a right curly brace (}). You can also press the O key to select the current frame as the out point.

5. Specify any relevant clip information in the Clip Data areas of the Capture window (**Figure 2.2**).

TIP

▶ You can also use the Handles setting in the Capture window to automatically grab extra frames before the in point and after the out point.

6. If you need to capture only one clip from the tape, click the In/Out button in the Capture area in the lower-right corner of the window. If you want to store this clip data and specify the in and out points of other clips on this tape or another tape, click the Log Clip button in the Timecode area of the window, and proceed to log another clip.

Figure 2.2 The Clip Data areas are located at right in the Capture window.

7. Once the capture process starts, you should refrain from switching to other applications on your desktop. It's usually a good idea to close any email, instant messengers, and screensavers before proceeding to capture. The Capture window displays the status and progress of the captured clip above the preview area (**Figure 2.3**). If the status message reports dropped frames, exit the capture by pressing the Esc key and try again.

NOTES

▶ Dropped frames are usually a result of a bad tape recording or inadequate system resources to perform the capture. If the tape was damaged or the information was incorrectly recorded to tape, there's not much you can do to recover dropped frames. If the tape appears fine while you're watching it, make sure you have a fast hard drive (7200 rpm or higher), and close all other running applications—even applications running in the system tray.

Figure 2.3 The Capture window.

NOTES

▶ For more information on the Flash Video encoding process, read Chapter 3, "Compression Primer," and Appendix C, "Encoding Flash Video."

8. After the capture has finished, Premiere prompts you to specify a filename and other clip information (**Figure 2.4**). If you typed this information into the Clip Data fields before the capture started, the Save Captured Clip dialog is automatically populated.

Figure 2.4 The Save Captured Clip dialog.

9. After the clip is saved, the new source file is added to the current project.

You can now use the captured clip with other clips in the Premiere project or proceed to encode the clip as Flash Video if no additional editing is required.

CLOSE-UP

Audio Channel Manipulation

If you've used more than one microphone during a shoot with your camcorder, you may prefer to use the audio channel from one microphone in both the left and right channels of your final video clip. Adobe Premiere's Audio Mixer window (Window > Audio Mixer) lets you manipulate the audio for an entire sequence (**Figure 2.5**). To copy one audio channel into another channel, expand the Effects and Sends pane with the expand/collapse control on the left margin of the pane. In the Effects area, choose Fill Right to copy the right channel into the left channel, or choose Fill Left to copy the left channel into the right channel.

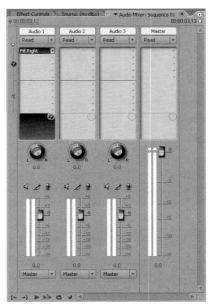

Figure 2.5 The Audio Mixer panel in Adobe Premiere Pro.

Processing Video with Adobe After Effects

Another amazing tool for video production is Adobe After Effects, available on both Windows and Mac systems. After Effects does for video what Photoshop does for still images: With exacting control, you can layer video with other graphic elements and special effects. It's beyond the scope of this book to provide intricate details of an After Effects workflow, but you should know the basics of this tool set. Later in the book, you'll learn how to use Adobe After Effects and the Keylight plug-in to remove a green screen from video footage so you can overlay a final Flash Video file over other Flash elements.

▶ For a thorough production guide to After Effects, read Adobe After Effects 7 Studio Techniques by Mark Christiansen. Visit www.flashsupport.com/books for more information.

Rendered video effects vs. real-time Flash effects

Before you approach After Effects to perform video production, you should ask yourself whether the Flash Player is capable of performing the equivalent effect faster, more efficiently, or programmatically with ActionScript. With Flash Player 8 or higher, you can add several real-time effects to Flash elements. Filters such as blur, drop shadow, and glow can be added to your Flash Video without using After Effects. Although After Effects can render SWF or Flash Video files, you may not want to render your effects directly into the video output that will eventually become a Flash Video file. You have greater flexibility adding effects with the Flash authoring environment. Before you use After Effects to add any effect or treatment, here's a list of factors to consider:

▶ **Can the effect be accomplished by the Flash Player?** Determine whether the effect you want to create in After Effects is something that's within the realm of the Flash Player's capabilities. I've provided a list of Flash Player effects in the next section.

▶ **Will the effect be processor-intensive if performed by the Flash Player?** Several visual effects can be accomplished in a Flash movie, but multiple effects layered on one another can quickly bring the Flash Player's performance to a crawl. If you're planning to layer several effects on top of your video footage (and they're constrained to the video area frame), consider rendering them directly into your video footage with After Effects.

▶ **Will the effect be visually sharper if rendered by the Flash Player?** Some visual aids used in broadcast TV, such as captions and callouts, can be more faithfully rendered in Flash than as rendered pixels in your video footage. Text overlays that are rendered by video applications don't compress well, especially at lower bitrates and smaller frame sizes. Regardless of how heavily compressed your video footage is, Flash can create text and vector graphics that are clean and crisp at any resolution.

You should also know what kind of effects you can easily apply to Flash Video, requiring no advanced knowledge of ActionScript:

▶ **Desaturation:** You can create a black-and-white (gray-scale) version of your Flash Video by using the Adjust Color filter in the Filters tab of the Property inspector of the Flash authoring environment.

▶ **Blur and fade effects:** If you want to blur in or out Flash Video, you can create a Flash tween with the Blur filter in the Filters tab of the Property inspector. You can also adjust the alpha property of a Flash Video clip with a tween.

▶ **Captioning:** Don't be tempted to add text tracks to your video source material in an editor like Premiere or Final Cut Pro. Flash can add text fields on top of Flash Video with the help of an application like Captionate, discussed in Appendix C, "Encoding Flash Video." Flash CS3 features a new FLVPlaybackCaptioning component, discussed in Chapter 10, "Constructing Banner Ads and Captioned Video."

Basic video effects

Perhaps a misnomer, the basic video "effects" that Adobe After Effects can perform on your video source material can dramatically improve the quality of the video experience. Although it may seem like overkill to use After Effects to perform mundane image-manipulation tasks, the computations used by After Effects are among the best in the industry;

TIP

▶ Flash CS3 features a new FLVPlaybackCaptioning component, which enables you to add caption text that is synchronized to your video. Learn more about this component in Chapter 10, "Constructing Banner Ads and Captioned Video."

there is a difference between a professional tool like After Effects and an inexpensive bargain video application geared for an amateur audience. Here's a short list of basic tasks After Effects can perform:

▶ **Color temperature correction:** It's fairly common for pro-sumer camcorders to inaccurately detect the color temperature of a scene. There are two general categories for color temperature: daylight (outdoor) and tungsten (indoor). If you're shooting outside at dusk or dawn or under heavy cloud cover, a camcorder's auto mode may presume that you're shooting indoors—contributing to an overly blue-looking scene. Likewise, if you shoot indoors with a daylight setting, colors in the scene may be overly warm (or yellow). Photo Filter in After Effects can convert improperly gauged color temperatures in your source material. Later in this chapter, you'll learn how to use the Photo Filter to correct color temperature.

▶ **Deinterlacing:** One of the most common tasks you need to perform with video footage acquired from camcorders is deinterlacing. (I discussed the effect of interlacing in Chapter 1.) Because Flash Video is a video format designed for computer display, any signs of interlacing should be removed from your source footage before you process it with a Flash Video encoder. Most encoding tools, including Adobe Flash CS3 Video Encoder, On2 Flix Pro, and Sorenson Squeeze, can remove inter-lacing, but After Effects has a superior deinterlacing engine. You'll learn more about this procedure later in the chapter.

▶ **Color and levels adjustment:** If your video image requires more or less contrast, saturation, or any other color channel enhancement, use the image-adjustment tools in After Effects (located in the Effects > Color Correc-tion menu).

▶ **Noise removal:** If you notice unwanted digital noise in your video image, you can use the Remove Grain filter in After Effects to clean up the image. Digital noise can be a result of many factors, including low-quality analog source formats (such as VHS tape) or shooting in low-light conditions.

NOTES

▶ For excellent tips and tricks related to color adjustment and noise removal, refer to the book After Effects Studio Techniques, mentioned earlier.

Adjusting color temperature in After Effects

If your video footage appears to be overly bluish or yellow-ish, chances are your footage was exposed with an incorrect white-balance setting. When you are shooting video, don't rely on the camera's automatic white-balance settings for professional-quality video. However, if you shot some video with the wrong white-balance setting, you can save the footage by adjusting the color saturation in After Effects. For this fix, you could try to use color-correction filters in After Effects; but After Effects 7 makes the process simple with the Photo Filter. The following steps describe how to fix the color of an image to achieve a proper white balance:

1. Open the starter After Effects project file, color_temp_correct_starter.aep, from the ch02/color_temp folder of this book's DVD-ROM.

    When the file opens in After Effects, you may need to relink the stella_pan.mov source clip to the stella_pan.mov file located in the source/dv folder on the DVD-ROM. This QuickTime DV clip contains footage shot with an indoor white-balance setting, even though the footage was shot outdoors.

2. Double-click the stella_pan.mov clip in the Project window to preview the clip.

    Notice that most of the colors in the scene seem to have a blue wash—the dry grass and the dog's fur don't exhibit much yellow. This color imbalance indicates that an incorrect white-balance setting was used during shooting.

3. Resave the project file as a new file named color_temp_correct.aep to a location on your system, such as your desktop.

4. Drag the stella_pan.mov clip from the Project panel to the Timeline panel. If the Timeline panel isn't visible, choose Window > Timeline.

    When you drag a clip to the Timeline panel, After Effects automatically creates a new composition based on the source clip's settings. The length of the new composition (also called a *comp*) is automatically set to the length of the source clip. Your Timeline panel should now have a new layer named after the source clip (**Figure 2.6**).

Figure 2.6 The new stella_pan comp displayed in the Timeline panel.

5. Select the stella_pan.mov layer in the Timeline panel, and choose Effect > Color Correction > Photo Filter. The Effect Controls panel appears, by default, on the right of the Project panel.

   Here, you can control the settings for any effect you've added to a layer. In the Filter setting of the Photo Filter effect, you can choose from several presets to add a new color cast to your image. If you have footage using an indoor color temperature that should have an outdoor color temperature, choose from the Warming Filter options—the higher the value, the warmer the tone. If you have footage using an outdoor color temperature that should have an indoor color temperature, choose from the Cooling Filter options—the higher the value, the cooler the tone. For this footage, choose a Warming Filter (81) value in the Filter setting menu. Slightly decrease the density to 22.3 percent (**Figure 2.7**). You can preview the new filter effect by dragging the play-head in the Timeline panel to a new position.

Figure 2.7 The Effect Controls panel showing the Photo Filter settings.

NOTES

▶ For this shot, I didn't want any red hue added to the pavement color. If you change the Filter value to Warming Filter (85) and reset the density to 25 percent, you'll notice more magenta in the pavement color. This setting doesn't look natural for the scene.

6. Render the composition to a new DV file. Open the Render Queue panel by choosing Window > Render Queue.

By default, the Render Queue is located as a tab next to the Timeline panel tab. I prefer to undock the Render Queue by right-clicking or Control-clicking the Render Queue panel title and choosing Undock Panel. Expand the height of the undocked panel to see the user interface (**Figure 2.8**). You shouldn't have any existing comps in the Render Queue. Leave the Render Queue open for the remaining steps.

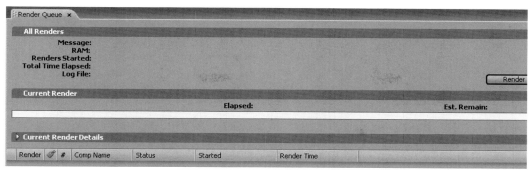

Figure 2.8 The undocked Render Queue panel.

7. Click the Project panel, and select the stella_pan comp item—don't select the stella_pan.mov clip.

   With the comp selected, choose Composition > Add to Render Queue.

8. In the Render Queue, you should see the stella_pan comp listed. Click the Render Settings drop-down menu, and choose DV Settings (**Figure 2.9**).

   If you want to review these settings, click the DV Settings text after you've added it as the Render Settings value.

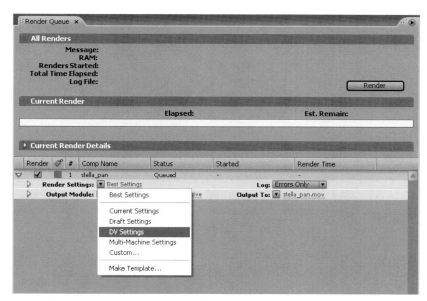

Figure 2.9 The Render Settings menu in the Render Queue panel.

9. Click the Output Module menu, and choose the Make Template option (**Figure 2.10**).

   In the Output Module Templates dialog, click the Load button, and browse to the Flash Video Studio Techniques–Output Modules.aom file located in the presets/After Effects folder of this book's DVD-ROM. When the templates load, you might receive a message about conflicting names—don't worry about this message. Close the Output Module Templates dialog.

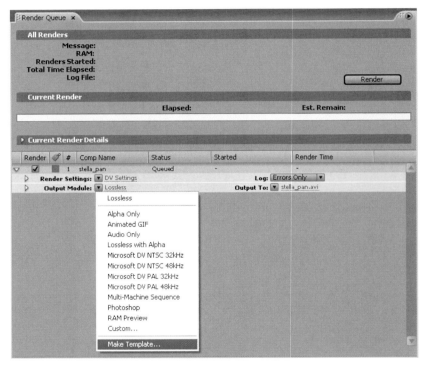

Figure 2.10 The Output Module menu.

10. Click the Output Module menu in the Render Queue again, and choose the newly added QuickTime – DV Interlaced module.

    This module creates a DV file with interlaced fields. (In the next section, you learn how to remove interlacing.)

11. Click the text to the right of the Output To field in the Render Queue.

    In the Output Movie To dialog, browse to a location on your system where you want to save the new file, and specify the filename stella_pan_color_corrected.mov.

12. Click the Render button in the Render Queue panel.

    After Effects creates a new QuickTime file with the new Photo Filter effect applied.

13. After the rendering has finished, browse to the location of the QuickTime movie, and play it. You can see the new color cast applied to the footage.

Deinterlacing video with After Effects

As you learned in Chapter 1, most video devices in North America and Japan capture video with interlaced fields. This system works great on most televisions, but the quality is less than ideal for computer displays. You should remove the effects of interlacing from *any* video footage you deploy on the Internet for computer displays. In this section, you learn how to retain a high-quality image with your interlaced video-source footage.

Before you learn how to remove interlacing, let's examine the problem. Seeing is believing, so follow these steps:

1. Open the ch02/deinterlace/flash_samples folder on this book's DVD-ROM, and load the demo.html file into your preferred Web browser.

2. When the Flash movie loads, select the Interlaced 640 by 480 item in the Left Video menu and the Deinterlaced 640 by 480 item in the Right Video menu.

3. Click the Play button to watch both samples play side by side. You can also click and drag on top of the video image to change the masked portion of each video.

    The left video sample exhibits horizontal lines where the subject matter is changing rapidly from one frame

NOTES

► You can find the completed After Effects project file and QuickTime movie in the ch02/color_temp folder on the DVD-ROM.

TIP

► There's more than one way to deinterlace video footage, all of which yield different results from one piece of footage to the next. For more detailed information about deinterlacing, read the deinterlacing articles listed in the Audio/Video Articles section of the links page for this book at www.flashsupport.com/links.

to the next—mainly the running dog (**Figure 2.11**). The right side, however, doesn't show any of these horizontal lines. When a video clip is deinterlaced, the two interlaced fields are joined into one frame.

Figure 2.11 The interlaced (left) and deinterlaced (right) video comparison.

You won't always notice the effects of interlacing with compressed Flash Video output. This is true in the following two cases:

▶ **Reduced frame size:** If your Flash Video output is 320 by 240 or less, you won't usually see the effects of interlaced fields, regardless of whether you deinterlaced the footage prior to Flash Video encoding. By reducing the horizontal resolution by half, you effectively eliminate one field from being processed by the encoder.

▶ **Little or no movement in the frame:** If your subject matter isn't moving or is moving very slowly, the edges of your subject aren't likely to change much from one field to the next. For example, if your footage shows an actor talking while sitting in a chair, there isn't much movement in the frame—unless you zoom in or out on the subject. Camera movements such as zooms or pans also add movement to the content in the frame.

If you know your video clip contains interlaced fields, you should deinterlace the content before encoding the content as Flash Video. The Macromedia Flash 8 Video Encoder can't deinterlace video content; the content, shown at left in Figure 2.11, was interlaced footage processed by Macromedia Flash 8 Video Encoder. Newer Flash Video encoders such as Adobe Flash CS3 Video Encoder, On2 Flix Pro, and Sorenson Squeeze do a reasonable job of deinterlacing, but you may prefer the quality you can achieve with Adobe After Effects.

To achieve optimal deinterlacing with a video clip in Adobe After Effects 7 or CS3, follow these steps:

1. In a new project, choose File > Import to bring in the interlaced video clip. You can use the ch02/color_temp/stella_pan_color_corrected.mov clip on this book's DVD-ROM.

2. In the Project panel, select the imported clip and choose File > Interpret Footage > Main (Ctrl/Cmd+F). You can also right-click (or Control-click on Mac) the clip and choose the same command. In the Interpret Footage dialog (**Figure 2.12**), select the Preserve Edges (Best Quality Only) check box. This setting enhances the image quality by only deinterlacing areas of the video frame that are moving.

3. Drag the new clip to the Timeline panel.

   After Effects automatically creates a new composition with settings based on the source clip. The clip becomes a new layer in the composition.

4. Double-click the Frame Blending box to access the layer. (The first click enables Frame Mix mode; the second click enables Pixel Motion mode, which is higher quality.) Frame blending is typically used when you want to slow down the frame rate of your video (for slow motion effects), but frame blending can also improve the quality of interlaced footage. Pixel Motion mode is a higher-quality frame blending technique than Frame Mix mode.

Figure 2.12 Preserve Edges enabled on the source clip

The Frame Blending box should have a solid forward slash (/) (**Figure 2.13**).

Frame Blending switch

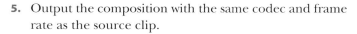

Figure 2.13 Frame Blending mode (second slashed box from the left) enabled on the source clip.

5. Output the composition with the same codec and frame rate as the source clip.

   Select the stella_pan_color_corrected comp in the Project panel, and choose Composition > Add to Render Queue.

6. For this example, you want to load specific Render Settings as well. Click the Render Settings menu in the Render Queue, and choose Make Template.

   In the Render Settings Template dialog, click the Load button, and browse to the Flash Video Studio Techniques – Render Settings.ars file located in the presets/After Effects folder on the DVD-ROM. (Don't worry about any warning messages that appear after loading the file.) Click OK to close the dialog. In the Render Settings menu, select the newly loaded DV Interlaced to DV Progressive template. This template turns off field rendering in the final output.

7. Click the Output Module menu, choose Make Template.

   In the Output Module Settings Template dialog, click the Load button, and browse to the Flash Video Studio Techniques – Output Modules.aom file located in the presets/After Effects folder on the DVD-ROM. (Don't worry about any warning messages.) Click OK to close the dialog. In the Output Module menu, select the QuickTime – Apple DV Progressive module.

8. Specify a new QuickTime file name in the Output To area.

9. Click the Render button to begin the process of creating the new deinterlaced QuickTime file.

NOTES

▶ If you're not familiar with the Render Queue window, review steps 6 through 12 in the earlier exercise in the section "Adjusting color temperature in After Effects."

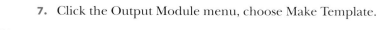

NOTES

▶ You can find the completed files for this project in the ch02/deinterlace folder of this book's DVD-ROM. You may need to relink the source video clips when you open the After Effects project file.

3

Compression Primer

Even with fast, fancy computers and digital devices, the simple fact is that digital video requires a lot of bits and bytes—there's no way to avoid throwing away visual and audio information. Storage is limited, and network bandwidth even more so. Compression is here to stay, and you need to know how to achieve the best results with the tools at your disposal. In this chapter, you learn how to make the right decisions when it comes time to compress digital video and audio into Flash Video files.

Distinguishing Source Files and Their Differences

Chapter 2, "Capturing and Processing Video," talked about the various video acquisition formats and their quality differences. When video is converted to, or acquired in, a digital format, a codec is used to effectively analyze the information in the video image and store that information on the digital tape, drive, or disc acquisition media. The term *codec* stands for *co*mpression and *dec*ompression: The source image is compressed during acquisition or capture and is later decompressed during playback.

A wide variety of video and audio codecs are available. Some codecs are used for professional video editing and output for TV broadcast, whereas other codecs are designed for low bitrates—ideal for video delivered over slower networks like the Internet or mobile phone networks. Video files don't contain the codec used to create them; the operating system or video-player application must have the codec installed in order to play back the video file. Luckily, since Flash Player 6, at least one video codec has been built into the player engine—the video codecs used by Flash Video aren't downloaded as separate files as they are with other video platforms or players.

▶ This chapter overlaps with Chapter 4, "Delivery and Deployment Primer." Before you decide on your Flash Video encoding strategy, be sure to read both chapters.

▶ You'll learn more about the video codecs available in the Flash Player later in this chapter.

▶ It's possible to capture video with QuickTime on Windows, but most native Window applications such as Adobe Premiere Pro use Microsoft Video for Windows (AVI) files.

▶ The VOB file extension stands for Video OBject.

Ideal source-file formats

Source video files, which are stored in a way specific to a codec, are commonly saved in Apple QuickTime (MOV files) and Microsoft Video for Windows (AVI files). You can also use the MPEG specification as a file format (MPEG or MPG files), especially for High Definition Video (HDV) or DVD Video files.

Apple QuickTime (MOV)

The QuickTime format, introduced by Apple in 1991, is more than just a video format. It's an entire multimedia architecture, supporting interactive sprite elements and text tracks along with audio and video. You can even add Flash movie tracks to QuickTime files! If you use a Macintosh, most video applications, including Apple Final Cut Pro and iMovie, use the QuickTime format for video captures. QuickTime is available for both Mac and Windows; it supports a wide range of video and audio codecs. The QuickTime format is popular for acquisition and delivery—many Web sites feature embedded QuickTime movies that use low bitrate video and audio codecs.

Microsoft Video for Windows (AVI)

Introduced in 1992, Microsoft's primary video-acquisition format is Video for Windows (AVI files). Most Windows-based applications save video captures in this format. AVI files are strictly audio/video content—you won't likely deploy AVI files on Web sites. You can play the AVI file format with the QuickTime Player on both Mac and Windows, but some codecs used for the AVI format aren't available in QuickTime. Adobe Premiere Pro uses the AVI file format on Windows as the native capture-file format.

MPEG

The MPEG file extension can be used on any video file that uses an MPEG video codec. Many MPEG video files are guised as AVI or MOV files. If you capture footage from an HDV camcorder, the source-file format is MPEG. The MPEG format is also used for VOB files on DVD Video discs. Most MPEG filenames don't indicate the version of the MPEG codec used by the video.

Ideal source-file codecs

Now that you know the three primary source-file formats, we can review the common codecs you'll find with high-quality video source files.

DV codec

The DV codec is used by miniDV and DVCAM camcorders to capture digital video. The DV codec has a constant (fixed) data rate of 25 Mbps for video and 5 Mbps for audio. The audio data rate can be split over four 12-bit channels or two 16-bit channels.

The DV codec has several software versions, usually specific to each vendor. The Apple DV codec was initially one of the more popular versions used in nonlinear video editing, but many video professionals prefer the Avid DV codec to other versions. The Microsoft DV codec is used by most Windows video applications to capture DV footage.

Modern computers can play DV content without any proprietary equipment or software. Most Flash Video encoders handle DV footage well.

DVCPro and DVCPro HD codecs

Panasonic introduced the DVCPro codec for standard definition video in 1995. DVCPro equipment can play DV tapes, but not vice versa. A DVCPro recording uses twice as much tape as an equivalent DV recording. Although DVCPro equipment isn't as popular as DV equipment, the newer DVCPro HD format (also called DV100) can record high-definition video at a variety of frame sizes and frame rates. DVCPro HD is considered a higher-quality HD video source than HDV sources; it can achieve data rates as high as 100 Mbps.

Unfortunately, the DVCPro HD codec isn't distributed with all video-editing or -player software. The best way to capture and edit DVCPro HD content is to use Final Cut Pro HD 5.0 (or higher) on a Mac.

NOTES

▶ The Apple DV codec ships with standard and professional versions of the QuickTime Player. The Avid DV codec is available free on Avid's Web site at www.avid.com. Visit the Audio/Video Articles section of this book's links page at www.flashsupport.com/links to find a direct link to these codecs.

NOTES

▶ I define a source video file as any file you want to compress as a Flash Video file. Most Flash Video encoders accept more than just MOV and AVI files. Other formats, such as Windows Media Video (WMV), can be recompressed into Flash Video formats. However, these formats usually introduce low bitrate compression to the video material, and further recompression into Flash Video reduces the quality of the image. With each decompression and recompression there is a loss of quality called generation loss. As I reiterate throughout this chapter, always try to get the highest quality source file available.

MPEG codecs

One of the most confusing video codecs is the MPEG codec, mainly because there are so many varieties. The most popular in use today is the MPEG2 codec, used by DVD Video discs, digital cable, and digital satellite broadcasts, as well as High Definition TV (HDTV) broadcasts. Many standards are evolving around the MPEG4 specification, including Apple QuickTime video.

Most MPEG video data is *multiplexed*, which means the video track is tightly interleaved with the audio track, making it more time intensive (and problematic) for many video-encoding utilities. The process of separating MPEG video from a sync audio track is known as *demuxing*. If you've ever tried to reencode an MPEG file to another format and lost the audio track, it's likely that the encoder couldn't demux the audio track from the video track.

Many Flash Video encoders use QuickTime as the underlying video architecture to help convert source files into the Flash Video (FLV) format. If you have MPEG2 footage (including HDV footage), you may need the QuickTime MPEG2 Playback Component. You can buy this component from Apple's site at www.apple.com/quicktime/mpeg2. The MPEG2 codec doesn't ship with either the standard or professional version of QuickTime Player.

If you have a DVD Video disc to encode into Flash Video, you may need to demux the audio and video tracks of the MPEG files (stored as VOB files on DVD Video disc) before you take the footage into a Flash Video encoder. Many DVD Video discs use difficult audio codecs, such as AC3 audio encoding, which isn't recognized by Macromedia Flash 8 Video Encoder, Sorenson Squeeze, or On2 Flix Pro. Several tools are available to transcode MPEG files to another video format before you bring it into a Flash Video encoder:

▶ **MPEG Stream:** This free QuickTime-enabled utility, created by Squared 5 (www.squared5.com), enables you to convert MPEG files into other video formats. As mentioned earlier, if you plan to use MPEG2 footage with QuickTime, you need the QuickTime MPEG2 Playback Component installed on your system.

▶ **DVDxDV:** This Mac OS X trialware utility enables you convert an entire DVD Video disc to QuickTime file formats. If you need to transcode more than a short section of video from a DVD Video disc into Flash Video, DVDxDV can reduce the work of splicing several MPEG2 files together. Visit the Web site at www.dvdxdv.com.

▶ **Cinematize 2:** This Mac OS X and Windows utility can also convert an entire DVD Video disc to QuickTime file formats. For more information, go to www.miraizon.com.

Motion JPEG (M-JPEG) codecs

Before the advent of the DV and HDV formats, many ana-log capture devices used Motion JPEG (M-JPEG) codecs. M-JPEG codecs have been available in QuickTime since version 2.5. If you have source footage in this codec, you shouldn't have a problem converting it to Flash Video.

Hardware-specific codecs

Many high-end professional video solutions use hardware codecs, which means that any video file using the codec must be played on a system with the hardware installed. To convert a hardware codec source file to Flash Video, you must run the Flash Video encoder on the same system.

Understanding Video File Bitrates

The *bitrate* of any video is the amount of data transmitted in a given unit of time, usually expressed in kilobits per second (Kbps) or kilobytes per second (KB/s). The term *data rate* is synonymous with *bitrate*. Every video file on your computer has a specific bitrate. DV clips, for example, have a data rate of 25 Mbps (megabits per second), whereas a broadband-quality Web video clip can have a data rate of 384 Kbps.

The bitrate of a video clip largely determines the visual quality of the video image. No matter how you slice it, a clip encoded with a lower bitrate shows less detail com-pared to the same clip encoded with a higher bitrate. However, each video codec can utilize the same bitrate

NOTES

▶ Depending on whom you ask, a kilobit equals either 1024 bits or 1000 bits. Sorenson Squeeze and On2 Flix Pro define a kilobit as 1024 bits.

differently. One codec may be able to store more information per kilobit than another codec.

Variations within clip properties

Video bitrate is a unit of measure used to quantify how much information is stored within one second of video. You can use that quantity any way you want. Think of data rate like a specific length of material—you can have three feet of high-quality rope or three feet of low-quality binder's twine. How well you use the bitrate of a video clip can determine the quality of the video a viewer experiences. Three factors determine how your video's bitrate is utilized:

▶ **Frame rate:** The frequency of video frames in your clip determines its frame rate, expressed as frames per second (fps). Higher frame rates have a lower bitrate per frame of video, whereas lower frame rates allow more data to be allocated per frame. Higher frame rates have smoother motion, and lower frame rates can exhibit jerky and unnatural-looking motion. Your content largely determines how much you can reduce the frame rate without destroying the flow of the clip.

▶ **Frame size:** The width and height of your video clip determine the number of pixels in each video frame. You can think of video pixels like an allotment of grass seeds for a yard. For any given bitrate, you have only so many seeds. If you spread those seeds over a large area, your yard will be splotchy with large gaps between the blades of grass. If you concentrate the seeds, the yard will be smaller but the grassy area will be rich.

▶ **Codec compression:** Each video codec has its own method of compressing data. For Web video formats, two types of compression are usually applied: *spatial* (intraframe) and *temporal* (interframe). Spatial compression is similar to JPEG image compression: Redundant color information is thrown away to reduce storage requirements. Temporal compression stores only the changed information from frame to frame. More efficient codecs require less storage and deliver higher quality but usually require more processing power and computer memory (RAM) for video playback.

Every codec has an ideal bitrate after you've determined which frame size and frame rate you want to use. The following formula can help you determine if your bitrate is acceptable:

```
(Width x Height x Frame rate x 8 ) ÷ Compression =
➥Bitrate (Kbps)
```

If you want to compress a Flash Video file at 320 by 240 with 29.97 fps, the following formula is an acceptable average bitrate for the Sorenson Spark codec, where 48000 indicates the compression divisor for Spark:

```
(320 x 240 x 29.97 x 8 ) ÷ 48000 = 384 Kbps
```

Because the On2 VP6 codec requires less data rate for the equivalent quality, you can use a compression divisor of 60000:

```
(320 x 240 x 29.97 x 8) ÷ 60000 = 307 Kbps
```

Each Flash Video encoding solution has its own set of compression profiles that try to match the best video width, height, and frame rate for each Flash Video codec.

Variations within subject matter

The amount of bitrate you need for a video clip depends on its content. I prefer to place video content into one of three categories:

▶ **Average movement:** If at least 25 percent of the pixels on any given frame of video remain the same, your video content isn't updating frequently. Much of the content visible on prior frame(s) can be reused on subsequent frames. The bitrate formula in the previous section assumes your video exhibits average movement. Most Flash Video encoders and their presets assume your content has average movement in the frame. For example, a shot of a person walking across the room to pick up a glass might contain average movement.

▶ In this equation, the dimensions and frame rate are multiplied by 8 to produce a data rate expressed in kilobits per second, because there are 8 bits to a byte.

▶ Just because a codec offers better compression doesn't mean you can ignore other factors in your video planning. You'll learn more about each codec's strengths and weaknesses in the section "Learning About Player Versions and Codec Options," later in this chapter.

▶ The Flash_Video_Bitrates.xls Excel file in the tools folder of this book's DVD-ROM compares the compression presets of Sorenson Squeeze, On2 Flix Pro, and Episode Pro. On the first page of this worksheet, you can calculate custom bitrates for your preferred video frame sizes and frame rates. On the second page, you can enter a preferred video width to see the corresponding height and frame rate for specific bitrate targets.

NOTES

▶ These are general classifications—a video clip may have variable movement from one scene to another. In such a case, you may consider breaking one clip into several clips and using a lower bitrate for clips containing slower-moving scenes and a higher bitrate for clips containing faster movement.

▶ **Slow movement:** If fewer than 15 percent of the pixels on any given frame change from frame to frame, your content is relatively stationary. For example, if your shot shows a person talking while sitting in a chair, the video frame is mainly updating around the person's face. If your content exhibits slow movement, you can adjust the bitrate formula by dividing the result in half.

▶ **Fast movement:** If more than 25 percent of the pixels on any given frame are changing, your content may be rapidly updating and requires more data to store the new information. A close-up shot of rushing water in a mountain stream exhibits fast movement. Fast movement clips can require up to twice as much bitrate. In the bitrate formula, be prepared to double the result.

Let's compare some samples of content containing different styles of movement. The following series of figures demonstrates a slow, average, and fast movement bitrate formula. Each sample uses the same frame width, frame height, and frame rate with the same quality of source material (HDV).

Figure 3.1 shows a slow movement profile applied to a clip containing little or no motion. In this example, a park trail is shown with slight movement in the trees. The bitrate used for this clip is 225 Kbps with the Sorenson Spark codec.

Figure 3.1 The bitrate is 225 Kbps, with the Sorenson Spark codec.

Figure 3.2 shows an average movement profile applied to a clip containing some movement. This clip of a waterfall spilling into a large pool uses twice the bitrate for the same clip characteristics: 450 Kbps with the Sorenson Spark codec.

Figure 3.2 The bitrate is 450 Kbps, with the Sorenson Spark codec.

Figure 3.3 illustrates a fast movement profile applied to a clip with several changing areas. This clip of rushing water uses a bitrate of 900 Kbps with the Sorenson Spark codec, twice that of the previous example.

Figure 3.3 The bitrate is 900 Kbps, with the Sorenson Spark codec.

But what happens if you use a slower bitrate with the rushing-water clip, leaving the frame width, frame height, and frame rate identical? The resulting video image suffers horribly (**Figure 3.4**).

Figure 3.4 The bitrate is 225Kbps, with the Sorenson Spark codec.

The formulas described in this section are by no means absolute—every piece of video is different. Use the bitrate formulas to help you establish reasonable start points in your compression tests.

Variations in connection speed

When you intend to deliver Flash Video over the Web, you should carefully consider how you want visitors to experience the video playback. Connection speeds on the Internet vary greatly; some people have fast cable modems, whereas others are still using slow 56 K dial-up modems. Two general methods are used to deliver video on the Web, and each method greatly affects how to compress your video:

- **One bitrate:** Only one bitrate is offered per piece of video content on the site. This is akin to a "one size fits all" approach, where you pick the quality of the video you want everyone to experience. If you choose a low bitrate, everyone sees a low-quality video, but the video content downloads quickly regardless of connection speed. If you pick a high bitrate, everyone can see a better-quality video, but visitors with slower connection

TIP

- As you can see with the DVD-ROM example, the On2 VP6 codec enables you to achieve the same image quality at a lower bitrate than that used by Sorenson Spark. You'll learn more about these codecs later in this chapter.

speeds have to wait for the video to download. As a video compressionist, you need to encode and upload only one video file per piece of content.

▶ **Multiple bitrates:** My preferred approach with most video content is to offer tiers of data rates. Visitors with fast Internet connections get high-quality, higher-bitrate video content; and visitors with slower Internet speeds get lesser-quality, low-bitrate video content. The video selection can be automated or user-initiated. For this approach, you must encode a separate Flash Video file for each targeted data rate.

If you decide to pick one bitrate for your Flash Video content, be aware of bandwidth problems that result. A high-bitrate video served over a slow Internet connection will result in long load times and possibly constant rebuffering during playback. When a Flash Video is sent from a server to a Flash movie, the video packets are temporarily stored in a memory buffer. If you play a video file and the buffer is empty or runs out, the video pauses until more video packets have downloaded.

To resolve this problem, make sure the video file's bitrate is less than the network connection speed. The video can then download to the user as it's played without as much risk that rebuffering will occur.

Learning About Player Versions and Codec Options

Now that you know what can affect the bitrate of a video clip, you need to learn the codec options for Flash Video before you start the compression process. Flash Video was first introduced with Flash Player 6, supporting the Sorenson Spark codec. The Spark codec is a derivative of the H.263 codec. At that time, Sorenson was well known for its high-quality, low-bitrate Sorenson Video 3 codec, which Apple licensed for QuickTime. Over the span of four releases of the Flash Player, four video codecs have been added to

▶ Regardless of your selected bitrate(s), you can always scale the size of your video clip beyond its original dimensions. For example, you can scale a 32 by 240 video clip to 640 by 480 in a Flash movie.

▶ You learn how to access and use the metadata of a Flash Video file in Chapter 7, "Building Your Own Video Player."

the Flash Video specification. **Table 3.1** lists the codecs supported in each version of the Flash Player. Each video codec and audio codec has a unique identifier that is stored in the metadata of a Flash Video file, as shown in **Tables 3.2** and **3.3**. In this section, you learn the strengths and weaknesses of each codec.

TABLE **3.1** Flash Video Codec Support

FLASH PLAYER VERSION	SORENSON SPARK	ON2 VP6	SCREEN VIDEO	SCREEN VIDEO V2
5 or earlier	○	○	○	○
6 and 7	●	○	●	○
8 and higher	●	●	●	●
FlashLite 1.0./1.1/2.0	○	○	○	○

TABLE **3.2** Flash Video: Video Codec Identifiers

CODEC	CODEC ID
Sorenson Spark (H.263)	2
On2 VP6 (no alpha)	4
On2 VP6 (with alpha)	5
Screen Video	3
Screen Video V2	6

TABLE **3.3** Flash Video: Audio Codec Identifiers

CODEC	CODEC ID
Uncompressed	0
ADPCM	1
MP3	2
Nellymoser 8 kHz	5
Nellymoser (non-8 kHz)	6

Sorenson Spark codec (H.263)

In 2002, when Flash Video first made its debut in Flash Player 6, Sorenson Spark was the video codec that made it all happen. If you need the widest range of compatibility for your Flash Video files, use the Sorenson Spark codec.

Strengths

The primary benefits of using Sorenson Spark as your Flash Video codec revolve around processing power:

▶ **Reduced processing:** The Spark codec requires less computer processing and memory (RAM) than the newer On2 VP6 codec. The rule of thumb is that Spark requires about half as much processing power and memory as On2 VP6. If you need to deploy Flash Video to a wide range of computers, including machines with processors slower than Pentium IIIs or Power Mac G4s, you should strongly consider using the Spark codec.

▶ **Widest acceptance:** As I mentioned earlier, Spark is available in Flash Player 6 and later versions.

▶ **Encoding products availability:** Many inexpensive (and open source) Flash Video encoding solutions only offer the Spark codec.

▶ **Speed of compression:** The Spark codec compresses video faster than the On2 VP6 codec. As a result, you can encode more content in less time.

▶ **Encoder and decoder solution:** The Sorenson Spark codec is the only codec whose compression encoder exists in the regular Flash Player. You can broadcast live video from a Web cam using the Sorenson Spark codec. The live video can be broadcast only to a Flash Media Server application.

Weaknesses

Despite the codec's wide availability and reduced demands on the processor, Spark has a few drawbacks:

▶ **Lower quality video:** Sorenson Spark's image quality is inferior to the newer On2 VP6 codec in Flash Player 8 and higher. If you want the best quality Flash Video for online distribution over low bitrates, you shouldn't use the Spark codec.

▶ **Inefficient compression:** You can achieve visual quality with Sorenson Spark on par with On2 VP6—at the cost of higher bitrates. You need about 20 percent more bitrate for Spark to produce the same quality with VP6. If you're distributing on fixed media such as CD/DVD-ROM and want the Flash Video to play on slower machines, storage and bitrate issues may be less important.

When to use it

In summary, the Sorenson Spark codec is ideal for projects requiring the following:

▶ **Wide range of playback platforms:** From Pocket PCs to mobile phones supporting the Flash Player (not Flash-Lite), Sorenson Spark is the only codec that performs well with slow processors.

▶ **Live video:** To broadcast live events from Flash applications, use Spark. You can purchase live encoding solutions for On2 VP6, but they're not cheap.

On2 VP6 codec

Sorenson Spark opened the possibility of video playback within a Flash movie, but the On2 VP6 codec included with Flash Player 8 inaugurated a new era of Web video. The superior image quality of the VP6 codec, combined with its efficient compression for low bitrates, has significantly increased the adoption of Flash Video.

Strengths

VP6 is a modern video codec, designed for fast processors and low bitrates. The following list provides an overview of its strength over other codecs:

▶ **Superior image quality:** Given equivalent bitrates, video using the VP6 codec is visually more stunning than video using Sorenson Spark.

▶ **Efficient compression:** On2 VP6 can more efficiently compress video data, resulting in smaller file sizes for equivalent bitrates.

▶ **Alpha channel support:** The VP6 codec implemented by Flash Player 8 and higher can utilize a transparency layer, also called an *alpha channel.* The alpha channel supports 256 levels of transparency, enabling you to add anti-aliased edges around subject matter in your video frame. An alpha channel makes regions of your video transparent, allowing Flash elements behind the video to show through.

Weaknesses

Although VP6 may seem like a natural one-size-fits-all Flash Video codec to use with your projects, consider the following drawbacks:

▶ **Higher processing and memory requirements:** Flash Video encoded with the On2 VP6 codec can require up to twice as much CPU power and memory (RAM) than equivalent Sorenson Spark Flash Video. Generally, your target platform for Flash Video encoded with VP6 should be a processor speed of 1.5 GHz or greater.

▶ **Longer encoding times:** Because its encoding algorithm is complex, the On2 VP6 codec requires more time to compress video footage than Sorenson Spark.

▶ **Player requirements:** Flash Video encoded with the VP6 codec can play only on Flash Player 8 or higher. If you're targeting devices with older players, the video track of the Flash Video files won't display (although the audio information will play).

When to use it

You should use the On2 VP6 codec with any Flash Video project that has the following criteria:

▶ **Best image quality available:** In most cases, your video material will look better with the VP6 codec. If your business clients want HD footage to look its best on the Web, use VP6.

▶ **Flash Player 8 deployment:** If you're targeting Flash Player 8 or higher, consider using the On2 VP6 codec over the Sorenson Spark codec.

▶ **Video compositing:** If you want to overlay Flash Video seamlessly with other media elements in a Flash movie, you need the alpha-channel support that's available only with the VP6 codec.

▶ **Desktop deployment:** If you're targeting modern-day desktop computers for Flash Video delivery, the On2 VP6 can decode video efficiently.

Screen recording codecs

Back when Flash MX and Flash MX 2004 were released, the QuickTime exporter plug-in for Flash Video included the option to compress Flash Video files with the Screen Recording codec. Adobe removed this codec from its encoding products, and you won't usually find the codec as an option in the Adobe Flash Video encoding product.

The Screen Recording codecs, Screen Video and Screen Video V2, are included with the Flash Player for playback of Adobe Acrobat Connect Professional (formerly known

NOTES

▶ For a detailed breakdown of the inner workings of On2's video compression, read the article at www.on2.com/technology/why-compress-video.

as Macromedia Breeze Meeting) screen-capture streams, during desktop sharing sessions. If you have access to the older Flash MX 2004 or Flash MX video compression plug-in for QuickTime-enabled applications, you can convert screen-capture files to Flash Video with this codec. You can use Spark or VP6 for screen captures as well, but the Screen Recording codecs are optimized for desktop application screens. The text in application windows appear sharper with the Screen Recording codecs than the other Flash Video codecs. Due to the large frame sizes of desktop screen captures, the frame rates of Flash Video for screen captures are usually low, from 1–6 fps.

Audio codecs

The Flash Player's audio codec offerings haven't changed since Flash Player 6. The following describes each codec:

▶ **MP3:** By far the best "bang for the byte" audio codec is MP3. Based on the same MPEG Audio Layer 3 used with early Video CD discs, this popular audio codec has made its way into just about every digital device on the market. You should always compress the audio track of a prerecorded video clip with the MP3 codec.

▶ **Nellymoser Speech codec:** Introduced in Flash Player 6, the Speech codec is designed for encoding voice audio in real time with little processing overhead. The compression ratio of the Speech codec isn't as good as the MP3 codec, however. You should only use the Speech codec for live video broadcasts to a Flash Media Server application. Most Flash Video encoders don't offer the Speech codec in the audio-compression options.

▶ **Uncompressed audio:** Some third-party Flash Video encoders offer the option to output an uncompressed audio track that doesn't use a codec or compression. The resulting Flash Video file is large and not fit for distribution over the Web. You should use the uncompressed audio option only if you plan to embed Flash Video in a Flash movie—the Flash authoring environment recompresses audio in Flash Video when you publish the Flash movie (SWF) file.

NOTES

▶ Although the ADPCM (Adaptive Differential PCM, or Pulse Code Modulated) codec is listed in Table 3.3 as a Flash Video audio codec, it's unlikely you'll find a Flash Video encoding product that uses it. ADPCM has a lower compression ratio than MP3, but it's usually less processor intensive.

Determining Your Video Compression Profiles

Now that you have a thorough understanding of your files, bitrates, and codecs, you're ready to create one or more compression profiles for your Flash Video content. A compression profile specifies, at minimum, the bitrate (or data rate), frame size, frame rate, and keyframe interval for the compressed video output, in addition to the bitrate of the audio track. Some Flash Video encoders also let you specify constant bitrate (CBR) or variable bitrate (VBR) encoding. You should plan your compression profile before you encode your Flash Video.

Total bitrate

The first number you need to determine for a compression profile is how much bandwidth your video clip requires for delivery. You can then divide the total bitrate between the video and audio tracks.

The bandwidth you should require from a viewer isn't necessarily equal to the bitrate you use for a clip. Many video producers prefer to specify a total bitrate between 70 and 80 percent of the target bitrate. For example, if you're targeting cable-modem viewers with a tested 768 Kbps download rate, you use a total bitrate of 614 Kbps. Some video producers require twice as much available bandwidth as the video clip requires.

Audio bitrate

Of course, most video content isn't complete without the audio track. After you've determined the total bitrate, determine the bitrate necessary to reasonably reproduce the audio content of your original source. Unless you're targeting dial-up modem connection speeds, you should use at least 24 Kbps for a mono (single-channel) audio track. Higher-fidelity audio tracks, such as music soundtracks, benefit from higher audio bitrates, such as 96 Kbps. Whatever audio bitrate you use, subtract the value from your total bitrate value to determine how much bitrate is left for the video bitrate.

NOTES

▶ Always include an audio track with your Flash Video clip. The audio track of a Flash Video helps govern the frame rate during playback. Without an audio track, the frame rate of a Flash Video clip can be slower than you specified in your compression profile. If your original video source didn't have an audio track, use a video editor to insert a silent audio track, and export a new source file to use with your Flash Video encoder. You should use the lowest audio data rate supported by your encoder for silent audio tracks, to allow more data rate to be used by the video track.

Video bitrate

As you learned earlier, the video track has its own specific bitrate or data rate. The bitrate you choose for a piece of content should support the frame size and frame rate you want to use. If you specify too little bitrate, the visual quality of your video content suffers. The bitrate for a video file should be based on the bandwidth demands you're willing to require from your target audience.

Frame size

The width and height of video destined for computer playback should be kept to a square pixel aspect ratio. Any nonsquare pixel aspect video, such as DV or HDV, should be adjusted for computer playback. For example, a DV source file with a 720 by 480 frame size can be resized to 640 by 480, 480 by 360, 320 by 240, 160 by 120, and so on. Similarly, HDV content with a 1440 by 1080 frame size should be resized to 1920 by 1080, 960 by 540, 480 by 270, 240 by 135, and so on. You should determine the frame size of your video content in conjunction with the frame rate of the video, as you learned earlier with compression formulas.

Frame rate

The frame rate of the video content should be in multiples of the source frame rate. For example, if the original video frame rate was 30 fps (or 29.97 fps), you should use 30 fps, 15 fps, or 10 fps. The frame rate should reasonably convey the sense of movement in the original content. If your content contains fast-moving subjects, use a higher frame rate. However, as you increase the frame rate, you may need to reduce the frame size of the video to retain reasonable visual quality for a specific bitrate.

Keyframe interval

Video keyframes are a lot like keyframes in Flash tweens; a keyframe specifies a significant point of action in a range of frames in the video clip. A *keyframe*, also called an *i-frame* (short for *intraframe*) is used as a starter frame, drawing the initial visual layer of the video. The following frames, also called *p-frames* (short for *predictive frames*), only store the

▶ The general rule for frame size is to use width and height values that are divisible by 4, 8, and 16. The second page of the Flash_Video_Bitrates.xls Excel file in the tools folder of this book's DVD-ROM displays these values in green text, and unacceptable values in red. Video content that adheres to optimal dimensions usually plays more efficiently.

changes in the video frame from the previous keyframe. When you compress video to Flash Video, your encoder enables you to specify the frequency of keyframes in your clip. Keyframes are best inserted in multiples (or fractions) of your compressed file's frame rate. For example, if you're using a frame rate of 15 fps, you might use a keyframe interval of 150 frames (one keyframe will be generated every 150 frames). Some encoders allow you to select automatic or *natural* keyframes, which essentially tell your encoder to make a keyframe whenever enough of the video frame has changed.

One important consideration for keyframe intervals used with Flash Video is the ability to seek to more points of the video clip. With ActionScript, you can only seek to keyframes within the video clip—if you try to seek to a time in the clip that doesn't contain a keyframe, the Flash Player jumps to the closest keyframe. You may notice this phenomenon when you scrub a Flash Video clip; the frequency of updates while scrubbing indicates the number of keyframes. However, if you use enhanced seek with Flash Video content served by Flash Media Server, the server can generate keyframes on the fly—enabling a viewer to scrub the video more smoothly.

NOTES

▶ Don't use a low keyframe interval for your video content. As you add more keyframes to a Flash Video compression profile (without boosting the bitrate), the overall visual quality of each keyframe starts to diminish.

CBR and VBR encoding

Most Flash Video encoders support two types of video data rates: CBR (Constant Bit Rate) and VBR (Variable Bit Rate). If you intend to stream Flash Video files from a Flash Media Server or Flash Video Streaming Service provider, you should use CBR encoding. CBR encoding ensures a stable predictable bitrate, which means that potential pitfalls with rebuffering can be avoided. If you intend to serve Flash Video content from a Web server (over HTTP) or a local source such as a CD-ROM or DVD-ROM, use VBR encoding. VBR encoding enables the encoder to spike the data rate for more complex areas of the video clip and reduce the data rate for visually simpler parts.

Some Flash Video encoders let you choose one- or two-pass encoding procedures with CBR or VBR encoding. You'll usually see better visual results with any two-pass encoding

► You'll learn more about deployment options for Flash Video in the next chapter. For more information on video encoding procedures, refer to Appendix C, "Encoding Flash Video."

setting. Using two-pass encoding requires twice as much time to encode to Flash Video as one-pass encoding. A two-pass encoding procedure involves one pass where the encoder analyzes the video content to see where bitrate peaks can be optimally applied, and a second pass where the information gathered during the analysis pass is applied to video output. A bitrate peak is a point or span of time in the content that more data than the average bitrate value allows. With VBR encoding, a section of video that requires less bitrate to encode can offer more bitrate to a more difficult section of video. Consider a video clip showcasing a segment with a talking head video, and another segment with fast paced action scenes. The talking head footage may not need as much bitrate as the action content. Therefore, the bitrate savings in the talking head footage can be applied to the action content, allowing the action content to have a data rate in excess of the average bitrate of the entire video clip.

Delivery and Deployment Primer

Creating video files with a video-compression tool is only one step in the process of taking your video content to the Web. To enable the best user experience for visitors watching your videos, you need to know how to distribute your video files on Web servers, streaming servers, or possibly even a content distribution network (CDN) such as Akamai, LimeLight, and others. In this chapter, you'll learn the differences between distribution file formats and protocols for Flash Video, along with their advantages and disadvantages.

File Formats: SWF, FLV, and HTML

In order for Flash Video to play properly on a Web site, you need at least one Flash movie, or SWF file, that contains the scripting code to initiate loading and playback. You have two options with Flash Video playback in a SWF file: embedded or external video.

Embedded video (SWF)

The Flash Video content (FLV file) is imported into a Flash document (FLA file) and published as a Flash movie (SWF file). Some Flash Video encoder tools automatically embed Flash Video content in a SWF file. This option is backward-compatible with Flash Player 6 or higher, and you need to keep track of only one media file. However, your Flash Video content significantly increases the file size of the SWF file, and you can't replace the Flash Video content without republishing the Flash movie.

For most Flash Video projects produced by interactive agencies, embedded video isn't the preferred approach for deployment. Most Flash Video content used by Web sites such as Google or YouTube is distributed as FLV files.

> **TIP**
>
> ▶ To send a Flash Video file to someone who is inexperienced with Flash authoring and development, use an embedded video in a Flash movie to enable easier playback of the Flash Video. Unfortunately, most computers aren't set up to play FLV files natively—you can't drag an FLV file into a Web browser window to play. However, with a SWF file, you can either drag the file into a Web browser window or play it with a standalone Flash Player or projector.

> **TIP**
>
> ▶ For the examples in the book, I use the SWFObject JavaScript code created by Geoff Stearns, a former co-worker of mine at Schematic. Geoff's code is used by many popular sites, including Amazon.com, Adobe, and the Library of Congress Web site. You can find the swfobject. js code included in many samples on this book's DVD-ROM. For more information about SWFObject, see Geoff's site at http://blog.deconcept. com/swfobject.

External video (FLV)

The Flash Video content (FLV file) is loaded as a separate asset into the SWF file at runtime when the Web page loads. The FLV file can be loaded with your own custom programming in ActionScript, the scripting language for the Flash platform, or with a prebuilt Flash component. I explore both techniques in later chapters.

There are advantages to using an external video file. For example, the FLV file can be preloaded into the Flash movie shell. You can also more easily swap out the video content with a new FLV file if necessary. In addition, you have much more control over your Flash Video when you load and control the video with ActionScript. Publishing times are drastically reduced when the Flash Video isn't embedded in the Flash document.

The disadvantage of using an external video file in the FLV format is that you must use Flash Media Server to stream playback if you need Flash Player 6 compatibility with your Flash Video content. (I talk more about Flash Media Server later in this chapter and throughout the book.) FLV files can be uploaded to a Web server, a Flash Media Server, or a Flash Video Streaming Service provider.

Video playback (SWF)

Regardless of which file format you use for your Flash Video content—SWF or FLV—you can control the playback and display of Flash Video with another Flash movie (SWF). Usually, this shell Flash movie is the SWF file you specify in your HTML document to initiate the Flash Player.

Web page (HTML)

For deployment on a Web site, the Flash Video, including the player movie (SWF) and Flash Video content (SWF or FLV), are shown on an HTML page. The <OBJECT> or <EMBED> tag can display plug-in content, including the Flash Player. Most Web sites use JavaScript in the HTML document to detect whether the browser has the Flash Player (and the required version of it) installed.

Protocols: HTTP vs. RTMP

When you use the FLV file format as your distribution method for Flash Video content, you have two options for serving the Flash Video over the Internet: HyperText Transfer Protocol (HTTP) and Real Time Messaging Protocol (RTMP). You can use one or both protocols to serve Flash Video to your Internet audience.

HTTP

Most content viewed on a Web site is served over HTTP. Any Web server, such as Apache or Microsoft Internet Information Services (IIS), can deliver Flash Video (FLV or SWF) files. The best reasons to use a Web server with HTTP protocol for hosting Flash Video content are simplicity and cost. If you know how to transfer files to a Web server using a File Transfer Protocol (FTP) client, for example, you can put Flash Video files on a Web site and make the content accessible to visitors. Another advantage of HTTP is cost: Most Web hosting providers offer cheap storage and large transfer quotas that allow you to host numerous media files and serve them to your visitors.

From a site visitor's point of view, one advantage of using HTTP is access. Many corporate networks use firewalls to block specific content from entering. Popular methods of blocking are protocol and port restrictions. Some firewall rules allow only HTTP content served over port 80. Almost all Web servers use port 80 to serve content, but a Web server can be set up to serve HTTP content over custom ports such as 8080, 8081, or 8500. These ports are usually used by test or development servers. Some firewall rules allow only specific MIME types, such as text/html (HTML documents), and common image formats (image/gif, image/jpeg, and image/png). By far, Flash Video served over HTTP on port 80 has the best chance of being viewed by a visitor.

However, Flash Video content delivered using HTTP lacks intellectual property (IP) protection. There is no way to limit offline access to Flash Video content served over HTTP: The Web browser caches Flash Video files in its

Runtime vs. Authortime Assets

Any asset that you load into a Flash movie (SWF) while it's running in a Web browser with the Flash Player is considered a *runtime asset*. If you load an FLV file into a SWF file at runtime, both files must be located on a Web server. If you import an asset into your FLA file, this asset is called an *authortime asset*. When an asset is embedded in your FLA file and placed on the timeline, it's automatically included with the published Flash movie.

The shell SWF and the FLVs can be served from different locations. For example, you can use a lower-cost Web server for your FLV files and a more robust and reliable Web server for your site hosting. Furthermore, you can use a CDN to serve your progressive video content, such as Amazon's S3 service. Sites such as Travelistic.com use Amazon's CDN for cost-effective progressive delivery of Flash Video. You can find a link to Amazon's S3 service on this book's links page at www.flashsupport.com/links.

▶ Any Flash Video embedded in a SWF file must be delivered by a Web server over HTTP. Also, most characteristics of HTTP delivery of Flash Video can be applied to local file playback. For example, the ActionScript code required to play FLV files from fixed or removable storage, such as FLV files on a CD-ROM or DVD-ROM, is identical to the code required for HTTP playback from a Web server.

temporary storage, which can be accessed by the user after browsing the site. As such, content producers and licensees don't distribute Flash Video content over HTTP; RTMP is the preferred protocol.

Another drawback to HTTP-delivered Flash Video is access to all parts of the video file. With Flash Video served over HTTP, the video file (FLV or SWF) progressively downloads to the Web browser's cache. The viewer can access only the portion of the video that has already downloaded. For example, if you have a 30-minute training video, and the viewer wants to view only the last five minutes of the video, they have to wait until the first 25 minutes have downloaded to the browser cache. For longer videos, you should consider using RTMP instead of HTTP.

RTMP

You can serve Flash Video over the Internet using RTMP, a special protocol for real-time server applications ranging from instant messaging to collaborative data sharing to video streaming. Whereas HTTP-delivered Flash Video is referred to as *progressive download video*, RTMP-delivered Flash Video is called *streaming video*. However, because the term *streaming* is so often misused, I prefer the term *real-time streaming video*.

NOTES

▶ You'll learn more about the ActionScript code required to play real-time streaming Flash Video in Chapter 7, "Building Your Own Video Player."

RTMP delivery of Flash Video is provided by licensed server software from Adobe, notably Flash Media Server (FMS). FMS is installed on a networked server and manages streaming Flash Video separately from the Web server hosting the Flash movie (SWF) and other HTML content (see **Figure 4.1**). Licensing FMS for high volume Web sites, though, can be prohibitively expensive, but you can find affordable shared hosting FMS services for less demanding sites from providers such as Influxis.com. Using a Flash Video Streaming Service (FVSS) provider is a better option for high volume Flash Video deployment, and I discuss this option later in the chapter.

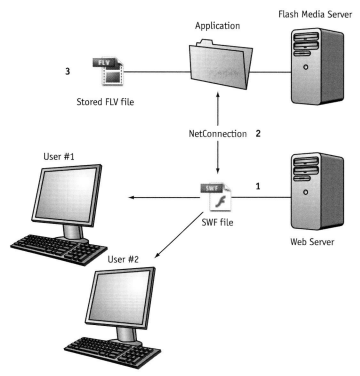

Flash Media Server

Application

3

Stored FLV file

NetConnection 2

User #1

SWF file

1

Web Server

User #2

Figure 4.1 When a user views real-time streaming Flash Video content, a Flash movie (SWF) is downloaded from a Web server (step 1), and a NetConnection instance created in the movie's ActionScript code makes a connection to the FMS application or FVSS provider (step 2). The Flash Video content (FLV) is then streamed packet by packet to the Flash Player (step 3).

One of the benefits of RTMP delivery for the viewer is near-instantaneous playback of video, provided the Flash Video file is encoded with a bitrate appropriate to the viewer's connection speed. Real-time streaming video can also be seeked to any point in the content. This feature is particularly advantageous for long-duration content because the viewer doesn't have to wait for the video file to load before jumping ahead, as is the case for HTTP-delivered video.

Content producers who want to protect video from local playback can opt to use real-time streaming video—in any video format, not just Flash Video. When RTMP-based video

NOTES

In the world of digital video editing, the word *seek* means to jump to a new time in a video clip, and yes, video is *seeked*, not sought.

streams into the Flash Player, the audio and video data is only stored in the Flash Player's memory buffer. The entire Flash Video file is never copied or stored to the Web browser cache.

Protocol usage

The protocol you use can affect your Flash Video deployment strategy. Be sure to carefully analyze your objectives before picking a protocol.

Encoding parameters

If you encode your Flash Video files with a compression tool, you should determine which protocol(s) to use before you create the FLV files. Because RTMP connections send video data from a remote server to a temporary player buffer, the Flash Video's data rate should be predictable throughout the entire duration of playback. This data rate consistency can only be accomplished with constant bitrate (CBR) encoding. Nearly all Flash Video encoders offer the option of selecting constant bitrate or variable bitrate (VBR) encoding. If your Flash Video encoding tool doesn't offer a choice, it's probably using CBR encoding.

If your Flash Video content is encoded with a VBR setting, your file may have extreme data spikes that exceed the average bitrate of the video. These spikes can abruptly empty the Flash Player's buffer and result in temporarily stalled playback and an annoying pause-play-pause experience.

However, if your Flash Video content won't be delivered over RTMP, you can safely use VBR encoding for standard HTTP delivery on a Web server. Because the Flash Video progressively downloads and is stored in the Web browser cache, data spikes probably won't occur during playback— provided the bitrate you're using is suitable to the viewer's connection speed.

Guaranteed access

For security reasons, some internal networks, or intranets, control the type of content that can enter the network from remote locations. In large corporations, these intranets can

NOTES

▶ You can use ActionScript to control the amount of Flash Video buffered into the Flash Player memory. Technically speaking, the buffer is temporarily written to the user's hard drive but isn't stored as complete, intact, or playable FLV file. You'll learn more about buffering strategies for real-time streaming Flash Video in Chapter 8, "Integrating Multiple Bitrates."

block much of the content available on the Web. Firewalls and proxies that allow Internet traffic accept HTTP connections over port 80 from remote servers, so you're nearly guaranteed that viewers behind these firewalls can access Flash Video delivered over HTTP.

However, this luxury isn't always shared with RTMP-delivered Flash Video. The default port for RTMP connections is 1935, which may not be allowed on tight firewalls. If the Flash Player's first attempt to play video over port 1935 fails, the Flash Player automatically tries to connect to the video stream with RTMP over port 80. If this second try fails, the last resort available for the Flash Player is to try an HTTP-tunneled connection over port 80. A *tunneled connection* means the RTMP data packet is wrapped (or *masked*) in an HTTP data packet. Some firewalls allow this traffic, because the data packet appears to be normal HTTP Web traffic. If the firewall inspects the HTTP data, though, it still may reject the connection, and the Flash Video won't play.

The bottom line: If you don't want to deal with firewalls and proxies, you should serve your Flash Video from a Web server over HTTP.

Content protection

Some video formats available over the Internet use digital rights management (DRM) to control access. Microsoft Windows Media and Apple QuickTime use encrypted keys to limit many factors of media usage, including the number of computers that can view the content and how long the content can be viewed. Flash Video hasn't included such ironclad content protection measures in any past releases of the Flash Player, including Flash Player 9.

If you must control access to Flash Video content, and you don't want users to fish FLV files out of their Web browser cache, you must use real-time streaming Flash Video. As soon as you put your FLV files in a publicly accessible location on a Web server, you're allowing users to copy the FLV files and do whatever they want with them. Mind you, lots of Flash Video files on the Web—even from high-volume sites—aren't real-time streaming Flash Video. Google's Video

NOTES

▶ Don't be disheartened by firewall security measures. As Flash Video becomes more popular, especially with business use and real-time video conferencing, more and more firewalls and proxies are allowing RTMP traffic.

search and YouTube.com are prime examples of sites offering browser-cacheable, do-as-you-please FLV files. However, real-time streaming Flash Video is usually the only viable option for companies and organizations (such as movie studios and broadcast networks) that need to control the way their content is viewed and accessed by the public.

Online or offline playback

If your Flash application is designed to run from a local source such as a user's hard drive or fixed media (CD/DVD-ROM), you may want the Flash Video content to coexist with other local files used for the application. Unless you want to require an Internet connection for the Flash application to run, you don't need to store Flash Video files on remote Web servers (HTTP) or real-time streaming servers (RTMP).

Duration of content

As the length of a video file increases, so should the likelihood of using real-time streaming Flash Video (RTMP) over a progressively downloaded Flash Video (HTTP). Regardless of the data rate used by the video file, longer files have larger file sizes. When an HTTP-delivered Flash Video starts to download into the Flash Player, by default the file continues to download to the browser cache regardless of whether the user watches the content. If you host large FLV files on your Web server, the Web server's data-transfer bytes will increase quickly, potentially raising the financial cost of hosting the files. If you host large FLV files on an FMS (or Flash Video Streaming Service), your data-transfer cost includes only the portions of the Flash Video watched by each user.

Delivery: Web Server, Flash Media Server, or CDN?

Determining where and how to host your Flash Video content means considering both the target audience and your budget. You can store Flash Video files on your own or a hosted Web server, your own or a hosted FMS, or on a CDN. Each of these options has specific deployment objectives.

▶ Although real-time streaming Flash Video isn't stored as an accessible FLV file after it's viewed by the user, hackers can make copies of any video stream, regardless of file format or delivery. Most content providers offering licensed content use real-time streaming Flash Video because the protection measures can adequately prevent most users from illegally reusing content, despite the current lack of a true licensing management system in the FLV file format and the Flash Player.

Low-volume Web site with limited video

If your Flash site uses a few pieces of video content, all of short duration and with small file sizes (less than 30 MB), you can probably store your FLV files on a standard Web server. Be sure to check the hosting plans from popular companies such as godaddy.com, dreamhost.com, or 1and1.com.

Examples of smaller sites include portfolio sites with short pieces of video work, small businesses with short video introductions by representatives of the company, and so on.

Low-volume Web site with protected or long content

For a small Web site that includes video content with playback restrictions or long-duration video content (more than 10 minutes per file), you should consider a hosted FMS account. You don't need to buy a licensed FMS—it's much simpler and more affordable to use a third-party FMS hosting company, such as influxis.com or mediatemple.com. You can usually find an FMS hosting company outside the United States with a bit of searching on the Web.

A low-volume site might belong to a musician who lets visitors watch music videos or listen to audio streams that can't be downloaded and repurposed by users. Or, a film production company's Web site may showcase a short film or documentary project—for example, www.teachnow.org allows visitors to watch the full 30-minute documentary *Teach*.

High-volume Web site with distributable content

Some large Web sites use a variety of video on their sites, from short product demonstrations to user-generated content (UGC). High-volume sites that receive thousands—if not millions—of visits per day require large CDNs to mirror content around the nation or globe. When content is *mirrored*, copies of the content are spread across several servers located throughout the country of origin or throughout the world. Each user is served content from the fastest server or the one closest to their network connection. Sites that don't require content protection, such as YouTube.com,

► The default file-cache limit varies from one browser to another, usually in the range of 30 MB to 50 MB. If your Flash Video file size exceeds 30 MB, you may want to consider using real-time streaming. Also, in ActionScript, you can specify large buffer sizes for real-time streaming Flash Video, potentially incurring higher streaming costs.

► FMS can also real-time stream MP3 audio files to a Flash movie, protecting the MP3 file from being downloaded directly to the user.

don't need FMS to serve millions of videos per day—but they do need first-class Web servers to host and deliver terabytes of Flash Video.

High-volume Web site with protected content

If a large Web site is showcasing protected video content consumed by thousands of people per day, an FVSS provider is required to manage hundreds of simultaneous connections. FVSS providers are licensed by Adobe to carry FMS technology on hundreds of servers to meet the demands of high-volume Web sites. Many popular CDNs are also FVSS providers, such as Akamai (www.akamai.com) and Limelight Networks (www.limelightnetworks.com). Many broadcast and cable networks use these CDNs to distribute popular TV shows on their Web sites.

Playback: Live Streaming vs. Prerecorded

You can not only compress and deploy FLV files from your own source video files, but also stream live video from your Web cam to an FMS application. This application in turn can redistribute your live video stream to other users. FMS can even record the live stream for later playback!

Requirements for live streaming

In order to stream live video and audio from a camera and microphone on a computer or device, you need the following:

- ▶ Flash Player 6 or higher
- ▶ Flash Communication Server (FCS) 1.0 or higher, or FMS 2.0 or higher
- ▶ Reasonably fast Internet connection from Flash Player to the FCS/FMS application, with a recommendation of at least a 128Kbps or faster upload rate for minimum quality video and audio and ideally a 384Kbps or higher upload rate
- ▶ Compatible USB or FireWire Web cam or video source
- ▶ Microphone connected to sound card or audio-in port, USB headset/microphone, or a Bluetooth headset/microphone

CLOSE-UP

When Do You Need Your Own Flash Media Server?

The exception, rather than the rule, is that any Web site offering Flash Video requires the site developers to invest in their own FMS license and hardware. Flash developers can download and install the free developer version of FMS to build prototypes for their business clients. Some media companies are investing in FMSs that work in tandem with larger CDN servers to distribute content with less administration hassle. Or, you can develop a custom real-time Flash application that handles multiple live video streams originating from users' Web cams. Such real-time applications require more than just video-streaming services, and they utilize the data-sharing capabilities of FMS. Jump to the next section to learn more about live video streams.

▶ A Flash movie (the *publisher*) that negotiates the connection to a FCS/FMS application and publishes the video and audio stream to the server

▶ A Flash movie (the *subscriber*) that connects to the FCS/FMS application and plays back the live video and audio stream

You don't need your own FCS or FMS license in order to stream a live audio and video feed over the Internet. You can use a hosted FCS or FMS account, as I mentioned earlier in the chapter. However, most FVSS providers do *not* offer live streaming capabilities.

Built-in real-time compression

Luckily, you don't need special hardware to compress the live video from a Web cam (or video source; see "Not Just for Web Cams"). Flash Player 6 and higher have a built-in Sorenson Spark video encoder, as well as a Speech codec that can encode audio.

Using ActionScript, you can control the quality and bitrate of the live video and audio stream published from a Flash movie. You can control all aspects of the video stream, including frame rate, frame size, bitrate (or data rate), or quality. The audio stream can be published in the following kilohertz rates: 5, 8, 11, 22, or 44.

Currently, the Flash Player doesn't ship with a built-in On2 VP6 encoder. However, Adobe has released Flash Media Encoder, a free standalone application that can encode live video as a real-time stream to an FMS. On2 sells Flix Live 8 for Windows, an application that streams live VP6-encoded video directly to an FMS application. Both of these applications allow you to take advantage of the higher quality of the On2 VP6 codec with live streams. You'll find links to these applications at www.flashsupport.com/links.

Live streaming video from prerecorded Flash Video

Live streaming Flash Video has a few key differences from prerecorded Flash Video content. Live streaming video can only be compressed and streamed by the Flash Player in the Sorenson Spark codec. Although you have substantial

NOTES

▶ The Flash Player can't stream live audio and video with only a Web server. You must have access to a FCS or FMS application to stream live video and audio content from the Flash Player. Red 5 is an open-source RTMP server that can stream live video with the Sorenson Spark codec. You'll find more information about Red 5 at www.osflash.org/red5.

NOTES

▶ I don't explore the use of live streams with Flash content in this book, but you can read more about the ActionScript Camera and Microphone classes in a series of tutorials I wrote for Community MX. You can find a list of my articles and tutorials at www.flashsupport.com/cmx.

Not Just for Web Cams

The video source for a Flash Player published stream can be a wide range of devices, including Web cams and digital video inputs on your computer. On both Windows and Mac computers, you can plug in a DV camcorder with a FireWire (iLink or IEEE 1394) connection and stream taped or live feeds from the camera. You can also use USB video capture devices for just about any analog video source, such as a videotape or older camcorder, with live streaming. Some screen-capture applications also install a video-capture driver that is accessible from Flash Player, such as TechSmith's Camtasia software on Windows.

To see if your device is supported by Flash Player, open any Flash movie in the Flash Player via a Web browser or standalone Flash Player. Right-click (or Control-click on Mac) the movie's stage, and choose Settings from the Flash Player contextual menu. In the Settings dialog, click the Web cam icon to view the available video sources on your computer. For more information on these settings, visit www.adobe.com/support/flashplayer/help/.

control over many aspects of live streaming compression, you can use only CBR encoding with live video—no VBR encoding is available for live streams.

One of the most critical operational differences is control of bitrate. With live streaming video, the published video is being pushed to the FCS or FMS application at a specific bitrate. If the bitrate of the publisher stream is too high for a subscriber, then that user's viewing experience of the live stream will suffer. FCS or FMS can't adjust a published stream's bitrate on the fly—at best, it can only drop frames on that subscriber's stream. You should either use a bitrate for your live stream that is compatible with all subscribers or publish more than one stream. To publish more than one stream, you need more than one video camera or source connected to your computer: one for each published stream. This is also true for audio streams—you need one audio device for each audio stream published. You can also craft subscriber movies that turn off the video portion of a stream and play only the audio portion if the subscriber's bitrate can't support both data streams.

Budgets: Bandwidth and Transfer Rates

Flash Video offers a unique experience for Web site visitors to view a wide range of video content: full episodes of TV shows, movie trailers, how-to videos and tutorials, music videos, home-grown video clips, and more. As long as Flash Player 6 or higher is installed on the user's computer, you can serve some type of Flash Video for their enjoyment.

But all video, regardless of whether or not its format is Flash Video, has a financial price. Depending on your content length and audience, the additional cost of hosting and serving Flash Video can range from zero to thousands—if not millions—of dollars *per month*. The more popular your video content, the more likely you'll need to pay extra hosting fees on top of your regular bill. Let's look at how you can estimate how much Flash Video deployment could end up costing you.

Before you encode your Flash Video content, you should determine how much of your site budget will be used for video, and estimate how much traffic you want to accommodate.

Real-time streaming video

To calculate the average transfer rate of real-time streaming video from your site per month, use the following formula for *each* video file to determine the number of bytes:

(Bitrate in bps ÷ 8) × Average viewing time in seconds × Viewers

So, if you have 3000 users (100 users a day over a 30-day period) watching a 500-Kbps Flash Video clip for an average duration of three minutes, the Flash Media Server (or equivalent FVSS provider) would have streamed around 31.4 GB of data:

(500,000 ÷ 8) × 180 seconds × 3,000 = 33,750,000,000 bytes = 32,186 MB = 31.4 GB

Depending on your service plan, this *one* video clip could cost you over $150 per month.

Progressive-download video

To calculate the average transfer rate of Flash Video from a Web server per month, use the following formula for each video file:

File size of video clip × Viewers

If 3,000 users (100 users a day over a 30-day period) watch a Flash Video clip that is 35 MB (roughly 500 Kbps at 10 minutes in length), the Web server streams around 102.5 GB of data:

35 × 3,000 = 105,000 MB = 102.5 GB

Depending on your Web hosting plan, this *one* video clip could cost you anywhere from $3 to $10 a month to host with popular Web hosting packages.

Why should you use the total file size for the progressive video calculation and not the average time watched by the viewer? Remember, with progressive video file formats,

NOTES

▶ Don't be intimidated by the results of your calculations. You should prepare these estimates ahead of any encoding procedures. After you've gauged the cost of Flash Video, you can head into a Flash Video encoding tool knowing the highest bitrates you should use.

after the Flash Player begins to download the video file to the browser cache, it doesn't stop. The file continues to load in the background while the viewer watches the content. Regardless of how much of the video the viewer watches, the entire Flash Video file is downloaded to the cache—unless the viewer unloads the Flash movie and continues to another Web page or closes the browser window.

Bottom line: estimate your transfer rates

Regardless of which method of delivery you use for your Flash Video content, prepare transfer estimates so you can forecast how much of your budget you need to allocate to Flash Video. If you're developing Flash Video for a business client, include these data-transfer estimates in your project plans. Each client will have a different hosting agreement with their CDNs, and those agreements vary dramatically based on the size of the company, the size of their audience, and the type of content they're providing.

PART II

Production Essentials

Chapter 5   Placing Flash Video on a Web Page   79

Chapter 6   Exploring the FLVPlayback Components   111

Chapter 7   Building Your Own Video Player   159

Chapter 8   Integrating Multiple Bitrates   179

5

Placing Flash Video on a Web Page

All Flash Video content needs a Flash movie (SWF file) to play in a Web browser. In HTML documents, you don't link directly to FLV files. Instead, you can add a Flash movie to the document and load the Flash Video content into that Flash movie using `<object>` and `<embed>` tags. You can also embed Flash Video into a SWF file, but embedded Flash Video is mostly a thing of the past—it's easier to manage Flash Video content by loading the FLV files into Flash movies. In this chapter, you learn how to set up Flash movie video players using Adobe Dreamweaver® and Adobe Flash.

Integrating Flash Video with Dreamweaver

If you have Dreamweaver 8 or Dreamweaver CS3, you can quickly add a Flash Video clip to an HTML document. Using Dreamweaver's media extensions, you're just a few clicks away from Flash Video deployment. Also, after you've set up a Flash Video player in Dreamweaver, you can reuse those SWF files with other HTML code editors.

Setting up the FLVPlayer SWF

To add a Flash Video element to an HTML document, follow these steps:

1. Launch Dreamweaver, and open or create an HTML document. When you create a new file, save it as `basic_player.html`.

2. To place the Flash Video element in a preexisting HTML document, make sure the cursor is located in the container element (table cell, `<div>` element, and so on). You can also insert the Flash Video anywhere between the opening and closing `<body>` tags

NOTES

▶ You can find all the source files for this chapter's exercises in the ch05 folder of this book's DVD-ROM.

▶ All the progressive-download URLs in this chapter contain relative paths (../flv) to the FLV files in the flv folder on the DVD-ROM. Depending on how you structure your local system folders and files, you may need to adjust the sample paths to point to FLV files on your system.

▶ You can use the Dreamweaver Flash Video extension with progressive-download Flash Video, but make sure you use an appropriate bitrate for your target audience. The Dreamweaver Flash Video extension isn't as full-featured as the FLVPlayback component available in Flash 8 or Flash CS3. I recommend the FLVPlayback component for better control over real-time streaming Flash Video.

of your document. (If necessary, switch to Code view to make sure you're inserting the Flash Video element exactly where you want it.)

3. To insert the video, choose Insert > Media > Flash Video. In the Insert Flash Video dialog (**Figure 5.1**), select either Progressive Download Video or Streaming Video from the Video Type combo box. Then, type the path to your FLV file in the URL field, or click the Browse button and locate the file. Select a look-and-feel for the video control bar in the Skin combo box. Click the Detect Size button to auto-fill the Width and Height values. If you want the video to begin playback as soon as the Web page loads, select the Auto Play check box. If you want the video to go back to the first frame when playback has finished, select the Auto Rewind check box. The Flash Player detection option is automatically selected. With this option enabled, JavaScript code is added to the document to determine which Flash Player version the user has and whether it needs to be updated in order to play the video. You can alert users that they need to upgrade by adding your own text to the alert dialog. Click OK to accept the settings.

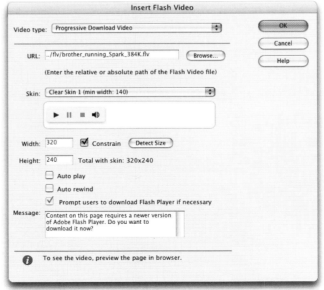

Figure 5.1 The Insert Flash Video dialog.

4. Your HTML document now contains the necessary HTML and JavaScript code to load your FLV file. Unfortunately, there's no going back to the Insert Flash Video dialog if you need to change the settings. However, you can select the Flash Video element on the stage and change the settings in the Property inspector (**Figure 5.2**).

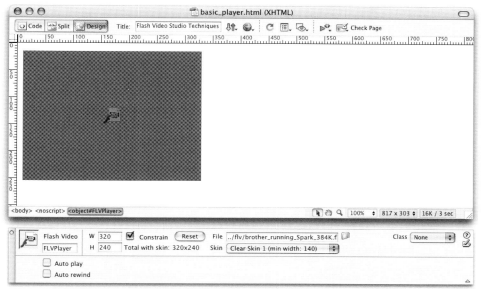

Figure 5.2 The Flash Video object's settings in the Property inspector.

5. Open the HTML file, and watch the Flash Video by choosing File > Preview in Browser > [Your Preferred Browser]. The video control bar appears only when the user's mouse hovers over the Flash Video clip (**Figure 5.3**).

6. Dreamweaver automatically copies two SWF files to the same location as your HTML file: FLVPlayer_Progressive.swf (or FLVPlayer_Streaming.swf, if you chose a Streaming Video type in the settings) and a SWF file including the skin you selected in the Insert Flash Video dialog. Dreamweaver also creates a Scripts folder and a file named AC_RunActiveContent.js. Upload these files, your FLV file, and the Dreamweaver HTML, JavaScript, and SWF files to your Web server for final deployment. Make sure you replicate the Scripts folder

Figure 5.3 The Flash Video content playing in a Web browser.

► You can download the 8.0.2 updater for Macromedia Dreamweaver 8 from www.adobe.com/support/ dreamweaver. Among other fixes, this free update changes the way in which a piece of Flash content (SWF file) is added to an HTML document. The 8.0.2 update integrates the AC_RunActiveContent.js file—a set of JavaScript functions that detects the Flash Player version and dynamically writes the <object> or <embed> tags for the HTML document at runtime. The Dreamweaver examples discussed in this chapter can use either Dreamweaver 8.0.2 or Dreamweaver CS3.

in the Web directory containing the HTML, SWF, and FLV files, and keep the AC_RunActiveContent.js file in the Scripts folder.

Detecting Flash Player with SWFObject

Even though the Flash Video playback works with the JavaScript and HTML code created by Dreamweaver, it's not the best real-world solution. There are problems with the way Dreamweaver embeds a Flash Video player in HTML:

► **Duplicate parameters for <object> and <embed> tags:** When you look at the Dreamweaver code, all the Flash Video settings are passed via the flashvars parameter in the <object> and <embed> tags. If you want to edit the code by hand, you have to change the HTML code in both tags.

► **Version detection of the Flash Player:** The Dreamweaver detection script used doesn't allow you to specify alternate HTML content if the required Flash Player version isn't installed.

► **Search engine optimization (SEO) of the Flash content:** If you want non-Flash content to be indexed by search engines, you must create hidden HTML text on your Web page. Most search engines can't index Flash content very well.

What's a Web designer or developer to do? Luckily, there's a great open-source JavaScript library called SWFObject, created by Geoff Stearns. You can download SWFObject at http://blog.deconcept.com/swfobject.

Geoff provides a thorough description and several tutorials for SWFObject on his site; in this section, you'll learn how to use SWFObject with the FLVPlayer SWF files generated by Dreamweaver. The basic principle of SWFObject is simple: Dynamically add a Flash movie to a <div> container on your page. The <div> tag specifies alternate HTML content that is seen only by users who don't have the required Flash Player version. If the user has the required version of Flash Player, the JavaScript code from SWFObject replaces the content of the <div> tag with your Flash movie. SWFObject fixes the Dreamweaver problems I mentioned earlier:

▶ **One script to specify settings for the Flash movie:** You don't need to write your own `<object>` and `<embed>` tags in the HTML document; SWFObject does the work for you. You need to specify Flash movie attributes, such as width, height, and source file, in only one place: the JavaScript code block that instantiates the Flash movie.

▶ **Easy Flash Player version detection:** The SWFObject Java-Script code enables you to specify the required version of the Flash Player, including minor releases, such as 6.0.79. If the required version isn't installed, the HTML content specified in the `<div>` tag is displayed. In addition, a special feature called ExpressInstall is available in Flash Player 6 and higher. I describe how SWFObject can use ExpressInstall later in the chapter.

▶ **HTML content is visible to search engines:** Search engines don't execute JavaScript code in a Web page during the indexing process. The search engine has no clue that there's a Flash movie on the page—the search engine crawler only looks at the HTML content in the `<div>` tag. You should include a description of your Flash content in the `<div>` tag, as well as instructions on how to update or install the Flash Player.

Let's start by replacing the Dreamweaver code for the Flash Video extension with the SWFObject code:

1. Open the HTML document with the Dreamweaver-created code, and resave the document as `swfobject_player.html`.

2. Delete the `<script>` block containing the JavaScript function named `MM_CheckFlashVersion` (approximately 33 lines of code).

3. Delete the following `<script>` tag just before the closing `</head>` tag (don't type the ➥ character, which indicates a continuation of the same line of code):

```
<script src="Scripts/AC_RunActiveContent.js"
➥type="text/javascript"></script>
```

4. Delete the `onload` handler from the `<body>` tag.

5. Delete all the HTML and JavaScript code between the opening `<body>` and closing `</body>` tags.

NOTES

▶ In response to a lawsuit against Microsoft, Microsoft changed the way browser plug-ins (ActiveX controls) initialize in Internet Explorer for Windows (IE Win). If you don't use JavaScript to dynamically write the `<object>` tag needed for a particular plug-in, the user must first click the embedded content before mouse events can be passed to the user interface (if any) of the embedded content. If you only include `<object>` tags on your HTML page for Flash content, you're making the IE Win users click the Flash movie before they can use it.

▶ SWFObject 1.5 is included in the ch05 folder on the DVD-ROM. The swfobject.js and expressinstall.swf files in ch05 are the same files distributed by Geoff Stearns on his site. You can also find the swfobject.js file in the scripts folder on the DVD-ROM.

6. You're ready to add the SWFObject functionality to the document. Above the closing </head> tag, add the following line of code:

```
<script src="swfobject.js"
➥type="text/javascript"></script>
```

7. Below the opening <body> tag and before the closing </body> tag, create a <div> tag containing your alternate HTML content, displayed to users (or search engines) lacking the required Flash Player version. Feel free to replace or modify the HTML content between the <div></div> tags to suit your particular needs.

```
<div id="flashcontent">
    <p><strong>You need to upgrade your Flash
    Player.</strong><br/>
    This is replaced by the Flash content. <br/>
    Place your alternate content here and users
    without the Flash plugin
    or with <br/>
    Javascript turned off will see this. Content here
    allows you to
    leave out <code>noscript</code> <br/>
    tags. To bypass Flash Player detection,
    <a href="swfobject_player.html?detectflash=false">
    ➥click here</a>.</p>
</div>
```

8. After the closing </div> tag, you need to write the JavaScript code that invokes the SWFObject constructor, contained in the swfobject.js file. Place the following code after the closing </div> tag and before the closing </body> tag. This code takes the same flashvars parameters used by the Dreamweaver code and dynamically passes them to the new Flash object created by the SWFObject code. Notice that the streamName variable specifies the FLV filename. Don't include the .flv file extension in the streamName value:

```
<script type="text/javascript">
// <![CDATA[
```

```
var so = new SWFObject("FLVPlayer_Progressive.
➥swf", "main", "320", "240", "7", "#FFFFFF");
so.addVariable("MM_ComponentVersion", "1");
so.addVariable("skinName", "Clear_Skin_1");
so.addVariable("streamName", "../flv/brother_
➥running_Spark_384K");
so.addVariable("autoPlay", "false");
so.addVariable("autoRewind", "false");
so.write("flashcontent");
// ]]>
</script>
```

9. Save the HTML file, and test the new document in a Web browser. You should see the video appear on the page, just as you did with the Dreamweaver-created version.

Using ExpressInstall with SWFObject

When Flash Player 8 was released, Adobe (then Macromedia) released a new feature called ExpressInstall. This feature automatically prompted anyone with Flash Player 6 r65 or higher to the current release of Flash Player. It eliminated the need for the user to manually download and launch a Flash Player installer file. Unfortunately, Mozilla-based browser users must close the browser while the in-place installation is processing.

Combined with the power of the SWFObject script, Express-Install enables the following Flash Player detection process:

1. The user loads the Web page with Flash content.

2. SWFObject checks for the presence of the Flash Player. If the required version is available, the Flash content is automatically displayed without user intervention. If Flash Player 6 r65 is installed, and a higher version of Flash Player is required, such as Flash Player 6 r79 or Flash Player 8, SWFObject loads a special SWF file (expressinstall.swf) instead of your Flash SWF file.

3. When the expressinstall.swf file loads, the user is presented with a dialog prompting them to upgrade to the latest version of the Flash Player (**Figure 5.4**).

CLOSE-UP

Locating the Origin of the SWF Files from Dreamweaver

If you happen to need copies of the FLVPlayer_Progressive.swf or skin SWF file that Dreamweaver provided, or you lost the ones that Dreamweaver created, you can find the files in the Dreamweaver application folder. Browse to the Dreamweaver application folder on your system:

Windows
C:\Program Files\Adobe\Dreamweaver CS3
C:\Program Files\Macromedia\Dreamweaver 8

Mac
[Startup disk]: Applications: Adobe Dreamweaver CS3
[Startup disk]: Applications: Macromedia Dreamweaver 8)

From the Dreamweaver application folder, you can find the FLVPlayer SWF files in:

Configuration\Templates\Video_Player

The skin SWF files can be found in:

Configuration\Templates\Video_Controls

4. If the user chooses to upgrade, the latest Flash Player installer file downloads behind the scenes. The user sees the download progress displayed in the dialog (**Figure 5.5**). If the user chooses not to upgrade, or an error occurs during the update process, Geoff's default expressinstall.swf movie throws a JavaScript alert notifying the user. I've updated the expressinstall.swf movie to go to another frame displaying an upgrade notification, instead of using a JavaScript alert.

Figure 5.4 The ExpressInstall dialog.

Figure 5.5 The download progress of the new Flash Player plug-in.

5. After the download finishes, the installation process begins. Mozilla-based browser users must quit the browser before beginning the installation.

6. After the installer finishes, the Web browser reopens (if it had to quit) and redirects back to the original Web page with the Flash content.

It's quick to add ExpressInstall functionality to any SWFObject implementation. In the following steps, you'll modify the code created in the last section to use ExpressInstall:

1. In Dreamweaver or your preferred HTML editor, open the swfobject_player.html file you built in the last section. Resave the document as `swfobject_expressinstall_player.html`.

2. If you added a detection-bypass link in your alternative HTML code contained in the <div> tag, update the document reference in the anchor <a> tag, such as

```
<a href="swfobject_expressinstall_player.html?
➥detectflash=false">
```

3. Below the closing `</div>` tag, update the `<script>` block that instantiates the SWFObject instance to use Express-Install, as shown in bold black text in the following code (don't type the ➥ character):

```
<script type="text/javascript">
// <![CDATA[
    var so = new SWFObject("FLVPlayer_Progressive.
    ➥swf", "main", "320", "240", "7", "#FFFFFF",
    ➥true);
    so.addVariable("MM_ComponentVersion", "1");
    so.addVariable("skinName", "Clear_Skin_1");
    so.addVariable("streamName",
    ➥"../flv/brother_running_Spark_384K");
    so.addVariable("autoPlay", "false");
    so.addVariable("autoRewind", "false");
    so.useExpressInstall("expressinstall.swf");
    so.write("flashcontent");
// ]]>
</script>
```

4. Copy the expressinstall.swf file from the ch05 folder on the DVD-ROM to the location of your local files. Make sure you upload the expressinstall.swf file along with the rest of the HTML, SWF, and JavaScript files.

5. Save the HTML document, and test the file in a Web browser that's using Flash Player 6. You can test the in-place upgrade process with any plug-in version that's lower than the required version specified in your SWFObject code.

Playing Video with Flash CS3 Components

If you want more control over Flash Video playback, use the components included with Flash CS3. By building your own Flash document with components, you can customize graphics and text that appear around, below, or above the video content. You don't have to own Dreamweaver to add Flash Video content to a Web site. You can build a Flash document that uses one of the Flash Video components.

NOTES

▶ To easily switch the Flash Player version used by the Firefox browser, I highly recommend using the Flash Switcher extension for Firefox on Windows. You can download this free extension at: https://addons.mozilla.org/firefox/3649/.

If you're using a Mozilla-based browser, you can create a folder of archived versions of Flash Players by downloading older Flash Player installers from Adobe's Web site. You can find the link for archived Flash Player installers at www.flashsupport.com/links.

► You can also build your own Flash Video player with Action-Script. Jump to Chapter 7, "Building Your Own Video Player," for more information. You'll also learn how to use more component features in Part III of this book.

► You can change the Flash Player version used by a Flash document at any time. Choose File > Publish Settings, and, in the Publish Settings dialog, click the Flash tab and change the Flash Player version. Changing the Flash Player version makes the Components panel automatically display suitable components.

Picking a Flash Player version

Before you create a new Flash document, you should determine which version of the Flash Player you want to require for the project. You can choose from one of three components to play video in Flash movies. In Flash CS3, the list of items in the Components panel (Ctrl/Cmd+F7) varies depending on which Flash Player and ActionScript version you use. When you launch Flash CS3, you can choose two Flash document types:

► **Flash File (ActionScript 3.0):** Select this document type if you want to use Flash Player 9 or higher for your video clip. One of the new features enabled by Flash Player 9 is full-screen playback. If you want users to be able to scale a video to take over the whole screen, use this document type.

► **Flash File (ActionScript 2.0):** This document type enables you to use components compatible with Flash Player 6, 7, or 8 in your Flash movie. If you need to target any of these player versions, select this document type.

In the following sections, you learn how to build a variety of Flash Video players using the components that ship with Flash CS3. The Flash Player 8, 7, and 6 video players can also be built using the components that ship with Flash Professional 8.

All the player examples can use either progressive-download or real-time streaming FLV file paths. If you plan to use real-time streaming FLV files, format the path of the FLV file as rtmp://<server url>/<application path>/<FLV file>.

For example, the path to an active FLV file residing on this book's Flash Media Server account on Influxis.com is:

```
rtmp://flashvideo.rtmphost.com/samples/
➥river_Spark_384K.flv
```

If your real-time streaming URL fails, try omitting the .flv extension from the path:

```
rtmp://flashvideo.rtmphost.com/samples/
➥river_Spark_384K
```

Playing video with the FLVPlayback component for Flash Player 9

If you're building an ActionScript 3.0 project (writing advanced code contained in classes), or if you want to enable full-screen playback for your Flash Video content, the new and improved FLVPlayback component for Flash Player 9 is for you. In this section, you learn how to build a static Flash Video player, which plays an FLV file you specify when you author the Flash document. You'll also learn how to build a Flash Video player that is passed from the URL to an FLV file via HTML parameters, just like the Dreamweaver Flash Video player.

Building an FLV player with authortime-assigned FLV

To create a Flash Player 9 movie (SWF file) that plays a Flash Video file specified during the authoring process, follow these steps:

1. Create a new Flash document, click Flash File (Action-Script 3.0) on the Flash CS3 welcome screen, or choose File > New and select Flash File (ActionScript 3.0). Save the new file as `flvplayer_fp9.fla`.

2. Rename Layer 1 to `flvPlayer`.

3. Open the Components panel (Ctrl/Cmd+F7). Open the Video group, and drag the FLVPlayback component to the stage of your Flash document.

4. Select the new instance of the FLVPlayback component on the stage, and open the Property inspector (Ctrl/Cmd+F3). Name the instance `flvPlayer`. If you only want to place a Flash Video clip in your Flash movie, place the instance at the top-left corner of the stage.

5. In the Parameters tab of the Property inspector, select a player skin. Double-click the `skin` property. In the Select Skin dialog (**Figure 5.6**), choose a skin with the player controls necessary for your project. If you don't have embedded cue points in the FLV file(s) played by the component, you don't need the skins sending in `All`, because these skins feature cue-point navigation buttons. For a general-purpose skin, choose the

NOTES

▶ You learn how to modify and create your own custom skins for the FLVPlayback component in Chapter 6, "Exploring the FLVPlayback Components."

SkinOverPlaySeekFullScreen.swf file. This skin features a play/pause button, a seek (or scrub) bar, and a full-screen button. You can also choose a skin background color here. Click OK.

Figure 5.6 The Select Skin dialog.

6. If the skin floats on top of the video area, set the skinAutoHide value on the Parameters tab to true, so the skin is visible only if the user mouses over the video area. You can also customize the skin background alpha and color.

7. On the Parameters tab, choose an FLV file to play in the component. Double-click the source property to browse to an FLV file, or type the path to the FLV file (**Figure 5.7**). By default, the Match Source FLV Dimensions option is selected; it automatically resizes the FLVPlayback instance to the frame size of the FLV file.

Figure 5.7 The Content Path dialog.

8. If you don't want to add any other Flash elements around the Flash Video content, change the size of your Flash document's stage to match the size of the

FLVPlayback component instance. Choose Modify > Document (Ctrl/Cmd+J), and change the Match value to Contents. This option automatically changes the width and height of the stage to the size of your FLVPlayback instance. You can also type a title and description for your Flash movie (**Figure 5.8**).

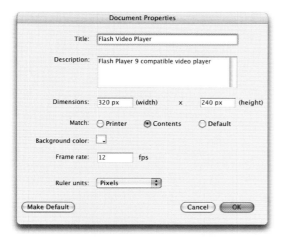

Figure 5.8 The Document Properties dialog.

9. Save the Flash document. Your stage should resemble **Figure 5.9**.

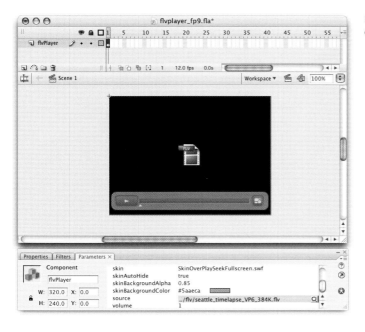

Figure 5.9 The FLVPlayback instance on the stage.

91

10. Choose File > Publish Settings to access the Publish Settings dialog. Select the HTML tab, and choose Flash with Full Screen Support from the Template drop-down menu (**Figure 5.10**). This template enables the full-screen functionality of the FLVPlayback component for Flash Player 9 by adding the `allow-FullScreen` parameter to the `<object>` and `<embed>` tags of the HTML document published by Flash CS3.

Figure 5.10 The HTML tab of the Publish Settings dialog.

Figure 5.11 The Flash Video content playing in the component.

11. Save the Flash document again, and choose File > Publish Preview > Default to view the Flash movie in a Web browser. Make sure you have Flash Player 9 installed in your default browser. You should see the video clip appear in the component instance (**Figure 5.11**). When you click the Full Screen button on the player skin (on the far right), the video scales to the full size of your monitor.

Creating an FLV player with an HTML-assigned FLV

After you've built the FLV player in the preceding section, you need only a few additional steps to enable HTML parameters that assign any of the properties listed in the Parameters tab for the FLVPlayback component. In the next exercise, you learn how to migrate two properties to HTML: the FLV source and the skin SWF file. You can also use this process with other properties such as `autoPlay` and `autoRewind`.

To assign properties of the FLVPlayback instance with HTML parameters, follow these steps:

1. Open the flvplayer_fp9.fla file created in the last section. You can also find this file in the ch05 folder of this book's DVD-ROM. Resave this file as `flvplayer_params_fp9.fla`.

2. Create a new layer named `actions`, and place this layer at the top of the layer stack.

3. Select frame 1 of the actions layer, and open the Actions panel (F9, or Option+F9 on Mac). The following code retrieves the parameters passed by the HTML document, using the new `LoaderInfo` class in Action-Script 3.0. Every object that inherits from the `Display` class, including the `MovieClip` class, has a `loaderInfo` property value. The main timeline of the Flash movie, `this`, qualifies as a `MovieClip` instance. Add the following code to the script pane:

```
// Retrieve the class for the FLVPlayback component
➥import fl.video.FLVPlayback;

// Do not scale Flash movie contents
➥this.stage.scaleMode = "noScale";

// Create a reference to the FLVPlayback instance
var fvp:FLVPlayback = this.flvPlayer;

// Retrieve the HTML parameters
var li:LoaderInfo = this.loaderInfo;
var flashvars:Object = li.parameters;
var flvURL:String = flashvars.flvURL;
var skinURL:String = flashvars.skinURL;
```

```
// Set the new source files for the player
if(flvURL != null) fvp.source = flvURL;
if(skinURL != null) fvp.skin = skinURL;

// Enable auto hide on skin
fvp.skinAutoHide = true;

// Resize FLVPlayback instance to
// match the size of the stage
fvp.setSize(this.stage.stageWidth,
➥this.stagestageHeight);

// Position the video within the instance
// to the top left corner
fvp.align = "topLeft";
```

4. Open the Publish Settings dialog (File > Publish Settings), and uncheck the HTML option in the Formats tab. You'll use an HTML file provided on this book's DVD-ROM. Click OK to close the Publish Settings dialog.

5. Save the Flash document, and test the movie (Ctrl/Cmd+Enter). You'll likely see errors in the Output panel, because no valid URL is passed to the FLVPlayback instance. You'll fix that in the next few steps.

6. You need to create an HTML document that embeds the flvplayer_params_fp9.swf file and passes two parameters to the movie: flvURL and skinURL. In the ch05 folder on the DVD-ROM, you'll find a modified version of the SWFObject example used in the Dreamweaver section of this chapter. Copy the flvplayer_params_swfobject_fp9.html, swfobject.js, and expressinstall.swf files to the same location as your Flash document on your local system. Open the HTML file in Dreamweaver or your preferred HTML editor. Jump to the JavaScript code below the closing </div> tag, and you'll see how the flvURL and skinURL parameters are passed to the Flash movie:

```
<script type="text/javascript">
// <![CDATA[
    var so = new SWFObject("FLVPlayer_Progressive.
    ➥swf", "main", "320", "240", "9.0.28",
    ➥"#FFFFFF", true);
```

```
      so.addParam("allowFullScreen", "true");
      so.addParam("salign","tl");
      so.addVariable("skinURL",
      ➥"SkinOverPlaySeekFullScreen.swf");
      so.addVariable("flvURL",
      ➥"../flv/seattle_timelapse_VP6_384K.flv");
      so.useExpressInstall("expressinstall.swf");
      so.write("flashcontent");
// ]]>
</script>
```

Notice that Flash Player 9 r28 ("9.0.28") is specified for the version requirements. Earlier minor releases of Flash Player 9 didn't offer the full-screen functionality. The allowFullScreen parameter must be set to true in order for the plug-in to scale Flash content to full screen. The salign parameter controls the alignment of the Flash movie's content. To position the video correctly, this property is set to tl, which means content is sized from the top-left corner of the stage. Finally, the skinURL and flvURL values are specified.

You can now easily deploy Flash Video files for Flash Player 9 by reusing the SWF, JS, and HTML files, and specifying new skinURL and flvURL values in the HTML document. If you're using a larger video frame size, be sure to adjust the width and height values in the SWFObject code.

Using the FLVPlayback component for Flash Player 8

You may not be able to target Flash Player 9 for your Flash Video deployment. Perhaps your business client doesn't feel Flash Player 9 has reached an appropriate saturation point with its number of installations. Maybe you don't want to code your own ActionScript with ActionScript 3.0 (AS3)—if you use the FLVPlayback component for Flash Player 9, you need to write all your code in AS3. Whatever your reason, you can use the FLVPlayback component for Flash Player 8 to accomplish nearly all the same functionality that the FLVPlayback component for Flash Player 9 offers. The FLVPlayback component for Flash Player 8 uses ActionScript 2.0 (AS2).

TIP

▶ If you want a copy of one of the skin SWF files that Flash CS3 uses for the FLVPlayback component for Flash Player 9, browse to the Flash application folder on your system and look in the following folder path: Configuration\FLVPlayback Skins\ActionScript 3.0\. On Windows systems, first look for a language folder (en) in the Flash application folder.

▶ If you own Flash Professional 8, you can create a Flash Video player following the steps in this section. When you create a new Flash document in Flash Professional 8, the default settings are already set up for Flash Player 8 and ActionScript 2.0.

▶ This version of the component is different from the FLVPlayback component discussed in the previous sections of this chapter. Flash CS3 automatically changes the component version when you're using a Flash document with AS2.

▶ You learn how to modify and create your own custom skins for the FLVPlayback component in Chapter 6.

Making an FLV Player with an authortime-assigned FLV

If you need a quick way to integrate an FLV file with a Flash Video player, and don't want to worry about passing variables via HTML code, you can use the Parameters tab of the Property inspector to get up and running in no time.

To build a Flash Video player for Flash Player 8, follow these steps:

1. Create a new Flash document by clicking Flash File (ActionScript 2.0) on the welcome screen of Flash CS3 or choosing File > New and selecting Flash File (ActionScript 2.0). Save the new file as `flvplayer_fp8.fla`.

2. Rename Layer 1 to `flvPlayer`.

3. Open the Components panel (Ctrl/Cmd+F7). Open the Video group, and drag the FLVPlayback component to the stage of your Flash document.

4. Select the new instance of the FLVPlayback component on the stage, and open the Property inspector (Ctrl/Cmd+F3). Name the instance `flvPlayer`. Place the instance at the top-left corner of the stage if you only want to place a Flash Video clip into your Flash movie.

5. In the Parameters tab of the Property inspector, pick a player skin that suits your needs. Double-click the `skin` property. In the Select Skin dialog (**Figure 5.12**), choose a skin with the player controls required for your project. If you don't have embedded cue points in the FLV file you want to play with the component, you don't need the skins ending in `All`, because they feature cue-point navigation buttons. For a general-purpose skin, choose the SteelOverPlaySeekMute.swf file. This skin features a play/pause button, a seek (or scrub) bar, and a mute button. Click OK.

6. If the skin floats on top of the video area, set the `skinAutoHide` value to `false`, so the skin is visible only if the user mouses over the video area. You can find this property on the Parameters tab.

Figure 5.12 The Select Skin dialog for the AS2 version of the FLVPlayback component.

7. On the Parameters tab, choose an FLV file to play in the component. Double-click the `contentPath` property to browse to an FLV file, or type the path to the FLV file (**Figure 5.13**). By default, the Match Source FLV Dimensions option is selected; it automatically resizes the FLVPlayback instance to the frame size of the FLV file.

Figure 5.13 The Content Path dialog.

8. If you don't want any additional Flash elements around the Flash Video content, change the size of your Flash document's stage to match the size of the FLVPlayback component instance. Choose Modify > Document (Ctrl/Cmd+J). Change the Match value to Contents to automatically change the width and height of the stage to the size of your FLVPlayback instance. You can also type a title and description for your Flash movie (**Figure 5.14**).

97

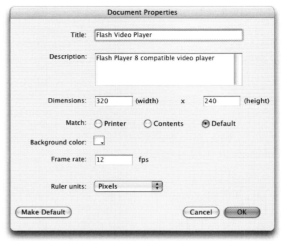

Figure 5.14 The Document Properties dialog.

9. Save the Flash document. Your stage should resemble **Figure 5.15**.

Figure 5.15 The FLVPlayback instance on the stage.

10. Open the Publish Settings dialog (File > Publish Settings), and select the Flash tab. Change the Flash Player version to Flash Player 8. The ActionScript version option should already be set to ActionScript 2.0.

11. Choose File > Publish Preview > Default to view the Flash movie in a Web browser. Make sure you have Flash Player 8 or higher installed in your default browser. You should see the video clip appear in the component instance (**Figure 5.16**).

Figure 5.16 The Flash Video content playing in the component.

Creating an FLV player with an HTML-assigned FLV

Now that you've built the FLV player for Flash Player 8, you need to complete only a few additional steps to enable HTML parameters that assign any of the properties listed in the Parameters tab for the FLVPlayback component. In the following exercise, you learn how to migrate the FLV source and skin SWF file parameters to HTML. As I mentioned in the Flash Player 9 section, you could use this process with other properties such as `autoPlay` and `autoRewind`.

To assign properties of the FLVPlayback instance with HTML parameters, follow these steps:

1. Open the flvplayer_fp8.fla file created in the last section. You can also find this file in the ch05 folder on the DVD-ROM. Resave the file as `flvplayer_params_fp8.fla`.

2. Create a new layer named `actions`, and place it at the top of the layer stack.

3. Select frame 1 of the actions layer, and open the Actions panel (F9, or Option+F9 on Mac). Add the following code to the script pane. This code retrieves the parameters passed by the HTML document:

```
// Retrieve the class for the FLVPlayback component
import mx.video.FLVPlayback;

// Do not scale Flash movie contents
Stage.scaleMode = "noScale";

// Create a reference to the FLVPlayback instance
var fvp:FLVPlayback = this.flvPlayer;

// Retrieve the HTML parameters
var flvURL:String = this.flvURL;
var skinURL:String = this.skinURL;

// Set the new source files for the player
if(flvURL != null) fvp.contentPath = flvURL;
if(skinURL != null) fvp.skin = skinURL;

// Enable auto hide on skin
fvp.skinAutoHide = true;

// Resize FLVPlayback instance to
// match the size of the stage
fvp.setSize(Stage.width, Stage.height);
```

4. Open the Publish Settings dialog (File > Publish Settings), and uncheck the HTML option in the Formats tab. You'll use an HTML file already provided on the DVD-ROM. Click OK to close the Publish Settings dialog.

5. Save the Flash document, and choose File > Publish (Shift+F12) to publish the movie.

6. You need to create an HTML document that embeds flvplayer_params_fp8.swf and passes two parameters to the movie: flvURL and skinURL. In the ch05 folder on the DVD-ROM, you'll find a modified version of the SWFObject example used in the Dreamweaver section of this chapter. Copy the flvplayer_params_swfobject_fp8.html, swfobject.js, and expressinstall.swf files to the same location as your Flash document on your local system. Open the HTML file in Dreamweaver or your preferred HTML editor. Jump to the JavaScript code below the closing </div> tag, and you'll see how the flvURL and skinURL parameters are passed to the Flash movie:

TIP

▶ If you want a copy of one of the skin SWF files that Flash uses for the FLVPlayback component for Flash Player 8, browse to the Flash application folder on your system and look in the following folder paths. On Windows systems, first look for a language folder (en) in the Flash application folder.

For Flash CS3: Configuration\FLVPlayback Skins\ActionScript 2.0\

For Flash 8: Configuration\Skins

```
<script type="text/javascript">
// <![CDATA[
    var so = new SWFObject("FLVPlayer_Progressive.
    ➥swf", "main", "320", "240", "8", "#FFFFFF",
    ➥true);
    so.addParam("salign","tl");
    so.addVariable("skinURL",
    ➥"SteelOverPlaySeekMute.swf");
    so.addVariable("flvURL",
    ➥"../flv/los_angeles_timelapse_VP6_384K.flv");
    so.useExpressInstall("expressinstall.swf");
    so.write("flashcontent");
// ]]>
</script>
```

Flash Player 8 is specified for the version requirements. The salign parameter controls the alignment of the Flash movie's content. To position the video correctly, this property is set to tl, which means content will be sized from the top-left corner of the stage. Finally, the skinURL and flvURL values are specified.

You can now deploy Flash Video files for Flash Player 8 by reusing the SWF, JS, and HTML files, and specifying new skinURL and flvURL values in the HTML document. If you want a larger video frame size, adjust the width and height values in the SWFObject code.

Navigating the MediaPlayback component for Flash Players 6 and 7

With components, you can even play video destined for Flash Player 6 and 7. The MediaPlayback component, available since Flash MX 2004, can play both MP3 and FLV files. The component is usually used for FLV playback, and it offers basic play controls for your video content. There are some caveats to the MediaPlayback component:

▶ **Sorenson Spark codec:** If you're publishing content for Flash Player 6 or 7 compatibility, you can use only FLV files that have been encoded for the Sorenson Spark codec. If you have On2 VP6-encoded FLV files, you must target Flash Player 8 or higher.

▶ **Progressive-download FLV for Flash Player 7:** If you want to load FLV files from a standard Web server over HTTP, you must target Flash Player 7. You can also use real-time streaming FLV files when you target Flash Player 7.

▶ **Real-time streaming FLV for Flash Player 6:** The Media-Playback component can't handle FLV content unless the video is delivered over RTMP from a Flash Communication Server, Flash Media Server, or a Flash Video Streaming Service (FVSS) provider.

▶ **Limited skinning options:** Modifying the look and feel of the MediaPlayback component isn't as easy as changing skin SWF files, as the FLVPlayback components offer. You learn more about changing the skin of the Media-Playback component in Chapter 6.

If you want a quick way to publish a Flash Video player that's compatible with Flash Player 6 or higher, the Media-Playback component may be your best choice.

Making an FLV player with an authortime-assigned FLV

To build a Flash Video player for Flash Player 6 or 7, follow these steps:

1. On the welcome screen of Flash CS3, click Flash File (ActionScript 2.0), or choose File > New and select Flash File (ActionScript 2.0) to create a new Flash document. Save the new file as `flvplayer_fp6-7.fla`.

2. Rename Layer 1 to flvPlayer.

3. Open the Components panel (Ctrl/Cmd+F7). Open the Media group, and drag the MediaPlayback component to the stage of your Flash document.

4. Select the new instance of the MediaPlayback component on the stage, and open the Property inspector (Ctrl/Cmd+F3). Name the instance flvPlayer. If you only want to place a Flash Video clip into your Flash movie, place the instance at the top-left corner of the stage.

5. Open the Component Inspector panel (Window > Component Inspector, or Shift+F7). With the flvPlayer instance selected, click the Parameters tab of the Component Inspector. On the Parameters tab, type the path to an FLV file to play in the component. Set Control Visibility to On. Review the settings shown in **Figure 5.17**.

6. The MediaPlayback component settings don't automatically resize your component instance to fit the frame size of your specified FLV file. Instead, you need to set the width and height of your instance in the Property inspector. Because of the frame border and controls used by the MediaPlayback component, you need to add 20 pixels to the width and 80 pixels to the height of your instance. For example, if you want to play a 320-by-240 video in the MediaPlayback instance, you need to set the width to 340 and the height to 320.

7. If you don't want any other Flash elements around the Flash Video content, change the size of your Flash document's stage to match the size of the MediaPlayback component instance. Choose Modify > Document (Ctrl/Cmd+J), and change the Match value to Contents. This option automatically changes the width and height of the stage to the size of your FLVPlayback instance. You can also enter a title and description for your Flash movie (**Figure 5.18**).

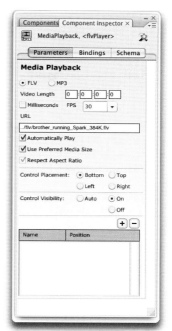

Figure 5.17 The Parameters tab of the Component Inspector panel.

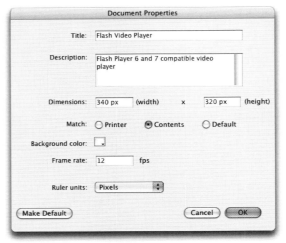

Figure 5.18 The Document Properties dialog.

8. Save the Flash document. Your stage should resemble **Figure 5.19**.

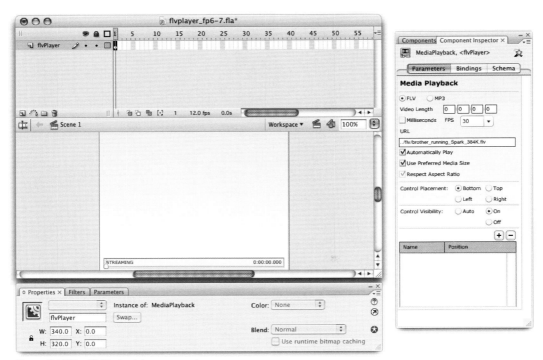

Figure 5.19 The FLVPlayback instance on the stage.

9. Open the Publish Settings dialog (File > Publish Settings), and click the Flash tab. Set the Version to Flash Player 6, and select the Optimize for Flash Player 6 r65 option (**Figure 5.20**). The MediaPlayback component requires Flash Player 6 r65 or higher. Click OK to close the dialog.

▸ Even though you're publishing a Flash Player 6–compatible SWF file, you must require Flash Player 7 in your HTML code to play progressive-download FLV files in the MediaPlayback component.

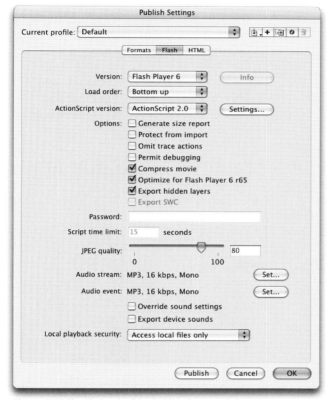

Figure 5.20 The Flash tab of the Publish Settings dialog.

10. Save the Flash document, and choose File > Publish Preview > Default to view the Flash movie in a Web browser. As the files publish, you may receive a warning about publishing to Flash Player 6 r65. Click OK to proceed with publishing the content. You should see the video clip appear in the component instance (**Figure 5.21**).

Figure 5.21 The Flash Video content playing in the component.

Constructing an FLV player with an HTML-assigned FLV

Now that you've built the FLV player for Flash Player 6 and 7, you can build HTML parameters that assign many of the properties listed in the Parameters tab of the Component Inspector for the MediaPlayback component. In the following exercise, you'll migrate the FLV source and skin SWF file parameters to HTML. As I mentioned earlier, you could continue this process with Flash Player 8 and 9 with other properties such as autoPlay.

To assign properties of the MediaPlayback instance with HTML parameters, follow these steps:

1. Open the flvplayer_fp6-7.fla file created in the last section. You can also find this file in the ch05 folder on the DVD-ROM. Resave this file as `flvplayer_params_fp6-7.fla`.

2. Create a new layer named actions, and place this layer at the top of the layer stack.

3. Select frame 1 of the actions layer, and open the Actions panel (F9, or Option+F9 on Mac). Add the following code to the script pane. This code retrieves the parameters passed by the HTML document:

```
// Retrieve the class for the MediaPlayback component
import mx.controls.MediaPlayback;

// Do not scale Flash movie contents
Stage.scaleMode = "noScale";

// Create a reference to the MediaPlayback instance
var fvp:MediaPlayback = this.flvPlayer;

// Set media type to FLV
fvp.mediaType = "FLV";

// Retrieve the HTML parameters
var flvURL:String = this.flvURL;

// Set the new source files for the player
if(flvURL != null) fvp.contentPath = flvURL;
```

```
// Always show player controls
fvp.controllerPolicy = "on";

// Resize video to match HTML parameters
fvp.autoSize = false;

// Resize MediaPlayback instance to
// match the size of the stage
fvp.setSize(Stage.width, Stage.height);
```

4. Open the Publish Settings dialog (File > Publish Settings), and turn off the HTML option in the Formats tab. Use the HTML file provided on the DVD-ROM. Click OK to close the Publish Settings dialog.

5. Save the Flash document, and publish the movie by choosing File > Publish (Shift+F12).

6. You need to create an HTML document that embeds flvplayer_params_fp6-7.swf and passes one parameter to the movie: flvURL. In the ch05 folder on the DVD-ROM, you'll find a modified version of the SWFObject example used in the Dreamweaver section of this chapter. Copy the flvplayer_params_swfobject_fp6-7.html, swfobject.js, and expressinstall.swf files to the same location as your Flash document on your local system. Open the HTML file in Dreamweaver or your preferred HTML editor. Go to the JavaScript code below the closing </div> tag, and you'll see how the flvURL parameter is passed to the Flash movie:

```
<script type="text/javascript">
// <![CDATA[
    var so = new SWFObject("flvplayer_params_fp6-7.swf",
    ➥"main", "340", "320", "7", "#FFFFFF", true);
    so.addParam("salign","tl");
    so.addVariable("flvURL",
    ➥"../flv/brother_running_Spark_384K.flv");
    so.useExpressInstall("expressinstall.swf");
    so.write("flashcontent");
// ]]>
</script>
```

Note that the Flash movie accommodates the 20 extra pixels on the width and the 80 extra pixels on the height that the MediaPlayback component requires for its user interface. Because this sample uses a progressive-download FLV file and not a real-time streaming FLV file, Flash Player 7 is specified for the version requirements. The `salign` parameter controls the alignment of the Flash movie's content. To position the video correctly, this property is set to `tl`, which means content is sized from the top-left corner of the stage. Finally, the `flvURL` value is specified.

You can now deploy Flash Video files for Flash Player 6 or 7 by reusing the SWF, JS, and HTML files, and specifying a new `flvURL` value in the HTML document. If you want a larger video frame size, adjust the width and height values in the SWFObject code, making sure to pad the width and height values for the MediaPlayback user interface.

Gathering Files for Deployment

If you've built all the examples in this chapter, you have a wide range of Flash Video players at your disposal. In this section, I've provided a checklist for each player to help you determine which files you need to upload to your server for final deployment.

Dreamweaver Flash Video Player

Make sure you upload the following files for Dreamweaver Flash Video Player:

▶ HTML file containing `<object>` and `<embed>` code for the Flash movie, or `<div>` and `<script>` tags if you're using SWFObject

▶ AC_RunActiveContent.js file, if you used the Dreamweaver 8.0.2 or Dreamweaver CS3 built-in method of Flash Player detection

▶ swfobject.js file, if you used the SWFObject code for Flash Player detection

▶ FLVPlayer_Progressive.swf or FLVPlayer_Streaming.swf (provided by Dreamweaver)

▶ Skin file (provided by Dreamweaver), such as Clear_ Skin_1.swf

▶ FLV file specified for the Flash Video player, uploaded to your Web server if delivered as a progressive download, or uploaded to your Flash Media Server or FVSS provider's account if delivered as a real-time streaming video

FLVPlayback for Flash Player 9

For FLVPlayback for Plash Player 9, upload these files:

▶ HTML file containing `<object>` and `<embed>` code for the Flash movie, or `<div>` and `<script>` tags if you're using SWFObject

▶ swfobject.js file, if you used the SWFObject code for Flash Player detection

▶ flvplayer_fp9.swf or flvplayer_params_fp9.swf containing the FLVPlayback component instance

▶ Skin file, such as SkinOverPlaySeekFullScreen.swf

▶ FLV file specified for the Flash Video player, uploaded to your Web server if delivered as a progressive download, or uploaded to your Flash Media Server or FVSS provider's account if delivered as a real-time streaming video

FLVPlayback for Flash Player 8

Put these files online for Flash Player 8:

▶ HTML file containing `<object>` and `<embed>` code for the Flash movie, or `<div>` and `<script>` tags if you're using SWFObject

▶ swfobject.js file, if you used the SWFObject code for Flash Player detection

▶ flvplayer_fp8.swf or flvplayer_params_fp8.swf containing the FLVPlayback component instance

▶ Skin file, such as SteelOverPlaySeekMute.swf

▶ FLV file specified for the Flash Video player, uploaded to your Web server if delivered as a progressive download, or uploaded to your Flash Media Server or FVSS provider's account if delivered as a real-time streaming video

MediaPlayback for Flash Player 7

Upload these files for Flash Player 7:

▶ HTML file containing <object> and <embed> code for the Flash movie, or <div> and <script> tags if you're using SWFObject

▶ swfobject.js file, if you used the SWFObject code for Flash Player detection

▶ flvplayer_fp6-7.swf or flvplayer_params_fp6-7.swf containing the MediaPlayback component instance

▶ FLV file specified for the Flash Video player, uploaded to your Web server if delivered as a progressive download, or uploaded to your Flash Media Server or FVSS provider's account if delivered as a real-time streaming video

6

Exploring the FLVPlayback Components

In Chapter 5, "Placing Flash Video on a Web Page," you learned how to build basic Flash Video players in Dreamweaver and Flash. For Flash Video placement on Web pages, these players can provide quick and easy solutions. However, for more customized playback experiences, you may need to go under the hood of these components. In this chapter, you learn how to use additional features of the FLVPlayback components that ship with Flash CS3.

Overview of the Components

As you remember from Chapter 5, Flash CS3 ships with two versions of the FLVPlayback component. One is built in ActionScript 3.0 (AS3) for Flash Player 9 or higher movies, and the other is built in ActionScript 2.0 (AS2) and shipped with Flash Professional 8. Some of the reasons you'd use one version over the other are as follows:

▶ **Full screen functionality:** If you want to play video outside of the browser window and scale the video's frame size to fill the entire screen area, you should use the AS3 FLVPlayback component for Flash Player 9.

▶ **Skinning options:** The AS3 FLVPlayback component has more parameters that control the background color and alpha of the player controls, eliminating the need to build your own custom skin SWF file.

▶ **Player compatibility:** To target Flash Player 8, you should use the AS2 FLVPlayback component. Also, if you want to integrate video with older projects build in AS2, you can use the AS2 FLVPlayback component.

You can't mix and match AS3 code with AS2 code.

On the DVD-ROM

▶ You can find all the source files for this chapter's exercises in the ch06 folder of this book's DVD-ROM. All the FLA files are referenced in the ch06.flp file. You can open these files in the Project panel of Flash CS3.

Caution

▶ All the sample progressive-download URLs used in this chapter contain relative paths (../flv) to the FLV files that reside in the flv folder of this book's DVD-ROM. Depending on how you structure your local system folders and files, you may need to adjust the sample paths to point to FLV files that reside on your system.

▶ If you want to learn how to place an FLVPlayback component into a Flash document (FLA file), review the Flash CS3 coverage in Chapter 5.

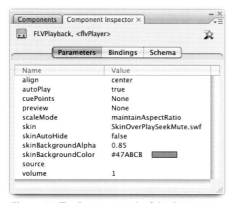

Figure 6.1 The Parameters tab of the Component Inspector.

Configuring the Component

Many of the parameters for the FLVPlayback component, regardless of version, are similar if not identical. In this section, you learn how to use each setting in the Parameters tab.

For the FLVPlayback component (AS3)

You can control many of the features available in the AS3 FLVPlayback component using the Property inspector and the Parameters tab. The Parameters tab is available in the Property inspector as well as the Component Inspector (Window > Component Inspector).

If you need to control only one video clip (FLV file) with the FLVPlayback component, you don't have to delve into the complexities of ActionScript in order to get up and running. I suggest you open a Flash document that has an instance of the FLVPlayback component already placed on the stage to become familiar with each parameter.

Try the following:

1. Copy the following files from the book's DVD-ROM to a local folder on your computer:

   ch06/flvplayback_fp9_authortime_params.fla
   flv/MightyCo1947_VP6_384K_CBR_Cues.flv

2. Open your local copy of the flvplayback_fp9_authortime_params.fla document in Flash CS3, and select the FLVPlayback instance on the stage.

3. Open the Component Inspector (Window > Component Inspector, or Shift+F7). In the Parameters tab, you should see all the settings for the FLVPlayback component (**Figure 6.1**).

4. Double-click the Value column for the source parameter. Click the folder icon to browse to your local copy of the MightyCo1947_VP6_384K_CBR_Cues.flv file, and click OK.

We'll now review each of the parameter names and values using this sample instance of the FLVPlayback component:

► `align`: This parameter controls how the video clip's edges align to the bounding area of the FLVPlayback component. You can choose `center`, `top`, `left`, `bottom`, `right`, `topLeft`, `topRight`, `bottomLeft`, or `bottomRight`. The default value is `center`. You'll notice changes to the alignment only if your FLVPlayback instance is sized larger than the native frame size of the video and you selected `noScale` for the `scaleMode` value.

► `autoPlay`: This parameter determines when the video clip starts to play when the FLVPlayback instance appears on the stage. The default value is `true`, which means the video plays automatically without the user having to click a Play button. If the value is set to `false`, the video doesn't play automatically, but the first frame of the video is displayed in the component.

► `cuePoints`: This parameter displays any cue points in the selected source clip. You can double-click this value to view the cue points. You can only add ActionScript-based cue points in the Flash Video Cue Points dialog. You can disable embedded cue points (discussed later in this chapter) and view extended parameters of cue points (**Figure 6.2**). If you have navigation cue points in your FLV file, you can seek to each navigation cue point using the Seek Forward and Seek Backward buttons featured in several skins of the FLVPlayback component.

Using the Video Import Wizard

Flash CS3 and Flash Professional 8 offer a Video Import Wizard to help beginners more easily integrate FLV files into their Flash documents. When you choose File > Import > Import Video, Flash walks you through the process of selecting an existing FLV file or a source video file and placing it into an instance of the FLVPlayback component. The Video Import Wizard can even handle basic video-encoding of source video files and add cue points to the resulting FLV file.

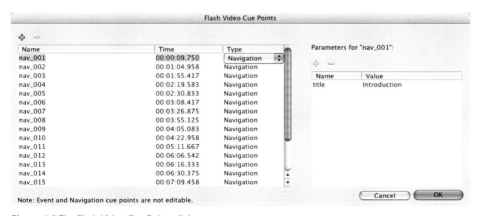

Figure 6.2 The Flash Video Cue Points dialog.

► You can only use the new preview feature with progressive-download Flash Video files. The feature doesn't work with real-time streaming Flash Video source files.

► `preview`. This exciting new parameter of the FLVPlayback component for AS3 enables you to preview a still frame of the video clip on the stage of your Flash document. Double-clicking this value opens the Select Preview Frame dialog (**Figure 6.3**). You can play the video clip and pause on the frame you want to preview in context on the Flash document stage. The preview image serves as a nice visual aid for selecting the skin color and alpha values, which I describe later in this list. The preview image is used only in the authoring environment—it isn't used by the SWF file. You can, however, click the Export button in the Select Preview Frame dialog to save a JPEG image of the current preview frame. You learn how to use a preview image later in this chapter.

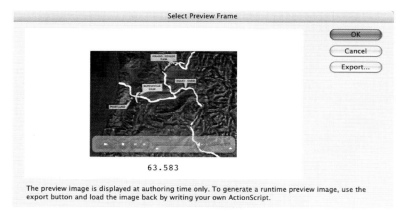

Figure 6.3 The Select Preview Frame dialog.

► `scaleMode:` This parameter controls how the video content scales within the boundary area of the FLVPlayback instance.

The default value is `maintainAspectRatio`, which enables the video content to scale to the width and height of the instance without distorting the original aspect ratio of the video clip. To enlarge or shrink a video's frame size, make sure you use the `maintainAspectRatio` value.

The `noScale` value prevents the video content from being resized within the boundary area of the FLVPlayback instance. For example, if your video clip dimensions are

320 by 240 and you size the FLVPlayback instance to 400 by 300, and you choose noScale for the scaleMode parameter, the video clip still displays at 320 by 240. The alignment is controlled with the align value. You can't use noScale mode to crop your video image—if you size the FLVPlayback component instance smaller than the native video size and use a scaleMode value of noScale, the instance is resized to the native video size.

The other value used by the scaleMode parameter is exactFit. Use this value to stretch the video frame size to meet the exact dimensions of your FLVPlayback instance. In this case, image distortion can occur if the instance's aspect ratio differs from the video's aspect ratio.

▶ skin: This parameter determines which external SWF file is used to display the playback controls for the FLVPlayback component. Double-click this value to open the Select Skin dialog (**Figure 6.4**). You can choose from 34 different skin variations.

Figure 6.4 The Select Skin dialog.

Any skin with the All keyword has the following controls: play/pause button, stop button, seek forward button (cue points only), seek backward button (cue points only), seek bar (for scrubbing the video), mute button, sound volume slider, full screen button, and caption display

NOTES

▶ You must upload the skin SWF file along with your Flash movie SWF file and support HTML documents to the Web server for a site. The skin file is loaded at runtime. If you don't see the skin displayed when you test your Flash movie live, make sure the skin SWF has been uploaded to the Web server. The skin file you select in the API is automatically copied to the same directory as your saved FLA file.

▶ If you choose a skin that appears below the video area, be sure to accommodate this extra height with respect to other elements on the Flash stage. The component instance's height, as reported by ActionScript or the Property inspector, doesn't take into account the pixel height of skin controls that appear below the video area. Any ActionScript 3.0 FLVPlayback skin file whose name contains the word "Under" is 44 pixels in height, which includes the drop shadow behind the background chrome.

button. Other skins feature subsets of these buttons and can be quickly previewed in the Select Skin dialog.

You can also preview and select a background color for the skin in this dialog. This background color value is copied to the skinBackgroundColor parameter, described later in this list.

If you don't want to use a preconfigured skin SWF, choose the None value in the Skin menu of the dialog. If you've created your own skin SWF file, you can choose Custom Skin URL in the Skin menu and type the relative or full path to the file. You learn how to modify and create your own version of a skin SWF later in this chapter.

▶ skinAutoHide. This parameter determines when the skin controls are displayed to the user. If the parameter is set to false (the default value), the controls are always displayed to the user. If the parameter is set to true, the controls are shown to the user only when the user moves the cursor into the boundary area of the FLVPlayback component. When the user's cursor moves off the instance, the skin fades out and remains hidden until the mouse reenters the area of the instance.

▶ skinBackgroundAlpha. This value controls the opacity of the background fill color used by the prebuilt skin SWF files. You can choose a value between 0 and 1. An alpha of 0 is equivalent to a fully transparent (or clear) background fill area. An alpha of 1 is a fully opaque background fill area. The default value, 0.85, is partially transparent (85 percent opaque).

▶ skinBackgroundColor. This value controls the background fill color used by the prebuilt skin SWF files. You can use any 24-bit RGB color value, represented in the Parameters tab as a hexadecimal string.

▶ source. This parameter sets the video clip used by the FLVPlayback component instance. If you want to use a relative path to an FLV file residing on your local system, be sure to save your Flash document (FLA file) before setting the source value. Double-click the source value to open the Content Path dialog (**Figure 6.5**). You can click the folder button to locate and select a Flash Video (FLV) file on your local system, or you can type a path, such as a real-time streaming URL:

```
rtmp://flashvideo.rtmphost.com/samples/MightyCo1947_
➥VP6_384K_CBR_Cues.flv
```

After you've specified the path to an FLV file, select the Match Source FLV Dimensions check box; Flash can automatically resize the FLVPlayback instance to the width and height of the video. If you specify a remote location such as a Real Time Messaging Protocol (RTMP) path, you can also enable the Download FLV for Cue Points and Dimensions option. Flash resizes the component instance (if required) after you click OK and the FLV data is analyzed.

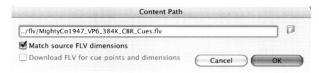

Figure 6.5 The Content Path dialog.

▶ **volume.** The last parameter is the volume level of the FLV file's audio track. The default value is 1, or 100 percent of the original volume. You can set a value between 0 and 1, where 0 indicates no volume (mute) and 1 indicates full volume. This setting doesn't control the system volume on your computer; it tells the Flash Player how to handle the volume level of the FLV file.

For the FLVPlayback component (AS2)

If you're targeting Flash Player 8 and want to use a component for FLV files, you're in luck—Adobe included the original FLVPlayback component shipped with Flash Professional 8 in the new Flash CS3 edition. Or, you can use the FLVPlayback component installed with Flash Professional 8. This version of the component is built in AS2 code.

Most of the parameters for the FLVPlayback (AS2) are identical to those of FLVPlayback (AS3). Open a Flash document with the AS2 FLVPlayback component on the stage as you read about each parameter of the component:

NOTES

▶ To learn how to place an FLVPlayback component into a Flash document (FLA file), review the Flash CS3 coverage in Chapter 5.

TIP

▶ If you're using Flash Professional 8, download and install the updated FLVPlayback component, version 1.0.1. This update fixes several bugs with the original version that shipped with Flash Professional 8. If you're using Flash CS3, you don't need this update. You can find the free updated version at www.adobe.com/support/flash/downloads.html.

1. Copy the following files from this book's DVD-ROM to a local folder on your computer:

   ch06/flvplayback_fp8_authortime_params.fla
   flv/MightyCo1947_VP6_384K_CBR_Cues.flv

2. Open your local copy of the flvplayback_fp8_authortime_params.fla document in Flash CS3 or Flash Professional 8, and select the FLVPlayback instance on the stage.

3. Open the Component Inspector (Window > Component Inspector, or Shift+F7). In the Parameters tab, you see all the FLVPlayback component settings (**Figure 6.6**).

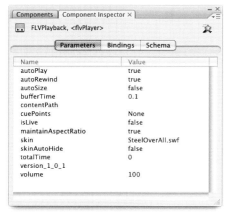

Figure 6.6 The Parameters tab of the Component Inspector.

4. Double-click the Value column for the `contentPath` parameter. Click the folder icon to browse to your local copy of the MightyCo1947_VP6_384K_CBR_Cues.flv file, and click OK.

You can now review each of the parameter names and values using this sample instance of the FLVPlayback component:

▶ `autoPlay`: This parameter controls automatic playback, as described in the preceding section.

▶ `autoRewind`: This parameter, when set to `true` (the default value), forces the video to seek back to the first frame when the end of the video is reached. If this value is set to `false`, the video stops when the last frame of the clip is played.

NOTES

▶ If you set `autoRewind` to `true`, the video doesn't automatically play after returning to the first frame, regardless of what the `autoPlay` value may be.

- `autoSize`: This parameter, combined with the `maintainAspectRatio` parameter, behaves similarly to the `scaleMode` parameter of the AS3 FLVPlayback component. If `autoSize` is set to `true`, the FLV file's frame width and height dictate the dimensions of the FLVPlayback component instance, regardless of the width and height assigned to the instance in the Property inspector or in ActionScript code. If `autoSize` is set to `false`, the video clip's dimensions scale to fill the dimensions of the instance. The `maintainAspectRatio` parameter, described later, controls how the content fills the boundary area of the instance.

- `bufferTime`: This parameter determines how much of the video content must download to the Flash Player memory buffer (for real-time streams) or to the browser cache (for progressive-download video) before playback can begin. The default value is 0.1, or one-tenth of a second. This parameter affects real-time stream playback and performance more than progressive-download playback. If you're delivering high-bitrate, real-time streaming content to low-bitrate connection speeds, you may need to increase the `bufferTime` value substantially.

- `contentPath`: This parameter behaves identically to the `source` parameter of the AS3 FLVPlayback component. Refer to the preceding section's list of parameters for more information.

- `cuePoints`: This parameter behaves identically to the `cuePoints` parameter of the AS3 FLVPlayback component. Refer to the previous section's list of parameters for more information.

- `isLive`: This parameter informs the instance about the nature of a real-time stream set as the `contentPath` value of the instance. To use the component to display a live video stream delivered from a Flash Media Server (FMS) or Flash Video Streaming Service (FVSS) provider, set this parameter's value to `true`. Otherwise, leave the setting at its default value, `false`. When `isLive` is set to `true` and a live stream is played, the scrub bar (if part of the selected skin) is disabled.

TIP

- For optimum real-time streaming performance, you should create multiple bitrates (several FLV files) per piece of video content and serve the most appropriate bitrate video to the user. You learn more about multiple bitrate scenarios in Chapter 8, "Integrating Multiple Bitrates."

▶ `maintainAspectRatio`: This parameter controls how the video clip frame size fills the boundary area of the FLVPlayback instance. The default value, `true`, informs the component instance to respect the original aspect ratio of the video clip. If you set `autoSize` to `false` and set `maintainAspectRatio` to `true`, the video clip content scales to the size of the component instance without distortion to the image aspect ratio. If `autoSize` is set to `false` and `maintainAspectRatio` is set to `false`, the video's frame size matches that of the instance exactly. In this case, image distortion may occur if the instance's aspect ratio differs from the video's aspect ratio.

▶ `skin`: This parameter determines which external SWF file is used to display the playback controls for the component, just like the AS3 version of the component discussed in the preceding section. Double-click this value to open the Select Skin dialog (**Figure 6.7**) to choose from 32 different skin variations.

Figure 6.7 The Select Skin dialog for the FLVPlayback AS2 component.

Any skin with the All keyword has the following controls: play/pause button, stop button, seek forward button (cue points only), seek backward button (cue points only), seek bar (for scrubbing the video), mute button, and a sound volume slider. Other skins feature subsets of these buttons, and can be quickly previewed in the Select Skin dialog.

If you don't use a preconfigured skin SWF, choose None in the dialog's Skin menu. If you've created your own skin SWF file, you can choose Custom Skin URL in the Skin menu and enter the relative or full path to the file. You learn how to modify and create your own version of a skin SWF later in this chapter.

▶ `skinAutoHide`: This parameter behaves identically to the `skinAutoHide` parameter of the AS3 version of the component, discussed in the previous section.

▶ `totalTime`: This parameter establishes the duration of the video clip played by the component instance. You don't need to set this parameter as long as your FLV file has accurate metadata created by your Flash Video encoding tool. If you do specify a value for `totalTime`, any metadata value for the video's `duration` metaproperty is ignored. If you're playing a real-time stream, the component instance attempts to retrieve the duration of the video using server-side code running in the FMS application or the FVSS provider account.

▶ `version_1_0_1`: This parameter lets you know that you're using the 1.0.1 version of the FLVPlayback component for AS2. If you don't see this parameter in the Parameters tab of the AS2 FLVPlayback component, update your version. For more information on this update, refer back to the beginning of this section.

▶ `volume`: This parameter controls the volume level of the audio track in the video clip. Unlike in the AS3 FLVPlayback component, the range of values is 0 to 100, where `100` represents full volume and `0` represents a muted audio track.

Enhancing Playback with Cue Points

When Flash Professional 8 was released, the Flash Video format changed in two significant ways: The On2 VP6 codec was introduced, and FLV files could contain embedded cue points on specific frames of the video. A *cue point* is essentially a marker in the video file, indicating a significant position. What makes the cue point significant is entirely up to you. Do you need to mark a position to enable the

NOTES

▶ The skin SWF file must be uploaded to the Web server along with your Flash movie SWF file and support HTML documents. The skin file is loaded at runtime. If the skin doesn't display when you test your Flash movie live, make sure the skin SWF has been uploaded to the Web server.

▶ If you choose a skin that appears below the video area, be sure to accommodate this extra height compared to the other elements on your Flash stage. The component instance's height, as reported by ActionScript or the Property inspector, doesn't take into account the pixel height of skin controls that appear below the video area. Any ActionScript 2.0 FLVPlayback skin file whose name contains the word "External" has a height of 44 pixels, which includes the drop shadow behind the background chrome.

TIP

▶ Although most FMS hosting providers and FVSS providers automatically include the server-side script necessary for the FLVPlayback component to determine the length of the video, you can find the server-side script file, main.asc, online at www.adobe.com/go/learn_fl_samples.

user to jump quickly to that position without scrubbing? Do you want to trigger an animation in your Flash movie when the video reaches a certain point? In this section, you learn about each cue point type and how to create them with your Flash Video content.

Planning cue point usage

Cue points in Flash Video distinguish the file format from other Web video formats, in that cue points enable you to build powerful synchronized video presentations that harness the power of ActionScript and utilize the wide array of graphic formats and filters that Flash Player supports. As you learn about cue points, you'll soon envision how you can take advantage of their capabilities in your own work.

Cue point types

Before you head into the Flash Video encoding tool to add cue points to your video clips, you need to learn about the three types of cue points you can use with the FLVPlayback components:

▶ **Navigation cue point:** Use this type of cue point to mark a seek frame, using the forward or backward button available in some FLVPlayback component skins. A suitable Flash Video encoding tool creates navigation cue points during the FLV file-creation process. These cue points are embedded in the final FLV file. A navigation cue point is similar to a chapter on a typical movie DVD-Video disc. You can create a table of contents for a video clip by reading the navigation cue points (described in Chapter 9, "Building a Video Index and Playlist").

In AS2, the value of the `type` property for a navigation cue point is a string value, `"navigation"`. In AS3, the value of the `type` property can also be referenced with the constant `CuePointType.NAVIGATION`.

▶ **Event cue point:** This type of cue point can be used to synchronize other Flash or HTML content with the video playback. Event cue points are created during the FLV file-creation process and are embedded in the FLV file. Event cue points aren't exposed to the user in the

FLVPlayback skin controls. For example, an event cue point could be used to trigger the fading up of a text label or caption above or below the video. You could also use an event cue point to display related content to the video. (In Chapter 10, "Constructing Banner Ads and Captioned Videos," you learn how to use event cue points to synchronize graphic overlays with Flash Video content.)

In AS2, the value of the `type` property for an event cue point is a string value, `"event"`. In AS3, the value of the `type` property can also be referenced with the constant `CuePointType.EVENT`.

▶ **ActionScript cue point:** A cue point can be created virtually in ActionScript code when you use the FLVPlayback component. An ActionScript cue point works like an event cue point for synchronization that doesn't require user intervention. You can add ActionScript cue points in the Parameters tab of the Component Inspector (or Property inspector) by double-clicking the Value field for the `cuePoints` parameter. You can also add ActionScript cue points with the `FLVPlayback.addASCuePoint()` method in your own code. ActionScript cue points exist only during runtime while the Flash movie is running in the Flash Player. These cue points aren't embedded in the FLV file.

In AS2, the value of the `type` property for an ActionScript cue point is a string value, `"actionscript"`. In AS3, the value of the `type` property can also be referenced with the constant `CuePointType.ACTIONSCRIPT`.

All cue points have properties that can be accessed in ActionScript. You can use these properties to handle a cue point when it's played:

▶ `time`: This property is the time at which the cue point occurs during playback of the video content. The unit of measure is seconds, reported as a decimal number.

▶ `name`: This property refers to the name assigned to the cue point in your Flash Video encoding tool. The name value is stored as a string, and it doesn't need to be unique. Your encoder may assign a default value, such as `Chapter`.

NOTES

▶ You can create an external data source such as an XML document to store cue point information. Using ActionScript, you can load the data and create ActionScript cue points for the FLVPlayback component or your own custom player.

▶ `type`: This property reports the string value assigned for the cue point type, as described in the previous list. For example, the type value of a navigation cue point is `"navigation"`.

▶ `parameters`: This optional property is an object data type, capable of storing one or more subproperties with string values. If you'd like to store additional data for a cue point, such as a text label or color value, you can use the `parameters` property to do so. The names of the properties in the `parameters` object are arbitrary.

To see cue point types and properties in action, follow these steps with the sample files provided on this book's DVD-ROM:

1. Copy the following files from the DVD-ROM to a local folder on your computer:

   ch06/flvplayback_fp8_cuepoint_events.fla
   flv/MightyCo1947_VP6_384K_CBR_Cues.flv

2. Open your local copy of the flvplayback_fp8_cuepoint_events.fla document in Flash CS3 or Flash Professional 8, and select the FLVPlayback instance on the stage.

3. Open the Component Inspector (Window > Component Inspector, or Shift+F7). In the Parameters tab, double-click the value for the `contentPath` parameter, and browse to the FLV file copied from the DVD-ROM. After you've selected the file, click OK. The `cuePoints` parameter in the Parameters tab updates to show the cue points stored in the sample FLV file.

4. Save the Flash document, and choose Control > Test Movie (Ctrl/Cmd+Enter) to test the movie. Do *not* use File > Publish Preview to test the Flash output, because the debugging output won't be displayed. As the video content plays in the Test Movie window, you should see cue point events traced in the Output panel. The ActionScript code placed on frame 1 of the actions layer is responsible for displaying this information.

Cue point behavior

When an embedded cue point is inserted into a Flash Video (FLV) file during the encoding process, some properties of the video clip are changed. At the point of insertion, a

NOTES

▶ You learn how to use cue point properties in Chapter 9, "Building a Video Index and Playlist," and Chapter 11, "Creating an Interactive Video Host."

keyframe is made in the video. The keyframe serves a critical purpose for cue points: It ensures that the cue point registers and fires an event to the ActionScript Virtual Machine (AVM). Unlike regular video frames, keyframes in Flash Video content are always played—the Flash Player won't drop a keyframe during playback. By creating a keyframe at the same point as a cue point, the Flash Video encoder builds a reliable framework for you to build a synchronized presentation with accurate seeking.

Even if you don't want to use the FLVPlayback component to play video clips, you can use the NetStream.onCuePoint() handler to detect when a cue point has played. You also don't have to wait for each cue point to play before you can access its data. All the cue point data arrives in the metadata stored at the beginning of the FLV file.

▶ You'll learn how to use the NetStream.onCuePoint() handler in Chapter 11.

To see all the cue point data as soon as the FLV file loads, follow these steps with the sample files provided on this book's DVD-ROM:

1. Copy the following files from the DVD-ROM to a local folder on your computer:

   ch06/flvplayback_fp8_cuepoint_summary.fla
   flv/MightyCo1947_VP6_384K_CBR_Cues.flv

2. Open your local copy of the flvplayback_fp8_cuepoint_summary.fla document in Flash CS3 or Flash Professional 8, and select the FLVPlayback instance on the stage.

3. Open the Component Inspector (Window > Component Inspector, or Shift+F7). In the Parameters tab, double-click the value for the contentPath parameter, and browse to the FLV file copied from the DVD-ROM. After you've selected the file, click OK.

4. Save the Flash document. To test the movie, choose Control > Test Movie (Ctrl/Cmd+Enter). Do *not* use File > Publish Preview to test the Flash output, because the debugging output won't be displayed. As the video content plays in the Test Movie window, you should see cue point events traced in the Output panel. The ActionScript code placed on frame 1 of the actions layer is responsible for displaying this information.

Creating embedded cue points

Several Flash Video encoding tools enable you to add embedded cue points in the compression settings before you output a Flash Video (FLV) file. In this section, you learn how to create navigation and event cue points for a sample video file in Adobe Flash Video Encoder, Sorenson Squeeze 4.5, and On2 Flix Pro 8.5.

Before you explore the cue point creation process, look at the sample files. Open the stella_tricks.mov file in the source/dv folder on the DVD-ROM. This short video clip demonstrates five tricks performed by my dog Stella. You learn how to create the following cue points with this clip:

▶ Five navigation cue points marking the beginning of each trick. Each navigation point has a parameter named `title` indicating the name of the dog trick, such as "Shake hands". This value can be used to build a marker index, as shown in Chapter 9.

▶ Five sets of 2 event cue points (10 total), each pair marking the in and out points of title text to appear over the video frame. The title text isn't created using Flash Video encoding tools—you can use ActionScript to create the text at runtime in the Flash movie. One event cue point introduces the text, and another event cue point removes the text. The introduction event cue point has a parameter named `title`, using the same value of the associated navigation cue point with the dog trick. You can use a different `title` value for title text if you so desire.

This section won't cover video bitrate and audio bitrate compression settings. For more information on bitrates (or data rates), read Chapter 3, "Compression Primer," and Appendix C, "Encoding Flash Video." Don't forget to carefully consider your video and audio compression settings for production-ready Flash Video files.

Adobe Flash CS3 Video Encoder

The Adobe Flash Video Encoder is included with Adobe Flash CS3 and delivers acceptable quality with Flash Video output. This encoder can add cue points in the compression settings, and you can import or export an XML document containing the cue point data.

To add cue points to a video clip, follow these steps:

1. Open the Adobe Flash CS3 Video Encoder, and drag the stella_tricks.mov file to the queue pane of the application window (**Figure 6.8**).

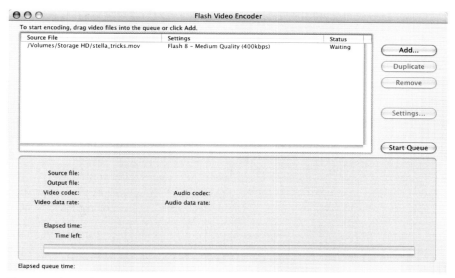

Figure 6.8 The newly added video clip in the queue.

2. Select the clip item in the queue, and click the Settings button. Or, double-click the clip item.

3. In the Flash Video Encoding Settings dialog, click the Cue Points tab (**Figure 6.9**).

4. Click the Add (+) button at left in the dialog to insert a new cue point on the first frame of the video. Change the Name value to trick_001, and switch the Type value to Navigation. In the Parameters area on the right side of the dialog, click the Add (+) button to add a new name/value pair. Change the Name row to title and the Value row to Lay down (**Figure 6.10**).

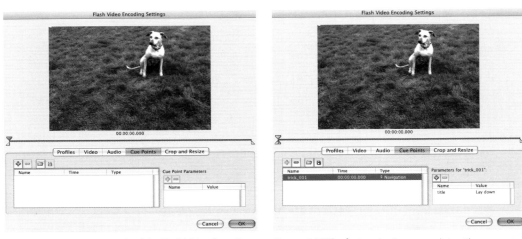

Figure 6.9 The Cue Points tab of the Flash Video Encoding Settings dialog.

Figure 6.10 The first navigation cue point settings.

5. Drag the yellow playhead indicator of the video scrub bar to 00:00:01.000 (**Figure 6.11**). Press the left or right arrow key to finesse the playhead time. Repeat step 4 using the cue point name `titleIn_001` and a cue point type of `Event`. Add a new parameter named `title` with a value of `Lay down`.

6. Drag the playhead indicator to 00:00:03.000. At this point, add a new event cue point named `titleOut_001` (**Figure 6.12**). No parameter information is necessary for this cue point.

Figure 6.11 The first event cue point settings.

Figure 6.12 The second event cue point settings.

7. Repeat steps 4 through 6 for each trick in the video. Refer to **Table 6.1** for a complete list of cue points and settings. If you'd prefer to import the cue point data, click the folder icon in the cue point toolbar on the left, and import the stella_tricks.xml file from the source/dv folder on the DVD-ROM. (You may need to delete duplicate entries after import, because you already created identical cue points in earlier steps.)

TABLE **6.1** Dog-Trick Clip Cue Point Settings

CUE POINT NAME	CUE POINT TIME	CUE POINT TYPE	PARAMETER NAME	PARAMETER VALUE
trick_001	00:00:00.000	Navigation	title	Lay down
titleIn_001	00:00:01.000	Event	title	Lay down
titleOut_001	00:00:03.000	Event	--	--
trick_002	00:00:04.738	Navigation	title	Shake hands
titleIn_002	00:00:05.244	Event	title	Shake hands
titleOut_002	00:00:07.244	Event	--	--
trick_003	00:00:13.780	Navigation	title	Hop
titleIn_003	00:00:14.259	Event	title	Hop
titleOut_003	00:00:16.259	Event	--	--
trick_004	00:00:23.423	Navigation	title	Speak softly
titleIn_004	00:00:23.922	Event	title	Speak softly
titleOut_004	00:00:25.922	Event	--	--
trick_005	00:00:33.834	Navigation	title	Speak loudly
titleIn_005	00:00:34.351	Event	title	Speak loudly
titleOut_005	00:00:36.351	Event	--	--

8. To save your cue point data—and I strongly recommend you save—so you can reuse the cue points with other compression settings for the same clip, click the Save (disk icon) button on the cue point toolbar. Use an .xml file extension when you save the file.

9. Click the Crop and Resize tab of the Flash Video Encoding Settings dialog. Select the Resize Video check box, and clear the Maintain Aspect Ratio check box. Enter a width of 320 and a height of 240 (**Figure 6.13**).

10. Click the Video tab of the dialog, and select the Deinterlace option (**Figure 6.14**). Click OK to close the dialog.

Figure 6.13 The Crop and Resize tab of the Flash Video Encoder Settings dialog.

Figure 6.14 The Video tab of the Flash Video Encoder Settings dialog.

▶ The Adobe Flash CS3 Video Encoder can't automatically interpret a video clip's pixel aspect ratio. Because this sample video clip is a DV clip, which uses nonsquare pixels, you must deselect the Maintain Aspect Ratio box to enter a 4:3 aspect ratio, such as 640 by 480, 320 by 240, and so on.

▶ You can find the completed FLV file from the Adobe Flash CS3 Video Encoder in the flv folder of this book's DVD-ROM. The file is named stella_tricks_ FVE_VP6_496K_CBR_Cues.flv.

11. Back in the main application window, click the Start Queue button to compress the final Flash Video (FLV) file. When the process has completed, you have a video clip with cue points. You'll use these cue points later, in the "Implementing Navigation Cue Points" section.

To export cue point data, follow these steps:

1. After you've added cue points on the Cue Points tab of the Flash Video Settings dialog, click the Save (disk icon) button.

2. Browse to a location on your system, and save the cue points file. Name the file with an .xml file extension.

3. To view the cue point data, open the XML file in a Web browser such as Mozilla Firefox. Each cue point's data is in its own child node, like this:

```
<CuePoint>
    <Time>0</Time>
    <Type>navigation</Type>
    <Name>trick_001</Name>
    <Parameters>
        <Parameter>
            <Name>title</Name>
            <Value>Lay down</Value>
        </Parameter>
    </Parameters>
</CuePoint>
```

▶ Flash CS3 Video Encoder features a profile named Flash 8 – DV Small (400 kbps) that uses the same settings as this sample. You can choose this option in the Profiles tab of the Flash Video Encoder Settings dialog.

4. You can reuse this cue point data with other compression settings in the Flash CS3 Video Encoder, or you can load this data into your Flash movie (SWF file) using ActionScript.

You can also create XML cue point data in a text editor or in a professional tool such as Adobe Dreamweaver.

To import cue point data, follow these steps:

1. After you've added a clip to the Flash CS3 Video Encoder queue, access its settings and click the Cue Points tab.

2. Click the folder icon in the cue points toolbar, and browse to an XML file containing the cue point data. The cue point data must be in the same schema as that used by the export process discussed in the last section.

3. The cue point data is displayed in the cue point list, and you can adjust the compression settings before outputting the final Flash Video (FLV) file.

Sorenson Squeeze

If you have Sorenson Squeeze 4.3 or higher, you can add cue points to your Flash Video output. Squeeze refers to cue point types a bit differently than Flash CS3 or the Flash CS3 Video Encoder. In Squeeze, a cue point is called a *marker*. A *chapter marker* is synonymous with a navigation cue point, and a *keyframe marker* is the same as an event cue point.

NOTES

▶ One reason Squeeze uses a nomenclature different from Adobe is that Squeeze can produce DVD-Video output complete with seekable chapter markers. The term cue point isn't an industry standard term, whereas the term marker is used in professional video-editing tools such as Apple Final Cut Pro.

▶ Sorenson Squeeze is frequently updated. Before every project, I download and install the latest updater on the Sorenson Squeeze Web site. Sometimes, the Web site doesn't list the minor release versions in the descriptions. Don't assume you have the latest version—download the latest updater and install it. You'll find a list of updates at www.sorensonmedia.com/downloads.

To add cue points to a video clip, do the following:

1. Open Sorenson Squeeze, and drag the stella_tricks.mov file to the job pane of the application window (**Figure 6.15**).

Figure 6.15 The newly added video clip in the job pane.

2. Make sure the marker type is set to Chapter. Click the drop-down arrow shown in **Figure 6.16**, and choose Chapter.

Figure 6.16 The marker type menu.

3. With the playhead indicator at the beginning of the clip, click the Add Marker button (**Figure 6.17**). An orange marker appears on the clip's scrub bar. Also, a new category named Markers is displayed below the clip name in the job pane.

Figure 6.17 The new chapter marker at the beginning of the clip.

4. Drag the video scrub bar's yellow playhead indicator to time 00:00:01.000 (**Figure 6.18**). Press the left or right arrow key to finesse the playhead time. Change the marker type to Keyframe, and click the Add Marker button to insert a new keyframe marker.

Figure 6.18 The new keyframe marker at time 00:00:01.00 of the clip.

5. Continue adding chapter and keyframe markers at the times listed in Table 6.1. You'll set the markers' names and parameters later. When you're finished, save the Squeeze project as `stella_tricks_markers.sqz`. Your scrub bar should resemble **Figure 6.19**.

Figure 6.19 The full set of markers on the clip.

TIP

▶ Instead of changing marker types as you add them, change the marker types later when you edit the settings.

6. To specify names and parameters for the new markers, double-click the Markers category below your clip name in the job pane. To edit a Position or Type value in the Edit Markers dialog, double-click the value and change the respective setting at the top of the dialog. (It's not exactly intuitive.) Unlike Adobe Flash CS3 Video Encoder, you can finesse the times of markers directly, without having to nudge marker icons on the scrub bar. Use the information in Table 6.1 to update all the markers (**Figure 6.20**). Remember, navigation cue points are chapter markers, and event cue points are keyframe markers. (Don't close the dialog just yet.)

7. To add the parameter name/value pairs in the Edit Markers dialog, click the Advanced button in the lower-left corner. Squeeze expands the dialog to show the Flash Cue Point Variables pane (**Figure 6.21**). Select the

markers that require a parameter (indicated by Table 6.1), clicking New in the Flash Cue Point Variables pane for each new `title` parameter. When you've added all the parameters, click OK to close the dialog.

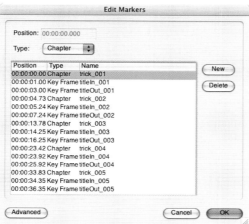

Figure 6.20 The Edit Markers dialog.

▶ A nice hidden feature of Squeeze project files is that they're actually XML files! You can open a Squeeze project (SQZ file) in a text editor and see the marker (cue point) data. If you're an ambitious ActionScript coder, you could even build an XML translator that interprets Squeeze project files into Flash CS3 Video Encoder–compatible cue point XML files, and vice versa.

Figure 6.21 The advanced settings of the Edit Markers dialog.

8. In the Format & Compression Settings pane, open the Macromedia Flash Video group, and drag the VP6_512K_Stream preset to the job pane. The Markers category is copied to the new preset. Toggle the preset

under the clip to reveal the audio, video, and marker categories (**Figure 6.22**).

9. Save the project, and click the Squeeze It! button to begin creating the final Flash Video (FLV) file.

Figure 6.22 The VP6_512K_Stream compression preset added to the job.

NOTES

▶ You'll find the completed FLV file in the flv folder of the book's DVD-ROM: stella_tricks_SQZ_VP6_512K_CBR_Cues.flv.

You'll find the Squeeze project file in the encoder_files folder: stella_tricks_markers.sqz.

Squeeze can't import or export marker (or cue point) data like Adobe Flash CS3—but it can save project files containing all of your marker settings. If you need to compress the video file with different FLV compression settings, reopen your Squeeze file and add a new preset to the clip in the job pane.

On2 Flix Pro

If you have On2 Flix Pro 8.5, you can also add cue point data to your compression settings for Flash Video output. The user interface (UI) for creating cue points is nearly identical to that of Flash CS3 Video Encoder.

To add cue points to a video clip, do the following:

1. Open On2 Flix Pro 8.5, and click the Browse button to the right of the Input field. Locate your local copy of the stella_tricks.mov file. If you want to change the output

FLV filename, modify the value in the Output field (**Figure 6.23**). Make sure the 512K Broadband High Video (Flash 8 FLV) preset is selected in the Presets menu.

Figure 6.23 The input and output video file settings in Flix Pro.

2. Click the Cue tab (or the Cue Points tab in the Windows version), and click the Add (+) button at the lower left of the application window to insert a new cue point on the first frame of the video. Change the Name value to trick_001, and select the check box in the Navigation column. In the Parameters area on the right side of the dialog, click the Add (+) button to add a new name/value pair. Change the Name row to title and the Value row to Lay down (**Figure 6.24**).

Figure 6.24 The first navigation cue point settings.

3. Drag the red line of the playhead indicator (located in the top half of the video scrub bar) to time 00:00:01.000 (**Figure 6.25**). Don't drag the gray arrow on the lower left of the scrub bar—that control sets the in point for the clip. Flix doesn't provide an exact indication of the playhead's current time. Repeat step 4, using the cue point name `titleIn_001` and a cue point type of Event. Add a new parameter named `title` with a value of Lay down.

4. Drag the playhead indicator to 00:00:03.000. At this point, add a new Event cue point named `titleOut_001` (**Figure 6.26**). No parameter information is necessary for this cue point.

Figure 6.25 The first event cue point settings.

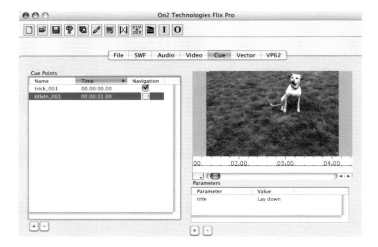

Figure 6.26 The second event cue point settings.

5. Repeat steps 2 through 4 for each trick in the video. Table 6.1 has a complete list of cue points and settings. Because Flix doesn't show you exact time values for the playhead indicator, drag the playhead to your best guess, and then click the Add (+) button. After you've named the cue point, double-click the value in the Time column to set it to the precise time shown in the table. When you're finished, your list of cue points should resemble **Figure 6.27**.

NOTES

▶ On2 Flix Pro can't automatically interpret a video clip's pixel aspect ratio. Because this sample video clip is a DV clip, which uses nonsquare pixels, you must select the No Constraints radio button in order to enter a 4:3 aspect ratio, such as 640 by 480, 320 by 240, and so on.

Figure 6.27 The complete list of cue points.

6. Click the Video tab, and select the No Constraints radio button in the Output Video Dimensions settings. Enter a width of 320 and a height of 240 (**Figure 6.28**). Change the Rate Control Mode from VBR (local playback) to CBR (streaming) if you intend to use the FLV file with real-time streaming services.

7. Click the Video Filters button on the Video tab, and enable the Deinterlace option (**Figure 6.29**). Click OK to close the dialog.

8. Choose File > Save Settings to save an FLX file containing your compression settings for this clip.

TIP

▶ Although it's best to perform deinterlacing using a professional video tool such as Adobe After Effects, the deinterlacing performed by Flix is acceptable if you're resizing your video below 50 percent of the original video dimensions. You may not notice any difference with Deinterlace turned on or off when you resize the video to a quarter of the original resolution, as you're doing in this example.

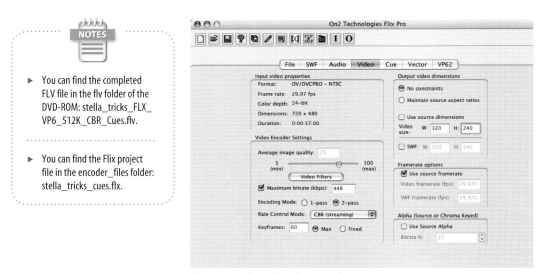

> **NOTES**
>
> ▶ You can find the completed FLV file in the flv folder of the DVD-ROM: stella_tricks_FLX_ VP6_512K_CBR_Cues.flv.
>
> ▶ You can find the Flix project file in the encoder_files folder: stella_tricks_cues.flx.

Figure 6.28 The Video tab in On2 Flix Pro.

Figure 6.29 The video filter options in On2 Flix Pro.

9. Click the File tab, and select the Encode button to compress the final Flash Video (FLV) file. When the process is complete, you'll have a video clip with cue points. You can use these cue points later in the "Implementing Navigation Cue Points" section.

Flix can't import or export cue point data like Adobe Flash CS3 can—but, like Sorenson Squeeze, Flix can save project files containing all your cue point settings. If you need to compress the video file with different FLV compression settings, reopen your Squeeze file, and change the preset (and/or individual settings) for the clip.

▶ Flix project files (FLX files) are XML files, just like Sorenson Squeeze project files. You can open a Flix project file in a text editor and see the cue point data.

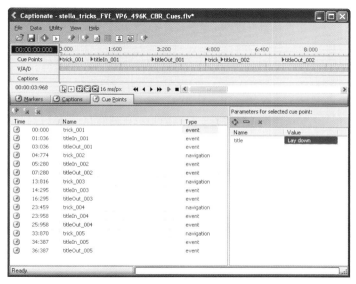

Figure 6.30 The cue point data from the dog-tricks FLV file.

Editing Cue Points with Captionate

Designers and developers working with Flash Video frequently complain that they can't edit existing metadata or cue points in Flash Video files. Luckily, there's Captionate, a tool specifically made to create captions for Flash Video. A new feature in Captionate 2 is the ability to add and modify cue points in FLV files. As shown in **Figure 6.30**, you can import a Flash Video (FLV) file and view the cue point data. Captionate can also export an XML file containing cue point data. Perhaps more important, Captionate was originally designed to build multilanguage captioning tracks for Flash Video content. Combined with its cue point capabilities, Captionate is a handy tool for any Flash Video professional. Captionate is available for Windows. You can download an evaluation copy of Captionate at www.captionate.com.

Implementing embedded cue points

After you've created a Flash Video (FLV) file with embedded cue points, you can quickly use them with the FLVPlayback component and any skin SWF that has seek forward and seek backward buttons. In this section, you create a Flash movie with the FLVPlayback AS3 component, capable of seeking to navigation cue points. I also include an ActionScript file that you can easily add to your document to display the title text for respective cue points on top of the video.

► You can use Flash Professional 8 with the ActionScript 2.0 version of the FLVPlayback component. The script to display the title text is different in AS2 but you'll find a Flash 8 version of the completed files in the ch06 folder of this book's DVD-ROM.

Before beginning this section, copy one of the dog-trick FLV files you created in either of the preceding cue point sections. This exercise uses the Flash CS3 Video Encoder version of the dog-trick FLV, which you'll find in the flv folder on the DVD-ROM: stella_tricks_FVE_VP6_512K_CBR_Cues.flv.

Follow these steps:

1. Open Adobe Flash CS3, and create a new Flash file (AS3). Save the file as `flvplayback_fp9_cues_title.fla`.

2. Rename Layer 1 to `flvPlayer`.

3. Open the Components panel (Ctrl/Cmd+F7), and open the Video group. Drag the FLVPlayback component to the stage.

4. Select the new instance on the stage. In the Property inspector, name the instance `flvPlayer`.

5. Open the Component Inspector panel (Window > Component Inspector, or Shift+F7), and click the Parameters tab. Double-click the value for the source parameter, and browse to your copy of the FLV file mentioned at the beginning of this section. Or, use one of your versions of the dog-trick FLV file. After you've selected the file, click OK. You should see the cuePoints parameter displaying information.

6. Double-click the value for the skin parameter. In the Select Skin dialog, choose a skin that displays seek buttons, such as SkinOverAll.swf. Click OK. Your Component Inspector panel should now have information related to your FLV file, cue points, and skin file (**Figure 6.31**).

7. Save the Flash document, and test the movie (Window > Test Movie or Ctrl/Cmd+Enter). As the video clip plays, click the seek buttons to jump to each navigation point created in the FLV file.

8. To show the title parameter stored in each event cue point whose name starts with `titleIn_`, you need to add a dynamic text field to the stage, above your FLVPlayback instance. Create a new layer named `titleField`, and place it above the flvPlayer layer.

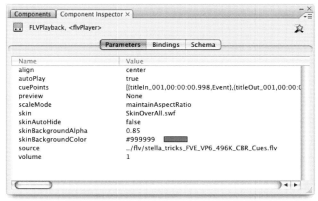

Figure 6.31 The new parameters in the Component Inspector panel.

9. Select the Text tool, and open the Property inspector. Set the Text Type menu to Dynamic Text, and choose a font name, size, and color. Click once with the Text tool on top of your FLVPlayback instance, and drag a text field out long enough to accommodate the titles used for the dog-trick clip. You can type temporary text into the field as you adjust the text settings. In the Filters tab of the Property inspector, feel free to add any filter effects, such as a drop shadow, to the text. Remove any text you added to the field when you're finished, without deleting the instance of the field.

10. With the new text instance selected, name the instance `titleField` in the <Instance Name> field of the Property inspector.

11. Make a copy of the VideoTitles.as file from the ch06 folder of this book's DVD-ROM to the same location as the saved FLA file you created in step 1. This Action-Script file will be used as the document class.

12. Deselect any items on the stage (for example, click the work area surrounding the stage), and open the Property inspector. In the Document Class field, type `VideoTitles` (**Figure 6.32**). This class file contains the code to read the event cue point data and display the `title` parameter in the `titleField`. To view the AS3 code in the VideoTitles.as file, click the pencil icon to the right of the Document Class field in the Property inspector.

NOTES

▶ The completed files for this example can be found in the ch06 folder of this book's DVD-ROM.

TIP

▸ You can modify the code in the VideoTitle.as file to add other ActionScript-based effects, such as fading the title text in and out. Check this book's forum at www.flashsupport.com/flvbook to find future updates to the VideoTitle.as file.

Figure 6.32 The Document Class value in the Property inspector.

13. Save the document, and test the movie. As the video clip plays, the `title` parameter value displays over the video area (**Figure 6.33**).

Dynamically Placing Video on the Stage

In all the Flash examples in this chapter, you've manually placed the FLVPlayback component on the stage of your Flash document. For many Flash Video presentations, this approach can serve you well. However, as your grasp of ActionScript becomes stronger, you may want to explore dynamic FLVPlayback instances created in ActionScript and never placed on your document's stage during the authoring process. Here's a list of examples that could use a runtime-created FLVPlayback component instance:

▸ **Video in a window:** You could include a button to your Flash movie that opens an internal Flash window displaying the video.

▸ **Video in another component:** You could display Flash Video in a data grid cell or other container.

▸ **Cleaner file structure:** Use ActionScript to control the layout and appearance of elements on the stage to avoid messy timelines in your Flash document.

Figure 6.33 The `title` parameter displayed in the text field.

Regardless of which Flash Player version you're targeting, you need to copy the skin SWF file that you plan to use to your project folder. The Flash authoring environment automatically copies skin SWF files to your FLA file location whenever you choose a new skin, but the ActionScript compiler doesn't do this. Be sure to copy your desired skin SWF file to the same location as your FLA file.

Building solutions with ActionScript 2.0

If you're planning to use the FLVPlayback component in Flash Player 8–compatible movies using AS2, you can create a new instance of the component using the `MovieClip.attachMovie()` method.

Attaching an instance on the first frame

With ActionScript, Flash Player 8 can attach many types of assets found in a movie's library. In the following steps, you learn how to create a new instance of the FLVPlayback component with code placed on the first frame of the main timeline (Scene 1):

1. In Flash Professional 8, create a new Flash document. In Flash CS3, create a new Flash file (AS2). Save the new file as `flvplayback_fp8_actionscript.fla`.

2. If you're using Flash CS3, open the Publish Settings dialog (File > Publish Settings), and click the Flash tab. Change the Flash Player version to Flash Player 8.

3. Rename Layer 1 to `actions`.

4. Open the document's Library panel (Ctrl/Cmd+L), and then open the Components panel (Ctrl/Cmd+F7). From the Video grouping (Flash CS3) or the FLV Playback−Player 8 grouping (Flash Pro 8), drag the FLVPlayback component into your Flash document's Library panel. If you drag the component onto the stage, delete the instance.

5. From your Flash application folder, browse to the location of the skin SWF files, and copy one to your FLA file's location. In Flash CS3, you can find the skins in the Configuration/FLVPlayback Skins/ActionScript 2.0 folder. In Flash Professional 8, you can find the skins in the Configuration/Skins folder. The sample code in this tutorial references the SteelOverAll.swf skin.

6. Copy an FLV file from the flv folder of this book's DVD-ROM to the location of your FLA file. You can use any FLV file. The sample code in this tutorial references the MightyCo1947_VP6_384K_CBR_Cues.flv file.

7. After the component is in the movie's library, you can create new instances of the component in ActionScript. Select frame 1 of the actions layer, and open the Actions panel (F9, or Option+F9 on Mac). Type the following

▶ The ActionScript code in the finished FLA file on this book's DVD-ROM uses a modified path for the FLV file, in order for the SWF file to play the video directly from the DVD-ROM.

code into the script pane. Notice how the same parameter names from the Component Inspector panel are used in the ActionScript code:

```
import mx.video.FLVPlayback;

var fp:FLVPlayback = FLVPlayback(attachMovie
➥("FLVPlayback", "fp", 1));
fp.skin = "SteelOverAll.swf";
fp.contentPath = "MightyCo1947_VP6_384K_CBR_Cues.flv";
fp.x = 20;
fp.y = 20;
```

8. Save the Flash document, and test it (Ctrl/Cmd+Enter). The Flash movie displays the FLVPlayback instance with the specified FLV file and skin SWF file.

Loading a preview Image

If you don't want to automatically begin playback of the FLV file as soon as the FLVPlayback component appears on the stage, and you want to display a nice video thumbnail to entice the user, you can dynamically load a JPEG, PNG, or GIF image or other Flash movie (SWF file) into the FLVPlayback instance. In the following steps, you learn how to load a thumbnail image for the Columbia River video clip:

1. Open your FLA file from the last section, or open a copy of the flvplayback_fp8_actionscript.fla file from the ch06 folder of this book's DVD-ROM. Resave this file as `flvplayback_fp8_actionscript_preview.fla`.

2. Copy the river_thumbnail.jpg image from the ch06 folder of this book's DVD-ROM to the location of the FLA file you saved in the last step.

3. Select frame 1 of the actions layer, and open the Actions panel (F9, or Option+F9). Below the existing code, add the following code. This code loads the river_thumbnail. jpg into a new `MovieClip` instance in the FLVPlayback instance. When the user clicks the Play button, the video thumbnail is hidden:

```
fp.autoPlay = false;

var thumb:MovieClip = fp.createEmptyMovieClip
➥("thumb", 999);
```

```
thumb.loadMovie("river_thumbnail.jpg");

fp.addEventListener("playing", onVideoPlay);

function onVideoPlay(e:Object):Void {
        thumb._visible = false;
}
```

4. Save the Flash document, and test it (Ctrl/Cmd+Enter). The video file starts to load into the Flash movie, but the video doesn't automatically play. The thumbnail image of the Columbia River loads into the FLVPlayback instance (**Figure 6.34**). When you click the Play button, the thumbnail is no longer visible, and the video content begins to play.

Figure 6.34 The loaded JPEG thumbnail image.

Producing results with ActionScript 3.0

If you're planning to use the FLVPlayback component in Flash Player 9–compatible movies using AS3, you can create a new instance of the component by using the new constructor with the FLVPlayback class.

Creating an instance on the first frame

In the following steps, you learn how to create a new instance of the FLVPlayback component with code placed on the first frame of the main timeline for a Flash file written in AS3:

1. In Flash CS3, create a new Flash file (AS3). Save the new file as flvplayback_fp9_actionscript.fla.

2. Rename Layer 1 to actions.

3. Open the document's Library panel (Ctrl/Cmd+L). Next, open the Components panel (Ctrl/Cmd+F7). From the Video grouping, drag the FLVPlayback component into your Flash document's Library panel. If you drag the component onto the stage, delete the instance.

4. From your Flash application folder, browse to the location of the skin SWF files, and copy the files to your FLA file's location. In Flash CS3, you can find the skins in the Configuration/FLVPlayback Skins/ActionScript 3.0 folder. The sample code in this tutorial references the SkinOverAll.swf skin.

WARNING

Caution

▶ You must have Flash CS3 to perform the steps in this exercise.

5. Copy an FLV file from the flv folder of this book's DVD-
    ROM to the location of your FLA file. You can use any
    FLV file. The sample code in this tutorial references the
    MightyCo1947_VP6_384K_CBR_Cues.flv file.

6. After you have the component in the movie's library,
    you can create new instances of the component in
    ActionScript. Select frame 1 of the actions layer, and
    open the Actions panel (F9, or Option+F9 on Mac).
    Type the following code into the script pane. Notice
    how the same parameter names from the Component
    Inspector panel are used here in the ActionScript code:

```
import fl.video.FLVPlayback;

var fp:FLVPlayback = new FLVPlayback();
fp.skin = "SkinOverAll.swf";
fp.skinBackgroundColor = 0x666666;
fp.source = "MightyCo1947_VP6_384K_CBR_Cues.flv";
fp.x = 20;
fp.y = 20;
addChild(fp);
```

NOTES

▶ The ActionScript code in the
finished FLA file on this book's
DVD-ROM uses a modified path
for the FLV file, in order for the
SWF file to play the video
directly from the DVD-ROM.

7. Save the Flash document, and test it (Ctrl/Cmd+Enter).
    The Flash movie displays the FLVPlayback instance with
    the specified FLV file and skin SWF file.

Loading a preview image

As demonstrated in the Flash Player 8 coverage earlier in
this section, you can dynamically load a JPEG, PNG, or GIF
image or other Flash movie (SWF file) into the FLVPlayback
instance. In the following steps, you learn how to load a
thumbnail image for the Columbia River video clip:

1. Open the FLA file you built in the last section, or open
    a copy of the flvplayback_fp9_actionscript.fla file from
    the ch06 folder on the DVD-ROM. Resave this file as
    `flvplayback_fp8_actionscript_preview.fla`.

2. Copy the river_thumbnail.jpg image from the ch06
    folder of this book's DVD-ROM to the location of the
    FLA file you saved in the last step.

3. Select frame 1 of the actions layer, and open the Actions
    panel (F9, or Option+F9). The following code loads

river_thumbnail.jpg into a new Loader instance added to the FLVPlayback instance. When the user clicks the Play button, the video thumbnail is hidden. Add the bold code shown in the following code block:

```
import fl.video.FLVPlayback;
import fl.video.VideoEvent;
import flash.net.URLRequest;
import flash.display.Loader;

var fp:FLVPlayback = new FLVPlayback();
fp.skin = "SkinOverAll.swf";
fp.skinBackgroundColor = 0x666666;
fp.source = "MightyCo1947_VP6_384K_CBR_Cues.flv";
fp.x = 20;
fp.y = 20;
fp.autoPlay = false;
fp.addEventListener(VideoEvent.PLAYING_STATE_ENTERED,
➥onVideoPlay);

var thumb:Loader = new Loader();
loadImage(thumb, "river_thumbnail.jpg");

addChild(fp);

function onVideoPlay(e:VideoEvent):void {
   thumb.visible = false;
}

function loadImage(loader:Loader, imageURL:String):
➥void {
   var urlRequest:URLRequest = new
   ➥URLRequest(imageURL);
      loader.load(urlRequest);
      fp.addChild(loader);
   }
```

4. Save the Flash document, and test it (Ctrl/Cmd+Enter). The video file starts to load into the Flash movie, but the video doesn't automatically play. The thumbnail image of the Columbia River loads into the FLVPlayback instance (**Figure 6.35**). When you click the Play button, the thumbnail is no longer visible, and the video content begins to play.

Figure 6.35 The loaded JPEG thumbnail image.

Modifying Skins

One of the best features of the skin SWF files used with the FLVPlayback component is that each one can be modified to suit the design and branding requirements for your video-playback presentation. Many designers and developers aren't aware that you can quickly change the look and feel of the skin for the FLVPlayback component. For example, you may want to:

► Add a logo or branding element

► Change a background color

► Change button shapes or icons

Creating a modified FLVPlayback skin for Flash Player 8

Adobe provides all the source Flash (FLA) files for each skin option for the AS2 version of the FLVPlayback component. You can find the source skin files in the following locations:

For Flash CS3 on Windows:

C:\Program Files\Adobe\Adobe Flash CS3\en\Configuration\FLVPlayback Skins\FLA\ActionScript 2.0\

For Flash CS3 on Mac:

[Startup drive]: Applications: Adobe Flash CS3: Configuration:FLVPlayback Skins:FLA:ActionScript 2.0:

For Flash Professional 8 on Windows:

C:\Program Files\Macromedia\Flash 8\en\Configuration\SkinFLA\

For Flash Professional 8 on Mac:

[Startup drive]: Applications: Macromedia Flash 8: Configuration: SkinFLA:

To modify a skin file for the AS2 version of the FLVPlayback component, follow these steps:

1. Make a copy of the original skin FLA file from the source folder mentioned previously. Copy the file to the location

of your other Flash documents. I used a copy of the
SteelExternalPlaySeekMute.fla file from the ch01 folder
on the DVD-ROM

2. Rename the copy of the skin file. This sample uses the
filename CustomExternalPlaySeekMute.fla.

3. Open the newly renamed file in Flash. You see every element of the skin's UI placed on the stage (**Figure 6.36**).
Most of the elements aren't exported on the stage,
though—they're placed on guide layers.

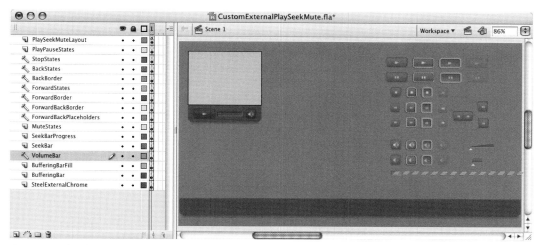

Figure 6.36 The skin elements on the main timeline.

4. To edit the look and feel of an element, double-click
the instance on the stage. Alternatively, you can open the
Library panel (Ctrl/Cmd+L) and edit the symbol
instances. Elements are grouped into various folders
and subfolders. Double-click the SteelExternalChrome
instance on the lowest layer of the main timeline.
Inside this symbol, unlock the Color Plate layer. Select
the rounded rectangle fill on the stage, and change the
background color. For this example, I used one of the
red colors from the Flash CS3 application icon, #AB111F
(**Figure 6.37**).

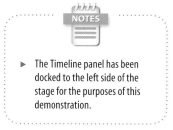

▶ The Timeline panel has been
docked to the left side of the
stage for the purposes of this
demonstration.

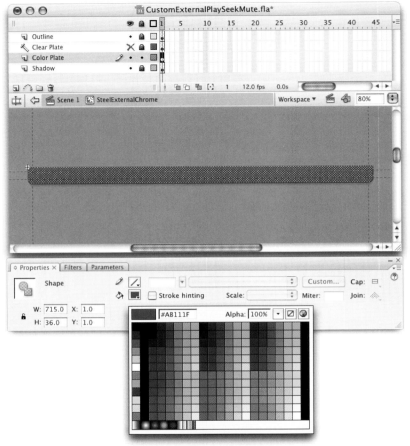

Figure 6.37 The contents of the `SteelExternalChrome` symbol.

5. Go back to the main timeline by clicking the Scene 1 tab at the upper left of the Timeline panel. You should see a preview of your new skin color at the upper left of the document stage. Note that the button colors on the right are semitransparent, showing through to the background gray color of the stage.

6. Save the Flash document, and publish the movie (Shift+F12). You now have a custom skin SWF file ready to use with the FLVPlayback component. Close the CustomExternalPlaySeekMute.fla document.

7. Open a Flash document containing an instance of the AS2 version of the FLVPlayback component. You can use

the starter file named flvplayback_fp8_custom_skin_starter.fla from the ch06 folder of this book's DVD-ROM, but resave your copy of the file as `flvplayback_fp8_custom_skin.fla`.

8. Select the FLVPlayback instance on the stage, and open the Component Inspector. Click the Parameters tab, and double-click the value for the `skin` parameter.

9. In the Select Skin dialog, choose Custom Skin URL from the Skin menu. In the URL field, type the name of the published SWF file from step 6. For this example, that SWF filename is CustomExternalPlaySeekMute.swf (**Figure 6.38**). Click OK when you're finished.

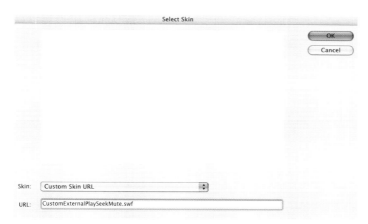

Figure 6.38 The Select Skin dialog.

10. Specify a Flash Video (FLV) file for the `contentPath` parameter in the Component Inspector.

11. Save the Flash document, and test the movie (Ctrl/Cmd+Enter). The new skin SWF file loads and displays with the FLVPlayback component (**Figure 6.39**).

Revising a FLVPlayback skin for Flash Player 9

Adobe also provides the skin source Flash (FLA) files for the AS3 version of the FLVPlayback component. In Flash CS3, you can find the source skin files in the following locations:

Figure 6.39 The customized skin SWF file.

For Flash CS3 on Windows:

C:\Program Files\Adobe\Adobe Flash CS3\en\
Configuration\FLVPlayback Skins\FLA\ActionScript 3.0\

For Flash CS3 on Mac:

[Startup drive]: Applications: Adobe Flash CS3:
Configuration: FLVPlayback Skins: FLA: ActionScript 3.0:

To modify a skin file for the AS3 version of the FLVPlayback
component, follow these steps:

1. Make a copy of the original skin FLA file from the source
   folder mentioned previously. Copy the file to the location
   of your other Flash documents. I used a copy of the
   SkinOverPlaySeekFullscreen.fla file.

2. Rename the copy of the skin file. This sample uses the
   filename CustomOverPlaySeekFullscreen.fla.

3. Open the newly renamed file in Flash. You see every
   element of the skin's UI placed on the stage.

4. To edit the look and feel of an element, double-click its
   corresponding instance on the stage. Alternatively, you
   can open the Library panel (Ctrl/Cmd+L) and edit the
   symbol instances. Elements are grouped into various
   folders and subfolders. For this example, open the
   Library, and expand the _SquareButton folder. This
   folder holds the background graphics used by all the
   control buttons.

5. Double-click the SquareBgOver symbol to edit its contents. Inside the symbol, select the green stroke on the
   Glow layer, and change its color. For this example, I used
   white (#FFFFFF) (**Figure 6.40**). If you'd like to change
   the down state of the button graphics, you can continue
   to edit the stroke colors of the SquareBgDown symbol.

6. Save the Flash document, and publish the movie
   (Shift+F12). You now have a custom skin SWF file
   ready to use with the FLVPlayback component. Close
   the CustomOverPlaySeekFullscreen.fla document.

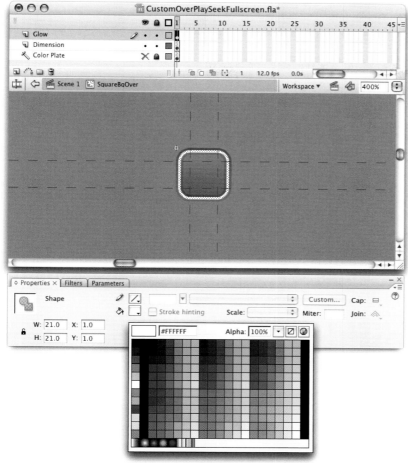

Figure 6.40 The new outline color for the button graphics.

7. Open a Flash document containing an instance of the AS3 version of the FLVPlayback component. You can use the starter file named flvplayback_fp9_custom_skin_starter.fla from the ch06 folder of this book's DVD-ROM. If you use this file, resave your copy of the file as `flvplayback_fp9_custom_skin.fla`.

8. Select the FLVPlayback instance on the stage, and open the Component Inspector. Select the Parameters tab, and double-click the value for the `skin` parameter.

9. In the Select Skin dialog, choose Custom Skin URL in the Skin menu. In the Custom URL field, type the name of

the published SWF file from step 6. For this example, that SWF filename is CustomExternalPlaySeekMute.swf. If you want a custom background color, select one from the Color pop-up menu as well. Click OK when you're finished.

10. Specify a Flash Video (FLV) file for the source parameter in the Component Inspector.

11. Save the Flash document, and test the movie (Ctrl/Cmd+Enter). The new skin SWF file loads and displays with the FLVPlayback component. Roll over the buttons in the skin, and the new white outline color is displayed.

Building a Player with Custom UI Components

You don't need a skin SWF file with your FLVPlayback instance. You can control the video clip loaded into an FLVPlayback component using custom UI components that ship with Flash CS3. The set of custom UI components for the FLVPlayback available in the Components panel (Ctrl/Cmd+F7) is nearly identical for the AS2 and AS3 versions. **Figure 6.41** shows the UI components that are included in the Video grouping for the AS3 version of the FLVPlayback component, and **Figure 6.42** shows those for the AS2 version.

NOTES

▶ If you're using Flash Professional 8, you can find the AS2 versions of the UI components in the FLV Playback Custom UI grouping of the Components panel.

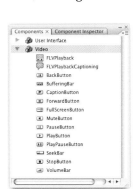 

Figure 6.41 The custom UI components for the AS3 version of the FLVPlayback component.

Figure 6.42 The custom UI components for the AS2 version of the FLVPlayback component.

The process of integrating a custom UI component with an instance of the FLVPlayback component is fairly straight-forward:

1. Add and name an instance of the FLVPlayback component on the stage.

2. Set the skin parameter to None.

3. Add and name each UI component you need on the stage.

4. Link each UI component to the respective property name of the FLVPlayback instance.

Now that you have an overview of the process, let's practice the steps with an example.

To use a custom UI component with the AS3 version of the FLVPlayback component, follow these steps:

1. Create a new Flash file (AS3). Save the file as flvplayback_fp9_custom_ui.fla.

2. Rename Layer 1 to flvPlayer.

3. Drag an instance of the FLVPlayback component from the Components panel to the stage. In the Property inspector, name this instance flvPlayer.

4. Select the Parameters tab of the Property inspector (or open the Parameters tab of the Component Inspector panel), and add an FLV file to the source parameter. Use one of your FLV files or a file copied from the book's DVD-ROM.

5. Double-click the skin parameter to open the Select Skin dialog. Set the Skin menu to None, and click OK.

6. Create a new layer named controls, and place this layer above the flvPlayer layer.

7. From the Video grouping in the Components panel, drag the PlayPauseButton component to the stage, and place it below the lower-left corner of the FLVPlayback instance. Name the new instance ppb in the Property inspector.

8. From the Video grouping in the Components panel, drag the SeekBar component to the stage, and place it to the right of the PlayPauseButton instance. Name the new instance sb in the Property inspector. You can stretch the width of the SeekBar instance using the Free Transform tool to fill the remaining width of the FLVPlayback instance (**Figure 6.43**).

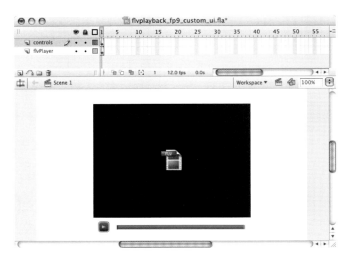

Figure 6.43 The newly placed custom UI components.

9. Create a new layer named `actions`. Place this layer at the top of the layer stack.

10. Select frame 1 of the actions layer, and open the Actions panel (F9, or Option+F9 on Mac). Add the following code to the script pane. Notice that the property names of the FLVPlayback controls mirror the names of the components in the Components panel—change the first letter of the name to lowercase. For example, PlayPauseButton becomes `playPauseButton`:

```
import fl.video.FLVPlayback;

var fp:FLVPlayback = flvPlayer;
fp.playPauseButton = ppb;
fp.seekBar = sb;
```

11. Save the Flash document, and test the movie (Ctrl/Cmd+Enter). When the Flash Video file loads into the FLVPlayback instance, use the newly added custom UI component instances to control the video's playback (**Figure 6.44**).

You can also edit the look and feel of the custom UI components by opening the Library panel and modifying the graphics inside the component's nested symbols. The custom UI components aren't compiled—you can view every asset of the controls directly in the Library panel.

Figure 6.44 The new components can control the video playback.

7

Building Your Own Video Player

Believe it or not, there may be times that your best choice for your video won't be the FLVPlayback components. For example, if you only want simple controls for your video playback, you can quickly build your own video player. You can, of course, continue to build on your video player code, and even add more advanced features. One of the best reasons to build your own basic video player is reduced complexity and file size. You can make a Flash movie (SWF file) smaller than 1 KB and play a video! Compare that to the size of the FLVPlayback component, which adds 32 KB to your Flash movie file size.

In this chapter, you learn how to use the NetConnection, NetStream, and Video classes to play a video. You also implement the VideoPlayer API to play a video. The VideoPlayer class is used by the FLVPlayback component.

Making a Connection

You need three ingredients in a Flash movie to play a Flash Video (FLV) file:

▶ Video **object:** This object is placed on the stage (or in a MovieClip instance) to display the video in the Flash movie. Any transformations you apply to the Video instance, such as width, height, position, or filter effects, are applied to the video displayed in the instance.

▶ NetConnection **object:** This object establishes the kind of network protocol the video file uses. Use the NetConnection instance to connect to an Adobe Flash Media Server application that hosts the video file(s) you want to play. If you're loading a video file from a local folder or a Web server, you can use a different connection technique. The NetConnection object is created in code only; it does not exist as an object placed on the stage.

NOTES

▶ After you've finished this chapter, you might want to jump to Chapter 10 to see how these production techniques apply to a video banner ad project.

NOTES

▶ Both of these FLV files are also hosted on the Flash Media Server for this book's examples. A warm thank-you to my friends at Influxis (www.influxis.com) for hosting the real-time streaming examples used in this chapter. The MPEG-1 source file for *Flight of Apollo 11* is available for download at www.archive.org/details/ flight_of_apollo_11. You can also find the MPEG-1 source file in the source/mpeg folder of this book's DVD-ROM. This NASA documentary is public-domain content.

▶ NetStream **object:** This object grabs the Flash Video file and controls its playback. The NetStream instance uses the NetConnection object to help it determine how to access a video resource. To display the video, the NetStream instance is attached to the Video instance. In fact, if you don't attach a NetStream object to a Video instance, you can play a video and hear its audio without even seeing it on the stage! Like the NetConnection instance, the NetStream instance only exists in the Flash Player memory—it is not a tangible object placed on the stage.

Of course, you can use either ActionScript 2.0 or ActionScript 3.0 code to build these objects in a Flash movie. You'll learn how to use both code versions in the following sections.

You can use the following FLV files from the book's DVD-ROM, located in the flv folder.

For Flash Player 8 or higher:

```
flight_of_apollo_11_SQZ_VP6_512K_CBR_Cues.flv
```

For Flash Player 6 (real-time streaming) or Flash Player 7:

```
flight_of_apollo_11_SQZ_Spark_512K_CBR_Cues.flv
```

ActionScript 2.0—Progressive Download Video

If you want to target Flash Player 7 or higher, use ActionScript 2.0 code to play a progressive-download Flash Video, which is an FLV file hosted on a Web server. However, you must use a Flash Video file encoded with the Sorenson Spark video codec to be compatible with Flash Player 7. If you want to play a progressive-download Flash Video file encoded with the On2 VP6 codec, you must target Flash Player 8 or higher.

To play a progressive video file in a Flash movie that uses ActionScript 2.0 code and targets Flash Player 7 or higher:

1. Create a new Flash document in Flash 8 or a new Flash file (ActionScript 2.0) in Flash CS3. Save as BasicPlayer_ Progressive_AS2.fla, to the same folder as the FLV file mentioned at the beginning of this section.

2. Choose File > Publish Settings to open the Publish Settings dialog. In the Flash tab, change the Flash Player version to Flash Player 7.

3. Open the Library panel (Ctrl/Cmd+L) and choose New Video from the options menu located at the top-right corner of the Library panel. The Video Properties dialog, shown in **Figure 7.1**, appears. You don't need to change any default value. Click OK. You now have a Video object in the movie's library.

TIP

On the DVD-ROM

► You can find all the source files for this chapter's exercises in the ch07 folder on this book's DVD-ROM. You can open the ch07.flp file in the Project panel of Flash CS3 to review all of the source files for this chapter.

► You can reuse one NetConnection instance with several NetStream objects.

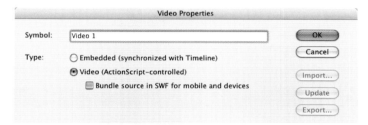

Figure 7.1 The Video Properties dialog.

4. Rename Layer 1 to vid. Drag the Video 1 symbol from the Library panel to the stage, on frame 1 of the vid layer.

5. Select the new instance on the stage, and name it vid in the Property inspector. Position the vid instance wherever you want on the stage.

6. Create a new layer named actions, and place it above the vid layer. Select frame 1 of the actions layer, and add the following code:

```
// Create a new NetConnection instance
var conn:NetConnection = new NetConnection();
// Connect with a null value for progressive FLV files
conn.connect(null);

// Create a new NetStream instance with the
➥NetConnection instance
var stream:NetStream = new NetStream(conn);

// Play the FLV file
stream.play("flight_of_apollo_11_SQZ_Spark_512K_CBR_
➥Cues.flv");
```

WARNING

► All the sample progressive-download URLs used in this chapter contain relative paths (../flv) to the FLV files in the flv folder of this book's DVD-ROM. Depending on how you structure your local system folders and files, you may need to adjust these sample paths to point to FLV files that reside on your system.

► Remember, if you're using a Flash Video file encoded with the On2 VP6 codec, you must target Flash Player 8 or higher.

```
// Create a reference to the Video instance on the stage
var vid:Video;
```

```
// Attach the NetStream instance to the Video instance
vid.attachVideo(stream);
```

7. Save the Flash document, and test the movie (Ctrl/ Cmd+Enter). When the Flash movie loads into the Test Movie window, you should see the *Flight of Apollo 11* video play in the vid instance. (There's no automatic control bar for the video playback with a Video instance. You need to build your own controls, as I describe later in this chapter.)

ActionScript 2.0—Real-time Streaming Video

With ActionScript 2.0 code, you can target Flash Player 6 or higher if your FLV file is encoded with the Sorenson Spark codec and hosted on a Flash Media Server (FMS) or Flash Video Streaming Service (FVSS). If you want to use a real-time streaming Flash Video encoded with the On2 VP6 codec, you must target Flash Player 8 or higher. For the following example, use the RTMP connection information shown in the sample code.

To play a real-time streaming Sorenson Spark Flash Video file in a Flash movie that uses ActionScript 2.0 code and targets Flash Player 6 or higher:

1. Continue working on the BasicPlayer_Progressive_ AS2.fla file you created in the last section. Alternatively, make a copy of this file from the ch07 folder on the DVD-ROM, and open it in Flash 8 or Flash CS3. Resave the document as BasicPlayer_Streaming_AS2.fla.

2. Select frame 1 of the actions layer, and open the Actions panel (F9, or Option+F9 on Mac). Change the existing code to the following code block. Notice that the FLV filename used in the NetStream.play() method does not include the .flv file extension when you play a stream over an RTMP connection.

```
// Create a new NetConnection instance
var conn:NetConnection = new NetConnection();
```

```
// Connect to the FMS application or FVSS provider
conn.connect("rtmp://flashvideo.rtmphost.com/samples");

// Create a new NetStream instance with the
➥NetConnection instance
var stream:NetStream = new NetStream(conn);

// Play the FLV file
stream.play("flight_of_apollo_11_SQZ_Spark_512K_
➥CBR_Cues");

// Create a reference to the Video instance on the stage
var vid:Video;

// Attach the NetStream instance to the Video instance
vid.attachVideo(stream);
```

3. Save the Flash document, and test the movie (Ctrl/Cmd+ Enter). The *Flight of Apollo 11* video streams from the Influxis server and is displayed in your Flash movie's vid instance. Because the Flash Video is streaming, your Internet connection speed must match or exceed the bitrate of the Flash Video file. If your Internet connection speed is slower, you will notice video playback pause as the video buffers.

ActionScript 3.0—Progressive Download Video

If you target Flash Player 9 or higher, you can use Action-Script 3.0 code to play a progressive-download Flash Video, which is an FLV file hosted on a Web server. Flash Player 9, like Flash Player 8, can play Flash Video files encoded with either the Sorenson Spark or On2 VP6 codec.

In ActionScript 3.0, you do not need to create a Video symbol in the Flash document's Library panel. You can create a new instance entirely in code.

To play a progressive video file in a Flash movie that uses ActionScript 3.0 code and targets Flash Player 9 or higher:

1. Create a new Flash file (ActionScript 3.0) file in Flash CS3. Save this document as BasicPlayer_Progressive_AS3.fla, to the same folder as the FLV file you copied at the beginning of this section.

NOTES

▶ This sample code does not provide a NetConnection. onStatus() handler for the *conn* instance. With this handler, you can determine if a connection is successful before you attempt to play a stream. The BasicPlayer_Streaming_ AS2_PauseOnLoad.fla file in the ch07 folder on the DVD-ROM demonstrates this handler's usage.

▶ You'll learn how to control and add dynamic buffering for a real-time streaming Flash Video in Chapter 8.

2. Rename Layer 1 to actions. Select frame 1 of the actions layer, and add the following code:

```
// Import AS3 class files
import flash.media.Video;
import flash.net.NetConnection;
import flash.net.NetStream;

// Create a new NetConnection instance
var conn:NetConnection = new NetConnection();
// Connect with a null value for progressive FLV files
conn.connect(null);

// Create a new NetStream instance with the
➡NetConnection instance
var stream:NetStream = new NetStream(conn);

// Play the FLV file
stream.play("flight_of_apollo_11_SQZ_Spark_512K_CBR_
➡Cues.flv");

// Create a Video instance on the stage
var vid:Video = new Video();

// Attach the NetStream instance to the Video instance
vid.attachNetStream(stream);

// Position the Video instance on the stage
vid.x = 20;
vid.y = 20;

// Add the Video instance to the display list
addChild(vid);
```

3. Save the Flash document, and test the movie (Ctrl/ Cmd+Enter). When the Flash movie loads into the Test Movie window, you should see the *Flight of Apollo 11* video play in the vid instance.

ActionScript 3.0—Real-time Streaming Video

You can also use ActionScript 3.0 code to play a real-time streaming Flash Video file, which is an FLV file hosted on a Flash Media Server (FMS) or Flash Video Streaming Service (FVSS) provider. As you learned in Chapter 4, Flash Video files hosted on such servers use a connection employing RTMP, or Real Time Messaging Protocol.

In ActionScript 3.0, you must wait for a successful connection from the server before creating a NetStream instance and playing the FLV file. The code to play a real-time streaming Flash Video file is more complicated.

To play a real-time streaming video file in a Flash movie that uses ActionScript 3.0 code and targets Flash Player 9 or higher:

1. Create a new Flash file (ActionScript 3.0) in Flash CS3. Save the document as `BasicPlayer_Streaming_AS3.fla`, to the same folder as the FLV file given at the beginning of this section.

2. Rename Layer 1 to `actions`. Select frame 1 of the actions layer, and add the following code:

```
// Import AS3 class files
import flash.media.Video;
import flash.net.NetConnection;
import flash.net.NetStream;
import flash.net.ObjectEncoding;
import flash.events.NetStatusEvent;

// Create a new NetConnection instance
var conn:NetConnection = new NetConnection();

// Create a handler for connection events
conn.addEventListener(NetStatusEvent.NET_STATUS,
➥onConnectStatus);

// Set the data encoding used by a FMS connection
conn.objectEncoding = ObjectEncoding.AMF0;

// Connect to the FMS application or FVSS provider
conn.connect("rtmp://flashvideo.rtmphost.com/samples");

// Create a new NetStream instance reference;
var stream:NetStream;

// Create a Video instance on the stage
var vid:Video = new Video();

// Position the Video instance on the stage
vid.x = 20;
vid.y = 20;
```

▶ When you test the Flash movie in Flash CS3, you may notice non-critical ActionScript 3.0 runtime error messages in the Output panel. The errors, labeled Unhandled AsyncErrorEvent, indicate that additional callback handlers are not defined on the NetConnection and NetStream instances. The video continues to play despite these error messages. You'll learn about more advanced status handlers later in this chapter and throughout the remainder of the book.

▶ You'll learn how to control and add dynamic buffering for a real-time streaming Flash Video in Chapter 8.

```
// Add the Video instance to the display list
addChild(vid);

// Define a handler for connection events
function onConnectStatus(e:NetStatusEvent):void {
    // Display the status in the Output panel
    trace("onConnectStatus > " + e.info.code);

    // If the connection is made to the server
    if(e.info.code == "NetConnection.Connect.Success"){

        // Create a new NetStream instance with
        ➥the connection stream = new NetStream
        ➥(e.currentTarget as NetConnection);

        // Play the FLV file
        stream.play("flight_of_apollo_11_SQZ_VP6_512K_
        ➥CBR_Cues");

        // Attach the NetStream instance to the Video
        ➥instance
        vid.attachNetStream(stream);
    }
}
```

3. Save the Flash document, and test the movie (Ctrl/Cmd+Enter). The *Flight of Apollo 11* video streams from the Influxis server and is displayed in your Flash movie's vid instance. Because the Flash Video is streaming, your Internet connection speed must match or exceed the bitrate of the Flash Video file. If your Internet connection speed is slower, you'll notice pauses in the video playback as the video buffers.

Building Basic Playback Controls

After you've set up a Flash Video file to play with a NetConnection, NetStream, and Video instance, you can start to add more playback control functionality to the Flash movie. In this section, you learn how to create an autoplay feature for the video (or pause the video upon loading), as well as add Play and Pause buttons to the movie.

Pausing the Video on Load

Many times, you may not want your Flash Video to auto-matically begin playing when the Video instance appears on the stage. To delay the video, add the following code features to the Flash movies we built earlier in this chapter:

- ▶ `autoPlay` **variable:** This variable controls whether the Flash Video plays automatically when the `NetStream.play()` method is invoked. If this variable is set to `false`, the first frame of the video is displayed and playback is paused.

- ▶ `firstPlay` **variable:** This variable remembers the first time the play event is fired on the `NetStream` instance. When the Flash movie (SWF file) initializes, the `firstPlay` variable is set to `true`. Then, when `NetStream.Play.Start` is received by the stream, the `firstPlay` variable is set to `false`.

- ▶ `NetStream.onStatus` **handler:** This method of the `NetStream` class can be used to detect any events that occur with Flash Video playback. If `autoPlay` is set to `false`, the `onStatus` handler will tell the stream to pause and seek to its first frame.

While there are differences between ActionScript 2.0 (AS2) and ActionScript 3.0 (AS3) status handlers, the approach does not vary with progressive-download video or real-time streaming video.

ActionScript 2.0

When targeting Flash Player 6 or higher, you can use ActionScript 2.0 to control video playback. Remember, available video codecs and delivery methods follow the same rules I mentioned in the previous exercises.

To pause a Flash Video on load and display the first frame of the video:

1. Open the BasicPlayer_Progressive_AS2.fla file from the ch07 folder on the DVD-ROM.

2. Resave this file as `BasicPlayer_Progressive_AS2_PauseOnLoad.fla` on your local system. Make sure the *Flight of Apollo 11* FLV file is in the same location as the FLA file.

3. Select frame 1 of the actions layer. Add the following code immediately after the `conn.connect(null);` line of code:

```
// Create a variable to control automatic playback
var autoPlay:Boolean = false;
// Create a variable to track playback
var firstPlay:Boolean = true;
```

4. After the `var stream:NetStream = new NetStream(conn);` line of code, add the following code:

```
// Listen for NetStream events to handle video playback
stream.onStatus = function(e:Object):Void {
    trace("stream.onStatus > " + e.code);
    // If this is the first time to load and play the
    ➥video
    if(e.code == "NetStream.Play.Start" && firstPlay){
        // If the video should NOT automatically play
        if(!autoPlay){
            // Pause the video
            this.pause(true);
            // Show the first frame
            this.seek(0);
        }
        // Establish that the video has loaded
        firstPlay = false;
    }
}
```

NOTES

▶ If you're using the FLA file from the book's DVD-ROM, you'll need to remove the `../flv/` path prefix in the `stream.play()` method on frame 1. Otherwise, the FLV file on your local system may not play.

On the DVD-ROM

▶ You can also find an updated version of this file for real-time streaming Flash Video files in the ch07 folder on the DVD-ROM. The BasicPlayer_Streaming_AS2_PauseOnLoad.fla file uses the same code as this example, but uses the connection method for a Flash Media Server.

5. Save the Flash document, and test the movie (Ctrl/Cmd+Enter). When the Flash movie loads into the Test Movie window, you should see the *Flight of Apollo 11* video load and pause in the `vid` instance.

ActionScript 3.0

If you're targeting Flash Player 9 or higher, use ActionScript 3.0 to control video playback. Remember, the same rules I described in the previous section' apply here as well.

To pause a Flash Video on load and display the first frame of the video:

1. Open the BasicPlayer_Progressive_AS3.fla file from the ch07 folder of this book's DVD-ROM.

2. Resave this file as `BasicPlayer_Progressive_AS3_PauseOnLoad.fla` on your local system. Make sure the *Flight of Apollo 11* FLV file is in the same location as the FLA file.

3. Select frame 1 of the actions layer, and add the following code just after the last `import` statement at the top of the script:

```
import flash.events.NetStatusEvent;
```

The `NetStatusEvent` class is used by the `NetStream` class.

4. Now, add the following code after the `conn.connect(null);` line of code:

```
// Create a variable to control automatic playback
var autoPlay:Boolean = false;
// Create a variable to track playback
var firstPlay:Boolean = true;
```

5. After the `var stream:NetStream = new NetStream(conn);` line of code, add the following:

```
// Create a listener for NetStream events
stream.addEventListener(NetStatusEvent.NET_STATUS,
➥onStreamEvent);
```

6. Finally, after the last line of code in the script, add the following function definition:

```
// Create the listener function for NetStream events
function onStreamEvent(e:NetStatusEvent):void {
    trace("stream.onStatus > " + e.info.code);
    // Set current stream
    var s:NetStream = e.currentTarget as NetStream;
    // If this is the first time to load and play the
    ➥video
    if(e.info.code == "NetStream.Play.Start" &&
    ➥firstPlay){
        // If the video should NOT automatically play
        if(!autoPlay){
            // Pause the video
            s.pause();
            // Show the first frame
            s.seek(0);
```

NOTES

▶ If you're using the FLA file from this book's DVD-ROM, you need to remove the ../flv/ path prefix in the `stream.play()` method on frame 1, or the FLV file on your local system may not play.

```
        }
        // Establish that the video has loaded
        firstPlay = false;
    }
}
```

The onStreamEvent function is specified in the code you added in step 4.

7. Save the Flash document, and test the movie (Ctrl/ Cmd+Enter). When the Flash movie loads into the Test Movie window, you should see the *Flight of Apollo 11* video load and pause in the vid instance.

Adding Play and Pause Buttons

It's all well and good to get a video to automatically play or pause on load, but what about the user? In this section, you learn how to add two buttons to the Flash movie to control Flash Video playback.

In the following two sections, you add two Button symbols to control the NetStream instance. The Flash movie will have these behaviors:

▶ **Enable or disable the buttons:** If the video hasn't loaded, the playback buttons should be disabled. After the video begins to load, enable the playback buttons. When the buttons are disabled, they appear faded and are not clickable. When the buttons are enabled, they appear opaque and are clickable.

▶ **Play video button:** Clicking the Play button starts playback of the Flash Video file.

▶ **Pause video button:** Clicking the Pause button halts playback of the Flash Video file.

ActionScript 2.0

To add Flash Video playback controls to a Flash Player 6 or higher movie:

1. Open the BasicPlayer_Progressive_AS2_PauseOnLoad. fla file from the ch07 folder on the DVD-ROM.

2. Resave this file as BasicPlayer_Progressive_AS2_ PlayPause.fla on your local system. Make sure the *Flight of Apollo 11* FLV file is in the same location as the FLA file.

3. Create a new layer named buttons. Place this layer below the actions layer.

4. Choose Window > Common Libraries > Buttons to open the Buttons library (**Figure 7.2**). Scroll down to the playback rounded folder, and drag the rounded gray pause and rounded gray play symbols to the stage.

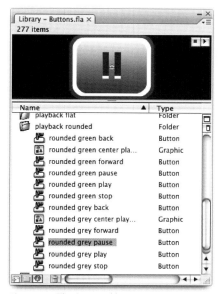

Figure 7.2 The Buttons library.

5. Position the Play and Pause buttons below the vid instance. In the Property inspector, name the Play button playBtn. Name the Pause button pauseBtn.

6. Select frame 1 of the actions layer, and add the following code just after the last line of code:

```
// Create references to the buttons
var playBtn:Button;
var pauseBtn:Button;

// Define button handlers
playBtn.onRelease = function():Void {
   stream.pause(false);
};
```

► If you're using the FLA file from the DVD-ROM, you must remove the ../flv/ path prefix in the `stream.play()` method on frame 1 of the actions layer, or the FLV file on your local system may not play.

```
pauseBtn.onRelease = function():Void {
    stream.pause(true);
};

// Disable buttons until video has loaded
enableButtons(false);

// Create a function to enable/disable buttons
function enableButtons(active:Boolean):Void {
    playBtn.enabled = active;
    pauseBtn.enabled = active;
    playBtn._alpha = active ? 100 : 50;
    pauseBtn._alpha = active ? 100 : 50;
}
```

7. Locate the `stream.onStatus()` handler, and add the new code before the closing curly brace (}) of the if statement:

```
// Listen for NetStream events to handle video playback
stream.onStatus = function(e:Object):Void {
    trace("stream.onStatus > " + e.code);
    // If this is the first time to load and play the
    ➥video
    if(e.code == "NetStream.Play.Start" && firstPlay){
        // If the video should NOT automatically play
        if(!autoPlay){
            // Pause the video
            this.pause(true);
            // Show the first frame
            this.seek(0);
        }
        // Establish that the video has loaded
        firstPlay = false;
        // Enable playback buttons
        enableButtons(true);
    }
}
```

8. Save the Flash document, and test the movie (Ctrl/Cmd+Enter). When the Flash movie loads into the Test Movie window, you should see the *Flight of Apollo 11* video load and pause in the `vid` instance, as shown in **Figure 7.3**. Now click the Play button to start playback

Figure 7.3 The Play and Pause buttons below the video.

of the Flash Video file. Clicking the Pause button halts playback of the file.

ActionScript 3.0

To add Flash Video playback controls to a Flash Player 9 or higher movie:

1. Open the BasicPlayer_Progressive_AS3_PauseOnLoad. fla file from the ch07 folder of this book's DVD-ROM.

2. Resave this file as `BasicPlayer_Progressive_AS3_ PlayPause.fla` on your local system. The *Flight of Apollo 11* FLV file must be in the same location as the FLA file.

3. To add control buttons to your movie, repeat steps 3 through 5 of the preceding section. Because this movie does not have an authortime Video instance on the stage, place the buttons in the top-left corner of the stage. You'll use ActionScript code to play the buttons in later steps.

4. Select frame 1 of the actions layer and add the following `import` statements at the top of the script, after the last `import` statement:

```
import flash.events.MouseEvent;
import flash.display.SimpleButton;
```

These classes are necessary for the button functionality you add in the next step.

5. After the `addChild(vid);` line of code, add the following code:

```
// Position the Button instances
playBtn.x = vid.x + (playBtn.width/2);
playBtn.y = vid.y + vid.height + (playBtn.height/2) + 5;
pauseBtn.x = playBtn.x + playBtn.width + 10;
pauseBtn.y = playBtn.y;

// Create listeners for the buttons
playBtn.addEventListener(MouseEvent.CLICK,
➥controlPlayback);
pauseBtn.addEventListener(MouseEvent.CLICK,
➥controlPlayback);

// Disable buttons until video has loaded
enableButtons(false);
```

NOTES

On the DVD-ROM

▶ You will find an updated version of this file for real-time streaming Flash Video files in the ch07 folder on the DVD-ROM. The BasicPlayer_Streaming_AS2_ PlayPause.fla file uses the same code as this example but uses the connection method for a Flash Media Server.

173

```
// Create a function to enable/disable buttons
function enableButtons(active:Boolean):void {
   playBtn.enabled = active;
   pauseBtn.enabled = active;
   playBtn.alpha = active ? 100 : 50;
   pauseBtn.alpha = active ? 100 : 50;
}

// Create a listener function for Button events
function controlPlayback(e:MouseEvent):void {
   // Set current button
   var btn:SimpleButton = e.currentTarget as
➥SimpleButton;
   // If button click is from the play button
   if(btn == playBtn && btn.enabled){
      // Resume playback
      stream.resume();
   // If button click is from the pause button
   } else if(btn == pauseBtn && btn.enabled){
      // Pause playback
      stream.pause();
   }
}
```

This code positions the buttons and enables their behaviors.

6. Locate the onStreamEvent function. Add the new code before the closing curly brace (}) of the if statement, as shown in the following code block.

```
// Create the listener function for NetStream events
function onStreamEvent(e:NetStatusEvent):void {
   trace("stream.onStatus > " + e.info.code);
   // Set current stream
   var s:NetStream = e.currentTarget as NetStream;
   // If this is the first time to load and play the
➥video
   if(e.info.code == "NetStream.Play.Start" &&
➥firstPlay){
      // If the video should NOT automatically play
      if(!autoPlay){
```

NOTES

► If you're using the FLA file from the book's DVD-ROM, you must remove the ../flv/ path prefix in the stream.play() method on frame 1. If you do not, the FLV file on your local system may not play.

```
        // Pause the video
        s.pause();
        // Show the first frame
        s.seek(0);
    }
    // Establish that the video has loaded
    firstPlay = false;
    // Enable buttons
    enableButtons(true);
    }
}
```

7. Save the Flash document, and test the movie (Ctrl/Cmd+Enter). When the Flash movie loads into the Test Movie window, you should see the *Flight of Apollo 11* video load and pause in the vid instance, as shown in Figure 7.3. Now click the Play button to start playback of the Flash Video file. Clicking the Pause button halts playback of the file.

Reading Metadata from a Flash Video

You can detect events related to video playback with the NetStream class, but you can also detect other significant events such as when the metadata of a Flash Video file has loaded. In this last section, you learn how to write the ActionScript code necessary to detect this event.

Most Flash Video encoders add standard metadata to the FLV file during the encoding process. Commonly used properties include:

▶ duration: This metadata information describes the length in seconds of the Flash Video file.

▶ width **and** height: This metadata describes the dimensions of the video.

▶ framerate: This metadata describes how fast, in frames per seconds (fps), the video frames play.

▶ videodatarate: The bitrate, in Kbps, of the file's video track.

▶ audiodatarate: The bitrate, in Kbps, of the file's audio track.

NOTES

▶ As I mentioned in prior AS3 examples, the Output panel displays runtime error messages related to undefined callback handlers for the NetStream and NetConnection instances. You can ignore these errors for this exercise.

....

On the DVD-ROM

▶ An updated version of this file for real-time streaming Flash Video files is in the ch07 folder of this book's DVD-ROM. The BasicPlayer_Streaming_AS3_PlayPause.fla file uses the same code as this example, but uses the connection method for a Flash Media Server.

▶ If you want to resize a Video instance in Flash Player 6 or 7, you need to nest the Video instance in a MovieClip instance, and then control the width and height of the MovieClip instance in ActionScript code.

ActionScript 2.0

In this example, you learn how to read the metadata from a Flash Video file in order to properly size the Video instance displaying the video. This code is compatible with Flash Player 8 or higher. These metadata properties are defined within an Object instance passed to the NetStream.onMetaData() handler.

1. Open the BasicPlayer_Progressive_AS2.fla file from the ch07 folder of this book's DVD-ROM.

2. Resave this file as BasicPlayer_Progressive_AS2_Metadata.fla.

3. Choose File > Publish Settings, and in the Publish Settings dialog, select the Flash tab. Change the Flash Player version to Flash Player 8.

4. Select frame 1 of the actions layer, and open the Actions panel (F9, or Option+F9 on Mac). Remove the ../flv path prefix from the stream.play() method in the script.

5. Move the var vid:Video; declaration to the top of the script. By placing the code at the top of the script, the vid instance is strongly typed for the code you enter in the next step.

6. Add the following code after the var stream:NetStream = new NetStream(conn); line of code:

```
// Detect when the FLV metadata loads
stream.onMetaData = function(meta:Object):Void {
    // show all metadata in Output panel
    for(var i in meta){
        trace(i + ": " + meta[i]);
    }
    // Resize vid instance if metadata exists
    if(meta.width > 0){
        vid._width = meta.width;
        vid._height = meta.height;
    }
};
```

This code captures the metadata event as it occurs on the NetStream instance.

7. Save the Flash document, and test it (Ctrl/Cmd+Enter). When the Flash Video file loads into the movie, the Output panel displays all the metadata available in the FLV file. The Video instance is also resized to the video's native width and height.

ActionScript 3.0

With Flash Player 9 or higher, you can use ActionScript 3.0 code to handle metadata events that occur on a `NetStream` instance.

1. Open the BasicPlayer_Progressive_AS3.fla file from the ch07 folder on the DVD-ROM.

2. Resave this file as `BasicPlayer_Progressive_AS3_Metadata.fla`.

3. Select frame 1 of the actions layer, and open the Actions panel (F9, or Option+F9 on Mac). Remove the ../flv path prefix from the `stream.play()` method in the script.

4. Move the `var vid:Video = new Video();` declaration to the top of the script, below the `import` statements. By placing the code at the top of the script, the `vid` instance is strongly typed for the code you enter in the next step.

5. Add the following code after the `var stream:NetStream = new NetStream(conn);` line of code. This code captures the metadata event as it occurs on the `NetStream` instance.

```
// Build an object to handle metadata events
var metaHandler:Object = new Object();
metaHandler.onMetaData = function(meta:Object):void {
    // show all metadata in Output panel
    for(var i in meta){
        trace(i + ": " + meta[i]);
    }
    // Resize vid instance if metadata exists
    if(meta.width > 0){
        vid.width = meta.width;
        vid.height = meta.height;
    }
};
```

Integrating the VideoPlayer Class

If you like the functionality of the FLVPlayback component but you'd prefer to build your own fully customized video player, you might want to take a look at the `VideoPlayer` class. This class is the foundation of the FLVPlayback component, and provides many of its core features. In the ch07 folder of this book's DVD-ROM, you can find some examples that use the `VideoPlayer` API. In Flash 8 Professional, you can import the `VideoPlayer` class directly from the default class path. However, in Flash CS3, you need to add the class files to your current document's location, or you can use the VideoPlayerBundle component I built from those very same classes. The VideoPlayer_AS3_starter. fla file contains the `VideoPlayer` class (and the associated `NCManager` class) in the library, within the VideoPlayerBundle component. If you want more information on the `VideoPlayer` class, search the Flash Help panel for the term `VideoPlayer`.

```
// Assign the handler to the stream
stream.client = metaHandler;
```

6. Save the Flash document, and test it (Ctrl/Cmd+Enter). When the Flash Video file loads into the movie, the Output panel displays all the metadata available in the FLV file. The Video instance is also resized to the video's native width and height. For this example, the default size of a new Video instance, 320 by 240, is the same as the native dimensions of the sample FLV file.

8

Integrating Multiple Bitrates

Most Web video formats, including Microsoft Windows Media and Real Video, have the capability to include multiple data rates, or multiple bit rates (MBR), for audio and video tracks within a *single* file. While Flash Video does not offer this feature, you can create the same user experience with a bit of ActionScript code and a SMIL file. SMIL, which stands for Synchronized Multimedia Integration Language, is a Web standard proposed by the W3C (World Wide Web Consortium), and most popularly used by Real Player and QuickTime Player. Traditionally, a SMIL file, which closely resembles the structure of an HTML document, is used to coordinate several pieces of media, including video, audio, animation, and text, in a presentation. For Flash Video and the FLVPlayback component, SMIL represents the opportunity to quickly enable a customized user experience, wherein the SMIL file enumerates two or more FLV files of the same piece of content encoded with different data rates.

In this chapter, you learn how to evaluate the needs of a project with respect to multiple data rates, how to build a SMIL file for both streaming and progressive Flash Video, and how to use a SMIL file effectively with the FLVPlayback components (AS2 and AS3).

Knowing When to Offer More than One Bitrate

Not every Flash Video project will require more than one FLV file per piece of content. You can determine if you need multiple FLV files per piece of content by answering these questions:

▶ **Do you intend to deploy real-time streaming FLV files?** If you're planning to host your Flash Video content on an Adobe Flash Media Server or Flash Video Streaming Service provider (such as Akamai or Limelight), you should consider providing at least two bitrates per piece of content. For example, you would encode a music video at 768 Kbps

On the DVD-ROM

► You can find all of the source files for this chapter's exercises in the ch08 folder of this book's DVD-ROM.

Caution

► All of the sample streaming and progressive-download URLs used in this chapter refer to FLV files that reside on this book's Web server (www.flashsupport. com) and hosted Flash Media Server account at Influxis.com. You're welcome to access these remote FLV files in your own tests, but you'll need to have access to a Web server and Flash Media Server (or FVSS provider) to create your own examples with different FLV files.

for high-quality video served to users with fast network connections, and another at 384 Kbps (or lower) for medium-quality video served to visitors with slower connections.

► **Will users with a wide range of Internet connection speeds be viewing the content?** Carefully examine the target audience who will be viewing the video content. What kind of connection speeds will those people have? For example, if you're building a Web site for a luxury foreign-car maker, chances are that the clientele visiting the site have broadband Internet connections. You might not have many dial-up users visiting a site selling luxury cars. On the flip side, if you're creating content for a public museum Web site or a company selling a wide range of projects (think JCPenney or Sears), then you're going to have people with a wide range of Internet speeds viewing the content.

► **Will you be serving Flash Video content to mobile devices?** While most mobile devices do not support Flash Video playback, some high-end PDAs or phones featuring Windows Mobile 5 or higher can use Flash Player 7. Some devices have Internet connection speeds in excess of 128 Kbps, but other devices may only have the equivalent of a 56 K modem connection. More importantly, mobile devices have limited storage capacity—serving real-time streaming video to these users can be more practical than serving large progressive-download video files that require storage on the device.

► **Do you want most, if not all, users to have an instant start and playback experience with video content?** This factor is perhaps one of the most important to consider when deciding to implement multiple bitrates with any Web video format. While everyone would prefer to get content faster on the Web, some audiences will grin and bear long wait times, especially for high-quality video. Just think of popular movie trailers on apple.com/quicktime. Some of these trailers are several hundred megabytes, and take a while to download before playback begins. However, for most video playback scenarios, your audience wants the experience to start as soon as possible, without any buffering (or waiting) in the middle of the experience.

▶ **Do you plan to serve video content with long durations?** If you're serving video content with lengths longer than a minute, then you'll likely want to consider both real-time streaming deployment and more than one bitrate per piece of content. The longer the content is, the higher the likelihood that the user will experience fluctuations with the Internet connection speed during playback. If you serve the right bitrate to each user, you can avoid playback hiccups.

▶ **Do you have the storage and encoding resources to batch-process multiple bitrates per piece of content?** Finally, you don't want to overlook the simple (but potentially costly) matter of encoding and storage requirements for a Flash Video project. If your project has hundreds of pieces of content (especially with long durations), you can easily require terabytes of server storage as you start to double, triple, and quadruple the data rates available for each clip. You'll also need more processing power to encode large volumes of video to each bit rate. Be sure to evaluate the hardware (and processing time) necessary to encode a collection of video clips.

If you answered yes to a majority of the questions in the list above, then your project meets the criteria to employ more than one bitrate (or data rate) for each piece of video content. In the next section, you'll learn how to pick the right data rates for your Flash Video content.

But first, you should understand that it's *never* a mandatory technical requirement to offer more than one data rate. The Flash Player will attempt to play any valid URL for an FLV file. As a general rule, progressive Flash Video can always play smoothly without interruption once enough of the video has downloaded and cached on the playback computer. However, real-time streaming video can complicate a playback scenario—you can only watch the video that's stored in the buffer. Without safety measures in place, the quality of that playback experience can vary from unwatchable to amazingly great. Offering more than one bitrate is one of the best safeguards you can employ for high-quality Web video experiences.

TIP

▶ If you're deploying video content on fixed media such as a CD/DVD-ROM, then you can forego considerations for multiple data rates. With fixed media, your only playback bottlenecks will be the size and speed of the fixed media and the processing power on the machine. Also, if you're deploying Flash Video for special-effects purposes, such as video with an alpha channel (for transparent backgrounds), you'll likely want to stick to one high-quality bitrate and use progressive-download Flash Video and/or well-buffered real-time streaming Flash Video. You'll learn more about buffering strategies later in this chapter.

Determining Which Bitrates to Offer

If you've decided that you want to deploy more than one bitrate for a Flash Video experience, you need to pick the bitrates you want to use in your preferred Flash Video encoding tool. There are four key factors to keep in mind: content scaling, content quality, connection speed, and capacity. (You can also remember them as the four "Cs" of bitrate decision-making.)

Content Scaling

As you're deciding which data rates to use with video on the Web, you need to plan how you will display different video sizes for the same video content. Will you use a fixed window size in your Flash movie or Web page, and scale the video content to that size, regardless of its native dimensions? Or, will you resize the video window to always use the native width and height of the clip, and reflow the rest of the Flash movie or Web page content around the video window? It's easier to use a fixed video window size, using the native frame size of your highest quality clip.

If you decide to scale lower quality video to a larger size, be sure to try out the smoothing property of the Video class. By enabling smoothing (that is, setting the smoothing value to true in ActionScript), the Flash Player applies an anti-aliasing filter to the scaled video. Therefore, the video looks better when scaled beyond its original frame size. Turning smoothing on has no effect on video that is played at its native width and height (or smaller). Smoothing does come at a price: More of the computer's processor power will be consumed by the Flash Player rendering the video.

Content Quality

Some video producers prefer to pick bitrate choices based on the range of qualities they want to offer for the content. With this approach, you make a judgment related to the quality of the video and audio. How good do you want the video to look?

Caution

▶ On slower computers (and most pre-Intel Macs), smoothing hobbles the video's frame rate, resulting in dropped frames.

On the DVD-ROM

▶ If you'd like to see how to enable smoothing with video played in the FLVPlayback component, review the MBR_AS3_Streaming_Smoothing.fla and MBR_AS2_Streaming_Smoothing.fla files in the ch08 folder of this book's DVD-ROM.

For example, if you know you want to deploy one tier of content with a 400 by 300 native frame size at 29.97 fps with the On2 VP6 codec, you would use an average video data rate of 480 Kbps plus the audio data rate for the content. Assuming your content was narration or speech, you could use a high-quality 48 Kbps audio date rate, bringing your total bitrate to 528 Kbps. The second tier of content could use a 240 by 180 native frame size at 15 fps with the On2 VP5 codec, using an average video data rate of 86 Kbps. Again, if the audio content was narration or speech, you could use a 20-Kbps audio bitrate, bringing the total bitrate to 106 Kbps.

Once you've determined the frame sizes and frame rates you want to use for each tier, you should pad the total bitrate with a minimum 20% overhead, as a safety net for fluctuations in connection speed during playback. (Always round your calculations up to the nearest kilobit as yet another safety measure.) So, with our previous example, the 528-Kbps tier should require a 634-Kbps connection speed—if the user's connection speed to the hosting video server doesn't match or exceed that data rate, then the lower tier will be delivered. Likewise, the 106-Kbps tier should require a 128-Kbps connection speed to play back efficiently.

Connection Speeds

You can pick data rates that match common connection speeds. Flash Video encoding solutions, including Adobe Flash Video Encoder, Sorenson Squeeze, and On2 Flix, offer many presets with this concept in mind. Being mindful of connection speeds, you can work backwards to calculate the proper video resolution and frame rate suitable for each connection speed you want to support.

I prefer to use this approach, picking anywhere from two to five connection speeds. At a minimum, I choose a medium broadband speed, such as 384 Kbps, and a high broadband speed, such as 768 Kbps. If a client demands a data rate that is compatible with 56 K dial-up modems, I add a low-quality 56 K tier, bringing the total connection count to three.

On the DVD-ROM

▶ You can use the Encoder Presets page of the Flash_Video_Bitrates.xls Excel spreadsheet located in the tools folder of this book's DVD-ROM to help you determine which bitrates you want to use.

▶ You can use the Excel spreadsheet located in the tools folder of this book's DVD-ROM to help you work backwards from a connection. The second worksheet page, Connection Speeds, lists the common connection speeds available on the Internet. You can simply type a video width to see an appropriate video height and frame rate. Watch the frame rate change with the width and height values—pick a width and height combination that yields your preferred frame rate. A green width color indicates that the value is optimized for playback performance. For Flash Video playback, you should use dimension values that are divisible by four and eight. Note that the audio bitrate is a constant value used across all of the calculations. You'll likely want to change the audio bitrate to suit your particular needs.

Capacity

The last "C" represents the capacity of your storage and encoding facilities. While you may want to offer seven data rates for each piece of Flash Video content, anything from the client's fiscal budget to time restrictions may stand in the way. Long pieces of content can take several hours (if not full days) to encode in a single bitrate. One 30-minute video can easily consume half a gigabyte or more of server storage space once it's encoded across three or five data rates.

To estimate file space requirements in megabytes, use this formula:

(Data rate × Duration) ÷ 8 bits/byte ÷ 1024 bytes/KB ÷ 1024 KB/MB

For example, a 15-minute video encoded at 500 Kbps would require about 55 MB of storage:

(512,000 bps × 900 seconds) ÷ 8 ÷ 1024 ÷ 1024 = 54.9 MB

Preparing SMIL Files

The FLVPlayback components (AS2 and AS3 versions) support a specific subset of SMIL tags and attributes. Because the layout of Flash elements within a Flash movie can be controlled in the timeline, on the stage, or with ActionScript, you won't use SMIL to control the X and Y position of video clips on the stage. You can, however, control many aspects of video behavior with a SMIL file:

▶ **Source location:** In the `<meta>` tag of a SMIL document, you can specify the host name of the server hosting your FLV files. For real-time streaming content, you need to specify the full path to the Flash Media Server application or Flash Video Streaming Service application, such as `rtmp://flashvideo.rtmphost.com/samples`. For progressive video, you can specify a path relative to the Flash movie (SWF file) or a fully qualified domain name and directory path, such as `http://www.flashsupport.com/video/`.

▶ **Video dimensions:** In the `<root-layout>` tag of a SMIL file, you can specify an absolute width and height (in pixels) for the video content listed in the SMIL file. Note that the AS3 version of the FLVPlayback component disregards a specified width and height unless you specifically create a handler to use the value, as shown later in this chapter.

▶ **Multiple bitrate-specific FLV files:** The fundamental reason to use a SMIL file is to enumerate the bitrates of a given piece of content on the server. The FLV files are listed in order of descending data rate. For each bitrate, you should specify the full filename, including the .flv file extension. Every FLV file item except the last should have a `system-bitrate` attribute, indicating the bits per second required for the video file. I recommend padding this value 20% higher (or more) than the actual video and audio bitrate used during encoding. The last FLV file is the default video file played if the other FLV bitrate values exceed the connection speed available to the user.

Now that you know which features of the SMIL specification you can use with the FLVPlayback component, let's look at a sample SMIL file. Make a local copy of the burnside_charlie_rtmp.smil file from the ch08 folder of this book's DVD-ROM. Open the SMIL file in Adobe Dreamweaver or your preferred text editor. (By default, Dreamweaver does not know that SMIL files are text files—you can just drag and drop a SMIL file into Dreamweaver to view and edit the code.) The SMIL file content is shown in the following code block. The ➥ character indicates a continuation of the same line of code.

```
<smil project="Flash Video Studio Techniques –
➥Streaming SMIL Example" ><head>
    <meta base="rtmp://flashvideo.rtmphost.com/
    ➥samples/" />
    <layout>
        <root-layout width="480" height="270" />
    </layout>
</head>
<body>
    <switch>
```

(Continues on next page)

Caution

▶ With real-time streaming content, the AS2 version of the FLVPlayback component can *not* use FLV filenames that end with the .flv file extension without an additional workaround in ActionScript code—this is a known bug of the AS2 version. I've provided a custom compiled `NCManager` class in the AS2 versions of this chapter's sample files. The custom class fixes this bug.

▶ For my own identification purposes, I add a project attribute to the starting `<smil>` tag to identify the content. This custom attribute is not used by the FLVPlayback component, nor does it interfere with the integration of the remaining data in the file.

On the DVD-ROM

▶ In Flash CS3, you can also open the ch08.flp project file from the ch08 folder of this book's DVD-ROM to view a sorted list of all the files discussed or mentioned in this chapter.

```
                          <video src="pb_burnside_charlie_SQZ_VP6_
                          ➥1Mbps_CBR.flv" system-bitrate="1250000" />
                          <video src="pb_burnside_charlie_SQZ_VP6_
                          ➥768K_CBR.flv" system-bitrate="870000" />
                          <video src="pb_burnside_charlie_SQZ_VP6_
                          ➥512K_CBR.flv" system-bitrate="524000" />
                          <video src="pb_burnside_charlie_SQZ_VP6_
                          ➥384K_CBR.flv" system-bitrate="397000" />
                          <video src="pb_burnside_charlie_SQZ_VP6_
                          ➥256K_CBR.flv" system-bitrate="220000" />
                          <video src="pb_burnside_charlie_SQZ_VP6_
                          ➥112K_CBR.flv" system-bitrate="103000" />
                          <video src="pb_burnside_charlie_SQZ_VP6_56K_
                          ➥CBR.flv" />
                      </switch>
                  </body>
              </smil>
```

WARNING

Caution

▶ While a SMIL file denotes multiple FLV files, only one FLV file is ever played per use. A SMIL file is *not* a playlist—it's just a collection of multiple bitrates from which the FLVPlayback component can choose the appropriate bitrate for a given user's connection speed. You need one SMIL file per piece of content. For example, if you have ten different training videos, you'll need ten SMIL files, each denoting the FLV files available for each video piece.

In this sample SMIL file, a Flash Media Server application is specified in the `<meta>` tag. Within the `<switch>` node, a series of `<video>` tags lists the available FLV files for this music video. The highest bitrate, encoded at 1 Mbps, requires a connection speed of 1.25 Mbps. If the user's connection speed matches or exceeds 1.25 Mbps, the highest quality FLV file plays. If the user's bandwidth falls between 1.25 Mbps and 870 Kbps, the 768-Kbps FLV file plays. This connection matching continues for the remaining ranges. If the user's connection speed is less than 103 Kbps, the lowest quality (56-Kbps) FLV file plays.

If you open the burnside_charlie_http.smil file, you'll notice that, when compared to the RTMP version of the SMIL file, only one attribute value changes: the base attribute of the `<meta>` tag. This is one of the advantages of SMIL files—the FLV file information can be identical for both Flash Media Server and Web server use.

If you have encoded your own series of FLV files, you can use the SMIL files included in the book's DVD-ROM as a template. Simply modify the following tags:

▶ `<meta base>`: Change the base attribute to point to your own Flash Media Server application, FVSS account, or Web server directory.

▶ `<root-layout>`: Specify a width and height you'd like to use for the video area in the Flash movie. Usually, you'll want to use the width and height of your highest bitrate FLV file.

▶ `<video>`: Modify all of the `<video>` tags, listing each FLV bitrate in its own node. You can use any number of `<video>` tags; you should have at least two in your SMIL document. You can substitute the `<ref>` tag name for `<video>` tags; the FLVPlayback component uses them interchangeably.

In the next section, you'll learn how to implement both of the SMIL files from the ch08 folder with working examples.

▶ There's more information regarding SMIL tag usage in the Flash Help panel. Search the help contents using the keyword SMIL.

Calculating Available Bandwidth

Once you have created a SMIL file for your Flash Video piece of content, you're ready to use the SMIL file with the AS2 or AS3 version of the FLVPlayback component. In order for the FLVPlayback component to properly select an FLV file from the list provided in a SMIL file, the component must determine the connection speed at runtime between the Flash Player and the remote server. This process is much simpler for FLV files hosted on a Flash Media Server (FMS) application or a Flash Video Streaming Service (FVSS) provider, because FMS applications can communicate bandwidth data between the server host and the Flash Player. You can also estimate bandwidth between a Web server (HTTP) and the Flash Player, but the process involves more custom ActionScript code in the Flash movie.

Placing Bandwidth Bets over RTMP

If your FLV files are hosted on a Flash Media Server account (such as those provided by Influxis.com or your own custom Flash Media Server installation) or on a Flash Video Streaming Service provider (such as Limelight Networks or Akamai), then you're in for a treat. As discussed in Chapter 4, both of these services use RTMP connections to stream Flash Video to the Flash Player. With a few steps, you can quickly transform the FLVPlayback component into a multi-bitrate Flash Video viewer.

Installing the Server-Side Script

In order for the FLVPlayback component to determine the connection speed between a Flash Media Server application and a Flash movie, client-side ActionScript must communicate with server-side ActionScript to time-test packets sent back and forth from the client and server. Fortunately, you don't have to do anything except upload a simple file to your Flash Media Server account. If you're using a Flash Video Streaming Service provider, the script file should already be in place for you to access.

If you have a Flash Media Server application hosting FLV files, download the samples.zip file, available at www.adobe.com/go/learn_fl_samples.

After you've extracted the files from the ZIP file, you'll find the main.asc file in the ComponentsAS2/FLVPlayback folder. Once you have this file, upload it to the root of the application folder on your Flash Media Server. This file is already in place on the Influxis.com account used for the sample SMIL files provided in this chapter. You may need to restart the application instance after you've uploaded the file, if you've accessed the application instance within fifteen minutes prior to uploading the file.

Setting up the FLVPlayback Component

After you have the main.asc file in place on the Flash Media Server (or if you're using an FVSS account with the same code base available), you can create a Flash movie with the FLVPlayback component tapping the SMIL resource. Before you begin these steps, make a copy of the sample burnside_charlie_rtmp.smil file from the ch08 folder of this book's DVD-ROM to a local folder on your computer.

1. In Flash CS3, create a new Flash document. If you're planning to use ActionScript 3.0 (AS3) code with other elements in your Flash movie and want to target Flash Player 9, create a new Flash file (ActionScript 3.0). If you want to use ActionScript 2.0 (AS2) code with other elements in your movie and want to target Flash Player 8, create a new Flash file (ActionScript 2.0).

On the DVD-ROM

▶ If you want to use the example FLV files referenced in the SMIL file on your own Flash Media Server or FVSS account, you can find them in the flv folder of this book's DVD-ROM.

2. Save the document as MBR_AS3_Streaming.fla if you selected AS3 as your code version. Save the document as MBR_AS2_Streaming.fla if you selected AS2 as your code version. Be sure to save the document in the same folder as the SMIL file you copied from the book's DVD-ROM.

3. Rename Layer 1 to flvPlayer.

4. Open the Components panel (Ctrl/Cmd+F7), and from the Video grouping (AS3 files only) or the FLV Playback–Player 8 grouping (AS2 files only), drag the FLVPlayback component to the stage.

5. Select the instance on the stage, and, in the Property inspector, name the instance flvPlayer.

6. Click the Parameters tab in the Property inspector, and choose a skin file for the instance. For more information on choosing a skin file, refer to Chapter 5 or 6 of this book.

7. Double-click the source parameter (AS3) or the contentPath parameter (AS2) in the Parameters tab. Type the path to the burnside_charlie_rtmp.smil file you copied to your local folder. As shown in **Figure 8.1**, deselect both options in the Content Path dialog before clicking OK.

> You cannot browse and select a SMIL file in the Content Path dialog. You need to type the path by hand.

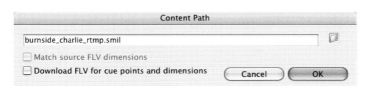

Figure 8.1 The Content Path dialog.

8. Configure any other options in the parameters panel, such as autoPlay and scaleMode options. If you're using the AS3 version of the FLVPlayback component and you set the scaleMode value to noScale, the instance will resize to the native width and height of the FLV file, regardless of your SMIL settings. If you're using the AS2 version of the FLVPlayback component and you set

On the DVD-ROM

> You can find the finished example files, MBR_AS2_Streaming.fla and MBR_AS3_Streaming.fla, in the ch08 folder of this book's DVD-ROM.

TIP

▶ If you open the MBR_AS3_ Streaming_SetSize.fla file in the ch08 folder of this book's DVD-ROM, you can view the ActionScript code necessary for the AS3 version of the FLVPlayback component to use the width and height values specified in a SMIL file.

the autoSize value to true, the instance will resize to the width and height values specified in the SMIL file.

9. Save the Flash document, and test the movie (Ctrl/ Cmd+Enter). Once the FLVPlayback component communicates with the Flash Media Server application (or FVSS provider) and determines your connection speed, you'll see the FLVPlayback component display the corresponding matched bitrate. If autoPlay is set to true, the FLV file automatically streams and begins playback. You may also notice debugging text shown in the Output panel, showing the results of server-side calls to retrieve the duration of the FLV file.

Estimating Bandwidth over HTTP

While Flash Media Server applications can talk back and forth with the FLVPlayback component, there's no such built-in communication available between the component and a regular Web server. To determine the available bandwidth to a Web server, you have to download some packets of data from the Web server and time the arrival before you load a SMIL file into the FLVPlayback component. With a little elbow grease, you can add bitrate detection to progressive-download FLV files and the FLVPlayback component. Here's a high-level overview of the procedure:

1. Create a thumbnail image (or still frame) from the original source video. Make the image dimensions equal to those of FLVPlayback instance dimensions, or of your highest resolution video bitrate. This thumbnail, saved as a JPEG or PNG file, will serve two purposes. First, it's a nice user interface (UI) addition to the Flash movie, as the image serves as a preview of the video file. Second, and more importantly, an image file has a decent amount of "weight" in bytes. The bigger the file, the more accurately you can determine a connection speed.

2. Put the thumbnail image on the same Web server that's hosting the FLV files. If you put the thumbnail image on a different server, the connection speed to that server could vary from the connection speed available on the server with the FLV files.

3. In the Flash movie, load the thumbnail at runtime, into a `MovieClip` instance (AS2) or a `Loader` instance (AS3). Mark the time at the beginning of the load, and mark the time when loading has finished. Subtract the start time from the end time to determine how much time was used to download the image file. Retrieve the total bytes of the image file, and calculate the bits per second (bps) for the transmission.

4. Set the `bitrate` property of the FLVPlayback component instance, specifying the value you calculated from the download of the image file.

5. Specify the SMIL file URL for the `contentPath` property (AS2) or the `source` property (AS3) of the FLVPlayback instance.

In the following sections, you learn how to apply this procedure in both ActionScript 2.0 and ActionScript 3.0. Both examples use a thumbnail image located here:

http://www.flashsupport.com/video/pbookmyer_music.jpg

and FLV files listed in this folder:

http://www.flashsupport.com/video/

You're welcome to use your own content for these examples—just be sure to upload the content to a Web server for accurate testing. If you load local files, you will not use an Internet connection to load the files. Therefore, you'll always see the highest bitrate video.

Monitoring Download Speed with ActionScript 2.0

In ActionScript 2.0, you can load a variety of image formats (JPEG, PNG, GIF, and SWF) into an empty `MovieClip` instance using the `MovieClipLoader` class. This class automatically fires event handlers when the loading begins and ends, making it ideal for helping us calculate the download speed to the Web server. In the following steps, you learn how to build a bandwidth detection mechanism for progressive-download Flash Video content.

NOTES

▶ To learn more about loading preview images for video, refer to Chapter 6.

WARNING

Caution

▶ Don't specify a contentPath (AS2) or source (AS3) value in the Parameters tab of an authortime placed instance of the FLVPlayback component. Doing so will result in the FLVPlayback component using an inaccurate connection speed.

1. Make a copy of the MBR_AS2_Progressive_starter.fla file from the ch08 folder of this book's DVD-ROM. This document contains an instance of the FLVPlayback component already placed on the stage, named `flvPlayer`. This file also contains modifications of the `NCManager` and `SMILManager` classes used by the FLVPlayback component. The rebuilt versions fix errors with FLV filenames. The classes are packaged as a compiled component named `NCManagerBundle` in the Flash document's library. Copy the ClearOverPlaySeekMute.swf skin file from the ch08 folder as well.

2. Open the copied file in Flash Pro 8 or Flash CS3. Save this file as `MBR_AS2_Progressive.fla`.

3. If you'd like to use a different skin for the component, select the FLVPlayback instance on the stage, and open the Parameters tab in the Property inspector. Change the `skin` value to your preferred skin.

4. Create a new layer named `actions`. Place this layer at the top of the layer stack.

5. Select frame 1 of the actions layer, and open the Actions panel (F9, or Option+F9 on Mac). Add the code shown in the following code block. This code performs each of the steps outlined in the last section. The ➥ character indicates a continuation of the same line of code.

```
//Import classes related to the FLVPlayback component
import mx.video.VideoPlayer;
import mx.video.FLVPlayback;
import com.flashsupport.video.INCManager;

// Use the rebuilt NCManager class to fix a SMIL bug
var forceFixedNCManager:com.flashsupport.video.
➥NCManager;
mx.video.VideoPlayer.DEFAULT_INCMANAGER =
➥"com.flashsupport.video.NCManager";

// Create a reference to the FLVPlayback instance
var fp:FLVPlayback = flvPlayer;
// Turn automatic playback off
fp.autoPlay = false;
```

```
// Retrieve the VideoPlayer instance inside the
➥component
var vp:VideoPlayer = fp.getVideoPlayer(0);
var vid:Video = vp["_video"];
// Turn smoothing on so that scaled video appears
better
➥vid.smoothing = true;

// Listen for any playback events with the
onVideoPlay
➥function
fp.addEventListener("playing", onVideoPlay);

// Create a variable to store the URL for the SMIL
file
var smilURL:String = "burnside_charlie_http.smil";

// Create an empty MovieClip instance for the
thumbnail
// inside of the FLVPlayback component
var thumb:MovieClip = fp.createEmptyMovieClip("thumb
",
➥999);

// Specify the URL of the image thumbnail
var imageURL:String = "http://www.flashsupport.com/
➥video/pbookmyer_music.jpg";
// For accurate connection speed detection,
// create a random string
var cacheBuster:String = "?cacheBuster= " +
escape(new
➥Date().toString());
// Append the string to the image URL
imageURL += cacheBuster;
// Set loading time values to zero
var startLoadTime:Number = 0;
var endLoadTime:Number = 0;
// Create a MovieClipLoader instance to load the
image
var mcl:MovieClipLoader = new MovieClipLoader();
// Invoke onLoadStart and onLoadComplete handlers
// during the load process
mcl.addListener(this);
```
(Continues on next page)

```
// Start loading the image file into the MovieClip
➥holder
mcl.loadClip(imageURL, thumb);

// Create a listener function to detect when loading
➥starts
function onLoadStart(mc:MovieClip):Void {
   // Mark the time when the first bytes of the
   // image file arrived to the Flash Player
   startLoadTime = getTimer();
}

// Create a listener function to detect when loading
➥finishes
function onLoadComplete(mc:MovieClip):Void {
   // Mark the time when loading finished
   endLoadTime = getTimer();
   // Compute the total time for loading the image
   var loadTime:Number = endLoadTime - startLoadTime;
   // Convert the load time to seconds from
   ➥milliseconds
   var loadSeconds:Number = loadTime/1000;
   // Retrieve the total bytes of the loaded image
   var totalBytes:Number = mc.getBytesTotal();
   // Calculate the connection speed
   calcBW(loadSeconds, totalBytes);
}

// Create a function to calculate connection speed
function calcBW(time:Number, bytes:Number):Void {
   // Convert bytes to bits
   var bits:Number = bytes*8;
   // Calculate bits per second
   var bps:Number = bits/time;
   // Display connection speed in Output panel
   trace("bps: " + bps);
   // Set the bitrate on the FLVPlayback instance
   fp.bitrate = bps;
   // Load the SMIL file into the FLVPlayback
   ➥instance
   fp.contentPath = smilURL;
}
```

```
// When video playback starts
function onVideoPlay(e:Object):Void {
    // Hide the thumbnail image
    thumb._visible = false;
    // Display the selected stream in the Output panel
    var ncManager:INCManager = e.target.
    ➥getVideoPlayer(0)._ncMgr;
    trace("selected stream: " + ncManager["_
    ➥streamName"]);
}
```

6. Save the Flash document, and then test the movie (Ctrl/Cmd+Enter). When the movie starts, the JPEG thumbnail image loads into the FLVPlayback instance. The measured bandwidth speed displays in the Output panel. When you click the Play button for the video, the selected stream appears in the Output panel, and the video begins to download and play. Because the movie has selected an appropriate FLV bitrate, you should not need to wait for playback to start once you've clicked the Play button.

On the DVD-ROM

▶ You can find the finished file, MBR_AS2_Progressive.fla, in the ch08 folder of this book's DVD-ROM.

Calculating Download Speed with ActionScript 3.0

With ActionScript 3.0, you can load an external image asset (JPEG, PNG, GIF, or SWF) into a Loader instance. This class contains a property named contentLoaderInfo, which is an instance of the LoaderInfo class. This class can fire event handlers when loading begins and ends, making it ideal for the task of calculating the download speed from the Web server. In the following steps, you learn how to build a bandwidth detection mechanism for progressive-download Flash Video content in ActionScript 3.0.

1. Make a copy of the MBR_AS3_Progressive_starter.fla file from the ch08 folder of this book's DVD-ROM. This document contains an instance of the AS3 version of the FLVPlayback component, already placed on the stage. This instance is named flvPlayer. Copy the SkinOverPlayStopSeekFullVol.swf skin file from the ch08 folder as well.

2. Open the copied file in Flash CS3. Save this file as MBR_AS3_Progressive.fla.

3. If you'd like to use a different skin for the component, select the FLVPlayback instance on the stage, and open the Parameters tab in the Property inspector. Change the skin value to your preferred skin.

4. Create a new layer named actions. Place this layer at the top of the layer stack.

5. Select frame 1 of the actions layer, and open the Actions panel (F9, or Option+F9 on Mac). Add the code shown in the following code block. This code performs each of the steps outlined in the last section. The ➥ character indicates a continuation of the same line of code.

```
//Import classes related to the FLVPlayback component
import fl.video.FLVPlayback;
import fl.video.VideoPlayer;
import fl.video.VideoEvent;
import fl.video.INCManager;
import fl.video.VideoScaleMode;

// Import classes for loading external assets
import flash.net.URLRequest;
import flash.display.Loader;
import flash.display.LoaderInfo;
import flash.events.Event;
import flash.utils.*;

// Create a reference to the FLVPlayback instance
var fp:FLVPlayback = flvPlayer;
// Turn automatic playback off
fp.autoPlay = false;

// Retrieve the VideoPlayer instance inside the
➥component
\var vp:VideoPlayer = fp.getVideoPlayer(0);
// Turn smoothing on so that scaled video appears
➥better
vid.smoothing = true;

// Listen for any play events with the onVideoPlay
➥function
fp.addEventListener(VideoEvent.PLAYING_STATE_ENTERED,
➥onVideoPlay);
```

```
// Detect when the SMIL has loaded with the
➥onVideoReady function.
// This listener fixes the SMIL width/height bug with
// the AS3 version of the FLVPlayback component
fp.addEventListener(VideoEvent.READY, onVideoReady);
// Create a variable to store the URL for the SMIL file
var smilURL:String = "burnside_charlie_http.smil";

// Create a Loader instance to store the image
var thumb:Loader = new Loader();
// Specify the URL of the image thumbnail
var imageURL:String = "http://www.flashsupport.com/
➥video/pbookmyer_music.jpg";
// For accurate connection speed detection,
// create a random string
var cacheBuster:String = "?cacheBuster= " +
➥escape(new Date().toString());
// Append the string to the image URL
imageURL += cacheBuster;
// Set loading time values to zero
var startLoadTime:uint = 0;
var endLoadTime:uint = 0;
// Start loading the image file
loadImage(thumb, imageURL);

// Create a function to handle loading requests
function loadImage(loader:Loader, imageURL:String):
➥void {
    // Create a new request instance
    var urlRequest:URLRequest = new
    ➥URLRequest(imageURL);
    // Create a reference to the LoaderInfo instance
    // within the Loader instance
    var li:LoaderInfo = loader.contentLoaderInfo;
    // Listen for the start of image loading
    li.addEventListener(Event.OPEN, onImgLoadStart);
    // Listen for the end of image loading
    li.addEventListener(Event.COMPLETE,
    ➥onImgLoadComplete);
    // Load the request into the Loader instance
    loader.load(urlRequest);
```

(Continues on next page)

```
        // Add the Loader instance to the display
        // list of the FLVPlayback component
        fp.addChild(loader);
    }

    // Create a listener function to detect when loading
    ➥starts
    function onImgLoadStart(e:Event):void {
        // Mark the time when the first bytes of the
        // image file arrived to the Flash Player
        startLoadTime = getTimer();
    }

    // Create a listener function to detect when loading
    ➥finishes
    function onImgLoadComplete(e:Event):void {
        // Mark the time when loading finished
        endLoadTime = getTimer();
        // Compute the total time for loading the image
        var loadTime:uint = endLoadTime - startLoadTime;
        // Convert the load time to seconds from
        ➥milliseconds
        var loadSeconds:Number = loadTime/1000;
        // Retrieve the total bytes of the loaded image
        var totalBytes:uint = (e.currentTarget as
        ➥LoaderInfo).bytesTotal;
        // Calculate the connection speed
        calcBW(loadSeconds, totalBytes);
    }

    // Create a function to calculate connection speed
    function calcBW(time:Number, bytes:uint):Void {
        // Convert bytes to bits
        var bits:uint = bytes*8;
        // Calculate bits per second
        var bps:Number = bits/time;
        // Display connection speed in Output panel
        trace("bps: " + bps);
        // Set the bitrate on the FLVPlayback instance
        fp.bitrate = bps;
        // Load the SMIL file into the FLVPlayback instance
        fp.source = smilURL;
    }
```

```
// Create a listener function to detect when the SMIL
➥has loaded
function onVideoReady (e:VideoEvent):void {
    // Create a reference to the FLVPlayback component
    var f:FLVPlayback = e.currentTarget as
    ➥FLVPlayback;
    // Retrieve the NCManager instance in the component
    var ncManager:INCManager = f.ncMgr;
    // Fetch the dimensions specified in the SMIL file
    var w:Number = ncManager.streamWidth;
    var h:Number = ncManager.streamHeight;
    // Make sure the video is not distorted in the new
    ➥size
    f.scaleMode = VideoScaleMode.MAINTAIN_ASPECT_RATIO;
    // Set the dimensions of the component to match
    ➥the SMIL
    f.setSize(w, h);
}

// When video playback starts
function onVideoPlay(e:Object):Void {
    // Hide the thumbnail image
    thumb.visible = false;
    // Display the selected stream in the Output panel
    var ncMgr:INCManager = (e.currentTarget as
    ➥FLVPlayback).ncMgr;
    trace("selected stream: " + ncMgr.streamName;
}
```

6. Save the Flash document, and test the movie (Ctrl/
    Cmd+Enter). When the movie starts, the JPEG thumb-
    nail image loads into the FLVPlayback instance. The mea-
    sured bandwidth speed displays in the Output panel.
    When you click the Play button for the video, the selected
    stream appears in the Output panel, and the video
    begins to download and play. Because the movie has
    selected an appropriate FLV bitrate, you should not
    need to wait for playback to start once you've clicked
    the Play button.

On the DVD-ROM

▶ You can find the finished file,
   MBR_AS3_Progressive.fla, in
   the ch08 folder of this book's
   DVD-ROM.

Enabling Dynamic Buffering with a Real-time Stream

One of the potentially problematic aspects of real-time video streaming is its ephemeral nature—you can only watch video that exists in the video player's buffer. This fact is true for any real-time streaming video format. Luckily, ActionScript enables you to have precise control with the video buffer settings.

If you're building your own video playback mechanism with the NetStream class, you can adjust the buffer time with the NetStream.setBufferTime() method in ActionScript 2.0 or the NetStream.bufferTime property in ActionScript 3.0. If you're using the FLVPlayback component (either version), you can use the FLVPlayback.bufferTime property. Setting this property controls the buffer values of the internal NetStream instance within the component. You can also check how much video content has buffered into the Flash Player by retrieving the NetStream.bufferLength property. This property returns the number of seconds in the buffer.

The default buffer time for the NetStream class or the FLVPlayback component is 0.1 second, or one-tenth of a second. While this low value is great for an instant-start experience, the video bitrate must be below the user's connection speed in order to maintain a steady and uninterrupted playback experience. Even if you pad your connection speed requirements with inflated SMIL system-bitrate values (as discussed earlier in this chapter), network connection speeds can vary widely, especially during peak traffic periods on your server.

You can ensure a smooth instant-start playback experience by performing four tasks with your video file:

▶ Always serve a video bitrate lower than the user's connection speed.

▶ Set an initial low value for the video buffer time.

▶ Reset the buffer time to a higher value after playback has started.

▶ If the buffered video runs out (or empties), reset the buffer time back to its initial low value.

▶ While you can control buffer times for both progressive-download and real-time streaming video, you may notice little or no effect when changing the buffer time for progressive-download video. Due to the fact that progressive video already cumulatively downloads to the Web browser cache, the "buffer" for a progressive video automatically grows as the file downloads. You may find some benefit to setting buffer times for progressive video played on slower machines, or for video files stored on fixed media such as a CD/DVD-ROM.

The process of fluctuating the buffer time based on the buffering state is known as *dynamic*, or dual, buffering. Many sites that deploy real-time streaming Flash Video use this technique. In the following sections, you learn how to employ dual buffering with the FLVPlayback component and SMIL-driven content in ActionScript 2.0 and ActionScript 3.0.

Dual Buffering with ActionScript 2.0

If you're using the ActionScript 2.0 version of the FLVPlayback component and targeting Flash Player 8, you can use the stateChange event emitted by the FLVPlayback component to capture buffer-related events and adjust buffer times accordingly. In this section, you learn how to change the buffer times of a SMIL-enabled streaming Flash Video experience, displaying the buffer time in a text field below the component.

To add dual buffering to a SMIL-driven FLVPlayback component (AS2):

1. Copy the MBR_AS3_Streaming_DualBuffer_starter.fla file from the ch08 folder on the DVD-ROM to your local system. Copy the ClearOverPlaySeekMute.swf and burnside_charlie_rtmp.smil files to the same location as well.

2. Open the MBR_AS2_Streaming_DualBuffer_starter.fla file in Flash Pro 8 or Flash CS3. Resave the file as MBR_AS2_Streaming_DualBuffer.fla.

3. The stage of this document already has an instance of the FLVPlayback component named flvPlayer, and a TextField instance named bufferField below the component. These instance names will be used in the code added in the next step. Notice that the stage of this document already has an instance of the FLVPlayback component named flvPlayer, and a TextField instance named bufferField below the component. These instance names will be used in the code added in the next step. The Library panel (Ctrl/Cmd+L) also contains the NCManagerBundle component, which contains rebuilt versions of the NCManager and SMILManager

NOTES

▶ If you'd like to learn more about the science behind dual buffering, read Fabio Sonnati's article "Implementing a dual-threshold strategy in Flash Media Server" on the Adobe Developer Center Web site. This article also provides sample code to control a NetStream instance directly, without using the FLVPlayback component. A link to this article can be found in the Audio/Video Articles category at www.flashsupport.com/links.

TIP

▶ The text field used with this example is not required for the dual buffering feature to work. The text field only displays the current state of the buffer. You can remove the text field and the interval function after you've learned how buffering works.

classes from the original FLVPlayback component. The NCManagerBundle component fixes a bug with the SMIL implementation of the ActionScript 2.0 version of the FLVPlayback component.

4. Create a new layer named actions. Select frame 1 of the actions layer and open the Actions panel (F9, or Option+F9 on Mac). Add the following code. Do not type the ➥ character, which indicates a continuation of the same line of code.

```
// Import classes related to the FLVPlayback component
import mx.video.VideoPlayer;
import mx.video.FLVPlayback;
import com.flashsupport.video.INCManager;

// Use the rebuilt NCManager class to fix a SMIL bug
var forceFixedNCManager:com.flashsupport.video.
➥NCManager;
mx.video.VideoPlayer.DEFAULT_INCMANAGER =
➥"com.flashsupport.video.NCManager";

// Create a reference to the FLVPlayback instance
var fp:FLVPlayback = flvPlayer;
// Create a reference to the text field on the stage
var bufferField:TextField;

// Retrieve the VideoPlayer instance inside the
➥component
var vp:VideoPlayer = fp.getVideoPlayer(0);
var vid:Video = vp["_video"];

// Turn smoothing on so that scaled video appears
➥better
vid.smoothing = true;

// Listen for any playback events with the
➥onVideoPlay function
fp.addEventListener("playing", onVideoPlay);
// Listen for any changes to the video state with
// the onVideoState function
fp.addEventListener("stateChange", onVideoState);
// Listen for finished playback of the video
fp.addEventListener("complete", onVideoComplete);
```

```
// Set the initial (low) buffer time
var startBufferTime:Number = 1;
// Set the increased (high) buffer time
var increaseBufferTime:Number = 10;
// Create a variable to store an interval ID.
// An interval will display the buffer length
// in a text field on the stage.
var bufferID:Number = 0;

// Create a variable to store the URL for the SMIL file
var smilURL:String = "burnside_charlie_rtmp.smil";

// Set the initial buffer time low
fp.bufferTime = startBufferTime;
// Set the content path to the SMIL file
fp.contentPath = smilURL;

// When video playback starts
function onVideoPlay(e:Object):Void {
    // Show the selected stream in the Output panel
    var ncManager:INCManager = e.target.
    ➥getVideoPlayer(0)._ncMgr;
    trace("selected stream: " + ncManager["_
    ➥streamName"]);
    // start showing buffer length in the text field

bufferID = setInterval(showBuffer, 100);
}

// When changes occur during video playback
function onVideoState (e:Object):Void {
    // Create a reference to the FLVPlayback component
    var fp:FLVPlayback = e.target;
    // If the video is starting to buffer
    if(e.state == "buffering"){
        // Show buffering value in Output panel
        trace("RESET buffer to low value: " +
        ➥startBufferTime);
        // Set the new value on the component
        fp.bufferTime = startBufferTime;
    // If the video has already buffered and playback
    ➥has started
    } else if(e.state == "playing"){    (Continues on next page)
```

```
        // Show buffering value in Output panel
        trace("INCREASE buffer to high value: " +
        ➥increaseBufferTime);
        // Set the new value on the component
        fp.bufferTime = increaseBufferTime;
    }
}

// When the video has finished playing
function onVideoComplete(e:Object):Void {
    // Stop updating the buffer time in the text field
    clearInterval(bufferID);
    bufferField.text = "";
}

// Display the buffer value
function showBuffer(e:Object):Void {
    // Retrieve the buffer length and display in the
    ➥text field
    bufferField.text = "Buffer: " + vp["_ns"].
    ➥bufferLength;
}
```

5. Save the Flash document, and test the movie (Ctrl/Cmd+ Enter). When the SMIL document loads, the FLVPlay- back component communicates with the Flash Media Server to determine the current connection speed, just as the previous streaming examples in this chapter have done. Once the bitrate is determined, the appropriate FLV file starts to buffer, using the initial buffer time specified by the startBufferTime variable. When the initial buffer is filled and the video begins to play, the onVideoState function fires and the bufferTime prop- erty of the component switches to the value of the increaseBufferTime variable, which is 10 seconds. Now, the video buffer can grow to store more video—if the connection speed falters momentarily, the buffer can accommodate the temporary dip and still continue to play the video. The first play event also triggers the setInterval() function within the onVideoPlay function, which continuously evokes the showBuffer() function. This function displays the current bufferLength value

of the internal `NetStream` instance of the component in the `bufferField` instance on the stage, as shown in **Figure 8.2**.

NOTES

On the DVD-ROM

▶ You can find the finished file, MBR_AS2_Streaming_ DualBuffer.fla, in the ch08 folder of this book's DVD-ROM.

Figure 8.2 The buffer length displayed below the AS2 version of the FLVPlayback component.

Dual Buffering with ActionScript 3.0

If you're using the ActionScript 3.0 version of the FLVPlayback component and targeting Flash Player 9, you can use the `VideoEvent.STATE_CHANGE` event emitted by the FLVPlayback component to capture buffer-related events and adjust buffer times accordingly. In this section, you learn how to apply the same buffer strategy shown in the last section, displaying the buffer time in a text field below the component.

To add dual buffering to a SMIL-driven FLVPlayback component (AS3):

1. Copy the MBR_AS3_Streaming_DualBuffer_starter.fla file from the ch08 folder of this book's DVD-ROM to your local system. Copy the SkinOverPlayStopSeekFullVol. swf and burnside_charlie_rtmp.smil files to the same location as well.

TIP

▶ As with the ActionScript 2.0 example, the text field used with this ActionScript 3.0 example is not required for the dual-buffering feature to work. The text field only displays the current state of the buffer. You can remove the text field and the interval function after you've learned how buffering works.

2. Open the starter file in Flash CS3. Resave the file as `MBR_AS3_Streaming_DualBuffer.fla`.

3. The stage of this document already has an instance of the FLVPlayback component named `flvPlayer`, and a `TextField` instance named `bufferField` below the component. These instance names will be used in the code added in the next step. (Note that the AS3 version of the FLVPlayback component does *not* need the `NCManagerBundle` component shown in the AS2 version.)

4. Create a new layer named `actions`. Select frame 1 of the actions layer and open the Actions panel (F9, or Option+F9 on Mac). Add the following code. Do not type the ➥ character, which indicates a continuation of the same line of code.

```
// Import classes related to the FLVPlayback component
import fl.video.FLVPlayback;
import fl.video.INCManager;
import fl.video.VideoPlayer;
import fl.video.VideoEvent;
import fl.video.VideoScaleMode;

// Import classes for timing events
import flash.events.TimerEvent;
import flash.utils.*;

// Create a reference to the FLVPlayback instance
var fp:FLVPlayback = flvPlayer;
// Retrieve the VideoPlayer instance inside the
➥component
var vp:VideoPlayer = fp.getVideoPlayer(0);
// Turn smoothing on for better scaled video
vp.smoothing = true;

// Listen for the SMIL data loaded to set proper
➥width and height
// with the onVideoReady function
fp.addEventListener(VideoEvent.READY, onVideoReady);
// Listen for any changes to the video state with
// the onVideoState function
fp.addEventListener(VideoEvent.STATE_CHANGE,
➥onVideoState);
```

```
// Listen for finished playback of the video
// with the onVideoComplete function
fp.addEventListener(Event.COMPLETE, onVideoComplete);

// Set the initial (low) buffer time
var startBufferTime:int = 1;
// Set the increased (high) buffer time
var increaseBufferTime:int = 10;

// Create a variable to store the URL for the SMIL file
var smilURL:String = "burnside_charlie_rtmp.smil";

// Set the initial buffer time low
fp.bufferTime = startBufferTime;
// Set the video source to the SMIL file
fp.source = smilURL;

// Create a timer to update the text field
// with the current buffer value
var timer:Timer = new Timer(100);
// Invoke the showBuffer function whenever
// the timer is running
timer.addEventListener(TimerEvent.TIMER, showBuffer);

// When the SMIL file has loaded
function onVideoReady (e:VideoEvent):void {
    // Create a reference to the FLVPlayback component
    var fp:FLVPlayback = e.currentTarget as FLVPlayback;
    // Access the NCManager within the component
    var ncManager:INCManager = fp.ncMgr;
    // Retrieve the width and height specified in the
    ➥SMIL file
    var w:Number = ncManager.streamWidth;
    var h:Number = ncManager.streamHeight;
    // Make sure the video scales properly in the new
    ➥size
    fp.scaleMode = VideoScaleMode.MAINTAIN_ASPECT_
    ➥RATIO;
    // Adjust the dimensions of the component to match
    // those specified in the SMIL file
    fp.setSize(w, h);
    // Start the timer to show the buffer value
    // in the text field
    timer.start();
}
```

(Continues on next page)

```
// When a change occurs to the video state
function onVideoState (e:VideoEvent):void {
   // Create a reference to the FLVPlayback component
   var fp:FLVPlayback = e.currentTarget as
   ➥FLVPlayback;
   // If the video buffer is starting to fill or is
   ➥empty
   if(e.state == "buffering"){
      // Display the buffer value in the Output panel
      trace("RESET buffer to low value: " +
      ➥startBufferTime);
      // Set the new value on the component
      fp.bufferTime = startBufferTime;
   // Otherwise, if the video has already buffered
   ➥and is playing
   } else if(e.state == "playing"){
      // Display the buffer value in the Output panel
      trace("INCREASE buffer to high value: " +
      ➥increaseBufferTime);
      // Set the new value on the component
      fp.bufferTime = increaseBufferTime;
   }

}

// When the video finishes playing
function onVideoComplete(e:Event):void {
   // Stop the timer from updating the text field
   timer.stop();
   // Clear the text field contents
   bufferField.text = "";
}

// Display the current buffer length in the text field
function showBuffer(e:TimerEvent):void {
   // Retrieve the bufferLength property from the
   // nested NetStream instance in the component
   // and display the value in the text field
   bufferField.text = "Buffer: " + vp.netStream.
   ➥bufferLength;
}
```

5. Save the Flash document, and test the movie (Ctrl/
Cmd+Enter). When the SMIL document loads, the
FLVPlayback component communicates with the Flash
Media Server to determine the current connection
speed, as previous streaming examples in this chapter
have done. Once the bitrate is determined, the appropriate FLV file starts to buffer, using the initial buffer
time specified by the startBufferTime variable. When
the initial buffer is filled and the video begins to play,
the onVideoState function fires and the bufferTime
property of the component switches to the value of the
increaseBufferTime variable, which is 10 seconds. Now,
the video buffer can grow to store more video—if the
connection speed falters momentarily, the buffer can
accommodate the temporary dip and still continue to play
the video. If the buffer does run out due to a decreased
connection speed, the buffer is reset to the initial value.
The first play event also triggers the timer.start() method
within the onVideoReady function. The TimerEvent.TIMER
event continuously evokes the showBuffer() function.
This function displays the current bufferLength value
of the internal NetStream instance of the component
in the bufferField instance on the stage, as shown in
Figure 8.3.

On the DVD-ROM

▶ You can find the finished
file, MBR_AS3_Streaming_
DualBuffer.fla, in the ch08
folder of this book's DVD-ROM.

Figure 8.3 The buffer length displayed below the AS3 version of the FLVPlayback
component.

PART III

Creative Explorations

Chapter 9   Building a Video Index and Playlist   213

Chapter 10   Constructing Banner Ads
             and Captioned Videos   239

Chapter 11   Constructing an Interactive Video Host   257

Chapter 12   Delivering a Reliable
             Video Experience   291

9

Building a Video Index and Playlist

After you've created Flash files that can load Flash Video files, using your own custom NetStream code or using FLVPlayback components, you're ready to tackle user interfaces that control more advanced video functionality. In this chapter, you learn how to read embedded cue points from a Flash Video file, display cue points in labeled buttons, and load XML playlists to cycle multiple video files.

Making a Marker Index for Video

If you encoded a Flash Video (FLV) file with embedded cue points, you can use ActionScript to retrieve all the cue point information you specified during the encoding process. Navigation cue points provide data values that enable the FLVPlayback component to seek to specific times in a Flash Video file. In this section, you learn how to:

▶ Use the metadataReceived and cuePoint events for the ActionScript 2.0 version of the FLVPlayback component.

▶ Build a list of buttons whose labels contain text retrieved from each cue point.

▶ Enable each button to seek to its assigned cue point time in the video.

▶ Highlight each button when each cue point is played.

Retrieving cue point data

Cue point information can be retrieved with two event handlers of the NetStream class: onMetaData and onCuePoint. These handlers are proxied to the FLVPlayback component class, where you can use listeners to catch the same events. The event names for the

On the DVD-ROM

▶ You can find all the source files for this chapter's exercises in the ch09 folder of this book's DVD-ROM. The ch09.flp file is a Flash Project file that you can open in Flash CS3 to view all the sample files related to topics discussed in this chapter.

▶ The examples in this chapter use the dog-trick video footage discussed in Chapter 7's cue point coverage. Each navigation cue point has a `title` parameter, which can be read with ActionScript. The `title` parameter specifies the name of the dog trick.

Caution

▶ The sample progressive-download URLs used in this chapter contain relative paths (../flv) to the FLV files in the flv folder of this book's DVD-ROM. Depending on how you structure your local system folders and files, you may need to adjust the paths to point to FLV files on your system.

ActionScript 2.0 version of the FLVPlayback component are `metadataReceived` and `cuePoint`. In the following steps, you learn how to use the first event, `metadataReceived`, with the sample dog-trick FLV file created in Chapter 6.

1. Make a copy of the MarkerIndex_AS2_starter.fla file from the ch09 folder on the DVD-ROM to your local system. Also, copy the ClearOverPlaySeekMute.swf file from the ch09 folder and the stella_tricks_FLX_VP6_512K_CBR_Cues.flv file from the flv folder.

2. Open the starter file in Flash Professional 8 or Flash CS3. Notice that the stage already includes an instance of the FLVPlayback (AS2) component, named `flvPlayer`.

3. Resave the starter file as `MarkerIndex_AS2.fla`.

4. Review the contents of the starter file's Library panel (Ctrl/Cmd+L), as shown in **Figure 9.1**. The IndexButton symbol is a MovieClip symbol set to export for use in ActionScript. The linkage identifier for this symbol is also IndexButton. You can edit the text field and background clip symbol inside the IndexButton symbol. You will use the IndexButton symbol in the next exercise.

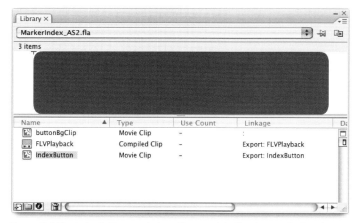

Figure 9.1 The IndexButton symbol and its associated background artwork, buttonBgClip.

5. Select the first frame of the actions layer, and open the Actions panel (F9, or Option+F9 on Mac). Add the following code to the frame script. This code creates

a `markerList` array to store the cue point data when the data is captured with the `onVideoMeta` listener function.

```
// Import class file for FLVPlayback component
import mx.video.FLVPlayback;

// Create a reference to the FLVPlayback component
// on the stage
var fp:FLVPlayback = flvPlayer;

// Create a variable to store the FLV file path
var videoURL:String = "../flv/stella_tricks_FLX_VP6_
➥512K_CBR_Cues.flv";

// Create a variable to store the navigation
// cue points from the FLV file
var markerList:Array;

// Start the movie
init();

// Initialize the movie
function init():Void {
   // Create a new cue point list
   markerList = new Array();
   // Create a listener to handle metadata
   // events from the FLV File
   fp.addEventListener("metadataReceived",
   ➥onVideoMeta);
   // Load the video into the component
   fp.contentPath = videoURL;
}

// When the FLV's metadata arrives
function onVideoMeta (e:Object):Void {
   // Retrieve the FLV's cue points
   var cues:Array =e.info.cuePoints;
   // Loop through the cue points
   for(var i:Number = 0; i < cues.length; i++){
      // Retrieve each cue point
      var cue:Object = cues[i];
      // If the cue point is a navigation cue point
      if(cue.type == "navigation"){
         // Retrieve the title parameter
         var title:String = cue.parameters.title; (Continues on next page)
```

```
                            // Retrieve the timestamp of the cue point
                            var time:Number = cue.time;
                            // Add the values to the cue point list
                            markerList.push( { label: title, data: time} );
                            // Display the title and time of the cue point
                            // in the Output panel
                            trace("title: " + title + ", time: " + time);
                        }
                    }
                }
```

6. Save the Flash file, and test the movie (Ctrl/Cmd+Enter). When the video loads into the FLVPlayback component, the Output panel displays the information retrieved from the FLV file's embedded navigation cue points.

```
title: Lay down, time: 0
title: Shake hands, time: 4.74
title: Hop, time: 13.79
title: Speak softly, time: 23.43
title: Speak loudly, time: 33.84
```

Creating buttons for each cue point

After you've created a routine to read the cue point information from the FLV file's metadata, you can use the cue point data with user interface controls, such as buttons that display names for each cue point and seek to the proper time in the video. To accomplish this goal, the following tasks need to be executed in ActionScript:

▶ Build an empty MovieClip instance to store new instances of the IndexButton symbol from the library.

▶ Determine the X and Y position of the MovieClip instance containing the buttons.

▶ Attach new instances of the IndexButton symbol to the list instance, after the cue point data has been read and stored in the markerList array.

▶ Assign a button handler to each newly attached IndexButton instance, enabling it to seek to its assigned cue point time.

NOTES

▶ Do not test the Flash file in a browser to see the trace() action output. You must test the movie with the Control > Test Movie command (Ctrl/Cmd+Enter) in order to see the Output panel display the trace() actions.

▶ You can find the completed file, MarkerIndex_AS2_Show_Cues.fla, in the ch09 folder of this book's DVD-ROM.

To add dynamic buttons that seek to each cue point:

1. Continue working with the Flash file built in the last section, or make a copy of the MarkerIndex_AS2_Show_Cues.fla file from the ch09 folder of the DVD-ROM. Open the file in Flash Professional 8 or Flash CS3.

2. Select frame 1 of the actions layer, and open the Actions panel (F9, or Option+F9 on Mac). After the `var markerList:Array;` line of code, add the following code. This code establishes the X and Y values used by the button container, as well as vertical spacing between the buttons. These X and Y values position the buttons along the right side of the FLVPlayback instance.

```
// Create a MovieClip reference to store
// the list of index buttons
var list:MovieClip;

// Create variables to store the position of the list
var listX:Number = fp.x + fp.width + 15;
var listY:Number = fp.y;

// Create a variable to control spacing
// between index buttons
var buttonVerticalSpacing:Number = 30;
```

3. After the closing curly brace (}) of the for loop of the onVideoMeta function and before the closing curly brace (}) of the function, add the following code, invoking a new function named buildList:

```
// Create the index buttons with the new list
buildList(markerList);
```

4. After the last line of code, add a new function declaration for buildList. This function takes the information added to the markerList array in the onVideoMeta function and creates a series of cue point buttons from the IndexButton symbol in the library.

```
// Make a series of index buttons from a list
function buildList(dp:Array):Void {    (Continues on next page)
```

217

```
// Create a new MovieClip instance to store the
➥buttons
list = createEmptyMovieClip("list", 1);
// Position the list instance
list._x = listX;
list._y = listY;

// Loop through the list items
for(var i:Number = 0; i < dp.length; i++){
   // Retrieve each list item
   var item:Object = dp[i];

   // Create an object to store initial
   // properties for the index button
   var initVal:Object = {
      // Set the Y position of the button
      _y: (i*buttonVerticalSpacing),
      // Create a property to refer to
      // the FLVPlayback component
      player: fp,
      // Create a property to refer to
      // the cue point's time value
      time: item.data
   };

   // Attach a new index button instance
   var button:MovieClip = list.attachMovie(
                        "IndexButton", // The
                        ➥linkage ID of the symbol
                        "indexBtn_" + i, // The
                        ➥new instance name
                        i, // The new depth of
                        ➥the instance
                        initVal // The initial
                        ➥properties
                     );
   // Add a mouse handler to the button
   button.onRelease = function():Void {
      // Seek to the cue point's time
      // when the button is clicked
      this.player.seek(this.time);
   };
```

```
    // Create a reference to the button's text field
    var field:TextField = button.labelField;
    // Set the text to the title of the marker
    field.text = item.label;
  }
}
```

5. Save the Flash file, and test the movie (Ctrl/Cmd+Enter). When the FLV file loads into the FLVPlayback component, the metadata is retrieved from the FLV file and the buildList() function is invoked. The buttons are created from the cue point data, displaying along the right side of the FLVPlayback component, as shown in **Figure 9.2**. When you click each button, the video jumps to the cue point's position.

> ► You can find the completed file, MarkerIndex_AS2.fla, in the ch09 folder on the DVD-ROM.

Changing the button color during playback

The last feature we want to add is to change the background color of each button when its cue point is played in the video file. You will create two variables to control the button color: a default color when the cue point is not active and a color to indicate which button's cue point was most recently played. As each cue point is played, a new button will be highlighted. The following tasks need to be executed in ActionScript:

Figure 9.2 The buttons corresponding to each cue point in the FLV file.

► Create two variables to define the color of the button states.

► Update the buildList function to add a Color instance as a new property to each button instance. This Color instance enables the background color to be changed in ActionScript.

► Define a function that controls the background color of every marker button, based on the time of the current cue point. If the cue point time matches that defined in a button instance, the color changes to the active color. Otherwise, the button's color is set to the default color.

► Define a function to listen to cue point events emitted by the FLVPlayback component. This function sends the cue point time to the function that controls the button background color.

▶ Update the button handler of each IndexButton instance to call the function that controls the button background color.

To control the button background color based on the current navigation cue point:

1. Continue working with the Flash file built in the last section, or make a copy of the MarkerIndex_Highlight_AS2_starter.fla file from the ch09 folder on the DVD-ROM. Open the file in Flash Professional 8 or Flash CS3.

2. Select the first frame of the actions layer, and open the Actions panel (F9, or Option+F9 on Mac). After the `var buttonVerticalSpacing:Number = 30;` line of code, add the following two variables to establish the color values for the button states. The default color specifies a light gray, while the cue color indicates a darker gray. You can use your own preferred colors.

```
// Create a variable to set the default
// button background color
var defaultColor:Number = 0x666666;
```

```
// Create a variable to set the button
// background color when the cue is played
var cueColor:Number = 0x333333;
```

3. Within the init function, after the `fp.addEventListener("metadataReceived", onVideoMeta);` line of code, add another listener function to capture cue point events.

```
// Create a listener to handle cue point
// events from the FLV file
fp.addEventListener("cuePoint", onVideoCue);
```

4. After the closing curly brace (}) of the onVideoMeta function, add the following onVideoCue function. When a navigation cue point is played, this function sends the time of the cue point to a function that is named highlightButton, defined later in this exercise.

```
// When a cue point is reached
function onVideoCue(e:Object):Void {
```

```
   // Retrieve the current cue point
   var cue:Object = e.info;
   // Retrieve the time of the cue point
   var time:Number = cue.time;
   // If the cue point is a navigation cue point
   if(cue.type == "navigation"){
      // Highlight the appropriate button's
      // background color
      highlightButton(time);
   }
}
```

5. Within the `buildList` function, add the following code after the `this.player.seek(this.time);` line of code in the `button.onRelease` handler. This code enables the background color of the button to change when clicked by the user.

```
// Highlight this button
highlightButton(this.time);
```

6. Within the `buildList` function and after the `button.onRelease` handler, add the following code. This code creates a new Color instance for the background clip of the button, which is a `MovieClip` instance named `bg`. The color of the background clip is set to the default color specified earlier in this exercise. A new property named `bgColor` is also added to the button, specifying the new Color instance. This property is used by the `highlightButton` function defined in the next step.

```
// Create a variable referencing the
// nested buttonBgClip within the
// IndexButton symbol
var bg:MovieClip = button.bg;
// Retrieve the Color instance for
// the button background clip
var clr:Color = new Color(bg);
// Change the button background color
// to the default value
clr.setRGB(defaultColor);
```

NOTES

▶ Before you proceed to step 8, you may need to alter the value of the videoURL variable defined near the top of the script. The starter file uses a relative path to the FLV file on the book's DVD-ROM.

▶ You'll find the completed file, MarkerIndex_Highlight_AS2. fla, in the ch09 folder on the DVD-ROM.

▶ You can find the file for Figure 9.4, MarkerIndex_List_AS2. fla, in the ch09 folder on the DVD-ROM. A variation of this file, MarkerIndex_Highlight_ AS2_ColorTransform.fla, uses the ColorTransform class instead of the older Color class for button color changes.

```
// Set up a background color property
// for the button
button.bgColor = clr;
```

7. After the closing curly brace (}) of the buildList function, define a function named highlightButton. The onVideoCue function and each button's onRelease handler use this function to set the background color of each button, based on the current cue point's time.

```
// Set the proper background color on each button
// based on the time of the cue point
function highlightButton(time:Number):Void {
    // Loop through the marker list
    for (var i:Number = 0; i < markerList.length; i++) {
        // Retrieve each marker's data
        var item:Object = markerList[i];
        // Retrieve each button
        var button:MovieClip = list["indexBtn_" + i];
        // If the button's time matches the current time,
        // use the cue color, otherwise use the default
        ➥color
        var colorVal:Number = (item.data == time) ?
        ➥cueColor : defaultColor;
        // Set the new color
        button.bgColor.setRGB(colorVal);
    }
}
```

8. Save the Flash file, and test the movie (Ctrl/Cmd+Enter). When the Flash Video file's metadata loads, the buttons are created and displayed to the right of the FLVPlayback component. As the video plays, the corresponding button for each navigation cue point is highlighted, as shown in **Figure 9.3**.

Figure 9.3 Each button's background color changes as the video plays.

You can apply this technique of listening to metadata and cue point events with other user interface elements such as a List component. **Figure 9.4** shows the same cue points displayed in a List component.

Figure 9.4 Cue points displayed in a List component.

Building a Video Playlist

You can create a list of several Flash Video (FLV) files and play them in succession, just like a music playlist. You can create lists of FLV files directly in ActionScript code or in an external document, such as an XML file. By using an XML file, you can more easily update the order and content of a video playlist—without opening and republishing a Flash document.

Determining an XML schema

XML, which stands for e*X*tensible *M*arkup *L*anguage, has become a corner store for data transfer on the Internet. Many Web-service providers offer XML data services to retrieve everything from product catalog information to satellite maps. One of the core strengths of the XML format is that you can create any structure, or schema, you need for your data. The schema of an XML document indicates the name and order of tags, or nodes, within the file. For this section, an XML schema has been determined and created for the examples. The schema uses the following node names:

▶ `<playlist>`: This node is the root of the XML document. An optional attribute, `id`, can specify an identifier for the playlist. With examples later in this chapter, attributes are added to this node to enable custom skin options.

▶ `<item>`: This node specifies each FLV file in the playlist. Each FLV file has its own `<item>` node, with up to four attributes: an identifier for the video (optional), a label for the video to display in the video list (required), the URL path to the video (required), and a thumbnail image to use in the playlist for the video clip (optional).

Review the sample XML file, animals.xml, in the data folder on the DVD-ROM. This playlist, shown in the following code block, specifies four FLV files.

```
<?xml version="1.0" encoding="UTF-8"?>
<playlist id="FVST Ch 09 Playlist Example" >

    <item id="feature-001" label="Squeak the Squirrel"
      src="../flv/squeak_the_squirrel_Spark_275K.flv"
      ➥/>
```
(Continues on next page)

NOTES

▶ For legibility here, some attributes are on a separate line. In the actual file, the attributes are written without line breaks. Also, the color coding used by Adobe Dreamweaver CS3 is used to help distinguish node names and attributes from values.

```
<item id="feature-002" label="Kitty Cleans Up"
src="../flv/kitty_cleans_up_Spark_275K.flv" />

<item id="feature-003" label="Food Getting Among
➥Animals"
   src="../flv/food_getting_among_animals_Spark_
   ➥275K.flv" />

<item id="feature-004" label="Safety with Animals"
   src="../flv/safety_with_animals_Spark_275K.flv"
   ➥/>
```

`</playlist>`

When you create an XML file for use in a Flash Player 6 or higher movie, use Unicode UTF-8 document encoding. In Dreamweaver CS3, Unicode UTF-8 is the default document encoding for new XML files. You can change the encoding by choosing Modify > Document. In Notepad (Windows) or TextEdit (Mac), you can choose Unicode UTF-8 in the Save As dialog.

Loading the playlist

After you have created an XML file specifying the FLV files in the video playlist, you're ready to build the Flash file that loads the XML data and displays the label values in a List component. For the examples in this section, you load the playlist data into a Flash Player 9 movie using Action-Script 3.0 code. To simplify this process, you'll use custom ActionScript 3.0 classes that I wrote to use with the AS3 FLVPlayback component. You can find these classes within the subfolders of the classes/AS3 folder on the DVD-ROM.

▶ `Playlist`: This class can load an XML file that uses the schema discussed in the previous section. More importantly, the class parses the XML file and creates an internal array enumerating each FLV file and its attributes. A Playlist instance has two important public properties: `selectedPlayItem` and `selectedPlayIdx`. The `selectedPlayItem` property indicates which item in the playlist is currently selected, and has property names that match the XML `<item>` node's attribute names. The `selectedPlayItem.src` value provides the path to the FLV

 TIP

▶ All the video samples are public-domain clips that you can find in the Prelinger Archive at www.archive.org. You can find more information about this site in Appendix A.

file. The `selectedPlayIdx` property indicates the index value of the currently playing video file, where 0 represents the first video, 1 represents the second video, and so on. This value can be used to align a List component's `selectedIndex` property with the playlist's index value.

▶ `BackgroundBox`: This class can create a filled rectangle behind the video player instance. You can specify a custom color in the constructor of this class.

To load the playlist in a Flash Player 9 movie using Action-Script 3.0:

1. In any location on your local drives, create a folder named `playlist`. In this folder, create four folders with the following names: `classes`, `data`, `flv`, and `swf`.

2. Copy the animals.xml file from the data folder on the DVD-ROM to your new data folder.

3. Copy the four FLV files shown in the previous XML code sample from the flv folder on the DVD-ROM to your new flv folder.

4. Copy the AS3 folder from the classes folder on the DVD-ROM to your new classes folder.

5. Open Flash CS3, and create a new Flash file (Action-Script 3.0). Save this document as `PlaylistExample_AS3.fla` in the new swf folder you created in step 1.

6. Choose File > Publish Settings, and select the Flash tab. Click the Settings button next to the ActionScript version menu. In the ActionScript 3.0 Settings dialog, type `PlaylistExample` in the Document class field. This name specifies a separate ActionScript (AS) file to be associated with the Flash file. (Do not include the .as file extension in the Document class field.)

7. Click the + button in the Classpath area of the dialog, and type `../classes/AS3/.` in the text field in the list, as shown in **Figure 9.5**. The Classpath tells Flash CS3 where it can find ActionScript classes to import into your own Flash files. Click OK to close the ActionScript 3.0 Settings dialog, and click OK again to close the Publish Settings dialog.

▶ These custom classes must be copied to your system, as instructed in step 4 below. These classes are not included with Flash CS3.

▶ If an ActionScript Class Warning dialog appears after you click OK in the ActionScript 3.0 Settings dialog, click OK again to dismiss the warning. Later in this tutorial, you will create the document class file referenced in the warning.

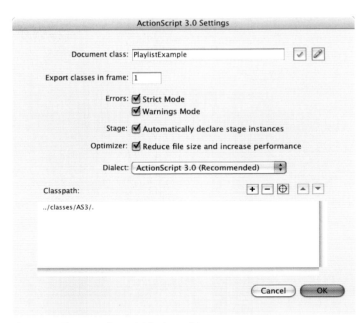

Figure 9.5 The ActionScript 3.0 Settings dialog.

8. Rename Layer 1 to flvPlayer.

9. Open the Components panel (Ctrl/Cmd+F7) and, from the Video grouping, drag the FLVPlayback component to the top-left area of the stage. Select the new instance, and open the Property inspector. Name the instance flvPlayer.

10. In the Parameters tab of the Property inspector, choose your preferred skin and skin options.

11. Create a new layer named videoList.

12. From the User Interface grouping in the Components panel, drag the List component to the right side of the FLVPlayback instance on the stage. In the Property inspector, name the List instance videoList.

13. Use the Free Transform tool to resize the width and height of the videoList instance to match the height of the FLVPlayback instance, as shown in **Figure 9.6**.

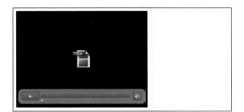

Figure 9.6 The videoList instance.

14. Now you're ready to create the document class file specified in step 6. Choose File > New and choose ActionScript File from the New Document dialog. Save this new script file as PlaylistExample.as in the same swf folder where you saved the PlaylistExample.fla file in step 5.

15. In the PlaylistExample.as file, add the following code. This code creates a new Playlist instance, which loads the XML file and starts playing the first video in the playlist. If you don't want to type this code, you can copy the PlaylistExample.as file from the ch09 folder on the DVD-ROM to your swf folder.

```actionscript
package {

  // Import the class files required for this movie
  import flash.display.Sprite;
  import flash.events.Event;
  import fl.video.FLVPlayback;
  import fl.controls.List;
  import com.flashsupport.video.Playlist;
  import com.flashsupport.video.BackgroundBox;

  // Declare the class name
  public class PlaylistExample extends Sprite {

    // Create a variable to store the playlist
    private var pl:Playlist;
    // Create a reference to the FLVPlayback
    ➥instance
    private var fp:FLVPlayback;
    // Create a reference to the List instance
    private var vl:List;

    // Create a variable to store the path to the
    ➥XML file
    public var xmlURL:String = "../data/animals.xml";

    // Declare the constructor for the class
    public function PlaylistExample(){
      // Start the movie
      init();
    }                                    (Continues on next page)
```

227

```
// Create a function to setup and start the movie
private function init():void {
    // Link the vl variable to the List instance
    // on the stage
    vl = videoList;
    // Create a listener function for the List
    ➥instance,
    // detecting when a user has selected a new
    ➥item
    vl.addEventListener(Event.CHANGE,
    ➥onItemClick);
    // Link the fp variable to the FLVPlayback
    ➥instance
    // on the stage
    fp = flvPlayer;
    // Create a listener function for the
    ➥FLVPlayback ➥instance,
    // detecting when the each FLV file has
    ➥finished playing
    fp.addEventListener(Event.COMPLETE,
    ➥onClipDone);
    // Create a new black background behind the
    ➥FLVPlayback instance
    var bg:BackgroundBox = new BackgroundBox(fp,
    ➥0x000000);
    // Create a new playlist
    pl = new Playlist();
    // Create a listener function for the
    ➥Playlist instance,
    // detecting when the XML file has loaded
    pl.addEventListener(Event.COMPLETE,
    ➥onListReady);
    // Create a listener function for the
    ➥Playlist instance,
    // detecting when a new FLV file has been
    ➥selected
    pl.addEventListener(Playlist.SELECT_LIST_
    ➥ITEM, onListItemSelect);
    // Load the XML file into the Playlist
    ➥instance
```

```
    pl.load(xmlURL);
}

// Define a listener function to detect when
// the playlist has loaded
private function onListReady(e:Event):void {
    // Retrieve the current playlist
    var pl:Playlist = e.currentTarget as Playlist;
    // Loop through the playlist items
    for(var i:int = 0; i < pl.length; ++i){
        // Retrieve each playlist item
        var item:Object = pl.getItemAt(i);
        // Add each label attribute to the List
        ➥instance
        vl.addItem({ label: item.label });
    }
}

// Define a listener function to detect when
// the user has selected a new item in the
➥playlist
private function onItemClick(e:Event):void {
    // Retrieve the List instance
    var list:List = e.currentTarget as List;
    // Change the playlist's selected index to
    ➥match
    // the selected index of the List instance
    pl.selectedIndex = list.selectedIndex;
}

// Define a listener function to detect when the
// selected index of the playlist has changed
private function onListItemSelect(e:Event):void {
    // Retrieve the current playlist
    var pl:Playlist = e.currentTarget as Playlist;
    // Set the List instance's index to the
    // Playlist instance's index
    vl.selectedIndex = pl.selectedIndex;
    // Play the new video file
    fp.source = pl.selectedItem.src;
}
```

(Continues on next page)

► You can find the complete files in the ch09 folder on the DVD-ROM.

Adding thumbnails to the playlist

The ActionScript 2 and ActionScript 3 versions of the List component can use custom cell renderers to dictate the format and layout of elements for each item in the list. I wrote a custom ActionScript 3.0 cell renderer class named `com.flashsupport.video.Thumbnail`. You can find the Thumbnail.as file for this renderer in the classes/AS3/com/flashsupport/video folder on the DVD-ROM. You can import this class into your own ActionScript 3.0 code, and set it as the cell renderer of your List component. In the data folder on the DVD-ROM, the XML schema of the sample animals.xml file has been updated in the animals_thumbnail.xml file, to include a `thumbnail` attribute. The JPEG images that are used as thumbnails are in the preview_images folder on the DVD-ROM. The XML `thumbnail` attribute is recognized by the `Playlist` class used in the last section. You can find a complete video playlist and thumbnail example in the ch09 folder. The PlaylistThumbnails_AS3.fla and PlaylistThumbnails.as files enable the cell renderer to work with the List component, as shown in **Figure 9.8**.

```
// Define a listener function to detect when
// the video has finished playing
private function onClipDone(e:Event):void {
    trace("onClipDone >");
    // If the current item selction is not the
    ➥last item
    // in the playlist
    if(pl.selectedIndex < pl.length - 1){
        // Jump to the next item in the playlist
        pl.selectedIndex++;
    } else {
        // Otherwise, cycle back to the first item
        // in the playlist
        pl.selectedIndex = 0;
    }
}
```

16. Save the ActionScript file, and test the Flash movie (Ctrl/Cmd+Enter). The playlist data loads into the List instance, and the first item is selected in the list, as shown in **Figure 9.7**. If you set the autoPlay parameter to true for the FLVPlayback instance on the stage, the first video automatically begins to play. Otherwise, the first frame of the video is displayed in the component. As each video completes playback, the next item starts to play. (Instead of watching the full length of each video, you can cheat by scrubbing to the end of the video, and play just the last few seconds of the video.)

Figure 9.7 The playlist data loaded into the List component.

Figure 9.8 The playlist and thumbnail data loaded into the List component.

Playing Video Ads during a Video Feature

One of the most powerful features of the FLVPlayback components is the ability to utilize multiple video players within a single instance of the component. Earlier in this chapter, you changed the contentPath property (AS2) or source property (AS3) of the FLVPlayback instance to change the current video playing in the component. If you do not need to maintain the previous video when you switch to another one, this approach works just fine. However, if you want to play multiple videos and be able to maintain the state (including playhead position) of previous video clips, an alternate technique is required.

In Chapter 7, "Building Your Own Video Player," the VideoPlayer class was described as the base of the FLVPlayback components. In fact, you can create more than one instance of the VideoPlayer class within the FLVPlayback component. Using the activeVideoPlayerIndex and visibleVideoPlayerIndex properties of the FLVPlayback component, you can create and control a new VideoPlayer instance. In this section, you learn how to build a Flash Video presentation that plays a feature presentation requiring the viewer to watch three video advertisements over the course of the feature. Each video ad plays only once throughout the playback of the featured clip.

A custom ActionScript 3.0 class named PlaylistManager contains the functionality to build this project. I wrote this class to work in conjunction with the Playlist class used in the last section's example. The PlaylistManager class does all the heavy lifting with the VideoPlayer instances within an FLVPlayback instance. Only two requirements are necessary to use the PlaylistManager class:

- ▶ An existing FLVPlayback instance, which is passed to the player property of the PlaylistManager instance
- ▶ A path to an XML document, which is used for the load() method of the PlaylistManager instance

The PlaylistManager class can also broadcast events related to its operations. The primary event, PlaylistManager.READY, is broadcast when the playlist XML data has been loaded and initialized. After this event has transpired, you can call the start() method of the PlaylistManager instance to begin playback of the feature video and its supporting ad units.

Defining the XML schema

The Playlist class supports additional XML nodes to enable the insertion of video ads during the playback of a featured video clip. Review the contents of the XML file for the example, labor_and_childbirth.xml, found in the data folder on the DVD-ROM. This file contains the following XML data:

NOTES

▶ The PlaylistManager class also uses the custom BackgroundBox class to add a black box behind the FLVPlayback component instance.

NOTES

▶ For legibility, some attributes are shown on a separate line. In the actual file, the attributes are written without line breaks. Also, the color coding used by Adobe Dreamweaver CS3 is used to help distinguish node names and attributes from values.

```xml
<?xml version="1.0" encoding="UTF-8"?>
<playlist id="FVST - Chapter 9 Feature Video with Ads"
    skin="SkinUnderPlaySeekMute.swf"
    skinAutoHide="false" skinBgAlpha="1"
skinBgColor="#666666" >

    <item id="feature-001" label="Labor and Childbirth"
        src="../flv/Laborand1950_SQZ_VP6_384K_CBR.
        ➥flv" >

      <inst skin="SkinAd.swf" >
        <ad id="ad-001" label="Beech-Nut Baby Food"
            src="../flv/Beech-NutBab_SQZ_VP6_384K_
            ➥CBR.flv"
            time="0" />
        <ad id="ad-002" label="Genteel Baby Bath"
            src="../flv/genteel_baby_bath_SQZ_VP6_
            ➥384K_CBR.flv"
            time="310" />
        <ad id="ad-003" label="Mennen Baby Magic"
            src="../flv/MennenBabyMa_SQZ_VP6_384K_
            ➥CBR.flv"
            time="590" />
      </inst>

    </item>

</playlist>
```

Each <item> node of the playlist XML file can specify a single child node named <inst>. Within this <inst> node, you can specify one or more <ad> child nodes, which represent the FLV files for the advertisements to play throughout the course of the featured video clip specified in the parent <item> node.

Both the root <playlist> node and the <inst> node require an attribute named skin. This attribute specifies the skin SWF file for the FLVPlayback instance managed by the PlaylistManager instance. The ad units use the skin specified in the <inst> node, while the featured video clip uses the skin specified in the <playlist> node. The <playlist> node also supports the following attributes related to the FLVPlayback component's skin properties of the same name: skinAutoHide, skinBgAlpha, and skinBgColor.

The <ad> child nodes can list four attributes:

▶ id: This optional attribute is not utilized by the PlaylistManager class. You can use this attribute to identify a clip for your own commenting purposes.

▶ label: This optional attribute specifies a label to be used with the video ad. The PlaylistManager class does not use this attribute.

▶ src: This required attribute specifies the path to the FLV file for the video ad.

▶ time: This required attribute indicates the time at which the video ad should play during the featured video clip's playback. The featured video pauses at this time value, while the video ad plays. The featured video resumes playback after the video ad has played.

You can change the XML data to use your own FLV files for the featured video clip and video ads. All the FLV files referenced in the sample XML file are located in the flv folder of this book's DVD-ROM.

TIP

▶ All these video samples are public-domain clips that you can find in the Prelinger Archive at www.archive.org. You can find more information about this site in Appendix A.

▶ You can find the source FLA file for the SkinAd.swf in the ch09 folder on the DVD-ROM. The SkinAd.fla assets can be changed to suit your own design requirements.

NOTES

▶ The PlaylistManager class uses the addASCuePoint() method of the FLVPlayback component to add the time values from each <ad> node as cue points for the featured video clip.

Instantiating the PlaylistManager class

You can use the `PlaylistManager` and `Playlist` classes with any ActionScript 3.0- and Flash Player 9-compatible project. In this section, you learn how to build a Flash file and a document class (AS file) that load and play the featured video and video ads specified in the XML file.

To add a `PlaylistManager` instance to a Flash file:

1. If you did not create the playlist and nested folder in the last section's exercise, repeat steps 1 and 4 from that exercise.

2. Copy the labor_and_childbirth.xml file from the data folder on the book's DVD-ROM to your data folder.

3. Copy the four FLV files shown in the previous XML code sample from the flv folder on the DVD-ROM to your flv folder.

4. Copy the custom skin SWF file, SkinAd.swf, from the ch09 folder also on the DVD-ROM to your swf folder. This SWF file is used by the video ad files.

5. Open Flash CS3, and then create a new Flash file (ActionScript 3.0). Save this document as `Sequencer_AS3.fla` in the swf folder you created earlier.

6. Choose File > Publish Settings, and select the Flash tab. Click the Settings button next to the ActionScript version menu. In the ActionScript 3.0 Settings dialog, type `Sequencer` in the Document class field. This name specifies a separate ActionScript (AS) file to be associated with the Flash file. (Do not include the .as file extension in the Document class field.)

7. Click the + button in the Classpath area of the dialog, and type `../classes/AS3/`. in the text field in the list, as shown in **Figure 9.9**. The Classpath tells Flash CS3 where it can find ActionScript classes to import into your own Flash files. Click OK to close the ActionScript 3.0 Settings dialog, and click OK again to close the Publish Settings dialog.

NOTES

▶ If an ActionScript Class Warning dialog appears after you click OK in the ActionScript 3.0 Settings dialog, click OK again to dismiss the warning. Later in this tutorial, you will create the document class file referenced in the warning.

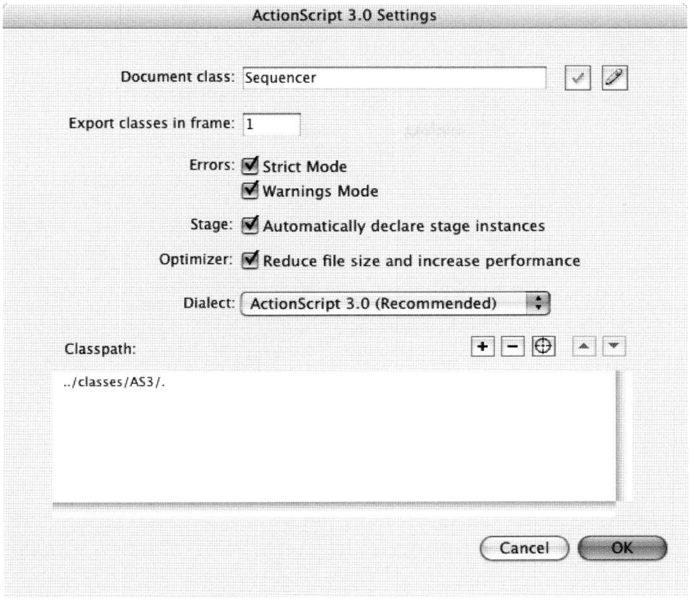

Figure 9.9 The ActionScript 3.0 Settings dialog.

8. Open the Components panel (Ctrl/Cmd+F7) and, from the Video grouping, drag the FLVPlayback component to the stage of your Flash file. Select the new instance, and delete it. You only need the FLVPlayback component in the file's Library panel to add dynamic instances of the component in ActionScript.

9. Now you're ready to create the document class file specified in step 5. Choose File > New, and choose ActionScript File from the New Document dialog. Save this new script file as Sequencer.as in the same swf folder where you saved the Sequencer_AS3.fla file in step 5.

10. In the Sequencer.as file, add the following code. This code creates a new FLVPlayback instance and centers it on the stage. A `PlaylistManager` instance is also created, which loads the XML file and processes the play order of the video ads and the featured video clip. If you don't want to type this code, you can copy the Sequencer.as file from the ch09 folder on the DVD-ROM

to your swf folder, overwriting the file you created in step 8.

```
package {
    // Import classes used in the movie
    import flash.display.Sprite;
    import flash.events.Event;
    import fl.video.FLVPlayback;

    // Import the custom class to manage playlists
    import com.flashsupport.video.PlaylistManager;

    // Declare the Flash file's class name
    public class Sequencer extends Sprite {

        // Create a variable to store the path to the XML
        public var xmlPath:String = "../data/labor_and_
        ➥childbirth.xml";
        // Create a variable to store the
        ➥PlaylistManager instance
        public var pm:PlaylistManager;

        // Create a constructor function
        public function Sequencer(){
            // Start the movie
            init();
        }

        // Create a function to initialize the movie
        private function init():void {
            // Make a new instance of the FLVPlayback
            ➥component
            var fp:FLVPlayback = new FLVPlayback();
            // Center the instance on the stage
            fp.x = (stage.stageWidth - fp.width)/2;
            fp.y = ((stage.stageHeight - fp.height)/2)
            ➥- 20;
            // Add the FLVPlayback instance to the
            ➥display list
            addChild(fp);

            // Create a new PlaylistManager instance
            pm = new PlaylistManager();
```

```
        // Pass the FLVPlayback instance to the
        // player property of the PlaylistManager
        ➥instance
        pm.player = fp;
        // Create a listener function to detect when
        // the XML data has loaded and initialized
        pm.addEventListener(PlaylistManager.READY,
        ➥onListReady);
        // Load the XML data
        pm.load(xmlPath);
    }

    // When the PlaylistManager instance is ready
    private function onListReady(e:Event):void {
        // Start the playlist
        pm.start();
    }
  }
}
```

11. Save the ActionScript file, and test the Flash movie (Ctrl/Cmd+Enter). The playlist data is loaded and initialized by the PlaylistManager instance, and the first video begins to play in the new FLVPlayback instance, as shown in **Figure 9.10**. When the first video ad finishes, the featured video clip begins to play with a different skin SWF file, as shown in **Figure 9.11**. If you scrub past the time values for other video ads specified in the XML data, the featured video clip pauses, and the respective video ad plays.

NOTES

▶ You can find the complete files in the ch09 folder of this book's DVD-ROM.

Figure 9.10 The first video ad with a custom skin SWF file.

Figure 9.11 The featured video clip with a standard skin SWF file.

10

Constructing Banner Ads and Captioned Videos

Most of the examples in this book use the FLVPlayback components for the heavy lifting of creating server connections, loading Flash Video (FLV) files, and controlling playback. There are projects, though, that require less overhead for video playback, such as a Web site banner ad featuring a short video clip. In the first half of this chapter, you learn how to build a simple yet effective video banner ad without using components. You also learn how to add simple captions below the video area in the banner. In the second half, you continue to learn how to caption video with the new AS3 FLVPlaybackCaptioning component that ships with Flash CS3.

Coding a Video Banner Ad

A trip to many popular Web sites will yield a wide range of banner advertisements, most of them running in Adobe Flash Player. Some Flash ads also include Flash Video, especially banner ads for upcoming movies. In this section, you learn how to build a light-weight Flash Video player for use in a banner ad (**Figure 10.1**).

Reviewing the technical requirements

For this project, the Flash banner (SWF file) needs to adhere to the following guidelines:

▶ **Flash Player 6 compatibility:** The Flash ad should be able to play in just about any Web site, without requiring the user to update or install Flash Player. Over 95 percent of computers connected to the Internet can play Flash Player 6 content.

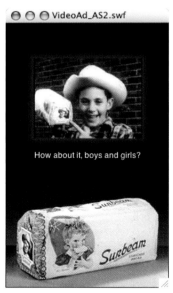

Figure 10.1 The banner ad featuring a video commercial.

NOTES

▶ You will find all the source files for this chapter in the ch10 folder on the DVD-ROM. The ch10.flp file is a Flash Project file that you can open in Flash CS3 to view the sample files discussed in this chapter.

▶ For testing in the Flash CS3 authoring environment, the Flash Video file is loaded locally. This approach, however, requires Flash Player 7 for actual deployment. The final delivery format, though, will be specified as an RTMP path, with parameters passed to the Flash movie in JavaScript and HTML.

▶ **Small file size:** The primary Flash movie (SWF file) must be 20 KB or less. This size does not include the Flash Video (FLV) file.

▶ **Low bitrate video:** The video asset should be targeted to a bandwidth of 112 Kbps or less.

▶ **Sorenson Spark codec:** Because the Flash ad must be Flash Player 6 compatible, the Flash Video file must use the Sorenson Spark codec, not the newer On2 VP6 codec.

▶ **Real-time streaming delivery:** The video asset should be able to stream from an Adobe Flash Media Server or a Flash Video Streaming Service (FVSS) provider such as Akamai or Limelight.

▶ **Synchronized captions:** The banner ad should display the narrator's script below the video area. The captions will be stored in an XML file that is loaded into the Flash banner ad at runtime.

▶ **Dynamic parameters passed via JavaScript:** Any external assets or resources used by the Flash banner ad should be assigned via JavaScript in the HTML document hosting the banner ad. These resources include the Flash Video URL, the URL to the XML file containing the video captions, and a click-through URL for the ad. A click-through URL is the destination Web site for the banner ad. In final deployment, this URL usually includes tracking information for usage metrics, where an intermediate server receives and processes the click request and redirects the browser to the appropriate destination.

Surveying the assets

The video ad uses graphics and animated elements already prepared in the starter file, VideoAd_AS2_starter.fla, located in the ch10 folder on the DVD-ROM.

If you open this file in Flash 8 or Flash CS3, the following layers are already placed in the main timeline of the file, as shown in **Figure 10.2**:

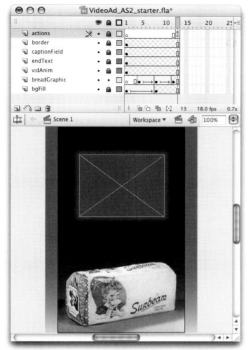

Figure 10.2 The contents of the starter file on frame 13.

▶ **border:** This layer contains the outline of the banner ad, as a simple black stroke. Most banner ads have a thin border to separate themselves from other elements on the page.

▶ **captionField:** This layer contains a dynamic text field named captionField in the Property inspector. This field uses the _sans device font for video captions displayed below the video area. A device font is used to lower the file size of the Flash movie.

▶ **endText:** This layer contains an instance of the symbol endTextAnim in the movie's library. The instance is named endText in the Property inspector. This symbol contains a text animation, fading the words "The bread you need for energy" onto the stage after the video has finished playing.

> **TIP**
>
> ▶ The starter file is based on the 240 by 400 ad template available in Flash CS3. To create a new file with this template, choose File > New, click the Templates tab, and select the Advertising category. In the Templates column, choose 240x400 (Rectangle). For this example, the ActionScript version was changed from 1.0 to 2.0 and the frame rate was changed from 12 fps to 18 fps.

NOTES

▶ All the sample progressive-download URLs used in this chapter contain relative paths (../flv) to the FLV files that reside in the flv folder on the DVD-ROM. Depending on how you structure your local system folders and files, you may need to adjust these sample paths to point to FLV files that reside on your system.

▶ The example in this section builds on the concepts in Chapter 7, "Building Your Own Video Player." If you need to learn more about the NetConnection, NetStream, and Video classes, please refer back to Chapter 7.

▶ Many thanks to Sean Porter for his time, advice, and design help with the banner ad created in this section's example. Sean is an art director and sound designer at Schematic (www.schematic.com).

TIP

▶ The video sample used in this section is a Sunbeam bread commercial, which is a public-domain clip that you can find in the Prelinger Archive at www.archive.org. You can find more information about this site in Appendix A.

▶ **vidAnim:** This layer holds an instance of the videoAnim symbol from the movie's library. The instance is named `vidAnim` in the Property inspector. This symbol contains another `MovieClip` instance named `holder`, which in turn holds the `Video` object named `vid`, which is responsible for displaying the video content. The `holder` instance, which is an instance of the videoClip symbol in the movie's library, contains a nested flickering animation for the background behind the video.

▶ **breadGraphic:** This layer contains instances of the breadGraphic symbol, featuring a still image from the video clip. Part of the background area in the image is transparent, as specified in the imported PNG file used for the graphic. This image animates on to the lower half of the movie's stage when the ad starts to play.

▶ **bgFill:** This layer contains the gradient background used behind all the other elements in the banner ad. This instance, named `bgFill` in the Property inspector, also acts as a button to receive mouse clicks from the user.

On the DVD-ROM, you can also find the Flash Video (FLV) file to accompany the video ad. The sunbeam_SQZ_Spark_112K_VBR.flv file is located in the flv folder. This file has been encoded with Sorenson Squeeze 4.5, and uses the Sorenson Spark codec to meet the requirements for this project. Because the clip is short, I used VBR encoding to produce better quality video over a low bitrate, 112Kbps. (VBR encoding for such a short clip will not complicate any real-time streaming delivery.)

Controlling playback of the interactive ad

In this section, you learn how to script the Flash banner to play the video file and execute actions relying on the video's events. The following tasks need to be executed in ActionScript:

▶ Create variables to track playback of the video stream. The `NetStream` instance dispatches a range of event codes, including `NetStream.Play.Start`, `NetStream.Play.Stop`, `NetStream.Buffer.Empty`, and `NetStream.Buffer.Full`. To detect when a video has finished playing, you need to listen for the `NetStream.Buffer.Empty` event that occurs after a `NetStream.Play.Stop` event. Because these actions occur asynchronously, two variables, `bufferEmpty` and `stopDetected`, are used to track the events.

▶ Create variables to determine the video's URL and the click-through URL. These variables can retrieve values passed by the HTML document hosting the banner ad.

▶ Define a function named `init` that initializes the video stream with `NetConnection` and `NetStream` instances. This function should be able to handle both RTMP and HTTP connections to FLV files. Remember, though, that progressive-download delivery requires Flash Player 7. Flash Player 6 must use RTMP for direct playback of FLV files.

▶ Define a function named `onStreamStatus` to handle and track events that occur with the video stream. When the video has finished playback, other ad elements must respond accordingly. The variables mentioned earlier in this list, `bufferEmpty` and `stopDetected`, are used in this function.

▶ Define a function named `onAdClick` to handle any mouse click on the ad. This function should open a browser window with the ad's destination (or click-through) URL.

▶ Define a function named `onVideoDone` to execute actions that occur with other ad elements when playback of the video has finished. This function should direct the `vidAnim` instance to play its exit frame, the `endText` instance to fade up, and the `captionField` instance to hide itself.

All this functionality has already been created in the VideoAd_ NoCaptions_AS2.as file provided in the ch10 folder on the DVD-ROM. The contents of this script are shown in the following code block. Note that the ➡ character indicates a continuation of the same line of code.

```
// Import the Delegate class to enable easier event
➡handling
import mx.utils.Delegate;

// Create a variable to remember if the
// video stream has initiated playback
var firstPlayEvent:Boolean = false;      (Continues on next page)
```

```
// Create a variable to remember if the
// video stream has stopped playing
var stopDetected:Boolean = false;
// Create a variable to track the
// buffer status of the video stream
var bufferEmpty:Boolean = true;

// Create a reference to the MovieClip instance
// containing the text animation to appear when
// the video completes playback
var endText:MovieClip;
// Create a reference to the Video instance on the stage
// which is nested inside of two MovieClip instances
var vid:Video = vidAnim.holder.vid;
// Create a reference to the background fill area
var bgFill:MovieClip;

// Create a variable for the NetConnection instance
var conn:NetConnection;
// Create a variable for the NetStream instance
var stream:NetStream;

// Create a stream URL variable
// If a value is passed via HTML parameters, use that
➥value.
// Otherwise, use a default value.
var streamURL:String = (_root.streamName !=
➥undefined) ? _root.streamName : "../flv/sunbeam_SQZ_
➥Spark_112K_VBR.flv";
// Create a click URL variable
// If a value is passed via HTML parameters, use that
➥value.
// Otherwise, use a default value.
var clickURL:String = (_root.clickPath != undefined)
➥? _root.clickPath : "http://www.flashsupport.com";

//Start the movie
init();
// Create a function to start the movie
function init():Void {

    // Create a function to handle mouse clicks on
    ➥the ad
    bgFill.onRelease = Delegate.create(this,
    ➥onAdClick);
```

```
// Create a new NetConnection instance
conn = new NetConnection();

// If the stream is served from a Flash Media Server
if(streamURL.toLowerCase().substr(0, 5) == "rtmp:"){
   // Parse the server application URL from the
   ➥stream path
   var connectURL:String = streamURL.substring(0,
   ➥streamURL.lastIndexOf("/"));
   // Retrieve the FLV file name from the stream
   ➥path
   ➥streamURL = streamURL.substr(streamURL
   ➥lastIndexOf("/") + 1);
   // If the stream name specifies the .flv
   ➥extension
   if(streamURL.substr(-4) == ".flv"){
      // Remove the .flv extension and reset the
      ➥streamURL value
      streamURL = streamPath.substr(0, -4);
   }
// Otherwise, the stream is hosted on a web server
} else {
   // Connect to a null value
   var connectURL:String = null;
}

// Connect to the appropriate delivery format
conn.connect(connectURL);

// Create a new NetStream instance with the
➥NetConnection instance
stream = new NetStream(conn);
// Pass the stream's status events to a function
➥named onStreamStatus
stream.onStatus = Delegate.create(this,
➥onStreamStatus);

// Turn on video smoothing for scaled video sizes
vid.smoothing = true;

// Attach the NetStream instance to the Video
➥instance
vid.attachVideo(stream);
```
(Continues on next page)

```
            // Load the video into the NetStream instance
            stream.play(streamURL);
         }

         // When an event occurs with the NetStream instance
         function onStreamStatus(e:Object):Void {
            //trace("onStreamStatus > " + e.code);
            // If a stop event has occurred
            if(e.code == "NetStream.Play.Stop"){
               // Track the stop with a variable
               stopDetected = true;
            // Otherwise, if a play event has occurred
            } else if (e.code == "NetStream.Play.Start"){
               // If this is the first play event
               if(!firstPlayEvent){
                  // Track the first play with a variable
                  firstPlayEvent = true;
                  // Invoke a function to handle operations
                  ➡that should
                  // only occur when the video has started
                  ➡playing
                  onVideoStart();
               }
               // Reset the stop detection variable
               stopDetected = false;
            // Otherwise, if the video's buffer has emptied
            } else if (e.code == "NetStream.Buffer.Empty"){
               // Reset the buffer variable
               bufferEmpty = true;
            // Otherwise, if the video's buffer is full
            } else if ( e.code == "NetStream.Buffer.Full"){
               // Set the bufferEmpty variable to false
               bufferEmpty = false;
            }

            // If the buffer is empty and the video has
            ➡finished playing
            if(bufferEmpty && stopDetected){
               // Invoke a function to handle operations that
               ➡should
               // only occur if the video has finished playing
               onVideoDone();
```

```
    }
}

// When the user has clicked the ad
function onAdClick():Void {
    // Create a new browser window and
    // navigate to the destination URL
    getURL(clickURL, "_blank");
}

// When the video has finished playback
function onVideoDone():Void {
    // Animate the video off the stage
    vidAnim.gotoAndPlay("exit");
    // Play the end text animation
    endText.play();
    // Hide the caption field
    captionField._visible = false;
}
```

To enable video playback within the banner ad:

1. In a preferred location on your computer, create a folder named video_ad. In this folder, create four folders with the following names: classes, data, flv, and swf.

2. Copy the sunbeam_SQZ_Spark_112K_VBR.flv file from the flv folder on the DVD-ROM to your new flv folder.

3. Copy the AS2 folder from the classes folder on the DVD-ROM to your new classes folder.

4. Copy the VideoAd_AS2_starter.fla and VideoAd_NoCaptions_AS2.as files from the ch10 folder also on the DVD-ROM to your new swf folder.

5. Open the VideoAd_AS2_starter.fla file in Flash CS3. Resave this document as VideoAd_NoCaptions_AS2.fla in the new swf folder you created in step 1.

6. Choose File > Publish Settings, and select the Flash tab. Click the Settings button next to the ActionScript version menu. In the ActionScript 2.0 Settings dialog, click the + button in the Classpath area of the dialog, and type ../classes/AS2/. in the new text field in the list,

as shown in **Figure 10.3**. The Classpath tells Flash CS3 where it can find ActionScript classes to import into your own Flash files, such as the custom `Captions` class used in the next section. Click OK to close the dialog.

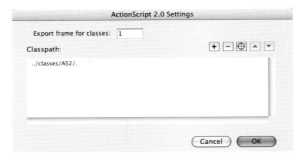

Figure 10.3 The ActionScript 2.0 Settings dialog.

7. Now, you're ready to implement the script discussed at the beginning of this section. Select frame 13 of the actions layer, and open the Actions panel (F9, or Option+F9 on Mac). Above the existing `stop()`; action, add the following line of code. The `#include` directive enables Flash CS3 to insert the contents of an Action-Script file into the current location:

```
#include "VideoAd_NoCaptions_AS2.as"
```

8. Save the Flash file, and test the movie (Ctrl/Cmd+Enter). When the Flash movie finishes the introductory animation, the video clip plays, as shown in **Figure 10.4**.

Adding captions to the ad

Captioning, or the display of transcribed text below or over the video image, is a useful feature for many Flash Video projects. Captions can serve as an accessibility option, enabling hearing-impaired users an alternative route to understand the content. For the banner ad example, captions can serve as a visual stimulus to catch the user's attention, especially if the user has turned down the computer's speaker (or headphone) volume.

Captions can be created in a number of ways. In this chapter, you employ two different XML schemas for captioned text: Captionate's schema and the W3C Timed Text schema.

Figure 10.4 The Flash banner ad displayed without captions.

In this section, you'll use the XML schema created by Captionate, a standalone third-party tool made specifically for building captions in Flash Video. If you don't want to use Captionate or another third-party solution, you can build your own XML schema and custom ActionScript code to implement caption loading, timing, and display. During the Flash Video encoding process, you can also create embedded cue points that contain captioned text.

Reviewing Captionate's XML schema

Captionate can create an XML version of caption text you've entered into the application to synchronize with a Flash Video's timing. Look at the sample XML document, bread_commercial.xml, in the data folder on the DVD-ROM. The following code block shows a snippet of the `<captions>` and `<caption>` nodes. Note that Captionate does not use tab indents in the XML data. Tabs have been added to this code block to make the information more readable:

```
<captions>
    <caption time="0">
        <speaker>0</speaker>
        <tracks>
            <track0>Hey young fella, that takes
            ➥ energy!</track0>
        </tracks>
    </caption>
    <caption time="3343">
        <speaker>0</speaker>
        <tracks>
            <track0>Better make sure you replace it.</
            ➥ track0>
        </tracks>
    </caption>
```

The nodes at the start of the XML document (not shown in the previous code block) provide additional information about the speakers, target words-per-minute, and more that can be used in the caption text and ActionScript for more advanced usage. For this banner ad example, only the `<caption>` node's `time` attribute and `<track0>` node value are implemented.

NOTES

► In Appendix C, you can find more information about Captionate's features. In Chapter 12, "Delivering a Comprehensive Video Experience," you learn how to build a hybrid embedded cue point and external XML file to display captioned text.

TIP

► You can download a trial version of Captionate from www.captionate.com. Links related to Captionate and its use can also be found at www.flashsupport.com/links.

Implementing the custom Captions class

In order to use the Captionate XML data, the captions file must be loaded at runtime into the Flash banner ad, parsed into native ActionScript objects, and set to synchronize with the timing of the Flash Video's playback. Captionate's documentation includes sample ActionScript code to help you get started. Using Captionate's example scripts as a starting point, I've created a custom Captions class (com.flashsupport.video.Captions) to simplify the task of using Captionate's XML data with Flash Video content. You'll find this class in the classes folder you created in the last section. While I won't dissect the code for the Captions class, you do learn how to implement the class with the banner ad.

In Flash Pro 8 or Flash CS3, open the VideoAd_AS2.as file from the ch10 folder on the DVD-ROM. Most of the code in this script is identical to the VideoAd_NoCaptions_AS2.as script shown in the last section, with the following additions:

▶ **New imported class:** The custom Captions class is imported on line 4. This class enables the loading of a Captionate XML file, as well as event dispatching for timed captions.

▶ **New variables:** Two variables, singlelineX (line 17) and multilineX (line 20), are declared to set the X coordinate for the captionField instance, based on the height of the caption text. These variables are used in the onCaptionDisplay function (line 178). The captionField instance is also declared on line 33, a captions variable to store new caption data on line 40, and a captionsURL variable on line 53 to reference the path to the XML file for the captions.

▶ **Updated init function:** The init function now creates a new instance of the Captions class (line 99), passes the captions XML file URL to the instance (line 101), assigns a listener function named onCaptionDisplay to receive timed captions events (line 103), assigns a listener function named onCaptionLoad to notify the movie when the captions XML file has loaded (line 105), and initiates the loading of the XML file (line 107). The stream.play(streamURL); line of code is also moved from the init function to the onCaptionLoad function (line 174).

▶ **Updated** `onVideoDone` **function:** On line 161, the `captionsField` instance is hidden, so that the last caption's text does not continue to display in the banner while the `endTextAnim` instance's text fades onto the stage.

▶ **New** `onVideoStart` **function:** Between lines 165 and 168, a function named `onVideoStart` is defined. This function is invoked by the `onStreamStatus` function when the video stream receives the first `NetStream.Play.Start` event. The `onVideoStart` function tells the `captions` instance to start timing caption text to the video (line 167).

▶ **New** `onCaptionLoad` **function:** As discussed earlier in this list, the `onCaptionLoad` function (lines 171-175) is designated as a listener for the `dataLoaded` event broadcast by the `captions` instance. When the captions data has loaded, the Flash Video file begins loading into the banner.

▶ **New** `onCaptionDisplay` **function:** This function, defined between lines 178 and 209, is designated as the listener function for the `update` event broadcast by the `captions` instance (line 103). Whenever a new caption's time matches the time of the `stream` instance, this function is invoked. The event object, specified by the argument named e, has a `text` value specifying the caption text. After the caption text is assigned to the `captionField` instance (line 185), the height of the text is measured to determine the X coordinate of the `captionField` instance.

To enable captions in the banner ad:

1. Open the VideoAd_NoCaptions_AS2.fla file you created in the last section. If you haven't built this file, make sure you performed steps 1 through 6 described in the last section as well.

2. Copy the bread_commercial.xml file from the data folder on the DVD-ROM to the data folder in your local video_ad folder.

3. Copy the VideoAd_AS2.as file from the ch10 folder on the DVD-ROM to your swf folder.

4. Resave the VideoAd_NoCaptions_AS2.fla file as `VideoAd_AS2.fla` in the swf folder.

Figure 10.5 The Flash banner ad displaying caption text.

NOTES

▶ You'll find the completed files for the banner ad in the ch10 folder on the DVD-ROM. You can also review the VideoAd_AS2.html file for the banner. This document uses the SWFObject JavaScript library, as discussed in Chapter 5, "Placing Flash Video on a Web Page," to pass custom FLV and XML file paths to the banner ad. The HTML document uses a real-time streaming video served from this book's Influxis.com account.

5. Now you're ready to implement the updated script. Select frame 13 of the actions layer, and open the Actions panel (F9, or Option+F9 on Mac). Replace the existing `#include` action with the following action. The `#include` directive enables Flash CS3 to insert the contents of an ActionScript file into the current location:

```
#include "VideoAd_AS2.as"
```

6. Save the Flash file, and test the movie (Ctrl/Cmd+Enter). When the Flash movie finishes the introductory animation, the video clip begins, and the captions display below the video area, as shown in **Figure 10.5**.

Controlling Captions with Timed Text XML

Flash CS3 provides you with a quick method of adding captions to video, if you're using ActionScript 3.0 and Flash Player 9. The new FLVPlaybackCaptioning component synchronizes captions with video playback. While you can use this component with your own custom video playback mechanisms, the FLVPlaybackCaptioning component has been designed to work in tandem with the ActionScript 3.0 version of the FLVPlayback component.

The FLVPlaybackCaptioning component can load a Timed Text XML file or read embedded cue points from your FLV file to display caption text for your video file. With or without the FLVPlayback component, you can also create your own TextField instance to control the look and feel of your captions.

In this section, you learn how to implement a Timed Text XML file with the FLVPlayback and FLVPlaybackCaptioning components to transcribe the audio track of newsreel footage depicting John F. Kennedy's inauguration as the 35th President of the United States, as shown in **Figure 10.6**.

Understanding the Timed Text schema

The FLVPlaybackCaptioning component can recognize most of the features described in the W3C's Timed Text format. The Timed Text (TT) format is an attempt to build a universal captioning schema for multimedia files. You can learn more about the Timed Text specification on these Web pages:

http://www.w3.org/AudioVideo/timetext.html

http://www.w3.org/TR/ttaf1-dfxp/

I provided a sample timed text file for this section's example. With a Web browser or your preferred XML editor, such as Adobe Dreamweaver CS3, open the jfk_inauguration.xml file from the data folder of this book's DVD-ROM. There are two primary sections to a TT XML file for use with the FLVPlaybackCaptioning component: the <styling> and <div> nodes. The component supports only one instance of each node. All other nodes will be ignored.

The <styling> node allows you to specify the text-formatting styles you want for the captions. The <styling> node is specified within the <head> tag of the document. The sample XML file uses the following styles. Note that the <style> tags use only one line of code in the actual XML file.

```
<styling>
    <style id="s1" tts:color="white" tts:
➥ fontFamily="sansSerif" tts:fontSize="12px" tts:
➥ textAlign="center" />
    <style id="s2" style="s1" tts:fontStyle="italic" />
</styling>
```

The first style, named s1, uses a white colored _sans device font, at 12 pixels, with center alignment. The s2 style is based on the s1 style but uses an italic style. The default style is not defined in the <styling> tags. Rather, it is defined in the <div> tag, discussed next.

The <div> node enumerates each caption as a separate <p> tag. The sample XML file starts with these captions:

```
<div xml:lang="en" style="s1">
    <p begin="00:00:01.00" dur="00:00:03.00"
➥ style="s2">[Music plays]</p>
    <p begin="00:00:05.00" dur="00:00:02.00">John F.
➥ Kennedy settles into office</p>
    <p begin="00:00:07.00" dur="00:00:02.50">as the
➥ 35th President of the United States,</p>
```

Figure 10.6 The FLVPlayback component displaying caption text.

▶ The video sample used in this section is a public-domain clip from the Prelinger Archive at www.archive.org. You can find more information about this site in Appendix A.

▶ You'll find a list of the tags and attributes of the Timed Text format supported by the FLV-PlaybackCaptioning component in the Flash CS3 Help panel. Search the help contents with the keywords timed text tags.

NOTES

▶ If you transcribe your own caption text, make sure you plan enough time to go through the video. For this example, I spent about an hour and sometimes two hours for *each minute* of transcribed video, testing and retesting the begin and dur values for each caption. Experienced transcribers will require less time to produce captions for video. Refer to Appendix C for more information about caption tools.

The <div> tag assigns a default style to each caption, using the style attribute. For this example, the s1 style is the default style. The first caption, however, uses the s2 style. Any caption that indicates an action within the video, or that is not in the narrator's voice, is displayed in italics, which is simply a convention used for this example. Each caption's <p> tag should specify a begin value, which indicates when the caption appears during video playback. The second value, dur, indicates the duration of the caption display. With this sample video, captions immediately follow one another. If you add the dur value to the begin value, you'll have the begin value for the next caption. The time values use a standard time-code format, hh:mm:ss.ss, where hh represents the hour, mm the minute, and ss.ss the second.

Integrating the FLVPlaybackCaptioning component

1. Create a folder named video_captions in a preferred location on your system. In this folder, create three folders with the following names: data, flv, and swf.

2. Copy the 1961-01-23_Inauguration_SQZ_VP6_512K_VBR.flv file from the flv folder on the DVD-ROM to your new flv folder.

3. Copy the jfk_inauguration.xml file from the data folder on the DVD-ROM to your new data folder.

4. In Flash CS3, create a new Flash file (ActionScript 3.0). Save this file as VideoCaptions_AS3.fla in the swf folder you created in step 1.

5. Rename Layer 1 to flvPlayer.

6. Open the Components panel (Ctrl/Cmd+F7), and expand the Video grouping. Drag the FLVPlayback component to the center of the stage.

7. Select the new instance on the stage, and open the Property inspector. Name the instance flvPlayer.

8. With the instance selected, click the Parameters tab of the Property inspector. Double-click the source value, and in the Content Path dialog, type the path to the FLV file you copied in step 2, as shown in **Figure 10.7**. Click OK to close the dialog.

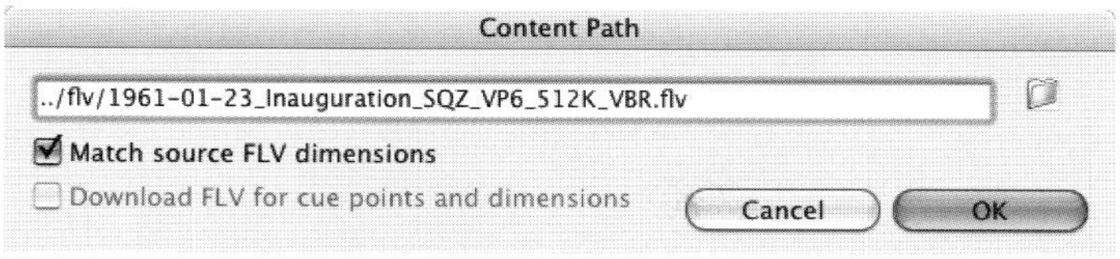

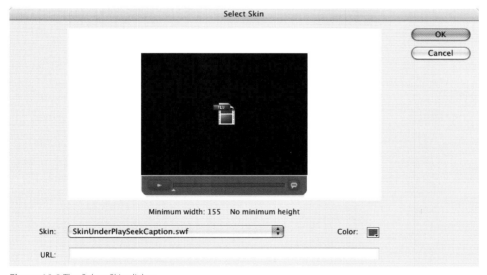

Figure 10.7 The Content Path dialog.

9. Double-click the skin value in the Parameters tab. In the Select Skin dialog, choose the SkinUnderPlaySeekCaption. swf skin, as shown in **Figure 10.8**. This skin features a caption toggle button, which works in tandem with the FLVPlaybackCaptioning component. Choose your preferred skin color as well. Whenever you're building a captioning system, I recommend using a skin that does not overlay the caption text. By default, the FLVPlaybackCaptioning component creates captions 40 pixels above the bottom border of the FLVPlayback component. Click OK to close the dialog.

Figure 10.8 The Select Skin dialog.

10. Now that you've created a player, you're ready to add the captioning component. Create a new layer named flvCaptions.

▶ You'll find the completed file, VideoCaptions_AS3.fla, in the ch10 folder on the DVD-ROM. Another example, Video-CaptionsOptimized_AS3.fla, uses a document class to instantiate the component instances. This optimized example also uses a custom skin SWF file, SkinUnderCaptions.swf. The document class file, VideoCaptionsOptimized.as, demonstrates how you can automatically turn on captioning whenever the user mutes the volume or sets the volume to 0.

11. From the Video grouping in the Components panel, drag an instance of the FLVPlaybackCaptioning component to the stage. While the component has an icon representation in the authoring environment, you won't see the component's icon in the final Flash movie. Place the instance off the right edge of the stage.

12. Name the FLVPlaybackCaptioning instance `flvCaptions` in the Property inspector.

13. With the new instance selected, click the Parameters tab of the Property inspector, and type `../data/jfk_inauguration.xml` for the source value. This path points to the XML file you copied in step 3. Leave the other parameters at their default values. (Note that the `auto` value for the `flvplayback` parameter enables the FLVPlaybackCaptioning component to automatically locate the instance of the FLVPlayback component.)

14. Save the Flash file, and test the movie (Ctrl/Cmd+Enter). As the Flash Video plays, the styled caption text displays above the skin controls, as shown in **Figure 10.9**.

Figure 10.9 The FLVPlaybackCaptioning component at work.

11

Constructing an Interactive Video Host

When Flash Player 8 added the On2 VP6 codec, Flash Video was enhanced by the ability to add transparency to the video image. This transparent area, called an *alpha matte* or *alpha channel*, can see through to underlying Flash elements, including Flash text, graphics, or another Flash Video clip.

Alpha channels for video can be created in a number of ways. If you're outputting a video sequence from a 3D modeling application, you can retain transparency for the background area behind a 3D object in the export settings. If you want to add an alpha channel to live-action video footage (that is, video depicting actors or subjects), you can shoot your subject on a chroma-key background, such as a green or blue screen. **Figure 11.1** shows a still frame of an actor (me!) against a green screen.

Once you've acquired the video footage, you can remove the chroma-key background in a tool such as Adobe After Effects or Serious Magic Ultra 2 (now owned by Adobe), and export a QuickTime movie with an alpha channel. After you've created the QuickTime file, you can process the footage in Adobe Flash CS3 Video Encoder or your preferred Flash Video encoder, retaining the alpha channel with the On2 VP6 codec.

In this chapter, you learn how to build a Flash movie featuring a video host that speaks words under the direction of the user. Visit the following URL to test the movie:

http://www.flashsupport.com/books/fvst/ch11/VideoWords_AS3.html

You can also load this file from the ch11 folder of this book's DVD-ROM. If you drag words to the input text area (or you can double-click each word for faster access) as

Figure 11.1 An actor in front of a green screen.

On the DVD-ROM

▶ You can find all of the source files for this chapter's exercises in the ch11 folder of this book's DVD-ROM. The ch11.flp file is a Flash Project file that you can open in Flash CS3 to view all of the sample files related to topics discussed in this chapter.

Caution

▶ All of the sample progressive-download URLs used in this chapter contain relative paths (../flv) to the FLV files that reside in the flv folder of this book's DVD-ROM. Depending on how you structure your local system folders and files, you may need to adjust these sample paths to point to FLV files that reside on your system.

shown in **Figure 11.2**, you can click the Play button to watch the video host speak the words. Notice that the words appear behind the actor until you roll over the video area. This presentation is referred to as "VideoWords" throughout this chapter.

Figure 11.2 The completed example.

Planning the User Interface

The user interface for the VideoWords example requires several elements to work cooperatively with one another. In this section, you learn about the requirements and objectives of the project.

Understanding the business objectives

The goal of the VideoWords example is to provide a fun activity for the user, and to create messages that can be played back for amusement. While the vocabulary of this particular implementation is generalized, the actor's script could be retooled to promote a product or service. The wardrobe of the actor could change with each word, or another background image (or video) could be inserted behind the words and the video. For example, for a Web site that books tropical vacations, the VideoWords content could feature words and actions related to the beach, such as "surfing," "tanning," "relaxing," and "cocktail."

Future iterations of the project should allow a new Flash Video asset to be inserted into the VideoWords user interface. Other enhancements, such as full-screen capability, emailing a friend with a custom video message, and localization (that is, customizing assets to foreign languages) should not require rewriting the initial code base. The project should also be able to work within a Flash application that uses the Adobe Flex™ framework, a development and deployment for state-of-the-art rich Internet applications (RIAs) on the Web.

Reviewing the technical requirements

For this project, the Flash content (SWF file) needs to adhere to the following guidelines:

▶ **ActionScript 3.0 code base:** To allow easier maintenance and compatibility with other ActionScript 3.0 content, such as a Flex application, all of the ActionScript code should be written in ActionScript 3.0.

▶ **Flash Player 9 compatibility:** The Flash movie uses ActionScript 3.0 code, which requires Flash Player 9.

▶ **Modest file size:** The primary Flash movie (SWF file) should load quickly over most broadband connections, 384 Kbps or higher. This size does not include the Flash Video (FLV) file.

▶ **High-quality video:** The video asset should exhibit a high-quality image, retaining the sharpness of the original source video. The voice track should not sound compressed—the tonal range of the source video should be kept intact.

▶ **On2 VP6 codec:** Because the Flash Video content requires transparency, the Flash Video file must use the On2 VP6 codec.

▶ **Embedded cue points:** Each spoken word in the Flash Video (FLV) file should be marked with cue points. The start time of each word should be marked by a navigation cue point, and the end time of each word should be marked by an event cue point. The navigation cue point should contain a parameter specifying the text of the spoken word. This text value will be retrieved with ActionScript and used to build the word collection behind the video of the actor.

▶ **Progressive download delivery:** The video asset should be able to seek quickly from one spoken word to the next. In order to achieve this effect, the entire Flash Video (FLV) file should download in its entirety before the user can engage the user interface.

Surveying the production requirements

The VideoWords project requires several production phases for completion, from video acquisition to ActionScript 3.0 code to HTML/JavaScript code. The amount of time required to complete each phase largely depends on the complexity of the actor's script and the number of words to display in the user interface. I undertook seven phases of production for this project:

▶ These phases represent an overview of the production cycle as implemented for this chapter's example, and are not absolute. You may want to add more phases to the cycle, such as a QA (Quality Assurance) period in which a test team thoroughly runs the content across a range of browsers and operating systems.

▶ **Scriptwriting:** You need to draft the words that will be spoken by the actor and displayed in the user interface. Each word adds to the length (and size) of the Flash Video (FLV) file.

▶ **Video production:** The live-action video requires a location suitable for chroma-key lighting, such as a well-lit sound stage or diffuse natural light outdoors. The crew should consist of an actor (or actors), camera operators, and sound technicians.

▶ **Video capture and editing:** After the video production has wrapped, post-production begins. The footage needs to be captured to a computer for video editing in a tool such as Adobe Premiere Pro CS3 or Apple Final Cut Pro. Depending on the quality of the acting, creating a sequence of separated words may take considerable time. When editing has finished, a new video file needs to be created from the edited original capture files.

▶ **Video effects generation:** The edited video footage is then processed in a video-effects tool capable of removing a chroma-key background. A wide range of software and hardware can remove the background, such as Adobe Premiere Pro, Adobe After Effects, Serious Magic Ultra 2, or Apple Motion. The tool should be able to produce a new QuickTime video file using the Animation codec with RGB and alpha channel support.

▶ **Flash Video encoding:** The alpha-enabled QuickTime video file is imported into a Flash Video encoding tool capable of outputting FLV files with the On2 VP6 codec and an alpha channel. The tool must be able to insert Flash Video cue points into the final file.

▶ **ActionScript code development:** At any point during the prior phases, the ActionScript code for the project can be written. The code needs to be able to load the FLV file and build the user interface for the VideoWords project.

▶ **HTML/JavaScript development:** The client-side HTML and JavaScript code can also be written at any point during the production cycle. This code needs to feature Flash Player version detection for Flash Player 9 r28 (or 9.0.28 in SWFObject parlance). The Flash movie should fill the entire area of the browser window without scaling the Flash assets. The movie should be centered in this area.

Producing the Video Footage

In this section, you learn how I created the video footage used in the VideoWords project. In the first part, I describe how the location was set up for the video shoot. In the second part, I provide an overview of the video-editing process in Apple Final Cut Pro. In the third part, I walk you through the steps to remove the chroma-key background in Adobe After Effects CS3.

NOTES

On the DVD-ROM

▶ You can find the source files for the After Effects project in the ch11 folder of this book's DVD-ROM.

Shooting the video

One of my intentions for producing the VideoWords example was to demonstrate that—by yourself—you can create a compelling interactive video experience. All you need is some equipment and a script! During an overcast spring day in Portland, Oregon, I shot the footage in my backyard, minimizing transportation time and location scouting.

> ▶ You don't have to purchase your own video and audio equipment. In most cities, you can rent equipment at reasonable prices. If you can spend time working on the weekend, you might even find discount weekend rates.

> ▶ If I had shot the footage with an assistant, I would have used a boom pole and a shotgun microphone, such as the Rode NTG-2 (under $300). You can purchase a boom pole for under $100. An assistant can hold the boom pole and microphone over the actor's head, keeping the mic and its shadow out of the video frame.

Reviewing the equipment and costs

The VideoWords footage was shot with prosumer video and audio equipment. The term *prosumer* describes equipment that is a blend of professional and consumer features, indicating a price range from $2,000 to $10,000. The term can also imply that, in today's market, it's possible to buy professional quality equipment at near-consumer prices.

Here's a summary of the equipment I used during video production. Refer to **Table 11.1** for a cost comparison between typical purchase and rental prices:

▶ **Video equipment:** The video was shot with a Sony HDR-A1U—an HDV camcorder. (For more information on the HDV format, refer to Chapters 2 and 3.) This camera can be purchased online at an estimated cost of $2,500. The camera features XLR audio inputs (discussed in the next bullet). The camera can also record High Definition (HD) or Standard Definition (SD) video. I used HD mode for this production. The camera was attached to a Slik Professional tripod—a heavy-duty tripod priced around $300.

▶ **Audio equipment:** I used a Shure UP4 portable UHF wireless receiver, connected to one of the XLR inputs on the Sony camera. I clipped a lavalier microphone to my shirt. The microphone was attached to a wireless transmitter clipped to my belt. The wireless receiver and transmitter sell as a kit for an average street price of $1,500.

▶ **Chroma-key background:** You can create a chroma-key background color behind a video subject in many ways. A simple technique is to paint a wall with Rosco video paint, which costs under $75 for a gallon bucket. An even cheaper alternative is to shoot your subject in front of a brightly lit white wall—you can attempt to create a chroma key with just about any color. For this project, I used a 6' × 9' Lastolite collapsible green screen, which costs approximately $300. I prefer a collapsible screen because the fabric is stretched tightly across its frame and does not need to be ironed or steamed for wrinkles. The screen was attached to two portable stands, which cost about $180. Because I shot the footage outdoors and the day was intermittently windy, the stands were weighted down with sandbags designed to keep them from tipping over.

▶ **Lighting equipment:** Natural outdoor light was the only light source used for this footage. Natural light refers to existing light available without additional equipment.

▶ **Miscellaneous equipment:** I used an inexpensive microphone stand (about $20) to hold a printed version of the script near the camera's lens. The script was printed at a large type size so that I could read the text during shooting. I kept two miniDV tapes on hand: one for recording, and another for backup. For makeup, I applied a light cosmetic powder to my face to reduce sheen on my forehead, nose, and cheeks.

TABLE 11.1 VideoWords Production Equipment Costs (US Dollars)

Item	Average street price	Average rental cost per day
Sony HDR-A1U camera	$2,500	$120
Heavy-duty tripod	$300	$10
Shure UP4 UHF kit	$1,500	$90
Lastolite 6′ x 9′ screen	$300	$40
Stands	$200	$20
MiniDV tapes	$15	Non-rental item
Total	$4,515	$295

Rolling the tape

Because I shot the footage without any assistants, I created a plan to shoot several takes in a row, repeating every word in the script until I had a good consistent take all the way through. Several takes were ruined by ambient noise created by overhead planes, crows fighting in a nearby tree, and my dog chasing squirrels along the fence.

Each take consisted of me reading aloud each word in the script, with a slight pause between each word. With forty-eight words in the script, I didn't want to spend hours in post-production removing long gaps between each word.

NOTES

▶ If I had an assistant on the shoot, I would have opted to use a bounce card or small fill light on my face, to remove the deep shadows below my eyebrow. A bounce card can be a simple piece of white foamboard or posterboard, held at an angle to bounce more existing light onto the subject. Bounce cards usually need to be held fairly close to the subject matter and remain out of the video frame.

In addition to bounce cards, I typically use my Lowel DV Creator 55 kit (approximately $1,500) to provide more fill light, properly adding filters (or gels) to the lights to accommodate the color temperature of the prevailing existing light sources. If the chroma-key background needs to be lit, you should properly balance the intensity across the entire background. Refer to the book's link page at www.flashsupport.com/links for an article on green screen lighting.

The best take had only one visual glitch—the wind had blown the script page corner in front of the lens, and I had to repeat one of the words. In post-production, I spliced the beginning of the next good take to the end of the last word's take.

After I shot the footage of the spoken words, I chose to tape some footage of my eyes wandering across the sky and my body shifting back and forth. This footage would be used for the waiting loop that plays while the user selects words. Unfortunately, the movements were overemphasized and difficult to use for a seamless repeating loop—you can see a frame shift between the end and beginning of the loop. If you're planning your own shoot for a customized loop, try to minimize movement, or try to create cuts from one position to another. Shoot a variety of poses to expand the potential of a more seamless loop during editing.

Editing the video

Immediately after shooting the footage, I watched it back on a video monitor. It's always a good idea to review as much footage as time allows between takes or before you strike (or take down) the set.

In Apple Final Cut Pro, I captured the best take of a consecutive spoken word sequence. I divided the take (named "Master" in **Figure 11.3**) into three clips:

- ▶ **part_i:** The first portion of spoken words before the visual glitch described in the prior section.
- ▶ **part_ii:** The second portion of spoken words after the visual glitch.
- ▶ **wandering:** The footage to be used as a waiting loop.

The clips were put into a sequence named Sequence 1 and exported as a new HD MPEG-2 clip. Because the editing involved only straight cuts (no effects were applied to the footage in Final Cut Pro), the exported MPEG-2 file did not suffer from any generation loss, or loss of audio/visual quality as a result of transcoding or re-exporting of footage.

On the DVD-ROM

▶ You can find the words used for the script in the VideoWords_script.doc located in the ch11 folder of this book's DVD-ROM.

On the DVD-ROM

▶ You can find the edited file, VideoWords_edit.mov, in the source/hdv folder of the DVD-ROM. Depending on your operating system and installed codecs, you may need to use MPEG Streamclip to create a playable version on your computer. For more information on this process, refer to Appendix C, "Encoding Flash Video."

Figure 11.3 The clips assembled in Final Cut Pro.

Processing the footage in After Effects

After an edited sequence has been created, you're ready to remove the green screen (chroma-key) background area from the footage. As mentioned earlier in this chapter, a wide range of tools can accomplish this task. In this section, you learn how to use Adobe After Effects CS3 and the Keylight 1.2 filter to remove the green screen area and create an alpha channel.

1. Create a folder named VideoWords on your computer to store the project assets.

2. If you're on a Mac with Apple Final Cut Pro 5 or higher installed, copy the VideoWords_edit.mov file from the source/HDV folder on the DVD-ROM to the new folder. If you're on a Mac without Apple Final Cut Pro or on a Windows computer, copy the VideoWords_edit.mp4 file from the source/HDV folder to the new folder.

3. Open Adobe Flash CS3, and choose File > Save As to save a project file named VideoWords_CS3.aep. Save the file in the folder you created in step 1.

NOTES

▶ If you'd prefer to jump straight into the Flash Video encoding tasks for the VideoWords project, you can skip this section and use the VideoWords_alpha_360x240.mov file located in the source/alpha folder on the DVD-ROM.

Also, you can use earlier versions of Adobe After Effects and the Keylight filter to accomplish the same tasks outlined in this section. Some of the Keylight properties have different names depending on the version of the plug-in.

NOTES

► The VideoWords_edit.mov file uses the Apple HDV codec, which is only available on a Mac with Apple Final Cut Pro installed. The VideoWords_edit.mp4 is a transcoded MPEG-4 version of the Apple HDV version. The MPEG-4 version has slightly reduced video quality as a result of the transcoding. During playback of the MPEG-4 version you may experience audio sync drift, where the audio track is not exactly matching the timing of the video track. This sync issue will not affect the final FLV output.

► If you're using the VideoWords_edit.mp4 file, change the Pixel Aspect Ratio option to Square Pixels in the Interpret Footage dialog.

4. Choose File > Import > File (Ctrl/Cmd+I), and browse to the folder you created in step 1. Select the file you copied in step 2. Click Open (Windows) or OK (Mac).

5. As you learned in Chapter 2, After Effects can deinterlace footage better than Flash Video encoders can. Because the source video is interlaced, right-click (or Control+click on Mac) the VideoWords_edit file in the Project panel, and choose Interpret Footage > Main. In the Interpret Footage dialog, make sure that the Separate Fields menu is set to Upper Field First. Select the Preserve Edges (Best Quality Only) option, as shown in **Figure 11.4**. Click OK.

Figure 11.4 The Preserve Edges option deinterlaces the footage file.

6. If the Timeline window is not open, choose Window > Timeline. Drag the VideoWords_edit file to the Timeline window. After Effects automatically creates a new composition based on the source footage settings, including frame size and duration. You can find the new composition, named after the footage file, in the Project panel.

7. Rename the new composition by selecting the composition item in the Project panel and pressing the Enter (or Return) key. Rename the composition HDV comp.

TIP

► A composition is also known as a comp in After Effects.

8. Click the Composition window, and choose View > View Options. In this dialog, you can make sure the Composition window properly displays the pixel aspect ratio of the footage file. In the Window area of the dialog, select the Pixel Aspect Ratio Correction option, as shown in **Figure 11.5**, and click OK.

The Timeline window, Composition window, and Project panel should now resemble **Figure 11.6**.

▶ The View Options modification affects only projects that use the VideoWords_edit.mov file, which uses a nonsquare pixel aspect ratio.

Figure 11.5 The View Options dialog.

Figure 11.6 The HD footage file (VideoWords_edit.mp4 version) added to the HDV comp.

NOTES

▶ Adobe After Effects 7 and earlier had different versions of the Keylight filter, 1.1 or 1.0. These versions of the filter can accomplish the same tasks with the VideoWords example.

9. Double-click the HDV comp in the Project panel to make sure this comp is active in the Timeline panel. In the Timeline panel, select the VideoWords_edit.mov (or VideoWords_edit.mp4) layer, and choose Effect > Keying > Keylight (1.2). The Effect Controls panel should now be active as a tab next to the Project panel tab. The Keylight filter settings should also be displayed in the Effect Controls panel, as shown in **Figure 11.7**. The Keylight filter is a professional keying filter that enables you to remove chroma-key backgrounds.

Figure 11.7 The Keylight filter settings in the Effect Controls panel.

10. The first step with the Keylight filter is to sample a green color from the VideoWords footage. Click the Eyedropper tool next to the Screen Colour option in the filter settings. Move the mouse cursor to a green area near the subject, as shown in **Figure 11.8**, and click with the eyedropper. The background area behind the actor changes to black, as shown in **Figure 11.9**. Alternatively, you can click the color chip next to the Screen Colour option, and enter the hex value, 2D7E3B.

Figure 11.8 The Eyedropper tool preparing to sample a green color in the video image.

Figure 11.9 The background color behind the actor has been removed.

11. To view the transparency grid instead of a background fill color, click the transparency grid icon in the settings area below the video image in the Composition window. Alternatively, click the options menu at the top-right corner of the Composition window, and then choose

269

Transparency Grid. The black background color changes to a transparency grid, as shown in **Figure 11.10**.

Figure 11.10 The transparency grid behind the actor.

12. Now you're ready to fine-tune the Keylight filter settings to create a better alpha channel for the video. There are several settings for the filter effect, but you only need to change a portion of the settings to achieve an excellent mask. To preview the screen mask (also called a matte), choose Screen Matte in the View menu of the Keylight filter settings. The Composition window now shows a grayscale rendition of the mask, as shown in **Figure 11.11**. An ideal mask should exhibit a contiguous white area for the subject and a solid black area for the mask area. An alpha channel can have 256 levels of transparency, where white represents full opacity and black represents full transparency. In the new Screen Matte view, you can see that the actor's shirt and face contain some blotchy gray areas, indicating partial transparency. Leaving this mask "as is" would create a ghost-effect for the final Flash Video file—other Flash elements behind the video would show through the shirt and face of the actor. You can use the Zoom tool to enlarge the view of the video in the Composition window, which allows

you to see subtle variations of gray within the mask. Leave the View menu of the filter set to Screen Matte for the next four steps.

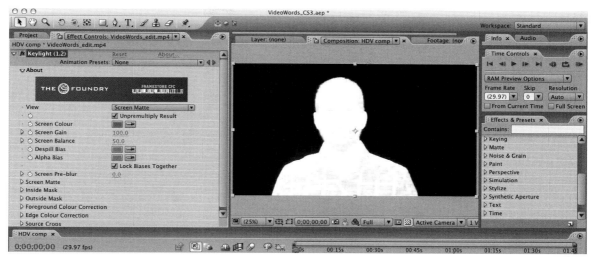

Figure 11.11 The Screen Matte view of the Keylight filter.

13. To clean up the black area of the mask (that is, the transparent area of the mask), increase the Screen Gain value of the Keylight filter to 133. Generally, you want to increase this value until the chroma-key area is solid black. Be careful not to increase the value too much—you can accidentally add transparency inside the edges of your subject matter.

NOTES

▶ Make sure you turn the View menu back to Final Result when you're ready to output a video file from After Effects.

14. Change the Screen Pre-blur value to 3.0. This value applies a blur effect to the footage before calculating the chroma-key mask. If your video footage was recorded with lossy compression codecs such as the DV codec (used by miniDV camcorders) or the MPEG-2 or MPEG-4 codec (used by High Definition, or HD, pro-sumer camcorders), use the Screen Pre-blur setting to improve the quality of the mask. Values between 1.0 and 3.0 subtly blur the video image and retain a clean edge on the subject. The blur effect is only applied to the video image for the purpose of generating a better mask—the final video image is not blurred.

▶ Feel free to toggle the View menu between Final Result and Screen Matte as you change settings, to view the effect on the footage. You should also drag the playhead indicator in the Timeline window to preview different times within the video footage. While one frame of video may have a clean mask, another frame may need stronger values. After you apply a stronger value to one setting at a particular frame, go back to the previous frame(s) to make sure the new values continue to work as expected.

15. Expand the Screen Matte area in the Keylight filter settings, and change the Clip White value to 50 for the VideoWords_edit.mp4 file, or 80.2 for the VideoWords_edit.mov file. The Clip White setting controls how the opaque (white) area of the mask is created. As you decrease the value of the Clip White setting, subtle gray (semi-transparent) colors within the boundary of the subject matter are added to the white portion of the mask.

16. Within the Screen Matte area of settings, change the Screen Shrink/Grow value to -1.5. This value, in pixels, shrinks the mask around the subject matter. I encourage you to use this setting with extreme care. For this particular piece of video, the edge of the shoulders exhibited a thin dark border without this change. For a review of all the changes in the Keylight filter, refer to **Figure 11.12**.

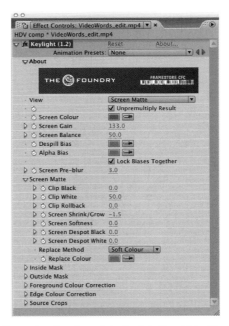

Figure 11.12 The updated settings of the Keylight filter (VideoWords_edit.mp4 footage).

17. After you have applied these changes, your video footage should have a clean mask, as shown in **Figure 11.13**. Change the View menu back to Final Result, as shown in **Figure 11.14**, before proceeding to the next step.

Figure 11.13 The improved alpha channel as displayed in the Screen Matte view.

Figure 11.14 The improved alpha channel as displayed in the Final Result view, with a different time position in the Timeline window.

NOTES

▶ The Preset name changes to Custom after you change the values as described in step 19.

TIP

▶ For your own video footage, you may find other settings in the Keylight filter helpful. The Replace Method menu in the Screen Matte area can help you remove color fluctuations in your subject matter. For example, during one of my Flash Video workshops, I taped a student wearing a yellow-orange shirt in front of the green screen. After using the same settings I discussed in steps 13 through 16, the output of the student displayed odd color noise in the shirt. I changed the Replace Method to Hard Colour, and voilà! The color oddity disappeared in the final output. Another nice settings area in the Keylight filter is the Source Crops area. These settings enable you to crop the video footage—but don't be tempted to create an After Effects mask for the footage layer to remove unwanted areas of the video frame from the final output.

18. Save the After Effects project file.

19. Now that you have a comp featuring a video file and a keying filter applied, you're ready to create a comp that has more appropriate dimensions for Web and Flash Video playback. The new comp will contain a nested copy of the HDV comp. Before you create a new comp, make a note of the duration of the HDV comp by selecting the comp in the Project panel and viewing its information in the preview area of the panel. The duration is 0;01;46;03, or 1 minute, 46 seconds, and 3 frames. Choose Composition > New Composition. In the Composition Settings dialog, type Web comp in the Composition Name field. In the Basic tab, choose the Web Video, 320 x 240 option in the Preset menu as a template. Deselect the Lock Aspect Ratio to 4:3 option, and change the Width value to 360 and the Frame Rate value to 29.97 frames per second. Make sure the Resolution menu is set to Full and the Duration field displays the same duration as the HDV comp. You can also type 14603 into the field, and After Effects automatically formats the value with the proper time-code notation. Review the settings as shown in **Figure 11.15**.

Figure 11.15 The Web comp settings.

20. The Timeline window should now display the new empty Web comp. Drag the HDV comp from the Project panel to the Timeline window, below the Source Name column. By default, the HDV comp is displayed at 100% size, 1920 by 1080, in the much smaller Web comp, 360 by 240, as shown in **Figure 11.16**. Choose Layer > Transform > Fit to Comp Height to resize the HDV comp within the Web comp. The HDV comp now fits vertically within the Web comp, as shown in **Figure 11.17**.

Figure 11.16 The HDV comp at 100% size in the Web comp.

Figure 11.17 The transformed HDV comp in the Web comp.

21. Drag the playhead indicator in the Timeline window to the time 0;01;40;00. Alternatively, you can double-click the time-code value at the top-left corner of the Timeline window to enter the value 14000 into the Go to Time dialog—After Effects can automatically format such a value into the proper time-code notation. At this new time, notice that the actor's right shoulder appears off frame in the Web comp. Choose the Selection tool and click the HDV comp in the Composition window. Use the Right Arrow key to nudge the comp to the right until the entire shoulder is in the viewing area of the Web comp, as shown in **Figure 11.18**. Nudge the comp just enough to show the right shoulder—if you move the comp too much to the right, then the actor's left shoulder as displayed in later frames will be cropped on the right edge of the Web comp.

Figure 11.18 The new position of the HDV comp.

22. Save the After Effects project file. The Web comp is now ready to be exported to a new QuickTime video file, which will be used in the Adobe Flash CS3 Video Encoder to create a Flash Video (FLV) file.

23. With the Web comp active in the Timeline window, choose Composition > Add to Render Queue. The Render Queue window should appear as a new tab with the Timeline window, with the Web comp added to the queue, as shown in **Figure 11.19**. Because the settings in the Render Queue require a lot of space on the screen (especially when I'm working on a laptop), I prefer to undock the Render Queue tab as a new window. Simply grab the gripper at the top-left corner of the Render Queue tab to undock it.

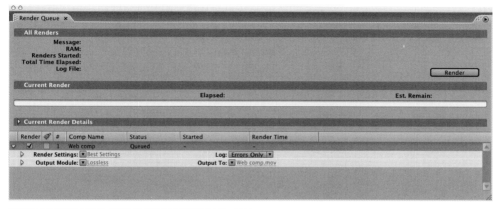

Figure 11.19 The Web comp in the Render Queue window.

24. To set up the output file with the correct codec settings for Flash Video encoding with alpha channel support, click the Lossless text to the right of the Output Module setting in the Render Queue. In the Output Module Settings dialog, make sure the Format menu is set to QuickTime Movie. Keep this dialog open for the next three steps.

25. In the Video Output area, click the Format Options button. In the Compression Settings dialog (shown in **Figure 11.20**), set the Compression Type menu to Animation and the Depth menu to Millions of Colors+. (The + value indicates the inclusion of an alpha channel.) To use lossless compression, make sure the Quality slider is set to Best. Lossless compression retains the original quality of the source footage without sacrificing detail through further recompression. Click OK to close this dialog.

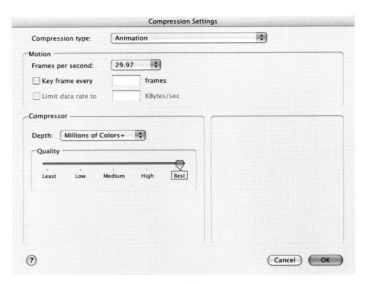

Figure 11.20 The Compression Settings dialog.

26. Back in the Output Module Settings dialog, change the Color menu to Straight (Unmatted). This value forces a clean alpha channel to be exported with the QuickTime file. A premultiplied color potentially introduces a black color fringe to your alpha channel, because After Effects multiplies the transparency value of the alpha channel with the default black background color of comps.

27. Select the Audio Output option, and change the sampling rate to 48.000 kHz, matching the original video footage's audio sampling rate. Make sure the bit depth is set to 16 Bit and the channels option is set to Stereo. Review these settings in **Figure 11.21**, and click OK when you are finished.

28. In the Render Queue window, click the filename to the right of the Output To setting. In the Output Movie To dialog, browse to your VideoWords folder (created in step 1), and name the filename VideoWords_alpha_360x240.mov. Click the Save (or OK) button.

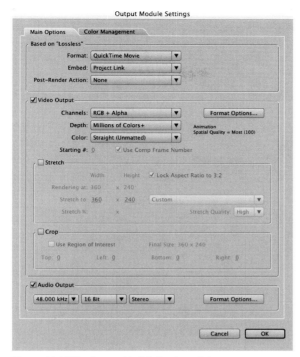

Figure 11.21 The Output Module Settings dialog.

29. After you've specified a filename, click the Render button in the Render Queue window. After Effects starts to process the comp, as shown in **Figure 11.22**. The amount of time required to render the comp will depend on the speed and memory capacity of your computer.

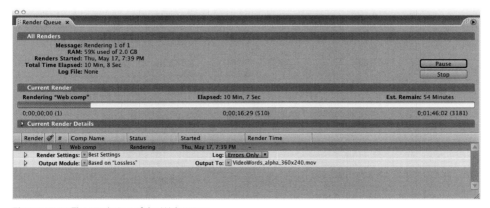

Figure 11.22 The rendering of the Web comp.

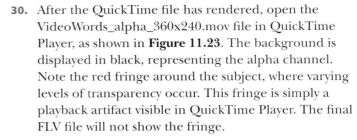

Figure 11.23 The rendered Quick-Time movie with an alpha channel.

On the DVD-ROM

► You can find two versions of the After Effects project file in the ch11 folder on the DVD-ROM. The VideoWords_CS3.aep file uses the HDV footage file, while the VideoWords_CS3_MP4.aep file uses the MPEG-4 version of the footage file. You can find the VideoWords_alpha_ 360x240.mov file in the source/alpha folder of the DVD-ROM.

30. After the QuickTime file has rendered, open the VideoWords_alpha_360x240.mov file in QuickTime Player, as shown in **Figure 11.23**. The background is displayed in black, representing the alpha channel. Note the red fringe around the subject, where varying levels of transparency occur. This fringe is simply a playback artifact visible in QuickTime Player. The final FLV file will not show the fringe.

31. Go back to After Effects, and save the project file.

Now that you have a QuickTime movie with an alpha channel, you're ready to process the video file in a Flash Video encoding tool.

Encoding the Flash Video

You can process a QuickTime video file that includes an alpha channel with several Flash Video encoders, including Adobe Flash CS3 Video Encoder, Sorenson Squeeze 4.2 or higher, and On2 Flix Pro 8 or higher. In this section, you learn how the final Flash Video (FLV) file for the Video-Words project is constructed.

Establishing specifications

As with most Flash projects, there's more than one way to design and develop a solution that works successfully. For the VideoWords project, the Flash Video file system could have been architected in more than one way. Here's a short list of the paths I considered:

► **Multiple FLV files delivered with HTTP:** Each word sequence from the VideoWords_alpha_360x240.mov file is edited to its own QuickTime file and encoded to a separate Flash Video (FLV) file, which is hosted on a Web server. The encoding process is more time-consuming for 48 video segments, and the client-side ActionScript code to preload and construct sequences is more difficult to write. An external data file, such as an XML file, contains the dictionary of words used by all of the clips and the URL to each clip's FLV file. This data source is loaded into the Flash movie (SWF) at the beginning of the experience. For this scenario, the initial VideoWords experience would load quickly. The user constructs a phrase, clicks Play, and waits for each clip to download before playback can begin.

▶ **One FLV file seeked with RTMP:** The VideoWords_alpha_360x240.mov file could be encoded to one Flash Video (FLV) file and streamed in real-time from a Flash Media Server. The encoding process is faster, and embedded cue points are specified at the start and end points for each word segment during the encoding setup. The client-side ActionScript code for video playback is not as difficult to develop—a NetStream playlist is built using the time of each word's starting cue point. Because Flash Media Server can jump (or seek) to specific times within a stream, each word segment can be streamed individually with a NetStream playlist. However, for immediate response times with user interaction, you would need to employ several bit rates (that is, one FLV file per target bit rate) or high buffer times in order to play word segments seamlessly. For this scenario, the experience loads quickly. The user constructs a phrase and clicks Play. Each word segment of the FLV file streams consecutively. However, longer pauses may occur between each word segment if the user's bandwidth fluctuates during the experience.

▶ **One FLV file delivered with HTTP:** The VideoWords_alpha_360x240.mov file is encoded to one Flash Video (FLV) file and hosted on a Web server. The encoding process is faster, and embedded cue points are specified at the start and end points for each word segment. The client-side ActionScript code for video playback uses the embedded cue point times to seek to each word segment. In order to have a seamless user experience, the entire FLV file needs to be downloaded before the experience can begin. The user waits for the FLV file to download (or preload), constructs a phrase, clicks Play, and watches the actor speak each word segment.

After weighing these options, I decided to implement the last option, where one FLV file is encoded with embedded cue points and seeked within the VideoWords experience

NOTES

▶ I don't discuss how to use Flash Media Server playlists in this book, but the NetStream.play() documentation in the Flash CS3 Help panel describes how to create a playlist with Flash Media Server streams.

TIP

▶ Another benefit of implementing a single FLV file for the experience is easier conversion to a real-time streaming environment. The same embedded cue point structure can be used with progressive-download or real-time streaming deployment.

after the FLV file has fully downloaded. The immediate gains are apparent, as there is only one FLV file asset to manage. The experience is very portable—you can host the files on Web servers without requiring additional Flash Media Server hosting costs. The only drawback to this approach is the initial download requirement, as a high-quality FLV file including the entire dictionary of words could easily weigh in at over 4 MB. The user may grow impatient as he waits for the FLV file to preload.

Adding cue points

In order to use a single Flash Video (FLV) file for deployment, a series of embedded cue points is created during the Flash Video encoding stage. The cue points require the following framework to function properly in the VideoWords experience:

▶ A navigation cue point at the start of each word segment. This cue point also includes a parameter indicating the term spoken in the segment. Each value is read from the `cuePoints` array delivered to the `NetStream.onMetaData` handler when the FLV file is initially loaded.

▶ An event cue point at the end of each word segment. This cue point indicates when the word segment has finished playing. When this cue point is detected in ActionScript during playback, the next word segment is played.

▶ Cue points at the start and end of the waiting segment at the end of the VideoWords_alpha_360x240.mov file. These cue points indicate the beginning and end of the loop cycle which plays as the user constructs phrases.

Because you already learned how to add cue points in the Flash CS3 Video Encoder in Chapter 6, I'll refrain from repeating the tasks for the 98 cue points required for the word segments. You can simply load the cue points XML file from the DVD-ROM to analyze the cue point structure, and proceed to encode your own FLV file.

1. Open Adobe Flash CS3 Video Encoder, and drag the VideoWords_alpha_360x240.mov file to the queue. Alternatively, you can click the Add button and browse to the QuickTime file.

On the DVD-ROM

▶ If you didn't create your own version of the VideoWords_alpha_360x240.mov file from After Effects, make a copy of the file from the source/alpha folder on the DVD-ROM to your own VideoWords folder.

2. Click the Settings button. In the Flash Video Encoding Settings dialog, choose the Flash 8 – Medium Quality (400kbps) preset in the Profiles tab as shown in **Figure 11.24**. In the Output filename field, type VideoWords_ FVE_VP6A_248K_CBR_Cues. This naming convention indicates the encoding tool (FVE, or Flash Video Encoder), the codec (VP6 with Alpha), the target bitrate (248 Kbps), the encoding type (CBR), and the inclusion of cue points. Note that you do not need to specify the .flv file extension for the filename, as the encoder automatically adds this suffix. Leave this dialog open for the next three steps.

Caution

▶ If you're using the Mac version of the Flash CS3 Video Encoder and your own QuickTime video file from After Effects does not display a gray background color in the Flash Video Encoding Settings dialog (as shown in **Figure 11.24**), you may have incorrectly exported the video footage. The gray background color represents the transparent areas in your video footage's alpha channel. If you're using Windows, the transparent area is represented by a black fill color.

Figure 11.24 The Profiles tab of the Flash Video Encoding Settings.

3. Click the Video tab. Select the Encode alpha channel option. Change the Quality menu to Custom and type 200 in the Max data rate field, as shown in **Figure 11.25**. Leave the other settings at their default values.

4. Click the Audio tab. Change the Data rate menu to 48 kbps (mono), as shown in **Figure 11.26**. The audio track for the video footage does not feature high-fidelity music or a wide range of tonality. As such, a lower bitrate can be allocated to the audio track.

▶ I used my Flash_Video_Bitrates. xls spreadsheet (located in the tools folder on the DVD-ROM) to determine an average bitrate of 200 Kbps for an On2 VP6 video sized at 360 by 240 with a frame rate of 29.97 fps.

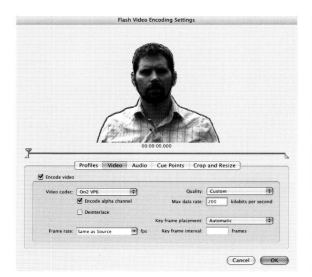

Figure 11.25 The Video tab of the Flash Video Encoding Settings.

Figure 11.26 The Audio tab of the Flash Video Encoding Settings.

NOTES

▶ One of the difficulties of this encoding task in the Flash CS3 Video Encoder is that the tool does not feature audio scrubbing while you drag the play-head in the Flash Video Encoding Settings dialog. Therefore, you can only use visual cues in the video frame to determine the start and end time of each spoken word.

On the DVD-ROM

▶ You can find the finished file, VideoWords_FVE_VP6A_ 248K_Cues.flv, in the flv folder of this book's DVD-ROM.

5. Click the Cue Points tab, and click the Load Cue Points button (the folder icon). Browse to the source/alpha folder of this book's DVD-ROM, and select the VideoWords_cue_points.xml file. Click Open (or OK) to import the cue point data. All 98 cue points load and display in the tab, as shown in **Figure 11.27**. If you select each navigation cue point, you can view the term parameter for the spoken word. Click OK to close the dialog.

6. Back in the main application window for the Flash CS3 Video Encoder, click the Start Queue button to begin encoding the Flash Video (FLV) file. The encoding progress is displayed in the lower part of the application window, as shown in **Figure 11.28**.

You should now have a Flash Video (FLV) file for the VideoWords project. In the remainder of this chapter, you learn how to integrate the FLV file with a Flash movie (SWF) for final deployment.

Figure 11.27 The Cue Points tab of the Flash Video Encoding Settings.

Figure 11.28 The encoding progress and preview area.

Developing the ActionScript 3.0 Code Base

The VideoWords project features several user-based interactions, such as dragging and dropping words and playing a specific sequence of video cue points. Each task requires several lines of ActionScript code. As discussed earlier in this chapter, the code base uses ActionScript 3.0 (AS3), which requires Flash Player 9. While I won't delve into a line-by-line code analysis in this section, I will walk you through a summary of the AS3 classes I built for the project, including the document class that initiates the experience.

Core Classes

The VideoWords code needs to accomplish several key operations in order to function properly. These tasks, in linear order as experienced by the user, are:

1. Load the Flash Video (FLV) file, and display the loading progress to the user.

2. Build the user interface, which includes the word collection behind the video actor, the video display (a `Video` instance) of the footage, the text area (a `TextArea` component) below the video, and the Play and Reset buttons (instances of the `Button` component) below the text area.

3. Enable a rollover effect with the video image, applying a hard light blend mode to the video container to allow every word in the word collection to be visible underneath the video.

4. Enable drag-and-drop functionality for each of the words in the word collection. Each word responds to double-clicking with the mouse as well.

5. Enable the Play and Reset buttons to respond to user clicks. When the Play button is pushed, each word added to the text area should play in correct sequence. When the Reset button is pushed, the text area should be cleared.

Let's look at how each of these responsibilities is handled by an ActionScript 3.0 class created for the project. Some of the classes handle more than one task.

In Flash CS3, open the ch11.flp project file from the ch11 folder of the DVD-ROM to review each of these classes as they are described in the following sections.

DraggableWord class

The simplest class is the DraggableWord class, which creates a TextField instance that can be dragged and dropped on the stage. The class is not specific to the VideoWords project— the DraggableWord class can be used with any Flash project that needs drag-and-drop text fields. Each instance of the class broadcasts two events utilized by other classes in the VideoWords project:

▶ DraggableWord.HIT **event:** This event is broadcast when an instance overlaps the DisplayObjectContainer instance specified by the *dragTarget* property of the DraggableWord class. Display objects such as the Sprite and MovieClip classes inherit from the DisplayObjectContainer class. In the WordCollection class (discussed in the next section), the *dragTarget* property is assigned the value of the TextArea component instance below the video image.

▶ DraggableWord.DOUBLE_CLICK **event:** This event is broadcast when an instance is double-clicked with the mouse. The WordCollection class uses the event to initiate the same set of actions invoked with a DraggableWord.HIT event.

WordCollection class

The next class in the hierarchy is the WordCollection class. This class takes a list of words (as an array) and builds a grid of DraggableWord instances. There are three notable features of this class:

▶ WordCollection.items **property:** This property specifies the text elements to be drawn on the stage. Each object in the items array has a property named term. The list of terms is gathered and created by the VideoWords class (described in the next section) from the Flash Video (FLV) file.

▶ WordCollection.dragTarget **property:** This property specifies the DisplayObjectContainer instance to be used as a hit target for each DraggableWord instance. The value is passed to the *dragTarget* property of each DraggableWord instance.

NOTES

▶ The DraggableWord class features another event— DraggableWord.PRESS— that is not used with the VideoWords project. This event is broadcast when a mouse-down action occurs on a DraggableWord instance.

▶ `WordCollection.HIT` **event:** This event proxies the
`DraggableWord.HIT` event. When the user drags a word
to the `dragTarget` instance (the `TextArea` instance) or
double-clicks a word, the `DraggableWord.HIT` event is
passed to and dispatched by the `WordCollection` instance.

VideoWords class

The class that brings all of the elements together is the
`VideoWords` class. In over 300 lines of code, this class creates
each display object, including the `WordCollection` instance
(which, in turn, creates the `DraggableWord` instances), the
`Video` instance to display the Flash Video file, the `TextArea`
instance to display the user's selected words, and the control buttons below the text. When the Flash Video file is
preloading, this class creates a `ProgressBar` instance to display the load progress of the FLV file. After the video finishes
loading, the video plays the waiting segment at the end of
the FLV file. When the user rolls over and off the video
image, this class controls the `blendMode` property of a `Sprite`
instance holding the `Video` instance.

▶ As the "master" class, the
VideoWords class contains
several code comments to help
you understand its functionality.

Despite the vast amount of code in the class, the `VideoWords`
class requires just two properties and one method call to work:

▶ `videoURL` **property:** This property sets the path to the
FLV file containing embedded cue points for each
spoken word.

▶ `videoWidth` **property:** This property controls the width of
the video display and the boundaries of the `WordCollection`
instance. While this value can be retrieved from the
FLV metadata, the direct specification of the width
allows the UI to be built before the video has loaded.

▶ `initialize()` **method:** This method starts the chain
of actions that build the user interface elements
(`createStyles` and `createView` functions) and start
loading the video (`createStream` function).

Document Class

The last class required for the `VideoWords` project is
the `VideoWordsExample` class. This class instantiates the

VideoWords class, specifying the FLV file path and the width of the video. The class also handles resize events, such as the user changing the size of the browser window or the stand-alone Flash Player. In the following steps, you learn how to implement the core classes and the VideoWordsExample class in your Flash file.

1. Copy the classes folder from the book's DVD-ROM to your VideoWords folder.

2. Create a folder named flv in your VideoWords folder. Copy the VideoWords_FVE_VP6A_248K_Cues.flv file that you created earlier in this chapter to the new flv folder.

3. In your VideoWords folder, create a folder named source. Copy the VideoWordsExample.as file from the ch11 folder of this book's DVD-ROM to your new source folder.

4. In Flash CS3, create a new Flash file (ActionScript 3.0). Save this file as VideoWords_AS3.fla in the source folder you created in step 2.

5. Choose File > Publish Settings, and select the Flash tab in the Publish Settings dialog. Click the Settings button next to the ActionScript version option. In the Action-Script 3.0 Settings dialog, type VideoWordsExample in the Document class field. This setting tells the Flash file to use the VideoWordsExample.as file you copied in step 2. Leave the dialog open for the next step.

6. In order for Flash to access the core classes you copied in step 1, you need to specify the class path for those files. Click the add (+) button in the Classpath area of the ActionScript 3.0 Settings dialog. Type ../classes/AS3/. into the new line below the Classpath heading. This relative path instructs Flash to look in the classes folder you copied in step 1. Review the ActionScript settings in **Figure 11.29**. Click OK to close the dialog, and click OK again to close the Publish Settings dialog.

TIP

▶ You can also specify the document class in the Property inspector. Make sure that you deselect any elements on the stage to reveal the document settings in the Property inspector.

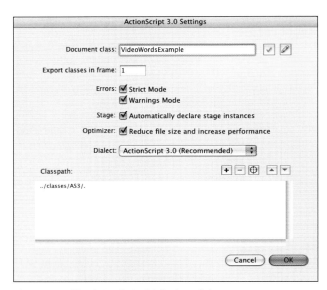

Figure 11.29 The ActionScript 3.0 Settings dialog.

On the DVD-ROM

▶ You can find the completed files in the ch11 folder of this book's DVD-ROM. This folder also contains an HTML file, VideoWords_AS3.html, which uses the SWFObject JavaScript library to detect the Flash Player version. Refer to Chapter 5 for more information on SWFObject. Note that the Flash movie fills the entire browser window without scaling the Flash content.

7. Add the necessary Flash CS3 components to the Flash file. From the User Interface grouping in the Components panel, drag the Button, ProgressBar, and TextArea components to the stage of the Flash file. Once they've been added to the stage, they're automatically copied to the file's Library panel and available for ActionScript. Keep the components in the Library panel, but remove the component instances from the stage.

8. Save the Flash file, and test the movie (Ctrl/Cmd+Enter). The Flash Video file loads into the movie, and the waiting loop begins to play. Drag words from the WordCollection instance to the TextArea instance, and click the Play button to watch the word segments play.

You now know the essential ingredients to create an interactive video host with Flash Video and ActionScript 3.0. If you have access to a video camera and video editing software, you can recreate the Flash Video footage on your own and reuse the existing VideoWords project code to have fun with the content!

12

Delivering a Reliable Video Experience

Flash Video offers a wide range of options for you to employ on and off the Internet. Unlike every other Web video format, the Flash Video (FLV) format is not simply one that plays in an audio/video player like Windows Media, QuickTime, and Real Player formats do, with limited interactivity. Because Flash Video is treated like any other external asset to the Flash Player, you need to create your own video player in ActionScript or use a pre-existing component or library in order to control a Flash Video experience.

As you've learned throughout this book, you can integrate Flash Video with other Flash content and use several techniques to play one or more Flash Video files. In this final chapter, you learn how to amalgamate the requirements for successful Flash Video deployment. From encoding multiple bitrates to ActionScript 3.0 development to JavaScript-based Flash Player detection, this chapter teaches you how to plan and execute a Web-based Flash Video experience. The example showcases the half-hour documentary, *Apollo 13: "Houston, We've Got a Problem."*, released by the National Aeronautics and Space Administration (NASA) in 1972. You can view the completed example (**Figure 12.1**) at the following URL:

http://www.flashsupport.com/books/fvst/ch12/ReliableVideo_AS3.html

On the DVD-ROM

▶ You can find all the source files
for this chapter's exercises in
the ch12 folder of this book's
DVD-ROM. The ch12.flp file is a
Flash Project file that you can
open in Flash CS3 to view all
of the sample files related to
topics discussed in this chapter.

Caution

▶ All of the sample streaming and
progressive-download URLs
used in this chapter refer to FLV
files that reside on this book's
Web server (www.flashsupport.
com) or my hosted Flash Media
Server account at Influxis.com.
You're welcome to access these
remote FLV files in your own tests,
but you'll need to have access
to a Web server and Flash Media
Server (or FVSS provider) to
create your own examples with
different FLV files.

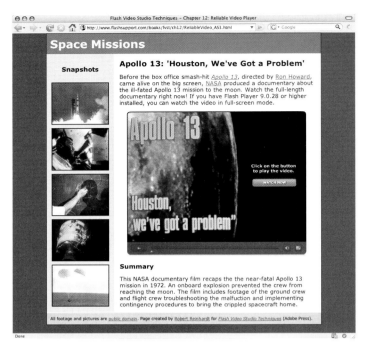

Figure 12.1 The finished content.

Creating a Deployment Plan

I designed the Apollo 13 example to demonstrate a foolproof
method of adding Flash Video content to an HTML page.
The primary Flash SWF file, ReliableVideo_AS3.swf, has only
one purpose: to load and control the video experience.
Everything else on the page is controlled with HTML, CSS,
and JavaScript. The page tries to handle most, if not all, user
and server conditions. For example, if the user does not have
the Flash Player installed or doesn't have the required Flash
Player version, JavaScript displays graphic and text elements
providing instructions for the user. If the user has the required
Flash Player version but the Flash Media Server (FMS) or
FLV file is unavailable, the Flash SWF file displays an error
message to the user. One of the objectives of the Apollo 13
example is to create a seamless experience for any user,
regardless of browser version, browser capability, or Flash
Player plug-in installation. The procedures that are required
to serve a better experience for fully-equipped users is often
referred to as *progressive enhancement*, which I discuss in the
next section.

Defining progressive enhancement

Wikipedia defines progressive enhancement (PE) as "a label for a particular strategy of Web design that emphasizes accessibility, semantic markup, and external stylesheet and scripting technologies, in a layered fashion that allows everyone to access the basic content and functionality of a Web page, using any browser or Internet connection, while also enabling those with better bandwidth or more advanced browser software to experience an enhanced version of the page."

A great example of PE that you have already learned from Chapter 5 is SWFObject. With SWFObject, you can easily display alternative content to users who don't have Flash Player installed, don't have the required version of Flash Player installed, or don't have JavaScript enabled in the browser preferences. The Apollo 13 example utilizes SWFObject to check for Flash Player 9.0.28—the minimum required version for full screen mode in ActionScript.

▶ You learn more about the specific details of the HTML and JavaScript utilized for the Apollo 13 example later in this chapter.

Examining the technical requirements

For this project, the Flash content (SWF file) is a full-featured video player that can be set up and controlled with HTML and JavaScript. The SWF file needs to adhere to the following guidelines:

▶ **ActionScript 3.0 code base:** To allow easier maintenance and compatibility with other ActionScript 3.0 content, such as a Flex application, all of the ActionScript code should be written in ActionScript 3.0 (AS3). The new version of the FLVPlayback component, included with Flash CS3, also requires ActionScript 3.0.

▶ **Flash Player 9.0.28 or higher compatibility:** The AS3 FLVPlayback component requires later versions of Flash Player 9. Earlier releases of Flash Player 9, such as 9.0.16, do not support functionality implemented by the FLVPlayback component.

▶ **Modest file size:** The primary Flash movie (SWF file) should load quickly over most broadband connections, 384 Kbps or higher. This size does not include the Flash Video (FLV) file.

▶ **Low-buffer video streaming:** The video asset should stream well over a wide range of connection speeds, ranging from high to low quality. The user should not have to wait more than a few seconds to begin playback of the video.

▶ **Real-time streaming delivery:** Due to the long duration of the Apollo 13 documentary, the video asset should be delivered from a Flash Media Server or equivalent streaming service. The video asset should be able to seek quickly from one time to another, regardless of the user's connection or the length of time the user has been watching the video.

▶ **ExpressInstall content:** If the user has Flash Player 6.0.65 or higher but not Flash Player 9.0.28 or higher, a custom SWF file with Apollo 13 graphics should be displayed prompting the user to upgrade to the latest Flash Player with ExpressInstall.

▶ **Poster content:** If the user has Flash Player 9.0.28 or higher, a poster SWF file with Apollo 13 graphics should be loaded and displayed before the user initiates playback. The poster SWF file serves as a promotional graphic for the content, featuring the video's title and a control to begin playback.

▶ **HTML-assigned parameters:** The primary Flash SWF file should be reusable with any progressive-download or real-time streaming Flash Video content. All parameters for the video experience, including the FLV file URL, skin SWF file URL, skin background color, skin background alpha, automatic playback, and more should be enabled via the `flashvars` parameter of the HTML plug-in tag or the `SWFObject.addVariable()` method.

Assessing the production requirements

The Apollo 13 example requires several production phases for completion, from video preparation to ActionScript 3.0 code to HTML/JavaScript code. The amount of time that's required to complete each phase largely depends on the duration of the video content and the complexity of the features added to the video player SWF file. I undertook four phases of production for this project:

▶ **Video transcoding:** The source MPEG-2 video file of the Apollo 13 documentary from archive.org exhibited exaggerated interlacing during playback, potentially indicating a bad transfer (or two) from the original film format to video. The footage would require retiming the 29.97 fps frame rate to its original 24-fps film frame rate.

▶ **Flash Video encoding:** The transcoded source footage requires several FLV bitrates for deployment to a range of connection speeds. An encoding profile for each supported bitrate needs to be planned and executed in a Flash Video encoding tool.

▶ **ActionScript code development:** At any point during the prior phases, the ActionScript code for the project can be written. The code needs to be able to load the FLV file and supporting assets.

▶ **HTML/JavaScript development:** The client-side HTML and JavaScript code can also be written at any point during the production cycle. This code needs to feature Flash Player version detection for Flash Player 9 r28 (or 9.0.28 in SWFObject parlance). Thumbnails created from the video footage should be specified in a sidebar of the HTML document. Each thumbnail can direct the Flash Video to seek to a specific time.

NOTES

▶ These phases represent an overview of the production cycle as implemented for this chapter's example, and are not absolute. You may want to add more phases to the cycle, such as a graphics production cycle to build the bitmap assets used in the poster and ExpressInstall content.

Encoding the Flash Video

In this section, you learn how the Apollo 13 documentary video file was transcoded to a better source file to use with a Flash Video encoder. You also learn the specifics of each connection-speed profile used with Sorenson Squeeze to create the Flash Video (FLV) files.

Establishing specifications

As I've discussed in examples throughout this book, there's more than one way to create a solution that delivers a high-quality Flash Video experience. For the Apollo 13 example, the Flash Video file system could have been architected in more than one way. Here's a list of the paths I considered:

▶ **Multiple short-duration FLV files delivered with HTTP:** The Apollo 13 documentary is edited into several individual source video files, each with a duration of five minutes or less. Each segment is then encoded to its own Flash Video (FLV) file, which is hosted on a Web server. The encoding process is more time-consuming for short video segments, and the client-side ActionScript code to pre-load and construct sequences is more intensive to write. An external data file, such as an XML file, contains a playlist of all the clips and the URL to each clip's FLV file. This data source is loaded into the Flash movie (SWF) at the beginning of the experience. To enable multiple bitrates for each clip, a comprehensive list of FLV files is specified in the data source. However, for a progressive-download delivery system, one high-quality series of FLV files could be implemented—users with slower connection speeds would be required to wait longer while each segment downloaded to the browser cache.

▶ **One FLV file delivered with HTTP:** The source video file is encoded to one Flash Video (FLV) file and hosted on a Web server. The encoding process is faster, with only one FLV file to output. However, one high-quality FLV file for a half-hour documentary can easily require over 100 MB of storage. The user cannot seek to times within the video that have not yet downloaded to the browser cache.

▶ **Multiple bitrate FLV files delivered with HTTP:** The source video file could be encoded to several Flash Video (FLV) files, each targeting a specific connection speed. Each FLV file is progressively downloaded from a Web server to the video playback movie. A SMIL file lists each FLV file and its required connection speed. The transfer speed at which the initial poster SWF downloads to the video playback movie could determine which FLV file is then downloaded and played. The ActionScript code already built into the AS3 version of the FLVPlayback component loads the SMIL file and determines the appropriate bitrate to play. With this solution, users would not be able to jump to a section of the video that had not yet downloaded from the Web server, and the entire FLV file is served to each user regardless of whether the user watches the full length of the video.

▶ **Multiple bitrate FLV files seeked with RTMP:** The source video file could be encoded to several Flash Video (FLV) files, each targeting a specific connection speed. Each FLV file is streamed in real time from a Flash Media Server

▶ With a little server-side scripting on a Web server, you can segment a large FLV file into smaller downloadable chunks. For more information on this technique, visit the "HTTP Streaming with Flash Video" section of links at this book's links page, www.flashsupport.com/links. This pseudo-streaming approach requires more legwork with FLV file preparation and server-side setup on your Web server.

(FMS). A SMIL file lists each FLV file and its required connection speed. The ActionScript code already built into the AS3 version of the FLVPlayback component loads the SMIL file and determines the appropriate bitrate with the FMS application.

After weighing these options, I picked the last option, requiring two or more FLV files to be encoded and specified within a SMIL file. I didn't want to break up the experience of the documentary into several small clips; I wanted the video to retain the appearance of one continuous video in the FLVPlayback component. The only drawback to this approach is the FMS requirement—I would need over 100 MB of file storage on an FMS hosting provider, supporting high bitrates for a high-quality video experience.

Improving the source video file

As I mentioned earlier in this chapter, the original MPEG-2 source file downloaded from archive.org showed signs of interlaced frames. **Figure 12.2** illustrates a sample frame where the interlaced artifacts are apparent. The man's face has a ghostlike copy trailing behind the previous frame.

In QuickTime Player (or your preferred media player), open and play the source file, Apollo_13_Houston_We_Have_A_Problem.mpeg, from the source/mpeg folder on the DVD-ROM. As you watch the video, notice that you can see interlacing appear throughout the footage. If you pause the video and advance the footage frame by frame (using the right arrow key), you can see that not every frame appears to exhibit the interlacing.

Telecine and 3:2 pulldown explained

While I do not know how the original film footage was transferred to video or how the MPEG-2 video file was created from the transferred footage, I do know that the original footage was shot on film, as indicated by the film grain and contrast in the footage. (Video was also not widely used in the early 1970s.) A typical frame rate for film footage is 24 fps. Whenever film is transferred to NTSC video, a process known as *telecine*, extra frames need to be added to accommodate the 29.97 fps frame rate specified by NTSC video. One method of telecine uses a technique that's

NOTES

▶ For more information on SMIL implementation, refer to Chapter 8.

NOTES

▶ Always seek out the best available source footage for your compression tasks. If a business client delivers poor-quality video source files, don't hesitate to ask if higher quality files are available. Be prepared to loan your business client a high-capacity external hard drive to store video source files.

Figure 12.2 A sample frame where interlacing can be seen.

▶ For more information on telecine and 3:2 pulldown, read the Wikipedia entry at http://en.wikipedia.org/wiki/Telecine. You can view diagrams of the telecine process at this wiki entry.

called *3:2 pulldown*, which stretches every four frames of footage into five frames by duplicating video fields. The process alternately places one film frame over two video fields, the next film frame across three video fields, the next across two, and so on.

Telecine is most useful for interlaced video display, such as video played on a regular standard definition (SD) television. For display on progressive-scan displays, such as a computer monitor or LCD, you can remove the 3:2 pulldown from the video and go back to the original 24-fps non-interlaced frame rate.

By reducing the frame rate of the source video, you can improve the overall video quality for a target bitrate. As I discussed in Chapter 3, the bitrate of a video is largely determined by the frame width, frame height, and frame rate of a video clip. If you reduce the frame rate of the source video from 29.97 fps to 24 fps (or 23.976 fps), you can use a larger frame size or reduce the overall bitrate required for a video clip. Perhaps more importantly, though, you can remove the effects of interlacing from the content, improving the overall quality of the video image.

Removing 3:2 pulldown in Adobe After Effects

▶ When you remove 3:2 pulldown from a source video that originated on film, the final frame rate is actually 23.976 fps. Some video applications automatically round this number to 24 fps.

The task of removing the effects of telecine from a source video file is not as simple as exporting a new video file with a reduced frame rate. Because the original film frames are mapped to interlaced video fields in a specific order during telecine, you need to use a program like Adobe After Effects to remove 3:2 pulldown with high-quality output. In the following steps, you learn how to prepare the Apollo 13 documentary footage in After Effects CS3.

1. Launch Adobe After Effects CS3. Save a new project file as `Apollo_13_transcode.aep`.

2. Choose File > Import > File, and browse to the location where you copied the file from the DVD-ROM or downloaded it from the archive.org site.

3. Right-click (or Control-click on Mac) the newly imported file in the Project panel, and choose Interpret Footage > Main. In the Interpret Footage dialog (**Figure 12.3**), click the Guess 3:2 Pulldown button. Note that the

Remove Pulldown menu selection changes to the phase type WSSWW. The letter W stands for whole frame, and the letter S stands for split frame. If you count the number of Ws and Ss in any of the options in this menu, you'll find that there will always be three Ws and two Ss, indicating a 3:2 pulldown. The video clip's first frame, though, may be an edit from a master source file, so the first three video fields may not be whole frames. Adobe After Effects can analyze the footage and try to determine the correct phase. Click OK to close the dialog.

Figure 12.3 The Interpret Footage dialog.

4. After you've applied a 3:2 pulldown setting in the Interpret Footage dialog, you can create a new composition (or comp) to output a new source file. Choose Composition > New Composition. In the Composition Settings dialog, type 24 FPS in the Composition Name field. In the Preset menu, choose NTSC DV. This preset sets up the correct frame dimensions and pixel aspect ratio. Change the Frame Rate value to 23.976 frames per second, as shown in **Figure 12.4**. When you change this value, the Preset menu name changes to Custom. In the Duration field, type 281004. This is the same duration as the Apollo 13 documentary footage. After Effects will automatically add the proper colons separating the time values. Click OK.

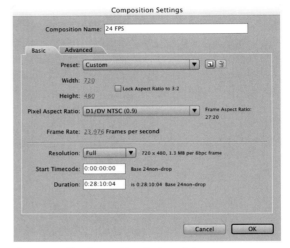

Figure 12.4 The Composition Settings dialog.

5. Double-click the new comp in the Project panel to make the comp active in the Timeline window. Drag the Apollo 13 footage file below the Source Name column in the Timeline window. The video clip is automatically centered in the new composition.

6. Expand the layer settings for the Apollo 13 clip, as shown in **Figure 12.5**. You can remove the uneven black borders of the video clip by scaling and repositioning the clip. Expand the Transform settings to reveal the Position and Scale properties. Change the X value of the Position settings to 355.5. In the Scale settings, change the X scale value to 103.3% and the Y scale value to 101.3%. When you are finished, the black borders of the video clip should no longer be visible in the comp.

Figure 12.5 The new Transform settings.

7. Now you can render the composition for a new and
   improved source file to use for Flash Video encoding.
   Choose Composition > Add to Render Queue. In the
   Render Queue window (Window > Render Queue), you
   can set up the render settings for the composition. Click
   the Lossless link to the right of the Output Module setting. In the Output Module Settings dialog, choose
   MPEG2-DVD from the Format menu. To conserve file
   size for the final output, I recommend keeping the new
   source file in the same codec as the original source file.
   You may achieve better results by rendering to a new
   QuickTime file with a lossless codec such as the Animation codec, but the file size for a half-hour documentary
   will be several gigabytes. Clear the Audio Output option,
   as shown in **Figure 12.6**. The audio from the original
   source can be extracted later in MPEG Streamclip,

without any loss of quality. Keep the Output Module Settings dialog open for the next step.

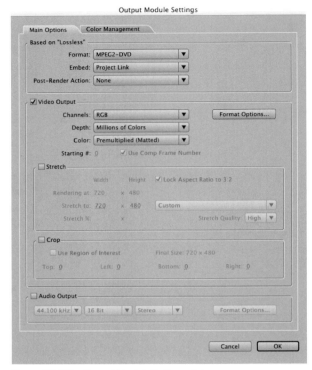

Figure 12.6 The Output Module Settings dialog.

8. Click the Format Options button in the Output Module Settings dialog. In the MPEG2-DVD dialog, click the Audio tab, and then clear the Export Audio check box. Click the Video tab, and change the Frame Rate menu [fps] to 23.976. Review these settings in **Figure 12.7**, and click OK to close the MPEG2-DVD dialog. Click OK again to close the Output Module Settings dialog.

9. In the Render Queue window, change the name of the output file for the 23 FPS comp to `Apollo_13_24fps.m2v` by clicking the text to the right of the Output To field. Specify a location on your computer that can accommodate 900 MB. The final MPEG-2 file will be about the same file size as the original source file.

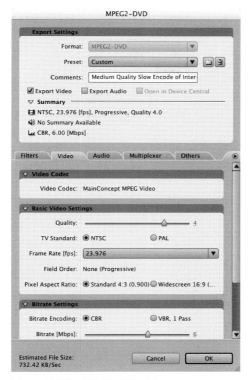

Figure 12.7 The MPEG2-DVD settings.

10. Save the After Effects project, and click the Render button. After Effects may need several hours to render the entire file. My MacBook with a 2 GHz Intel Core 2 Duo processor and 2 GB of RAM spent over five hours rendering the file. When the rendering is complete, you will have a new video file (without any audio) that you can merge with the original audio track in Sorenson Squeeze.

Extracting an audio track in MPEG Streamclip

If you're using MPEG source files for Flash Video compression, most Flash Video encoders won't be able to read the audio track of the MPEG file. One of the reasons I prefer to use Sorenson Squeeze for MPEG file processing is that the encoder can link separate video and audio files together

NOTES

On the DVD-ROM

▶ You can find the After Effects CS3 project file, Apollo_13_transcode.aep, in the ch12 folder of this book's DVD-ROM. The rendered video file, Apollo_13_24fps.m2v, is located in the source/mpeg/demuxed folder on the DVD-ROM.

NOTES

▶ MPEG Streamclip is a free Windows and Mac utility offered by Squared 5. You can download the software from www.squared5.com. You will need to have the Apple QuickTime MPEG-2 Playback Component. You can find more information on this component at www.apple.com/quicktime/mpeg2/. At the time of this writing, the component costs $19.99. If you need to process MPEG-2 video content frequently, you may find this component incredibly handy.

On the DVD-ROM

▶ You can find the extracted audio file, Apollo_13_24fps.aiff, in the source/mpeg/demuxed folder on the DVD-ROM. If you're using the Windows version of Sorenson Squeeze and experience difficulties linking the AIFF file to the MPEG-2 video file (as described later in this chapter), you may need to transcode the AIFF file to the WAV file format in an application such as Apple QuickTime Pro.

TIP

▶ I used my Flash_Video_Bitrates.xls Excel spreadsheet, located in the tools folder on the DVD-ROM, to help determine the frame dimensions and frame rates to use with each bitrate.

for output to other formats. In the previous section, you learned how to create a better MPEG-2 video file with Adobe After Effects. In this section, you learn how to use MPEG Streamclip to extract an AIFF or WAV file based on the MPEG audio track in the source file.

1. Launch MPEG Streamclip, and open the Apollo_13_Houston_We_Have_A_Problem.mpeg file that you copied from the DVD-ROM.

2. Choose File > Demux to AIFF. AIFF, or Audio Interchange File Format, is a common audio file format on Mac, the equivalent of the WAV file format on Windows. Specify a filename, such as `Apollo_13_24fps.aiff`, and a destination for the new AIFF file.

After MPEG Streamclip has processed the audio file, you're ready to head into Sorenson Squeeze to process the video footage.

Determining Encoding Profiles

After the source footage has been transcoded to separate MPEG-2 and AIFF files, the process of creating the Flash Video (FLV) files can begin. To support a wide range of connection speeds to the FMS application, I chose to create four profiles based on connection speeds.

Each profile uses a combined audio and video bitrate that is 80 percent of the required connection speed. This padded value accommodates fluctuations that may occur with the user's connection speed during the video experience. Also, each profile uses Constant Bit Rate (or CBR) encoding because the FLV files will be streamed from a Flash Media Server application.

While each profile features unique frame dimensions, the video size is scaled to fit the maximum dimensions, 512 by 384, during playback. You can review the encoding settings in **Table 12.1**.

TABLE 12.1 Apollo 13 Encoding Profiles

Connection Speed	Total Bitrate	Audio Bitrate	Video Bitrate	Audio Quality	Frame Size	Frame Rate
1 Mbps +	800 Kbps	48 Kbps	752 Kbps	22 kHz mono	512 x 384	24 fps
625 Kbps	500 Kbps	48 Kbps	452 Kbps	22 kHz mono	400 x 300	24 fps
375 Kbps	300 Kbps	32 Kbps	268 Kbps	22 kHz mono	288 x 216	24 fps
44 Kbps	35 Kbps	16 Kbps	19 Kbps	11 kHz mono	112 x 84	12 fps

High-quality 800 Kbps

If the user has a connection speed of 1 Mbps or higher to the FMS application hosting the Flash Video content, a Flash Video (FLV) file with a total bitrate of 800 Kbps is streamed to the user. This file has the following bitrates:

▶ **48 Kbps audio bitrate:** Because the original audio track is of fair quality and is comprised mainly of narration and radio transmission, a low bitrate can be afforded for the audio track. A sampling rate of 22 kHz is used for this bitrate. Because the original audio is not stereo sound, a single channel will be used in both the left and right speakers (mono sound).

▶ **752 Kbps video bitrate:** The remainder of the 800 Kbps bitrate is applied to the video track. Using the compression formula described in Chapter 3, I designated a frame size of 512 by 384 with a frame rate of 24 fps. In Squeeze, a frame-rate ratio of 1:1 is specified. Because Squeeze expresses kilobits per second as 1024 bits to a kilobit (instead of 1000 bits per kilobit) for the video track, Squeeze does not properly calculate kilobits per second. Therefore, the 752 Kbps video bitrate is specified as 734 Kbps in Squeeze. (752 Kbps multiplied by 1000 bits equals 752,000 bps, divided by 1024 equals 734 Kbps.)

High-quality 500 Kbps

If the user has a connection speed between 625 Kbps and 1 Mbps to the FMS application hosting the Flash Video content, a Flash Video (FLV) file with a total bitrate of 500 Kbps is streamed to the user. This file has the following bitrates:

▶ **48 Kbps audio bitrate:** The same audio quality specified by the 1 Mbps encoding profile is used with this profile.

▶ **452 Kbps video bitrate:** The remainder of the 500 Kbps bitrate is applied to the video track. The video has a frame size of 400 by 300, with a 1:1 frame rate ratio. In the Squeeze encoding profile, this bitrate is specified as 441 Kbps.

Medium-quality 300 Kbps

If the user has a connection speed between 375 Kbps and 625 Kbps to the FMS application hosting the Flash Video content, a Flash Video (FLV) file with a total bitrate of 300 Kbps is streamed to the user. This file has the following bitrates:

▶ **32 Kbps audio bitrate:** The audio quality is slightly reduced from the previous profiles in order to allocate more bitrate to the video portion of the FLV file.

▶ **268 Kbps video bitrate:** The remainder of the 300 Kbps bitrate is applied to the video track. The video has a frame size of 288 by 216, with a 1:1 frame rate ratio. In the Squeeze encoding profile, this bitrate is specified as 261 Kbps.

Low-quality 44 Kbps

If the user has a connection speed below 375 Kbps to the FMS application hosting the Flash Video content, a Flash Video (FLV) file with a total bitrate of 35 Kbps is streamed to the user. This file has the following bitrates:

▶ **16 Kbps audio bitrate:** The audio quality is greatly reduced from the previous profiles in order to allocate more bitrate to the video portion of the FLV file. The audio quality suffers from such compression, but is acceptable for a dial-up modem connection.

▶ **19 Kbps video bitrate:** The remainder of the 35 Kbps bitrate is applied to the video track. The video has a frame size of 112 by 84, with a 2:1 frame rate ratio, 12 fps. In the Squeeze encoding profile, this bitrate is specified as 18 Kbps.

Creating the compression presets in Sorenson Squeeze

Once the encoding profiles have been planned, you can execute the Flash Video encoding tasks in your preferred video encoding software. Because the Apollo 13 source file has been separated into video and audio files, the Flash Video encoding software needs to be able to link audio and video files as one source item.

For this chapter's source video, I used Sorenson Squeeze because it can link separated files and produce high-quality Flash Video output. I also like to build a project file (SQZ) in Squeeze specifying presets, which I can then send to a client to encode the source video file(s) with their resources and their own license of Sorenson Squeeze.

You can download a trial version of Sorenson Squeeze at:

www.sorensonmedia.com/freetrial

1. Launch Sorenson Squeeze, and save a new project file as `Apollo_13.sqz`.

2. The first important task is to build a group of presets to use for the project. As I mentioned at the beginning of this section, oftentimes I only build a project file with presets that I can provide to my client. Open the Macromedia Flash Video group in the Format & Compression Settings pane. You'll use four of the default presets as starting points for the encoding profiles outlined in the last section. Drag the following presets to the Job pane: VP6_768K_Stream, VP6_512K_Stream, VP6_256K_Stream, and VP6_56K_Dial_Up_Stream. When you are finished, the Job pane should resemble **Figure 12.8**.

TIP

▶ If you prefer to use another Flash Video encoding tool, you're not out of luck. You can create a QuickTime (MOV) reference file that links the M2V and AIFF files together. The reference movie for this Apollo 13 footage, Apollo_13_24fps_ref.mov, can be found in the source/mpeg/demuxed folder on the DVD-ROM.

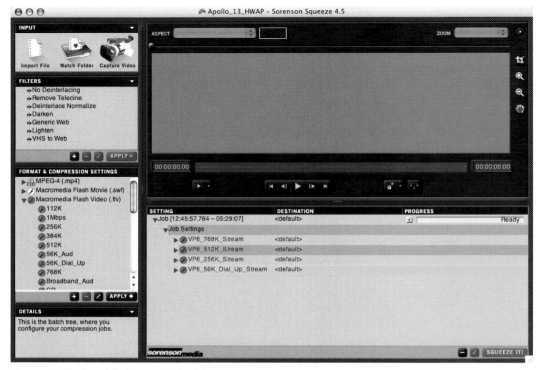

Figure 12.8 The four default presets in the Job pane.

NOTES

► If the Flash Video (FLV) file was being delivered from a Web server as a progressive download, a lower keyframe interval value would have been used to create more keyframes. Flash Player can only show keyframes during user operations such as scrubbing and seeking. Flash Media Server applications, on the other hand, can create keyframes on the fly. Because of this feature, the keyframe interval is not as critical during the encoding stage.

3. Rename the VP6_768K_Stream preset by expanding the preset in the Job pane (**Figure 12.9**) and double-clicking the MP3 or VP6 Pro property in the preset. In the Audio/Video Compression Settings dialog (**Figure 12.10**), type `SQZ_VP6_800K_CBR` in the Name field at the top left corner. The Name value is automatically added as a file suffix to the final FLV file. Apply the changes to the preset as indicated in the "Determining Encoding Profiles" section on page 304. Note that the Key Frame Every (or keyframe interval) is set to 240, a value that is ten times the frame rate of the source video. The Auto Key Frames Enabled option is also applied in the compression settings.

Figure 12.9 The expanded properties of the first preset.

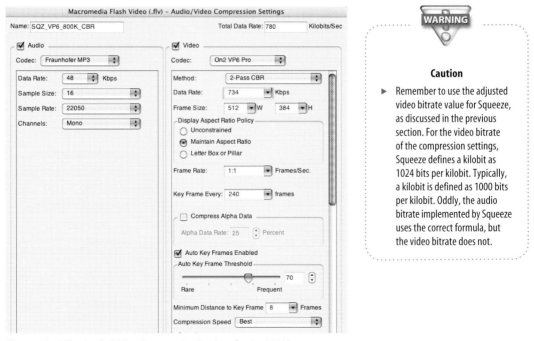

Figure 12.10 The Audio/Video Compression Settings for the 800 Kbps stream.

WARNING

Caution

▶ Remember to use the adjusted video bitrate value for Squeeze, as discussed in the previous section. For the video bitrate of the compression settings, Squeeze defines a kilobit as 1024 bits per kilobit. Typically, a kilobit is defined as 1000 bits per kilobit. Oddly, the audio bitrate implemented by Squeeze uses the correct formula, but the video bitrate does not.

On the DVD-ROM

► You can find a version of the Squeeze project file, 24fps_multibitrate.sqz, in the encoder_files folder on the DVD-ROM.

4. Repeat step 3 for the remaining presets, using the data from Table 12.1 and the profile descriptions from the previous section. Change the name of each preset to indicate the total bitrate of the output. Remember to use the Squeeze-adjusted video bitrate value for each preset. Note that the frame rate for the 35 Kbps preset is 2:1, unlike the other presets, which use 1:1. When you are finished, the Job pane should reflect the new preset names (**Figure 12.11**).

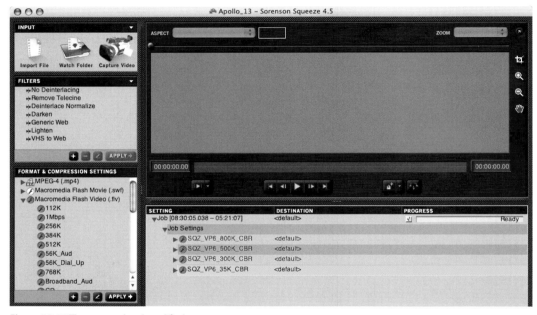

Figure 12.11 The renamed and modified presets.

► You can replace the audio track of any video source file with the Link Audio option, even if the imported video clip already has an existing audio track.

5. Save the project file.

6. Now you're ready to import the M2V and AIFF files for the Apollo 13 footage. Click the Import File button in the top left corner of Squeeze, or choose File > Import Source. Browse to the M2V file created by After Effects, or import a copy of the Apollo_13_24fps.m2v file from the book's DVD-ROM.

7. After the M2V file has been added to the Job pane, right-click (or Control-click on Mac) the filename,

and choose Link Audio (**Figure 12.12**). Browse to the AIFF file created by MPEG Streamclip, and import the file. The Job pane should now show both files as one item (**Figure 12.13**).

Figure 12.12 The Link Audio option for a source video clip.

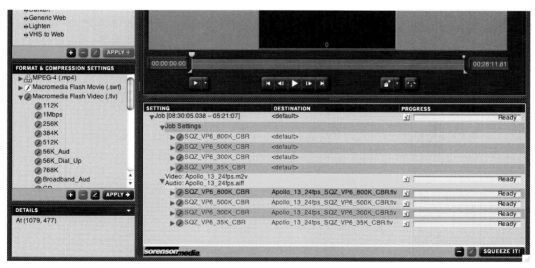

Figure 12.13 The updated Job pane.

NOTES

▶ If you're using the Windows version of Squeeze, you will need to convert the AIFF file created by MPEG Streamclip to a WAV file. You can use QuickTime Player Pro to do this. You can find a WAV-file version of the audio track in the source/mpeg/demuxed folder on the DVD-ROM.

8. The last task to complete before starting compression is to disable deinterlacing. Because the M2V file uses a 720 by 480 frame size, common for NTSC broadcast video, Squeeze will automatically apply deinterlacing to the content during encoding—even if it's already deinterlaced! Because the footage was already preprocessed with After Effects, deinterlacing does not need to be applied to this footage. In the Filters pane of Squeeze, click the add (+) button to create a new filter. In the Filter Settings dialog (**Figure 12.14**), name the filter No Deinterlacing. Make sure all options within the filter are disabled. Click OK to close the dialog.

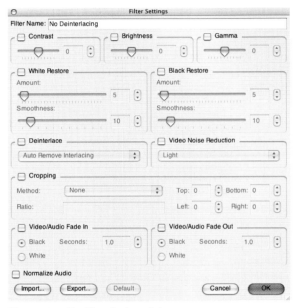

Figure 12.14 The Filter Settings dialog.

9. Make sure the Apollo 13 footage item is selected in the Job pane. Select the new No Deinterlacing filter in the Filters pane, and click the Apply button. The filter is now copied to all of the presets for the footage (**Figure 12.15**). By creating an empty filter and applying it to the footage, Squeeze will not preprocess the footage before encoding to Flash Video.

Figure 12.15 The new filter applied to the footage.

10. Click the Squeeze It button at the lower right corner of the Squeeze application window to begin encoding the four Flash Video (FLV) files. The encoding process may require several hours to complete.

When the encoding process is done, you'll have four FLV files that you can upload to a Flash Media Server account. For the remainder of this chapter, you can access the existing FLV files on this book's Influxis hosted account, as specified in the apollo_13_rtmp.smil file, located in the ch12 folder of the DVD-ROM.

NOTES

On the DVD-ROM

▶ You can find the finished Squeeze project file, Apollo_ 13.sqz, in the encoder_files folder on the DVD-ROM. The four FLV files located in the flv folder of the DVD-ROM.

Developing the Video Player

The Apollo 13 example features a video player that extends the functionality of the new ActionScript 3.0 version of the

FLVPlayback component. On its own, the FLVPlayback component can provide a wide range of options for a full-featured video playback experience, including the following capabilities required for the Apollo 13 example:

- ▶ Full screen video capability
- ▶ Multiple bitrates with SMIL files
- ▶ Automatic connection speed calculations with Flash Media Server
- ▶ Custom skin controls
- ▶ Comprehensive video event handling

However, other tasks require custom scripting. The video player for the Apollo 13 example needs to enable the following features:

- ▶ Configure options with HTML parameters
- ▶ Display preview content (or a poster SWF) before playback starts
- ▶ Display error messages to the user when video parameters are incorrect or a video connection fails
- ▶ Display custom graphics to users who have earlier versions of the Flash Player installed

As discussed earlier in this chapter, the video player code base uses ActionScript 3.0 (AS3), which requires Flash Player 9. While it's beyond the scope of this book to provide a line-by-line code analysis of each custom class, I'll walk you through a summary of the AS3 classes I built for the project, including the document class that initiates the experience.

FLA files

There are three Flash (FLA) files listed in the ch12.flp project file, each providing a specific task for a comprehensive and reliable video experience.

ExpressInstall file

If the user has Flash Player 6.0.65 or higher installed, a custom SWF file can initiate the ExpressInstall process to upgrade the user's Flash Player. The SWFObject.useExpressInstall() method in the JavaScript of the ReliableVideo_AS3.html document, discussed later in this chapter, specifies the apollo_13_expressinstall.swf file.

NOTES

- ▶ You can open each ActionScript (AS) class file to review the code. The ActionScript 3.0 classes for this chapter are located in the classes/AS3/com/flashsupport/video folder of the DVD-ROM. The ch12.flp project file located in the ch12 folder also provides quick and easy access to the Apollo 13 project files.

The apollo_13_expressinstall.fla file has custom graphics taken from the Apollo 13 documentary footage. The first frame of this file is shown to users with older Flash Players (**Figure 12.16**). If the user clicks the Yes, Install Now button, the ExpressInstall dialog is displayed, prompting the user to initiate the upgrade process (**Figure 12.17**). If the user clicks the No button in this dialog, a JavaScript alert dialog is displayed (**Figure 12.18**), indicating that the content requires the latest Flash Player. The second frame of the apollo_13_expressinstall.swf file is displayed for this condition as well (**Figure 12.19**), prompting the user to go to the Adobe Web site to download the Flash Player installer. If the user clicks the Yes button to begin the upgrade process, the plug-in is downloaded behind the scenes and installed. Mozilla-compatible browsers need to be closed before the upgrade can complete; these browsers are automatically restarted and taken back to the Apollo 13 Web page.

Figure 12.16 The first frame of the ExpressInstall movie.

Figure 12.17 The Flash Player's built-in prompt to upgrade to the latest version.

Figure 12.18 The JavaScript alert dialog.

Figure 12.19 The second frame of the ExpressInstall movie.

TIP

▶ The ApolloPoster document class extends a custom ActionScript 3.0 class named Poster. You can find the Poster.as file in the classes/as3/com/flashsupport/video folder on the DVD-ROM. The file can also be accessed from the ch12.flp project file. By extending the Poster class with your own document class, you can create your poster movie to work with the ReliableVideo class.

Poster file

If the user has Flash Player 9.0.28 or higher installed, the primary SWF file, ReliableVideo_AS3.swf (discussed in the next section), can load another SWF file acting as a preview frame (also called a poster frame) for the video clip. The poster SWF file is loaded as soon as the video player loads. The apollo_13_poster.fla file contains title graphics nearly identical to those used in the ExpressInstall movie. The ApolloPoster.as file serves as the ActionScript 3.0 document class for the poster movie. A Watch Now button in the poster movie enables playback of the video clip loaded by the primary SWF file.

Video player file

The heart of the video experience for the Apollo 13 example is the ReliableVideo_AS3.swf file. The Flash file, ReliableVideo_AS3.fla, uses the ReliableVideoExample.as file as the document class. The library of the ReliableVideo_AS3.fla file contains an instance of the FLVPlayback component. Nothing appears on the authortime stage of the Flash file—everything is created and placed on the stage with ActionScript.

Core Classes

The ReliableVideo_AS3.swf file must be able to process several operations in order to function properly. These tasks, in linear order as experienced by the user, are:

NOTES

▶ The BackgroundBox class is used by the Apollo 13 example but is not discussed in this chapter. For more information on this custom AS3 class, refer to Chapter 9.

1. Load the skin (SWF) file.

2. Load the SMIL or FLV file.

3. Load the poster (SWF) file.

4. Set up external calls to JavaScript.

5. Enable the Play control within the poster file.

Let's look at how each of these responsibilities is handled by an ActionScript 3.0 class created for the project. Some of the classes handle more than one task.

In Flash CS3, open the ch12.flp project file from the ch12 folder on the DVD-ROM to review each of these classes as they are described in the following sections.

ReliableVideo class

The core of operations can be found in the `ReliableVideo` class, which creates or loads all the assets required for the video playback experience. An instance of the `ReliableVideo` class has the following ten public properties that can be controlled via HTML `flashvars` parameters. Many of these properties control the same-named properties of the FLVPlayback instance created by the class:

> ► The ReliableVideoExample document class, discussed later in this chapter, does the job of parsing HTML `flashvars` parameters and passing them to an instance of the `ReliableVideo` class.

► `autoPlay`: This property controls the `autoPlay` property of the FLVPlayback instance, and determines if the FLV file (or SMIL file) automatically loads and plays. If the property is set to `true`, the video automatically plays when the user loads the player. If the property is set to `false`, the video does not play until the user clicks the play button in the skin or the Watch Now button in the poster SWF. The HTML `flashvars` name is `"autoPlay"`, which can use string values of `"true"` or `"1"` for `true`, and `"false"` or `"0"` for `false`.

► `flvURL`: This property controls the `source` property of the FLVPlayback instance, which specifies the FLV file (or SMIL) to load for playback. If a value for this property is not specified, the ReliableVideo instance displays the message, "The video can not start because a video URL was not specified." The HTML `flashvars` name is `"flvURL"`.

► `posterURL`: This property specifies the path to the poster SWF file. If you are using a real-time streaming FLV path for the `flvURL` property, the `posterURL` property is optional. However, for progressive-download FLV files, the poster SWF file's controls provide the only user interface to initiate playback of the FLV file. The HTML `flashvars` name is `"posterURL"`.

► `preferredWidth`: This property controls the width of the `ReliableVideo` instance, as well as the width of the nested FLVPlayback instance. This property can be controlled in HTML by specifying a pixel width for the plug-in `<object>` or `<embed>` tag, or with the width parameter for the `new SWFObject()` constructor in JavaScript.

► `preferredHeight`: This property controls the height of the `ReliableVideo` instance. The nested FLVPlayback instance uses this value to calculate its own height, which is 44 pixels shorter to accommodate a skin SWF that is displayed below the video area. This property can be controlled in HTML by specifying a pixel height for the plug-in `<object>` or `<embed>` tag, or with the height parameter for the `new SWFObject()` constructor in JavaScript.

▶ `skinAutoHide`: This property controls the `skinAutoHide` property of the nested FLVPlayback instance. For more information on this property, refer to Chapter 5. The HTML `flashvars` name is `"skinAutoHide"`.

▶ `skinBackgroundAlpha`: This property controls the `skinBackgroundAlpha` property of the nested FLVPlayback instance. For more information on this property, refer to Chapter 5. The HTML `flashvars` name is `"skinBackgroundAlpha"`, with a string representation of a decimal number between 0 and 1.

▶ `skinBackgroundColor`: This property controls the `skinBackgroundColor` property of the nested FLVPlayback instance. For more information on this property, refer to Chapter 5. The HTML `flashvars` name is `"skinBackgroundColor"`, with a string value indicating the hex value for the color, such as #666666. Note that the # character is optional in the `flashvars` value.

▶ `skinURL`: This property controls the `skin` property of the nested FLVPlayback instance, loading the user interface controls for video playback. The HTML `flashvars` name is `"skinURL"`.

▶ `videoSmoothing`: This Boolean property controls the `Video.smoothing` property of the `VideoPlayer` instance nested with the FLVPlayback instance. Smoothing improves the quality of scaled video but consumes more processing power from the computer. The HTML `flashvars` name is `"videoSmoothing"`, which can use string values of `"true"` or `"1"` for `true` and `"false"` or `"0"` for `false`.

Once these properties have been set on an instance of the `ReliableVideo` class, the `ReliableVideo.initialize()` method can be invoked to start loading the assets.

ApolloPoster and Poster classes

The poster file, apollo_13_poster.fla, uses the `ApolloPoster` document class, which extends the `Poster` class. The `Poster` class has the following features:

▶ `items` **property:** This property specifies an array of `DisplayObject` instances within the poster to be shown or hidden from the user. For the Apollo 13 example, the `headerField` instance, which is a `TextField` instance, and the `watchBtn` instance, which is a `MovieClip` instance, are the elements added to the `items` property from the `ApolloPoster` class.

▶ `displayControls` **method:** This method controls the visibility of the elements in the `items` array. When the poster SWF is loaded into the ReliableVideo_AS3.swf movie, the `ReliableVideo` class calls the `displayControls()` method, passing a `false` parameter to hide the elements. When the `VideoEvent.READY` event is broadcast from the FLVPlayback instance within the `ReliableVideo` instance, the `ReliableVideo.onVideoReady()` method is triggered, passing a `true` parameter to the `displayControls()` method. The controls should only be shown if the video URL is valid and ready to play.

▶ `Poster.VIEW_CLICK` **event:** This event is triggered from the `Poster` class when the `onViewClick()` method is invoked within the class. This method is utilized by the Watch Now button created by the `ApolloPoster` class, discussed next.

The `ApolloPoster` class extends the `Poster` class, which means that the `ApolloPoster` class inherits all the same properties and methods of the `Poster` class. The `ApolloPoster` class is specified as the document class for the apollo_13_poster.fla file. In addition to the features of the `Poster` class, the `ApolloPoster` class provides the following functionality for the poster SWF:

▶ **Creates a Play control and description text:** The `init()` method of the `ApolloPoster` class creates the elements added to the `items` array, as described in the previous list.

▶ **Creates button handlers for the Play control:** The `watchBtn` `MovieClip` instance is given mouse rollover and rollout

NOTES

▶ The controls are immediately shown if the flvURL property of the `ReliableVideo` instance indicates a progressive-download Flash Video file.

states that change the color of the button background. Most importantly, the button listens for the MouseEvent. CLICK event, which invokes the onButtonClick() handler. This handler, in turn, calls the onViewClick() handler of the Poster class.

ExpressInstall class

As I discussed earlier in this chapter, a customized Express-Install SWF, apollo_13_expressinstall.swf, is loaded by JavaScript with the SWFObject library if the user does not have Flash Player 9.0.28 or higher. The SWFObject source code, available from Geoff Stearns at blog.deconcept.com/ swfobject, includes an ExpressInstall class that you can use with your own ExpressInstall content. You can find a slightly revised version of Geoff's ExpressInstall class in the classes/AS2/com/deconcept/expressinstall folder of this book's DVD-ROM. A typical use of this class looks like this:

```
ExpressInstall.getInstance().loadUpdater();
```

That's it! With just one line of code in your own Express-Install movie, Flash Player 6.0.65 or higher can update the Flash Player for the browser.

I modified the ExpressInstall class to make it capable of broadcasting events related to the install status. In the apollo_13_expressinstall.fla file, the first frame's action includes the apollo_13_expressinstall.as file located in the ch12/includes folder. This ActionScript file creates button handlers for the Yes, Install Now button (the installBtn instance). The onRelease() handler is delegated to the onInstallClick function, which does the following:

```
function onInstallClick():Void {
    // start the update
    ExpressInstall.getInstance().loadUpdater();
    ExpressInstall.getInstance().addEventListener(
            "installStatus",Delegate.create(this,
            ➥onInstallStatus)
        );
}
```

> ▶ You can read more about SWFObject and ExpressInstall in Chapter 5.

If the ExpressInstall procedure fails or is cancelled by the user, the onInstallStatus function in the apollo_13_expressinstall.as code is called. This function tells the ExpressInstall SWF to go to and stop on the second frame, which directs the user to manually install the plug-in from Adobe's Web site.

```
function onInstallStatus(e:Object):Void {
  var msg:String = e.code;
  if(msg == "Download.Cancelled" || msg == "Download.
  ➥Failed"){
    this.gotoAndStop(2);
  }
}
```

ReliableVideoExample document class

The last class required for the Apollo 13 example is the ReliableVideoExample document class. This class instantiates the ReliableVideo class, specifying the ten properties previously described in my summary of the ReliableVideo class. Review the code from the document class in the following code block. Most of the script's actions are related to retrieving each property that is specified in the HTML flashvars parameters:

```
package {

  // Import intrinsic classes
  import flash.display.Sprite;
  import flash.display.LoaderInfo;
  import flash.display.StageScaleMode;

  // Import custom AS3 class for video playback
  // which requires the FLVPlayback component
  // to be added to the FLA file's library
  import com.flashsupport.video.ReliableVideo;

  // Declare the document class name
  public class ReliableVideoExample extends Sprite {

    // Define a constructor function
    function ReliableVideoExample(){
      // Start the movie
      init();
    }
```

(Continues on next page)

```
// Define a function to fire when the SWF loads
private function init():void {

  // Do not scale Flash movie contents
  this.stage.scaleMode = StageScaleMode.NO_SCALE;

  var rv:ReliableVideo = new ReliableVideo();

  // Set the width and height of the player
  rv.preferredWidth = this.stage.stageWidth;
  rv.preferredHeight = this.stage.stageHeight;

  // Add the instance to the display list
  addChild(rv);

  // Retrieve the HTML parameters
  var li:LoaderInfo = this.loaderInfo;

  // Retrive the flashvars properties
  var fv:Object = li.parameters;

  // Check and set each property for the
  ➥ReliableVideo instance

  if(fv.flvURL != null) rv.flvURL = fv.flvURL;
  if(fv.skinURL != null) rv.skinURL = fv.skinURL;

  if(fv.posterURL != null) rvPlayer.posterURL =
  ➥fv.posterURL;

  if(fv.autoPlay != null) rv.autoPlay =
  ➥evalBool(fv.autoPlay);
  if(fv.skinAutoHide != null)
  ➥rv.skinAutoHide = evalBool(fv.skinAutoHide);

  if(fv.skinBackgroundAlpha != null)
  ➥rv.skinBackgroundAlpha = Number(fv.
  ➥skinBackgroundAlpha);

  if(fv.skinBackgroundColor != null){
    var paramVal:String = fv.skinBackgroundColor;
    var hexVal:String = paramVal.indexOf("#") !=
    ➥-1 ? paramVal.substr(1) : paramVal;
    rv.skinBackgroundColor = parseInt("0x" +
    ➥hexVal);
  }

  if(fv.videoSmoothing != null) rv.videoSmoothing
  ➥= evalBool(fv.videoSmoothing);
```

```
    // Initalize the ReliableVideo instance
    rv.initialize();
  }

  // Convert string representations of Boolean values
  private function evalBool(val:String):Boolean {
    return (val.toLowerCase() == "true" || val ==
    ➥"1") ? true : false;
  }
 }
}
```

To see how the document class is specified for the FLA file, open the ReliableVideo_AS3.fla file in Flash CS3 and choose File > Publish Settings. Select the Flash tab in the Publish Settings dialog. Click the Settings button next to the ActionScript version option. In the ActionScript 3.0 Settings dialog (**Figure 12.20**), you can review the settings required to import the ReliableVideoExample class.

TIP

▶ You can also specify the document class in the Property inspector. Make sure you deselect any elements on the stage to reveal the document settings in the Property inspector.

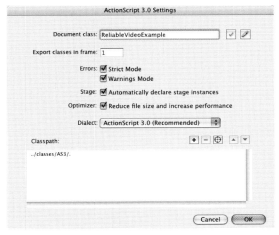

Figure 12.20 The ActionScript 3.0 Settings dialog for the ReliableVideo_AS3.fla file.

You now know the ingredients to build a Flash Video experience that evaluates the user's installed Flash Player and proceeds to deliver the appropriate content. Try reusing the ReliableVideo project files with your own Flash Video content. You can continue to add your own code, or revise existing portions of the class files to accommodate special features you'd like to integrate.

NOTES

On the DVD-ROM

▶ You can find the completed files in the ch12 folder on the DVD-ROM.

NOTES

▶ I'd like to extend my gratitude to Bruce Hyslop, Director of Interface Engineering at Schematic, for his assistance with the HTML, CSS, and JavaScript code used for this example.

On the DVD-ROM

▶ You can find the HTML, CSS, and JavaScript files for the example in the ch12 folder of this book's DVD-ROM.

▶ The changes to the CSS file are mostly cosmetic. You can review the style additions in the twoColHybLtHdr.css file in the ch12 folder on the DVD-ROM.

Customizing the Video Experience with HTML and JavaScript

Once the essential Flash SWF files are ready, you can build the HTML and JavaScript necessary to display the appropriate SWF content to the user. SWFObject handles the Flash Player detection and `flashvars` parameters, while additional JavaScript enables HTML elements to communicate with the ReliableVideo_AS3.swf file, controlling the seek time for the Apollo 13 footage.

HTML and CSS

I used one of the new HTML and CSS templates available in Adobe Dreamweaver CS3 to create the initial look and feel of the Apollo 13 page. In the New Document dialog (File > New), I chose a Page Type of HTML and a Layout of 2 column hybrid, left sidebar, header and footer (**Figure 12.21**). The DocType menu was set to XHTML 1.0 Strict, and the Layout CSS menu was changed to New File. The CSS file was saved with the default name, twoColHybLtHdr. css, and the HTML file as `ReliableVideo_AS3.html`. The modifications to the HTML document are discussed in the remaining sections of this chapter.

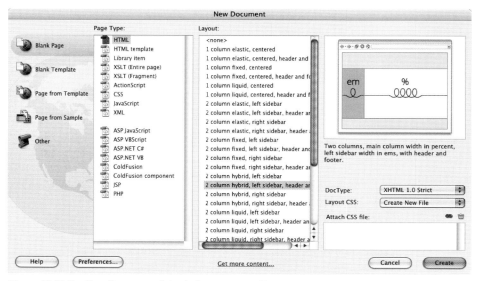

Figure 12.21 The New Document dialog in Dreamweaver CS3.

SWFObject Revisited

The Dreamweaver template automatically created a
`<div id="mainContent">` tag for the middle right area of
the HTML page. In this container, I created a nested `<div>`
tag to hold the alternate HTML content for the Flash Video
player, as shown in the following code. Everything in the
`videoContent` element will be replaced by SWFObject with
either the ExpressInstall SWF if Flash Player 6.0.65 or higher
is installed or the ReliableVideo SWF if Flash Player 9.0.28
or higher is installed.

```
<div id="videoContent">
   <div id="videoImage">
      <img src="web_images/Apollo_13_Houston_title.jpg"
      ➥width="360"
         height="430" alt="Poster image of Apollo 13
         ➥'Houston, We've Got
         a Problem'" />
   </div>
   <div id="noPlayerText">
      <p class="noPlayer">To watch the video, enable
      ➥JavaScript in your
         browser and install the latest Flash
         ➥Player.</p>
      <a href="http://www.adobe.com/go/getflashplayer">
         <img src="get_flash_player.gif" width="88"
         ➥height="31" alt="Get
         Adobe Flash Player" />
      </a>
   </div>
</div>
```

If JavaScript is disabled, Flash Player 6.0.47 or earlier is
installed, or no version of Flash Player is installed, the
browser displays this content (**Figure 12.22**) to the user.

At the bottom of the HTML document, before the closing
`</body>` tag, the JavaScript code is placed to create a new
SWFObject instance that checks the Flash Player version
and overwrites the `videoContent` element with the appropriate SWF content.

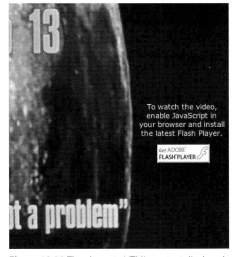

Figure 12.22 The alternate HTML content displayed
by the browser.

```
<script type="text/javascript">
  // <![CDATA[
  var so = new SWFObject("ReliableVideo_AS3.swf",
  ➥"flvMain", "512", "430", "9.0.28", "#FFFFFF",
  ➥true);
  so.addParam("allowFullScreen", "true");
  so.addParam("allowScriptAccess", "always");
  so.addParam("salign", "tl");
  so.addVariable("skinURL",
  ➥"SkinUnderPlaySeekMuteFullscreen.swf");
  so.addVariable("flvURL", "apollo_13_rtmp.smil");
  so.addVariable("posterURL", "apollo_13_poster.swf");
  so.addVariable("autoPlay", "false");
  so.addVariable("skinAutoHide", "false");
  so.addVariable("skinBackgroundColor", "#666666");
  so.addVariable("skinBackgroundAlpha", "1");
  so.addVariable("videoSmoothing", "true");
  so.useExpressInstall("apollo_13_expressinstall.swf");
  so.write("videoContent");
  // ]]>
</script>
```

All the properties required for the `ReliableVideo` class are created with the `SWFObject.addVariable()` method. Additional parameters, such as `allowFullScreen` and `salign`, enable full screen mode and SWF alignment, respectively. The `allowScriptAccess` parameter is required for the Action-Script `ExternalInterface` class and JavaScript, discussed next.

ExternalInterface and JavaScript

Since Flash Player 8, Flash SWF content has had the capability to communicate more easily with its host environment, such as a browser. The `ExternalInterface` class, enlisted in the `ReliableVideo` class, enables a Flash movie to map external functions in the hosting script environment, such as JavaScript, with internal functions in ActionScript.

The `ReliableVideo` class has the following two functions, which enable the class to communicate with a JavaScript function named `sendToActionScript`. When JavaScript sends arguments to the `sendToActionScript()` function, the ActionScript `receivedFromJavaScript()` function is invoked with the same parameters.

```
private function setupExternalInterface():void {
   Security.allowDomain("*");
   try {
      ExternalInterface.addCallback("sendToFlashVide
      ➥o", receivedFromJavaScript);
   } catch (error:SecurityError) {
      displayMessage("A SecurityError occurred: " +
      ➥error.message);
   } catch (error:Error) {
      displayMessage("An Error occurred: " + error.
      message);
   }
}

private function receivedFromJavaScript(command:
➥String, val:String):void {
   if(command == "seek" && !isNaN(Number(val))){
      playVideo();
      player.seek(Number(val));
   }
}
```

For the Apollo 13 example, only one feature is enabled with the `ExternalInterface` class: the ability to seek to a new time in the Flash Video. If JavaScript passes a `command` value of "seek" and a valid `Number` value for the `val` parameter, the FLV content seeks to the new position.

In the HTML document, the images in the `sidebar1` container are given `<a>` tags to pass seek values to the Flash SWF file. The images are stored in an unordered list for easier processing in JavaScript. Here's a sample seek command used by the first thumbnail image:

```
<li> <a href="no_js.html?cmd=seek&amp;val=154"
➥title="Seek to time

0:02:34"> <img src="web_images/Apollo_13_
➥thumbnail-001.jpg" width="160"

height="120" alt="Thumbnail of Apollo 13 launch" />
➥</a> </li>
```

NOTES

▶ The `Security.allowDomain()` method specifies which documents have access to the SWF file. For this example, the value of "*" enables all domains access.

▶ The setupLinks function requires functions defined in the external JavaScript file, flashvideo.js. This file can be found in the ch12 folder on the DVD-ROM.

The cmd and val values in the href attribute are parsed and used by the onclick handler assigned to each <a> tag when the document loads. The setupLinks and controlVideo functions defined at the top of the HTML document handle this task. When the user clicks a thumbnail, the seek value assigned to the image is passed to the Flash SWF file. If JavaScript is disabled in the browser, the no_js.html document loads into a new browser window, instructing the user that JavaScript is required for the operation.

You now know the breadth and depth of assets required to create a foolproof Flash Video player on an HTML page. Once you've tested your own solution, you can reuse the framework for a wide range of Flash Video projects.

Software Installation

This book's DVD-ROM includes sample files for several applications, including Adobe Flash CS3 Professional and Sorenson Squeeze. You can download trial versions for most of the applications discussed in the chapter's examples and walk-throughs.

Adobe Software

Adobe creates a wide range of Web design, print design, and video production tools. You can download time-limited versions of Adobe software at www.adobe.com/downloads.

I discuss the following Adobe products in this book:

► Adobe After Effects® CS3 Professional

► Adobe Dreamweaver® CS3

► Adobe Flash® CS3 Professional (includes Adobe Flash CS3 Video Encoder)

► Adobe Photoshop® CS3

► Adobe Premiere® Pro

► Macromedia Flash Media Server 2.0

Flash Video Encoders

If you're looking for an alternative to the Adobe Flash CS3 Video Encoder to produce FLV files, you can try out a third-party software product. These products offer a wide range of features that streamline your video production workflow.

► **Sorenson Squeeze:** You can download a trial version of Squeeze Compression Suite at www.sorensonmedia.com/freetrial. The Compression Suite edition includes presets to output other audio/video formats such as Windows Media, MPEG-4, and QuickTime.

The trial version adds a watermark at the corner of the video frame. Mac and Windows versions are available.

▶ **On2 Flix Pro:** You can download a trial version of On2 Flix Pro at www.on2.com/downloads. The trial version adds audio and video watermarks to the FLV output. Mac and Windows versions are available.

▶ **Telestream Episode Pro:** Another high-quality Flash Video encoding tool is Episode Pro, a compression product that can output a variety of video formats. You can download a trial version of this tool at www.flip4mac. com/episode_download.htm. The trial version is limited to 20 seconds of compressed video output. This encoding tool is available only for Mac systems.

Flash Video Utilities

No Flash Video production workflow is complete without products that can play and modify source video files before you process the footage with a Flash Video encoding tool.

QuickTime software

Most professional video production incorporates the QuickTime architecture for video playback. Here are the essential tools for QuickTime:

▶ **Apple QuickTime Player Pro:** While the basic QuickTime Player is available as a free download, you can unlock the Pro edition of the QuickTime Player by purchasing a license key from Apple. The Pro edition enables you to transcode video files from one codec to another. You can also combine or split audio and video tracks with source files. You can download the QuickTime Player at www.apple.com/quicktime, and purchase a QuickTime license from the online Apple Store at store.apple.com.

▶ **Apple MPEG-2 Playback Component:** If you want to be able to open MPEG-2 source files in QuickTime Player, you need to purchase this playback component from the online Apple Store. This component is also required to open MPEG-2 files in QuickTime-enabled applications such as MPEG Streamclip, discussed later in this list.

- **Perian QuickTime Component:** If you use the Mac version of QuickTime Player, you'll love this free component that enables playback of FLV files directly in the QuickTime Player application. You can drag and drop FLV files to QuickTime Player for quick playback and preview.

- **MPEG Streamclip:** This free utility, available for Windows and Mac, is a powerhouse MPEG converter. I use this tool most frequently to convert HDV capture files to MPEG program files (that is, an MPEG file with modified headers), or to demux a multiplexed MPEG file into separate MPEG-2 video (M2V) and audio (M2A) files. You can download this utility at www.squared5.com.

- **Miraizon Cinematize:** This cross-platform product enables you to extract MPEG-2 video files from DVD-Video discs. If a client wants you to create Flash Video (FLV) files from a DVD-Video disc, you can use this product to convert the VOB files on the DVD-Video disc to MPEG-2 program files or transcode to another file format and video codec. You can download an evaluation version of Cinematize at www.miraizon.com.

Adobe FLVCheck Tool

This new Windows command-line utility enables you to check and fix the FLV files created by your Flash Video encoding tool. At the time of this writing, this tool was in beta and available at http://labs.adobe.com/technologies/flvcheck.

Captionate

This Windows-only software product, created by the Manitu Group, can create caption and cue point data for Flash Video content. You can download a trial version of the tool at www.buraks.com or www.manitugroup.com. You can also download free FLV utilities such as the FLV MetaData Injector at www.buraks.com. If you'd like to be able to view FLV file details from Windows Explorer, you can download the free FLV MetaData Viewer for Windows at www.buraks.com/flvmdv. This add-on enables you to right-click an FLV file and access the file's FLV properties in an FLV Details tab.

NOTES

I've also provided a Microsoft Excel worksheet in the tools folder on this book's DVD-ROM. You can download a trial version of Microsoft Office at www.microsoft.com/office.

Public-Domain Video

Many of the sample video clips used in examples through-out this book are available for download on archive.org. This Web site features many public-domain video files that you are free to use and distribute with your own content. The Prelinger Archives at archive.org contain nearly 2000 pieces of content which are 100% royalty-free, public-domain content. You can search the collection at:

www.archive.org/details/prelinger

For an up-to-date list of links pointing to the specific clips used within this book, visit:

www.flashsupport.com/books/fvst

B

Flash Video Project Checklist

Before you start a Flash Video production, you should gather critical information related to your business client's requirements. Make sure you are given the answers to these questions before ramping up any Flash Video production. Each of these questions is just as important as the next.

▶ **How many Flash Video bitrates does your client want to support?**

For each piece of video content, how many FLV files will be available for the Flash movie to load? If your client wants to maintain only one FLV file per piece of content, you'll likely want to use a medium-quality bitrate, such as 384 Kbps. With only one bitrate per clip, you should deploy the FLV files from a standard Web server (over HTTP), so that the content can progressively download to the browser. The FLV file can then be viewed by anyone with any connection speed; slower connections will take longer to buffer the clip, while faster connections will play the FLV file more instantaneously. If you are encoding more than one bitrate per clip, you can deploy your content with a Web server (HTTP), a Flash Media Server (RTMP), or a Flash Video Streaming Service provider (RTMP and/or HTTP).

You should consider file-storage requirements for your client's video library. If your client has a vast collection of video to distribute online, encoding more than one bitrate per clip may be beyond their resources.

▶ **How will the Flash Video files be delivered?**

The delivery method you use for Flash Video content will depend on the demands of the potential audience for a Flash Video production. Most Flash Video content on the Web is delivered from standard Web servers over HTTP. This type of delivery ensures that just about everyone can download and view the Flash Video content. If the traffic to a Web site is light, you can host the FLV files on a regular Web hosting account. For high-volume Web sites, though, you should consider using a Flash Video Streaming Service provider such as Limelight or Akamai. These services use RTMP and/or HTTP delivery methods for Flash Video content.

The longer the Flash Video content, the more likely you should opt to use an RTMP delivery method. For example, if you want to offer a 30-minute video clip on the site, the content would be better served from an RTMP service.

If you're using a Web server for deployment (HTTP), you can encode the FLV files with VBR (Variable Bit Rate) compression if your Flash Video encoding software offers the option. If you're using a real-time streaming service (RTMP), then you should use CBR (Constant Bit Rate) encoding in your compression tool.

▶ **Does the video content require Digital Rights Management (DRM)?**

Many content creators do not want to enable viewers to illegally distribute or use their video content. The legal staff of your business client will likely want to evaluate any Internet-enabled delivery method for video content. Some businesses trust only the DRM solutions offered by Microsoft Windows Media, but *real-time streaming* Flash Video has gained more acceptance by the industry as a method to protect video content.

If your business client wants to protect video content, you should always use an RTMP delivery mechanism. Until Adobe offers a true DRM and licensing solution equivalent to Windows Media, there is no other way to protect Flash Video assets.

▶ **What kind of source video files can the client provide?**

Another consideration for Flash Video encoding is the quality of the video source file. If your client has only a low-quality source format, either as a videotape format or a digital file format, you may want to advise your client to produce new footage in a high-quality format. More and more video content is acquired in High Definition (HD), and the cost of HD equipment is becoming more affordable each day.

Before your client sends a large batch of video source files to you for encoding, request one source video file that's representative of the quality and duration of the video source collection. Create Flash Video samples from this source video file, which you can then demonstrate for the client.

▶ **What is the lowest acceptable video and audio quality for your business client's content?**

Every business client has different goals to achieve with their video content. For some, low-quality video is just fine—just take a look at YouTube.com or Google Video. These video files are hardly the best quality that can be achieved with Flash Video encoding software. Other clients, though, want to protect a brand image, and don't want to offer low-quality video. A quick trip to ABC.com's Full Episode Streaming site will show that you'd better have a fast Internet connection to watch their content. The lowest bitrate used by this site is 500 Kbps. Remember, video quality is determined by frame rate, frame size, and amount of motion in a clip.

The best way to gauge your client's appetite for quality is to produce a battery of sample files with their content. Make a Flash movie that shows a low, medium, and high bitrate sample for a few pieces of content. You can use the video comparison sample included in the ch02/deinterlace/flash_samples folder of this book's DVD-ROM to organize your clips—simply update the XML file with the names of your video files, and upload the new content files to your Web server for your client to view.

Not surprisingly, many content providers do not want to offer extremely low-quality content, such as a bitrate that's compatible with a 56 K dial-up modem connection. There are clients who may need low-bandwidth clips for their audience. If dial-up modem users are part of your target demographic, make sure you create content suitable for their connection speed. If you intend to push high-quality content to dial-up users, make sure the content is delivered by a Web server over an HTTP connection, so that the video file can progressively download to the user. Such users will still have to wait a longer time for content to download, but they can watch the content after it's cached in the browser.

▶ **What is the minimum version of the Flash Player that the client wishes to support?**

Before you encode your Flash Video content, you need to know the target Flash Player version. If your client wants to be backward-compatible to Flash Player 6, then you'll have limited options with your encoding and deployment strategy. Here's a quick summary of options available with each Flash Player version:

- ▶ **Flash Player 6:** Embedded video in SWF files and real-time streaming FLV files. Sorenson Spark video codec supported.

- ▶ **Flash Player 7:** Same options as Flash Player 6, with the addition of progressive-download FLV files.

- ▶ **Flash Player 8 or higher:** Same options as Flash Players 6 and 7, with the addition of On2 VP6 codec.

C

Encoding Flash Video

Throughout this book, I've discussed a variety of Flash Video encoding tools. This appendix summarizes and augments the compression coverage already provided in Chapter 3.

Overview of Common Features and Workflow

If you're in the market for picking a Flash Video encoding solution, you should weigh the factors that are most important for your typical day-to-day encoding needs. In this section, I review the features that you will use for most Flash Video projects.

Major Compression Controls

Regardless of which Flash Video encoding tool you use, every product enables you to control the bitrate (or data rate), frame size (width and height), and frame rate. Of all the settings in your compression preset, these properties have the most impact on the quality of the audio and video tracks.

▶ **Bitrate:** This value controls how much data, with respect to file size and transfer from the remote server, will be required per second of the video content. Every encoder enables you to allocate a bitrate for the video track and a bitrate for the audio track. Determining the bitrates you want to provide to your audience should be your first step in the compression process. If you are planning to deploy FLV files to a Flash Media Server (FMS) application or Flash Video Streaming Service (FVSS) provider, extra care should be given to creating ActionScript code that can detect the connection speed between the user's computer and the server. Streaming a video with a bitrate that exceeds the user's connection speed results in a disruptive viewing experience, where the user waits for longer periods of time for the video to buffer, play, and then buffer again.

TIP

▶ Use the Flash_Video_Bitrates.xls
spreadsheet in the tools folder
of this book's DVD-ROM to help
you determine the bitrate, frame
dimensions, and frame rate for
your video content.

▶ **Frame size:** Once you've determined a bitrate, you can calculate an appropriate width and height for your video. Use the compression formula in Chapter 3 to help you pick a frame size that maintains high quality for a given bitrate.

▶ **Frame rate:** The frame rate of your video should be based on a ratio of the original source video's frame rate, such as 1:1, 2:1, or 3:1. Lower frame rates allow you to maintain high quality and use a larger frame size for a given bitrate.

Other Factors

Not every encoding solution can control all aspects of the compression process. Here's a quick list of features that you may want on your shopping list for a Flash Video encoding tool:

▶ **CBR/VBR encoding:** Constant Bit Rate (CBR) encoding specifies that the output file evenly distributes the bitrate across a narrow span of time, usually four-to-six-second segments within the video. If the compression settings don't expose a CBR or VBR option, the encoder most likely uses CBR compression. CBR encoding should be used for FLV files that will be deployed with real-time streaming from FMS or FVSS. Variable Bit Rate (VBR) encoding enables the output file to use an average bitrate over the length of the entire video file, not just a narrow span of time like CBR encoding does. As such, less complex segments of video can underutilize the bitrate to allow more difficult segments to overutilize, or surpass, the average bitrate of the file.

▶ **Keyframe interval and automatic keyframes:** Most encoding products enable you to control how often a video keyframe (also known as an I-frame) is created within the video file. Keyframes require more bitrate than frames between keyframes, or P-frames. The general rule of thumb is to use a keyframe interval that is ten times the frame rate for the output file. So, if you specify a frame rate of 24 fps, you should implement a keyframe interval of 240 or less. Some encoders also enable you to specify a variability threshold to create additional keyframes, or automatic keyframes. If the content between two frames varies beyond the threshold value (usually specified as a percent of frame area), the encoder creates a new keyframe.

▶ **Cue points:** As you learned in Chapter 6, you can add navigation and event cue points during the encoding process. Cue points allow ActionScript and the FLVPlayback component to seek to specific times within the video (navigation cue points) or fire events to callback functions (event cue points). If you want to create navigation markers or synchronize other content with your Flash Video, you may want your encoder to support cue point creation.

▶ **Advanced codec settings:** Some encoders allow you to modify low-level processing and playback directives for the Sorenson Spark codec or the On2 VP6 codec. Most of your day-to-day compression tasks will not require you to alter such settings, but they can help you change output for special video deployment scenarios, such as high-bitrate DVD-ROM distribution.

Comparing Video Encoders

Each Flash Video encoder has a unique set of features. In this section, I summarize the strengths and weaknesses of four products that I use routinely in my Flash Video workflow. You can review the features for each encoder in **Table C.1**.

▶ **Adobe Flash CS3 Video Encoder:** The best feature about this tool is that it's automatically included and installed with Adobe Flash CS3 Professional. I also like the new cue point import and export feature, as discussed in Chapter 11. One drawback to this encoder is the lack of pixel-aspect-ratio detection. For example, when you import a DV source file with a nonsquare pixel aspect ratio, this encoder does not resize output automatically.

▶ **Sorenson Squeeze 4.5 (all editions):** Squeeze is my preferred Flash Video encoder because it looks and feels like other video applications. The application's panels are intuitive and easy to learn. Squeeze offers the most Flash Video presets, based primarily on bitrate, compared to any other Flash Video encoder. The ability to save a project file and share it with a co-worker or client is especially critical for large encoding jobs. Another nice feature of Squeeze is its ability to link audio and video source files together, as discussed in Chapter 12. The biggest drawback to Squeeze is its confusing bitrate values: The video bitrate setting for all compression presets is based on 1024 bits per kilobit, instead of the industry standard 1000 bits per kilobit. As such, any calculations involving the video bitrate need to be reverse-engineered for proper output, as discussed in Chapter 12. Oddly, the audio bitrate is based on 1000 bits per kilobit. Go figure. I have also experienced bugs with FLV output using the VP6 codec, an alpha channel, and embedded cue points, such as the video featured in the VideoWords project discussed in Chapter 11. When I tried to use Squeeze for that chapter's example, the seek points did not work correctly.

▶ **On2 Flix Pro 8.5:** Flix Pro has been a popular Flash Video encoding solution—even before Flash Video was an official file format! Flix produces consistent high-quality output. I like the variety of compression settings in Flix, but I'm not a big fan of its overall user interface. Flix also enables you to save a project file for reuse and portability to other computers.

▶ **Telestream Episode 4.3 (all editions):** Many of my broadcast TV clients use Telestream products for high-volume video encoding and distribution and swear by the quality achieved by Telestream products. The Encoded Movie Info feature now works with FLV files. This feature shows a graph of the finished output's bitrate from frame to frame across the video's duration, just like the Bandwidth Profiler in Flash CS3 does for a SWF file. (I would like to see this feature work with already-encoded FLV files, to compare bitrates from one project to another.) The primary drawback to Episode 4.3 is its Mac-only availability.

NOTES

▶ Adobe Flash CS3 Video Encoder is included with the purchase of Adobe Flash CS3 Professional. Telestream Episode (Standard edition) with Flash 8 encoder is available for $495.

TABLE C.1 Flash Video Encoder Comparison

FEATURE	ADOBE FLASH CS3 VIDEO ENCODER	SORENSON SQUEEZE 4.5 POWERPACK	SORENSON SQUEEZE 4.5 FOR FLASH	ON2 FLIX PO 8.5	TELESTREAM EPISODE PRO 4.3 WITH FLASH 8 ENCODER
Save project file	○	●	●	●	○
Export presets	○	●	●	●	●
Batch processing	●	●	●	●	●
Watch folder	○	●	●	○	○
Deinterlacing	●	●	●	●	●
Windows OS edition	●	●	●	●	○
Mac OS edition	●	●	●	●	●
Sorenson Spark support	●	●	●	●	●
Advanced Sorenson Spark settings	○	●	●	○	○
On2 VP6 support	●	●	●	●	●
On2 VP6 alpha channel support	●	●	●	●	○
Advanced On2 VP6 settings	○	●	●	●	●
CBR and VBR support	○	●	●	●	●
Video image adjustments	○	●	●	●	●
Flash cue point creation	●	●	●	●	○
Flash cue point import/export	●	●[1]	●[1]	●[1]	○
Output to other video formats	○	●	○	○	●
Chroma-key processing	○	○	○[2]	●	○
Pixel aspect ratio detection	○	●	●	○	●
Audio playback in preview window	○	●	●	○	●
Encoded movie information	○	○	○	○	●
Purchase price (US dollars)	N/A	$649 ($799 Mac)	$249	$249	$995

1 While Squeeze and Flix do not feature import/export cue point commands like Adobe Flash CS3 Video Encoder does, you can modify cue point data in the XML-based project files for Squeeze and Flix. For example, you can copy the cue point data from one project file into another project file.

2 The chroma-key processing in On2 Flix provides adequate alpha channels for well-shot green or blue screen footage, but Flix does not offer a full range of chroma-key filter options such as those found in Adobe After Effects. Refer to Chapter 11 for more information about using the Keylight filter in Adobe After Effects CS3.

Other Flash Video Utilities

If you're on the track to becoming a Flash Video expert, you'll likely need to provide solutions for a wide range of Flash Video projects. In this section, you learn about other tools that can help you with specific tasks in a Flash Video workflow.

QuickTime Export Components

You can create FLV files for many QuickTime-enabled applications if you have an export component installed on your system. There are two popular FLV exporter components available for QuickTime:

▶ **Adobe Flash CS3 Video Exporter:** If you have installed Flash CS3 Professional on your computer, you can export FLV files directly from video applications such as Adobe Premiere Pro, Adobe After Effects, Apple Final Cut Pro, Apple Compressor, and Apple QuickTime Player Pro. If you choose File > Export in these applications, you can select Flash Video (FLV) as an export format. The options for export are the same as those you find in the stand-alone Adobe Flash CS3 Video Encoder.

▶ **On2 Flix Exporter for Flash:** If you'd like to have more control over your FLV output from a QuickTime-enabled application, you can purchase and install the On2 Flix Exporter component for QuickTime. Most of the compression options available in On2 Flix Pro 8.5 are available in the Flix Exporter component. For more information, go to www.on2.com/products/flix/exporter.

On-Demand Compression

More and more content providers want to compress source video files to the FLV format directly from a public Web server. For example, sites that feature user-generated content (UGC) such as YouTube.com or blip.tv might want to convert a wide range of video file formats uploaded by their users to the FLV format. After conversion, the FLV file is used for public consumption by other visitors to the site, requiring only one plug-in, the Flash Player, instead of a player plug-in for the original source file uploaded by the user.

Two popular commercial products enable you to compress to the FLV file format directly from a Web server:

▶ **On2 Flix Engine:** If you need the most flexibility with processing video files directly from a Web server, you can license the Flix Engine from On2. There is no fixed price for the license, which varies based on the number of servers and the number of FLV files you want to encode. For more information, visit www.on2.com/products/flix/engine. On2 also offers a client-side encoder named On2 Flix Publisher for Flash, which can encode FLV files from a wide range of source video files directly in a Web browser. You can find more information about Publisher at www.on2.com/products/flix/publisher.

▶ **Sorenson Squish and SquishNet:** Sorenson provides a comprehensive solution that you can license for a Web site. Squish is the name of the browser plug-in that can encode video files to the FLV format directly on the user's machine. Squish can then upload the FLV file directly to a server. You can also tie Squish into Squish-Net, a hosted server solution where the content can be tagged and rated by users. For more information, visit www.sorensonmedia.com.

Open Source Tools

If you'd prefer to avoid paying license fees for FLV file output, there are a growing number of Flash Video utilities available under an open source license:

▶ **FFmpeg:** This popular command-line tool enables you to transcode video file formats, including FLV files. Finding a compiled program file of FFmpeg can be difficult, so I've created a Windows executable file for you to download at www.flashsupport.com/books/fvst. For more information on how to use FFmpeg, visit the official site at http://ffmpeg.mplayerhq.hu.

▶ **FLVTool2:** This tool can manipulate the metadata in an FLV file, including cue point data. For more information, visit http://inlet-media.de/flvtool2.

▶ **vixy.net flv2mpeg4:** This program enables you to convert FLV files to the MPEG-4 file format. For more information, visit http://sourceforge.net/projects/vixynet.

Caption Tools

As you learned in Chapter 10, you can create captions for Flash Video content, and display the caption text with your own custom ActionScript code or with the new FLVPlaybackCaptioning component available in Flash CS3. You can create caption text by hand with any text editor, but there are tools that can more efficiently organize and edit caption text for you. Note that neither of these tools can transcribe an audio track directly into caption text—you have to go through the video content by hand and type the caption text as you listen (or re-listen) to the audio track.

▶ **MAGpie:** This free tool, whose name stands for Media Access Generator, enables you to watch a video and add captions. The program requires the Java Runtime Environment (JRE), and lacks the sophistication of other captioning programs. It's a great tool to use if you want to practice the process of creating caption text. You can download the tool at http://ncam.wgbh.org/webaccess/magpie. MAGpie can run on Windows, Mac, or Linux.

▶ **Captionate:** This licensed tool, which is available at www.manitugroup.com or www.buraks.com, is a full-featured program that can enable captions for Flash Video. You can export an XML file of your captions, or directly embed caption text in an existing FLV file. Captionate can't encode Flash Video, but it can add or modify existing metadata to an FLV file that you have created with a Flash Video encoder. The tool's documentation includes sample ActionScript code that you can use to load external caption files into a Flash SWF file at runtime.

Troubleshooting Flash Video

While I've made every attempt to address structured workflows for Flash Video throughout this book, you may encounter problems during the encoding and deployment process. This appendix can help you find answers to common problems with Flash Video.

▶ **Why don't the controls for the FLVPlayback component appear when I test my Flash movie from a live site?**

You must upload the skin SWF file along with your Flash movie SWF file and support HTML documents to the Web server for a site. The skin file is loaded at runtime. If you do not see the skin displayed when you test your Flash movie live, make sure the skin SWF has been uploaded to the Web server.

▶ **I've added a filter effect to the FLVPlayback component (or a MovieClip instance containing a FLVPlayback component). Why is my video's frame rate so slow?**

Runtime filter effects are very processor-intensive. If you want to add a drop shadow or glow effect to a Flash Video, create a MovieClip instance (or Sprite instance in AS3) behind the video, and add the filter effect to the MovieClip or Sprite instance. You should also enable the Use Runtime Bitmap Caching option in the Property inspector for such MovieClip instances. In ActionScript, this option is controlled with the MovieClip.cacheAsBitmap or Sprite.cacheAsBitmap property.

▶ **Why is my FLV file's frame rate playing slower than what I specified during the encoding process?**

A few factors can affect the Flash Player's ability to keep the frame rate of a video consistent during playback. First, make sure your Flash Video file was encoded with an audio track, even if it's just audio of a looped silence track. The audio track is the governor for a Flash Video's frame rate; without it, the FLV file may not play smoothly. Another factor is the computer's processing speed. Slower computers such as a PowerMac G3s or Pentium II may not be able to play video files with large dimensions and fast frame rates. If you are experiencing choppy playback on slower computers, try testing a Flash Video encoded with the Sorenson Spark codec. The Spark codec is much less processor-intensive than the On2 VP6 codec.

▶ **How can I detect when a Flash Video file has finished playing?**

The NetStream class dispatches status codes during the initialization and playback of Flash Video (FLV) files. To know when a video has reached its end, you should check for two consecutive events: NetStream.Play.Stop and NetStream.Buffer.Empty. The NetStream.Play.Stop event occurs when the video stream has finished loading into the Flash Player buffer, but the video in the buffer has not yet played. Therefore, you can track the event and wait for the NetStream.Buffer.Empty event to know when the remaining video in the buffer has played.

▶ If you're using the FLVPlayback component, you don't have to monitor NetStream events. You can create a listener for the "complete" event (ActionScript 2.0) or Event.COMPLETE (ActionScript 3.0).

▶ If an FLV file has been encoded with an older encoder tool (two or three years old), you may not be able to accurately detect the end of playback. Badly encoded Flash Video files may not fire NetStream status events when the video has finished playing. Your best solution is to re-encode the source files with a current Flash Video encoding tool.

▶ **Why are cue points that I added to my Flash Video during the encoding stage not firing in ActionScript?**

You may have a problem with the Flash Video encoding software. Sorenson Squeeze, in all versions supporting cue points, may not correctly encode cue points for source video files containing an alpha channel. I've also experienced problems with Squeeze's Auto Keyframes Enabled property with alpha channel footage requiring cue points. If you are experiencing problems with cue point events in ActionScript, you may want to try encoding the Flash Video file with another encoder.

TIP

▶ You can solve some problems with older FLV files by checking and correcting any errors with the metadata. The FLV MetaData Injector for Windows, available for free at www.buraks.com, can analyze and fix metadata. Adobe released FLVCheck, a free command-line utility for Windows that also can check FLV files for errors. You can download this tool at http://labs.adobe.com/technologies/flvcheck/.

▶ **Why is my real-time streaming Flash Video file not playing smoothly on a variety of Internet connection speeds? The video seems to play for a few seconds and then pause for a while before restarting.**

Always be mindful of your Flash Video (FLV) file's bitrate. If you serve a high-quality, high-bitrate FLV file to a user with a slow Internet connection, the user will likely suffer through several long pauses while the video constantly buffers into the Flash Player and attempts playback. As soon as the buffer is exhausted, the video pauses and rebuffers. If you're deploying the video with real-time streaming solutions such as Flash Media Server or a Flash Video Streaming Service provider, you must pay careful attention to the viewer's available bandwidth and serve the appropriate bitrate to that viewer. As discussed in Chapters 8 and 12, you can use the SMIL file format to delineate two or more FLV files for the FLVPlayback component to choose from, selecting the best bitrate for the user's connection speed.

▶ **Why does my Flash Video encoding tool not let me encode the audio portion of an MPEG file?**

Most Flash Video encoders cannot fully process MPEG files. Most MPEG files are *muxed*, which means that the audio and video portions of the file are mixed into one track instead of two distinct and separate tracks. As such, most Flash Video encoders can only recognize the video portion and not the audio portion.

The best way to encode a muxed MPEG file is to demux, or separate, the audio and video portions into two separate files without recompressing the data. As discussed in Chapter 3, you can use MPEG Streamclip (http://www.squared5.com), a free tool, to demux MPEG files into video and audio files. Once you have an MPEG video file (usually a file with an .mpv extension) and an MPEG audio file (usually a file with an .mpa extension), you can use Sorenson Squeeze to encode the two files into an FLV file. Squeeze is one of the only Flash Video encoders that can import a video file and link an audio file to the video.

The other alternative is to transcode the MPEG file to another format, such as a QuickTime MOV file or a Windows AVI file, with a lossless or near lossless codec. Then, encode that video file to Flash Video with your preferred encoding tool.

▶ **When I preview a source file in QuickTime Player, I can hear the audio track but the video track displays nothing except a white background color. What's wrong?**

Typically, not being able to view the video portion of a source file indicates that your computer does not have the necessary video codec installed. You can find the video codec information in QuickTime Player by opening the file and choosing Window > Show Movie Info (free QuickTime Player) or Window > Show Movie Properties (QuickTime Player Pro only). Some Quick-Time codecs are not freely available for download, nor are they included with the QuickTime Player installer. For example, the Apple HDV codec and the DVCPro HD codec for QuickTime are only available if you have purchased and installed Apple Final Cut Pro on a Mac OS X computer.

▶ **After I've uploaded my FLV and SWF files to my Web server, the video does not load or play in the Flash SWF file when I'm testing the experience in a Web browser. How can I fix this problem?**

Confirm that you can access the FLV file directly in a Web browser by typing the full URL to the file in the Web browser. If the browser can locate and download the file, then you know that the URL is valid and should be accessible by the Flash SWF file.

If the browser can find the file but displays several lines of random text and numbers, your Web server is not configured correctly to serve FLV files. To fix this problem, you need to add a MIME type header for the .flv file extension. If you do not administer your own Web server, you may need to contact the technical support staff at your Web hosting service to add the MIME type. For more information on this procedure, visit the Flash Video Hosting Providers section on this book's links page at www.flashsupport.com/links.

NOTES

▶ For more Flash Video trouble-shooting tips, read my Flash Video FAQ at Community MX at www.communitymx.com/abstract.cfm?cid=ABB1B.

INDEX

A

accessing book's remote FLV files, 88, 180
AC_RunActiveContent.js file, 81, 82, 108
ActionScript. *See also* AS2 FLVPlayback component; AS3
  FLVPlayback component
    attaching FLVPlayback instance on first frame, 145–146,
      147–148
    buffering file sizes for real-time streaming, 71
    building progressive-download video player in, 160–162,
      163–164
    calculating download speed with AS2, 191–195
    calculating download speed with AS3, 195–199
    changing size of video frame in, 6–7
    classes used in Apollo 13 documentary, 316–323
    clearing Warning dialog, 225
    code base for interactive video host, 261, 285–290
    configuring AS3 FLVPlayback component, 112–117
    controlling Flash Video buffering with, 68
    core classes for interactive video host, 286–290
    custom classes for loading playlist, 224–225
    designing player for real-time streaming video, 162–163,
      164–166
    errors playing real-time streaming video, 166
    FLVPlayback component versions based on AS2 and
      AS3, 111
    inaccurate connection speeds for authortime placed
      instances, 191
    loading preview image, 146–147, 148–149
    modifying FLVPlayback skin for AS3 component,
      154–156
    pausing video on load, 167–170
    placing FLVPlayback component dynamically on stage,
      144–149
    reading metadata from Flash Video file, 175–178
    setting Classpath for AS3, 225, 234–235
    version 3.0 for deploying Flash Video successfully, 293
    virtual cue points with, 123
ActionScript 3.0 Settings dialog
    Classpath area, 225, 234–235, 289–290
    illustrated, 226
<ad> child node attributes, 233
Adobe Acrobat Connect Professional, 57–58
Adobe After Effects. *See* After Effects
Adobe Dreamweaver. *See* Dreamweaver
Adobe Flash CS3. *See* Adobe Flash CS3 Video Encoder; Flash CS3
Adobe Flash CS3 Video Encoder, 126–130
    audio scrubbing unavailable for, 284
    embedding cue points with, 126–130
    features of, 339, 341
    Flash 8 - DV Small profile, 131
    illustrated, 127
    processing alpha channel footage in, 257
    table of cue point settings entered with, 129
    unable to interpret clip's pixel aspect ratios, 130
Adobe Flash CS3 Video Exporter, 342
Adobe Flex, 259
Adobe FLVCheck tool, 331
Adobe Premiere Pro CS3. *See* Premiere Pro CS3
Adobe trial software, 329

ADPCM (Adaptive Differential Pulse Code Modulated)
    codec, 58
ads
    captioning banner, 248–252
    controlling playback of interactive banner, 242–248
    layers of sample starter file for banner, 240–242
    playing in video feature, 231–237
    synchronizing captions with banner, 240
    technical requirements for banner, 239–240
After Effects. *See also* Keylight filter
    about, 31
    adjusting color temperature, 33, 34–39
    basic effects performed by, 32–33
    deinterlacing video with, 33, 39–42, 266
    removing 3:2 pulldown in, 298–303
    removing chroma-key background with, 257, 260–261,
      265–280
    rendering Web comp, 277, 279
    Screen Matte view of Keylight filter, 270–271, 272–273
    useful settings in Keylight filter, 274
    using rendered or real-time Flash Player effects, 31–32
    using View menu to Final Result for video output, 271,
      272, 273
    verifying pixel aspect ratio in, 267
AIFF file conversion, 312
align parameter, 113
alpha channels. *See also* chroma-keyed video; green screen
    about, 257
    exporting, 6
    production requirements for using chroma-key
      lighting, 260
    using, 6
    using Keylight filter to adjust, 270–273
Apollo 13 documentary, 291–328
    creating compression presets in Sorenson Squeeze, 307–313
    customizing experience with HTML and JavaScript,
      324–328
    determining encoding profiles on connection speed,
      304–307
    developing video player for, 313–324
    encoding FLV files for, 295–313
    establishing specifications for encoded files, 295–297
    extracting audio track for, 303–304
    FLA files used for, 314–316
    HTML and CSS templates for, 324
    illustrated, 292
    improving source video for, 297–303
    JavaScript functions in ExternalInterface class, 326–327
    objective for files in, 292
    planning deployment for, 292–295
    production phases and requirements, 294–295
    removing 3:2 pulldown in After Effects, 298–303
    rendering improved source files, 301–303
    replacing videoContent element with SWFObject, 325–326
    source files for, 292
    technical requirements for SWF file, 293–294
    URL for completed, 328
ApolloPoster class, 316, 319–320
Apple DV codec, 45
Apple Final Cut Pro. *See* Final Cut Pro
Apple Motion
    Motion JPEG (M-JPEG) codecs, 47
    removing chroma-key background with, 260–261
Apple MPEG-2 Playback Component, 330

Apple QuickTime Player Pro, 330
applications
    determining connection speed between Flash movie
        and, 188
    MPEG codex utilities, 46–47
    specifying FMS application in SMIL file <meta> tag, 186
AS2 FLVPlayback component
    dynamically placing video on stage, 144–147
    parameters, 117–121
    versions on AS2 and AS3 code, 111
    viewing files in, 118
AS3 FLVPlayback component
    configuring, 112
    customizing UI component for, 157–158
    dynamically placing video on stage, 147–149
    modifying skin for, 154–156
    parameters, 113–117
    versions on AS2 and AS3 code, 111
aspect ratios
    Adobe Flash CS3 Video Encoder unable to interpret
        clip's pixel, 130
    On2 Flix Pro unable to interpret clip's, 139
    using After Effects for verifying pixel, 267
assets, runtime vs. authortime, 65
attributes
    <ad> child node, 233
    sample coding conventions using, 223
audio. See also microphones
    Apollo 13 bitrates for, 305–307
    balanced signals for, 19
    bitrates and compression, 59
    codecs for, 54, 58
    determining acceptable quality for, 335–336
    extracting Apollo13 track for, 303–304
    manipulating channels for, 30
    matching sampling rates for Premiere Pro and
        camcorders, 28
    quality in Apollo 13 encoding profiles, 305
    replacing in video source files with Sorenson Squeeze,
        310, 311
    scrubbing unavailable for Adobe Flash CS3 Video
        Encoder, 284
    streaming with Flash Player, 73
    troubleshooting encoding of, 347–348
    unbalanced signals for, 19–20
audio codecs
    about, 58
    identifiers for, 54
audio tracks, uncompressed, 58
Audio Mixer panel (Premiere Pro), 30
Audio tab (Flash Video Encoding Settings dialog), 284
Audio/Video Compression Settings dialog (Flash), 309
authortime assets, 65
authortime placed instances, 191
authortime-assigned FLV files, 89–92
    creating FLV Player with, 96–99
    Flash Player 6 or 7, 102–105
autoPlay parameter, 113, 118
autoPlay variable, 167
autoRewind parameter, 118
autoSize parameter, 119
AVI files, 44
Avid DV codec, 45

B
backdrops, 22
BackgroundBox class, 225, 232, 316
backing up capture files and source tape, 26
bandwidth, 187–200
    calculating download speed with AS2, 191–195
    calculating download speed with AS3, 195–199
    determining connection speed for FLVPlayback
        component, 188–190
    estimates using RTMP protocol, 187–190
    estimating over HTTP, 190–191
    installing server-side script, 188
banner ads, 239–252
    adding captions for, 248–252
    controlling playback of interactive, 242–248
    layers of sample starter file for, 240–242
    origin of starter file, 241
    technical requirements for, 239–240
bitrates, 47–53. See also multiple bitrates
    adjusting video bitrate for Sorenson Squeeze, 309
    amount needed for video clip, 49–52
    Apollo 13 video and audio, 305–307
    banner ad requirements, 240
    client's requirements for, 333
    compressing for encoded files, 337
    considering variations in connection speed, 52–53
    defined, 47, 48
    determining for codec types, 48–49
    planning video compression profile, 59–60
    setting for Dreamweaver Flash Video play, 80
    specifying constant or variable, 59
blur and fade effects, 32
bounce card, 263
browsers
    building archived Flash Players for Mozilla, 87
    default file-cache limit for, 71
    ExpressInstall with Mozilla, 85, 86
    Microsoft initialization of browser plug-ins, 83
    previewing Flash Video in, 81
    switching Flash Player version for Firefox, 87
    troubleshooting FLV and SWF playback on, 348
buffering. See dynamic buffering
bufferTime parameter, 119
building own video player, 159–178
    adding Play and Pause buttons, 170–175
    basic playback controls, 166–175
    creating progressive-download video files, 160–162, 163–164
    designing to play real-time streaming video, 162–163,
        164–166
    ingredients necessary, 159–160
    making decision to, 159
    pausing video on load, 167–170
    reading metadata from Flash Video file, 175–178
buildlist function, 219, 221–222
business objectives for presentation, 258–259
buttons
    adding to own video player, 170–175
    changing color of video index, 219–222
    creating video index, 216–219
    illustrated, 172
Buttons library, 171

C

cables for video devices, 24
calculating available bandwidth. *See* bandwidth
camcorders
    capture sensors for, 16–17
    connecting to computer, 24
    digital cameras as, 16
    exposure controls for, 18
    frame size for HDV, 13
    hard drives and storage for footage, 21–22
    lens quality of, 17–18
    matching audio-sampling rates with Premiere Pro, 28
    microphones, 18–20
    setting video-output mode for HDV, 27
    tripods and stands for, 21
    working with daylight and tungsten light sources, 20
Captionate
    about, 344
    downloading trial version of, 331
    editing cue points with, 141
    review of XML schema, 249
    using XML schema in, 248–249
captions, 252–256
    adding for banner ads, 248–252
    controlling with Timed Text XML, 252–256
    defined, 248
    implementing custom Captions class, 250–252
    synchronizing with banner ads, 240
    tools for creating and displaying, 344
    transcribing time for, 254
    turning on when volume muted or set to 0, 256
    using, 32
    ways to create, 248–249
Captions class, 250–252
Capture window (Premiere Pro), 29
capturing video, 23–30
    about, 23
    backing up capture files and source tape, 26
    connecting video device to computer, 24
    creating new project for, 27–28
    initiating capture process, 25–26
    preparing video device for, 26–27
    requirements for VideoWords presentation, 260
    running video capturing program, 24
    saving clip list, 26
    specifying capture location, 25
    starting capture process, 28–30
CBR (Constant Bit Rate)
    about, 61–62
    encoding using, 68
    using, 338
CDNs (content distribution networks)
    defined, 63
    delivering progressive video content with, 65
    options using, 70, 71, 72
chapter markers, 131, 133
choosing multiple bitrates. *See also* multiple bitrates
    based on range of content quality, 182–183
    content scaling and, 182
    determining capacity of storage and encoding facilities, 184
    picking rates matching common connection speeds, 183

chroma-keyed video
    creating background for, 262–263
    processing footage in After Effects, 265–280
    production requirements for, 260
    removing chroma-key background, 257, 260–261
    shooting against green screen, 257, 258
    using, 6
    viewing transparency grid behind images, 269–270
Cinematize 2, 47
Classpath area (ActionScript 3.0 Settings dialog), 225, 234–235
clients
    delivering FLV files to, 333–334
    lowest acceptable video and audio quality for, 335–336
    planning support for Flash Player, 336
    requirements for bitrate, 333
    source video files supplied by, 334–335
client-side code
    Apollo 13 in JavaScript and HTML, 295
    VideoWords presentation in HTML, 261
clip-list file, 26
clips. *See* video clips
CMOS (Complementary Metal Oxide Semiconductor), 17
codecs. *See also specific codecs*
    audio, 54, 58
    defined, 43
    determining bitrates for, 48–49
    DV, 14, 45
    DVCPro, 45
    hardware-specific, 47
    identifiers for audio and video, 54
    modifying from encoding tools, 339
    Motion JPEG, 47
    MPEG, 46–47
    On2 VP6, 49, 52, 54, 56–57
    options for Flash Video, 53–58
    Screen Video/Screen Video V2, 54, 57–58
    Sorenson Spark, 49, 50, 51–52, 53, 54–55
    troubleshooting missing, 348
    types of source file, 45–47
color
    adjusting in After Effects, 33, 34–39
    changing navigation cue point button background, 220–222
    sample coding conventions using, 223
companion DVD
    adjusting progressive-download URLs for FLV files, 80
    Flash_Video_Bitrates.xls file on, 49, 183, 304
    SWFObject files on, 64, 83
Complementary Metal Oxide Semiconductor (CMOS), 17
Component Inspector panel, 103, 112, 118, 143
Composition Settings dialog (After Effects)
    changing frame rate values in, 300
    Web comp settings in, 274
compositions. *See* comps
compression, 43–62. *See also* codecs
    about codecs, 43–47
    codec options for Flash Video, 53–58
    creating project presets in Sorenson Squeeze, 307–313
    determining profiles for, 59–62
    digital camera video, 16
    products for on-demand, 342–343
    ratios for frame rate, 338
    spatial and temporal, 48
    understanding video bitrates, 47–53

Compression Settings dialog (After Effects), 277–278
comps (compositions)
    creating from source clip, 34–35
    HDV, 265–274, 275, 276
    rendering Web, 277, 279
computers. *See also* Windows computers
    connecting video device to, 24
    disk space required for video, 25
    preparing for capture process, 25–26
    specifying capture location on, 25
connection speeds
    choosing multiple bitrates matching common, 183
    considering playback and variations in, 52–53
    determining encoding profiles based on, 304–307
    determining for FLVPlayback component, 188–190
    inaccurate speeds for authortime placed instances, 191
    picking data rates matching common, 183
    troubleshooting real-time streaming, 347
    when to offer multiple bitrates for, 180
Constant Bit Rate. *See* CBR
content
    batch-processing multiple bitrates per piece of, 181
    bitrate choices based on quality of, 182–183
    determining data rates and content scaling, 182
    FLV files for, 63
    indicating path to, 90, 97, 117, 189
    lowest acceptable video and audio quality for client's, 335–336
    protection offered with HTTP and RTMP protocols, 69–70
    providing lengthy, 181
    requiring Digital Rights Management, 334
    search engine optimization for Flash, 82
content distribution networks. *See* CDNs
Content Path dialog (Flash CS3), 90, 97, 117, 189
contentPath parameter, 119
contentPath value, 191
copying streaming video, 70
costs
    equipment purchase vs. rental, 262, 263
    video delivery, 74–76
Crop and Resize tab (Flash Video Encoding Settings dialog), 130
CSS templates, 324
cue points, 121–144. *See also* embedded cue points
    adding in frame, 127
    Adobe Flash CS3 Video Encoder for adding, 126–130
    behavior of, 124–125
    changing index button color during playback, 219–222
    creating buttons for video index, 216–219
    creating embedded, 126
    defined, 121
    editing with Captionate, 141
    encoding tools for adding, 339
    exporting data for, 130–131, 136
    implementing with FLVPlayback component, 141–144
    keyframes inserted with, 124–125
    making marker index from, 213–222
    markers vs., 131
    On2Flix Pro for adding, 136–141
    placing in interactive video host FLV file, 282–284
    properties for playing, 123–124
    saving settings for, 129
    settings with Adobe Flash CS3 Video Encoder, 129

    troubleshooting, 346
    types of, 122–122
    using for progressive-download and real-time streaming projects, 281
    using with FLVPlayback component, 141–144
    viewing, 124, 125
    when to set, 121–122
    working with in Sorenson Squeeze, 131–136
Cue Points tab (Flash Video Encoding Settings dialog), 128, 285
cuePoints parameter, 113, 119
customizing
    Flash Player interface, 156–158
    playback experience with HTML and JavaScript, 324–328

D

data rate. *See* bitrate
daylight, 20
deinterlacing
    After Effects for, 33, 39–42
    defined, 11
    disabling in Sorenson Squeeze, 312
    On2 Flix Pro for, 139
    VideoWords footage, 266
delivery of files, 70–76. *See also* deploying Flash Video reliably; progressive-download video; real-time streaming video
    estimating costs for, 74–76
    file formats for Flash movies, 63–64
    FLV files, 64, 67
    HTML file format for Web pages, 64
    HTTP vs. RTMP protocols, 65–70
    live streaming vs. prerecorded playback, 72–74
    multiple bitrate files delivered via RTMP protocol, 296–297
    multiple FLV files via HTTP protocol, 280–281, 296
    part of project's checklist, 333–334
    progressive video content delivered with CDNs, 65
    project delivery of FLV file seeked with RTMP protocol, 281
    providing FLV files to clients, 333–334
    sending single FLV file via HTTP protocol, 296
    single FLV file seeked with HTTP protocol, 281
    SWF files, 63, 64, 67
    using Web server, FMS, or CDN, 70–72
    VideoWords as progressive-download video, 259–260
    Web sites for, 71–72
demuxing, 46
deploying Flash Video reliably, 291–328
    compression presets for, 307–313
    customizing experience with HTML and JavaScript, 324–328
    determining encoding profiles based on connection speed, 304–307
    developing video player, 313–324
    encoding FLV files, 295–313
    FLA files used for Apollo 13 documentary, 314–316
    functions provided by ApolloPoster and Poster classes, 319–320
    operations processed by ReliableVideo_AS3.swf file, 316
    planning deployment, 292–295
    production phases and requirements, 294–295
    ReliableVideo class and properties for, 317–318
    technical requirements for SWF file, 293–294
    using ExpressInstall class for, 320–321
    using ReliableVideoExample document class, 321–323

desaturation, 32
Digital 8 format, 15
digital cameras
    exposure controls for, 18
    functioning as camcorders, 16
Digital Rights Management (DRM), 334
digitizing, 23
disk space required for video, 25
`<div>` node, 253–254
`<div>` tag, 254
`Document` class, 288–290
Document Class values (Property Inspector), 143–144
document files. *See* FLA files
Document Properties dialog (Flash), 91, 98, 104
downloading. *See also* progressive-download video
    calculating times in ActionScript, 191–199
    Captionate trial version, 249, 331
    and delivering FLV files, 64, 67
    MPEG Streamclip, 304
    On2 Flix Pro trial version, 330
    QuickTime tools, 330–331
    segmenting FLV files into chunks for, 296
    Sorenson Squeeze trial version, 307
    SWF files, 67
    time-limited versions for Adobe software, 329
`DraggableWord` class, 287
Dreamweaver, 79–82
    adding Flash Video element to HTML document, 79–82
    customizing video experience with HTML and JavaScript
        in, 324–326
    detecting Flash Player with SWFObject, 82–87
    locating origin of SWF files from, 85
    problems with embedded players in HTML, 82
    setting bitrate for Flash Video play, 80
    updating, 82
    uploading for Flash Video deployment, 108–109
    using progressive-download video with, 80
DRM (Digital Rights Management), 334
dropped frames, 25, 29
dual buffering. *See* dynamic buffering
duration of video playback, 70
DV codec, 14, 45
DV format, 14, 15
DVCPro codecs, 45
DVD format video recording, 15
DVDs. *See also* companion DVD
    backing up capture files and source tape to, 26
    multiple data rates unnecessary for fixed media
        deployment, 181
DVDxDV utility, 47
DVmag.com, 22
dynamic buffering, 200–209
    adding to SMIL-driven AS2 FLVPlayback component,
        201–205
    adding to SMIL-driven AS3 FLVPlayback component,
        205–209
    defined, 201

E

Edit Markers dialog (Sorenson Squeeze), 135
editing
    changing marker types while, 134
    cue points with Captionate, 141

Final Cut Pro for, 260, 264–265
Premiere Pro CS3 for, 260
symbol instances, 151–152
Effect Controls panel (After Effects), 36
embedded cue points
    adding in VideoWords presentation, 259–260
    behavior in FLV files, 124–125
    creating, 126
    retrieving information from navigation cue points, 215–216
    setting with Adobe Flash CS3 Video Encoder, 126–130
embedded video
    alternative to, 79
    HTTP protocol for SWF files delivered as, 65
    in SWF format, 63, 64
encoding files, 337–344
    alternative tools for Apollo 13 project, 307
    bitrate compression, 337
    caption tools, 344
    comparison of video encoders, 339–341
    establishing specifications for, 295–297
    FLV for interactive video host, 280–285
    frame size and rate, 338
    improving Apollo 13 documentary source video file,
        297–303
    on-demand compression, 342–343
    open source tools for, 343
    protocol considerations for, 68–70
    QuickTime exporter components, 342
    requirements for VideoWords presentation, 261
    troubleshooting audio encoding, 347–348
    useful utility features for, 338
equipment, 9–20
    about selection of, 9–10
    backdrops, 22
    camcorder capture sensors, 16–17
    exposure controls on, 18
    hard drives and storage, 21–22
    HD video, 10–13
    lens quality, 17–18
    lighting accessories, 20
    microphones, 18–20
    purchase vs. rental costs of, 262, 263
    requirements for live streaming playback, 72–73
    SD video, 13–16
    tripods and stands, 21
    used for VideoWords project, 262–263
event cue points
    adding at start of each VideoWord word segment, 282
    adding in On2 Flix Pro, 138
    inserting in sample file, 126–130
    keyframe markers and, 131
    synchronizing playback with, 122–123
exporting
    alpha channels, 6
    cue point data, 130–131, 136
    Web comp to QuickTime video file, 276
exposure controls on equipment, 18
ExpressInstall feature
    Apollo 13 documentary's use of, 294, 320–321
    using with SWFObject code, 85–87
`ExpressInstall` file, 314–315
eXtensible Markup Language. *See* XML

external video in FLV format, 64
ExternalInterface class, 326–327
extracting audio track, 303–304
Eyedropper tool, 268, 269

F

FCS (Flash Communication Server), 72, 73
FFmpeg, 343
files. *See also* SMIL files; XML; *and specific formats*
    AVI, 44
    backing up source tape and capture, 26
    clip-list, 26
    FLV, 64
    HDV, 12–13, 44
    HTML, 64
    MOV, 44
    MPEG, 44–45, 46–47
    protocol considerations for encoding, 68–70
    readability of MPEG audio by encoders, 303–304
    reading metadata from Flash Video, 175–178
    size of SWF file for deploying Flash Video, 293
    size requirements for banner ads, 240
    source video file, 44–45
    SWF, 63, 64
    technical requirements for VideoWords SWF, 259–260
    Timed Text (TT), 252–253
    uploading, 108–110, 116, 121
    XML cue point, 135, 141
film transfer to NTSC video, 297–298
Filter Settings dialog (Sorenson Squeeze), 312
Final Cut Pro
    editing VideoWords presentation in, 264–265
    using for video capture and editing, 260
Firefox browsers, switching Flash Player versions for, 87
firewall security
    HTTP vs. RTMP protocols and, 68–69
    using HTTP content with, 65
FireWire connections, 24
firstPlay variable, 167
FLA (Flash document) files
    authortime assets and, 65
    relationship among FLV, SWF, and, 63
    used for Apollo 13 documentary, 314–316
Flash 8 - DV Small profile (Adobe Flash CS3 Video Encoder), 131
Flash Communication Server (FCS), 72, 73
Flash CS3. *See also* Adobe Flash CS3 Video Encoder; Flash Professional 8
    changing component version when using document with AS2, 96
    playing video from, 87–108
    selecting Flash File document types, 88
    Video Import Wizard for, 113
Flash CS3 Video Encoder. *See* Adobe Flash CS3 Video Encoder
Flash File document types, 88
Flash Media Server. *See* FMS
Flash movies. *See* SWF files
Flash Player. *See also specific versions*
    adding clip to HTML document, 79–82
    assigning MediaPlayback instance properties with HTML parameters, 106–108
    building for authortime-assigned FLV, 89–92

    codec options for versions of, 53–58
    creating FLV Player with HTML-assigned FLV in, 93–95, 99–101, 106–108
    customizing interface, 156–158
    detecting with SWFObject, 82–87
    effects rendered in video vs., 31–32
    keyframe display in, 308
    making with authortime-assigned FLV, 96–99
    picking version for Flash CS3 video play, 88
    planning client support for, 336
    playback for, 109–110
    requirements for banner ads, 239–240
    skin SWF files needed for dynamically placing video on stage, 144
    source video files for, 74
    streaming video and audio with, 73
    switching version for Firefox browsers, 87
    uploading and playing files for versions of, 109–110
    versions for deploying Flash Video successfully, 293
    video sources for, 74
Flash Player 6/7
    authortime-assigned FLV files, 102–105
    creating FLV Player with HTML-assigned FLV, 106–108
    publishing content for, 102
Flash Player 8
    AS2 FLVPlayback compatibility with, 111
    creating FLV Player with HTML-assigned FLV, 99–101
    files needed to deploy FLVPlayback component for, 109
    modifying FLVPlayback skin for, 150–153
Flash Player 9
    creating FLV Player with HTML-assigned FLV, 93–95
    files needed to deploy FLVPlayback component for, 109
    loading playlist in movie for, 225–230
    playing video with FLVPlayback component, 89–95
    revising FLVPlayback skin for, 153–156
Flash Professional 8
    ActionScript attaching FLVPlayback instance on first frame, 145–146
    steps for creating Flash Video player, 96
    using with ActionScript 2.0 FLVPlayback component, 142
    Video Import Wizard for, 113
Flash Video. *See* Flash Player; FLV files
Flash Video Cue Points dialog, 113
Flash Video Encoding Settings dialog, 283–284
    Audio tab, 284
    Crop and Resize tab, 130
    Cue Points tab, 128, 285
    Profiles tab, 283
    Video tab, 130, 284
Flash Video Streaming Service. *See* FVSS
Flash_Video_Bitrates.xls spreadsheet, 49, 183, 304
Flight of Apollo 11 source file, 160
floating rectangular video display, 4–5
FLV (Flash Video) files. *See also* deploying Flash Video reliably
    about, 64
    accessing book's remote, 180
    adding listeners to handle cue point events from, 220, 222
    behavior of embedded cue points in, 124–125
    building player for authortime-assigned, 89–92
    changing properties in Dreamweaver, 81
    chroma-keyed video, 6

codec options for, 53–58

content protection for, 69–70

controlling buffering with ActionScript, 68

converting files to FLV using QuickTime, 46

costs of transferring, 74–76

delivering single file seeked with RTMP protocol, 281

delivery of client, 333–334

downloading and delivering files in, 64, 67

encoding interactive video host, 280–285

encoding VideoWords project, 261

exporter components for, 342

filenames included in AS2 FLVPlayback component, 185

floating rectangular display, 4–5

FLV Player creation with HTML-assigned, 93–95, 99–101, 106–108

HTTP and RTMP distribution methods for, 65–70

including host name in `<meta>` tag of SMIL document, 184

inserting in Dreamweaver HTML document, 80

integrating with Dreamweaver, 79–87

masked video display for, 5

multiple bitrates for real-time streaming, 179–180

nonfloating display for, 4

placing in FLVPlayback component using Video Import Wizard, 113

preparing for SMIL files, 185

problems with Dreamweaver-embedded players in HTML, 82

reading metadata from, 175–178

relationship among FLA, SWF, and, 63

resizable videos, 6–7

resizing FLVPlayback instance to match frame size, 90–91

segmenting into downloadable chunks, 296

troubleshooting problems playing on Web browser, 348

using with SMIL files, 186

viewing all cue points after loading, 125

FLV MetaData Injector for Windows, 346

FLV Player. *See* Flash Player

FLVPlayback component. *See also* AS2 FLVPlayback component; AS3 FLVPlayback component; building own video player; cue points

adding dynamic buffering to SMIL-driven, 201–209

building player with custom interface components, 156–158

configuring AS3, 112–117

controlling `NetStream` object without, 201

core features found in `VideoPlayer` class, 178

default buffer time for real-time streaming, 200

Dreamweaver Flash Video extension vs., 80

dynamically placing on stage, 144–145

files needed to deploy Flash Player v8 and v9, 109

implementing cue points with, 141–144

inaccurate connection speeds for authortime placed instances in, 191

installing server-side script determining connection speeds for, 188

modifying AS2 parameters for, 117–121

modifying skins, 150–156

multiple players for single instance of, 231–237

overview of, 111

playing video with Flash Player 9, 89–95

resizing instance to match FLV frame size, 90–91

retrieving cue point data with `metadataReceived` event,

214–216

server-side scripts for, 121

streaming Flash Video to Flash player via RTMP, 187–190

troubleshooting, 345

uses of `PlaylistManager` class in, 231–232

using FLV filenames with .flv extension in AS2 version of, 185

using with Flash Player 8, 95–99

versions of, 4

`FLVPlayback.bufferTime` property, 200

FLVPlaybackCaptioning component

about, 32

integrating in video, 254–256

loading Timed Text XML file with, 252

selecting from Select Skin dialog, 255

FLVPlayer_Progressive.swf, 85

FLVPlayer_Streaming.swf, 81

FLVTool2, 343

FMS (Flash Media Server)

author's hosted account with Influxis, 88, 160, 180

determining connection speed between Flash movie and applications on, 188

disadvantages of external video files with, 64

downloading files to, 67

investing in own, 72

keyframes created by FMS applications on fly, 308

RTMP and, 66

specifying FMS application in SMIL file `<meta>` tag, 186

streaming MP3 files to Flash movie, 71

using hosted FMS accounts, 70, 71

FMS hosts

accounts with, 70, 71

providing server-side scripts for FLVPlayback components, 121

Frame Blending box, 41, 42

frame rate

Apollo 13, 305

bitrates and, 48

changing values in After Effects, 299–300

compression ratios for, 338

determining for video compression profile, 60

factoring into bitrate choices, 182–183

HDV format, 13

SD video, 13

3:2 pulldown and, 298–303

troubleshooting slow, 345–346

frame size

Apollo 13, 305

bitrates and, 48

compressing, 338

determining for video compression profile, 60

factoring into bitrate choices, 182–183

FLVPlayback instance resized to match, 90–91

HDV camcorder, 13

interlacing effects on reduced, 40

frames. *See also* frame rate; frame size; keyframes

attaching FLVPlayback instance to first, 145–146, 147–148

bitrate for average, slow, and fast moving, 49–50

dropped, 25, 29

embedding cue points in, 126–130

interlacing unnoticable on slow moving, 40

Frames (continued)
    progressive and interlaced, 10
    smoothing and dropped, 182
FVSS (Flash Video Streaming Service)
    calculating available bandwidth on, 187
    providers of, 72, 73
    RTMP and, 66
    streaming Flash Video to Flash player via RTMP
        using, 187–190

G

green screen
    sampling color in VideoWords footage, 268, 269
    shooting against, 257, 258
    working with backgrounds using, 6
Guess24Pa Pulldown button (Interpret Footage dialog), 299

H

Handles setting (Premiere Pro), 28
hard drives
    specifying capture location on, 25
    storing footage on, 21–22
HDV (High Definition Video)
    formats for, 12–13
    frame size and rate for, 10–11
    HDTV display in pixels, 11
    MPEG source-file format for, 44
HDV comp
    adjusting video image in Timeline window, 276
    resizing within Web comp, 275
height
    accommodating extra for skins, 116, 121
    specifying with `<root-layout>` tag in SMIL files,
        184–185, 187
Hi 8 format, 15–16
high definition video. *See* HDV
HTML (Hypertext Markup Language)
    adding Flash Video element to document, 79–82
    Apollo 13 client-side code in JavaScript and, 295
    deploying Flash Video on Web pages, 64
    developing client-side code for VideoWords
        presentation, 261
    enabling all SWF file parameters with tags or methods, 294
    file format for Web pages, 64
    FLV Player creation with HTML-assigned FLV, 93–95,
        99–101, 106–108
    overlaying Flash Video with, 5
    problems with Dreamweaver-embedded Flash Video
        players in, 82
    using HTML and CSS templates for Apollo 13
        documentary, 324
HTTP (Hypertext Transport Protocol)
    calculating available bandwidth over, 190–191
    delivering projects as multiple FLV files via, 280–281
    delivering single Apollo 13 FLV files via, 296
    delivering single FLV file seeked with, 281
    duration of video playback and, 70
    HTTP streaming with Flash Video, 296
    multiple bitrate FLV files delivered via, 296
    option for delivering Apollo 13 multiple FLV files via,
        295–296
    picking RTMP or, 68–70, 333–334

progressive-download video and, 66
    viewing Flash files over, 65–66
Hypertext Markup Language. *See* HTML
Hyslop, Bruce, 324

I

i-frames. *See* keyframes
iLink, 24
"Implementing a dual-threshold strategy in Flash Media
    Server" (Sonnati), 201
index. *See* video index
IndexButton symbol
    about, 214
    assigning new instance to cue point, 216, 218–219
Influxis, 88, 160, 180
initiating capture process, 25–26
Insert Flash Video dialog, 80
instant-start video playback
    offering users, 180–181
    tasks ensuring, 200
intellectual property (IP) protection
    choosing protocols for, 69–70
    lacking in HTTP deliveries, 65
interactive video host, 257–290. *See also* producing interactive
  presentations; VideoWords presentation
    adding alpha channels for live-action footage, 257
    core ActionScript classes for, 286–290
    developing ActionScript code for user interactions, 285–290
    encoding Flash Video for, 280–285
    implementing core classes in FLV file, 289–290
    planning user interface, 258–261
    production phases for, 260–261
interlaced frames, 10
interlacing
    illustrated, 40
    improving quality of Apollo 13 source video files, 297–303
Internet connection speeds. *See* connection speeds
Interpret Footage dialog (After Effects)
    deinterlacing footage, 266
    removing 3:2 Pulldown, 298–299
isLive parameter, 113, 119

J

JavaScript
    detecting Flash Player with SWFObject, 83–85
    developing client-side code for VideoWords
        presentation, 261
    development of Apollo 13 client-side code in HTML
        and, 295
    parameters passed by, 240
    using functions in `ExternalInterface` class for Apollo 13
        documentary, 326–327
Job pane (Sorenson Squeeze), 308, 311

K

KB/s (kilobytes per second), 47
Kbps (kilobits per second), 47
keyframe markers, 131
keyframes
    controlling with encoding utilities, 338–339
    defined, 60
    determining intervals for video compression profile, 60–61

inserted with cue points, 124–125
intervals displayed in Apollo 13 encoding, 308
keyframes:natural, 61
Keylight filter (After Effects)
adjusting alpha channel for video with, 270–273
properties of earlier versions of, 265, 268
sampling green color from VideoWords footage, 268, 269
Screen Matte view of, 270–271, 272–273
settings displayed in Effects Control panel, 268
useful settings in, 274
kilobits per second (Kbps), 47
kilobytes per second (KB/s), 47

L

layers
sample banner ad, 240–242
settings for Apollo 13 clip, 300
lens quality of camcorder, 17–18
lighting
accessories for, 20
observing location's, 8
VideoWord project, 263
Link Audio option (Sorenson Squeeze), 310, 311
List component
custom cell renderers used in, 230
illustrated, 222, 230
listeners
adding to handle cue point events from FLV file, 220, 222
detecting playlist actions, 229–230
loader classes
Loader, 195
MovieClipLoader, 191
loading preview image
in FLVPlayback component using AS2, 146–147
in FLVPlayback component using AS3, 148–149
locations for shooting, 8–9
logging video footage, 24

M

Mac computers, alpha channel color for, 283
Macromedia Breeze Meeting. See Adobe Acrobat Connect Professional.
MAGpie, 344
main.asc file, 188
maintainAspectRatio parameter, 120
markers. See also cue points
changing types of, 134
chapter, 131, 133
cue points vs., 131
defined, 131
specifying names and parameters for new, 134
working with, 131–136
masked data packets, 69
masked video displays, 5
MBR. See multiple bitrates
media for SD video, 14–16
MediaPlayback component
assigning MediaPlayback instance properties with HTML parameters, 106–108
files needed for Flash Player 7, 110
navigating for Flash Players 6 and 7, 102
<meta> tag of SMIL document, 184, 186

metadata
listening to in cue point events, 220, 222
reading from Flash Video file, 175–178
retrieving cue point data with metadataReceived event, 214–216
metadataReceived event, 214–216
microphones, 18–20
balanced audio signals, 19
mixing audio from multiple, 30
shotgun vs. omnidirectional, 20
unbalanced audio signals for, 19–20
Microsoft DV codec, 45
Microsoft Video for Windows (AVI), 44
mini jacks, 19
miniDV format, 15
Miraizon Cinematize, 331
mirrored content, 71
mobile devices and multiple bitrates, 180
monitoring download speed
AS2 code for, 191–195
AS3 code for, 195–199
Motion
Motion JPEG (M-JPEG) codecs, 47
removing chroma-key background with, 260–261
MOV files, 44
MovieClipLoader class, 191
Mozilla browsers, 85, 86, 87
MP3 codec, 58
MPEG2-DVD dialog (After Effects), 302, 303
MPEG files
about, 44–45
audio tracks unreadable with most encoders, 303–304
codecs for, 46–47
MPEG Stream, 46
MPEG Streamclip, 303-304, 331
multiple bitrates (MBR), 179–209
about, 179
calculating available bandwidth, 187–200
capacity of storage and encoding facilities, 184
choosing, 182–184
enabling dynamic buffering for real-time streams, 200–209
estimating bandwidth over HTTP protocol, 190–191
knowing when to offer, 179–181
optimizing real-time streaming with, 119
picking rates matching common connection speeds, 183
preparing SMIL files, 184–187
unnecessary for fixed media, 181
multiplexed video tracks, 46

N

name property, 123
naming markers, 134
natural keyframes, 61
navigation cue points
adding for each VideoWord word segment, 282
adding in On2 Flix Pro, 137
chapter markers and, 131
controlling button background color based on current, 220–222
creating table of contents with, 122
inserting, 126–130, 259–260
retrieving information from embedded, 215–216

Nellymoser Speech codec, 58
NetConnection object
    creating NetStream instance with instance of, 161, 163
    reusing, 161
    uses for, 159
NetConnection.onStatus() handler, 163
NetStatusEvent class, 169
NetStream object
    attaching to video instance, 162, 163
    controlling without FLVPlayback component, 201
    creating instance with NetConnection instance, 161
    detecting end of video file play with, 346
    handling metadata events on instance of, 177–178
    reusing NetConnection instances with, 161
    uses for, 160
NetStream.bufferTime property, 200
NetStream.onCuePoint() handler, 125
NetStream.onStatus handler, 167
NetStream.pmMetaData() handler, 176
NetStream.setBufferTime() method, 200
New Document dialog (Dreamweaver), 324
New Project dialog (Premiere Pro), 27–28
NLE (nonlinear editors), 24, 25–26
nodes in XML, 249
noise
    observing location's, 8
    removing in After Effects, 33
nonfloating video displays, 4
nonlinear editors (NLE), 24, 25–26

O

omnidirectional microphones, 20
On2 Flix Engine, 343
On2 Flix Exporter for Flash, 342
On2 Flix Pro
    adding cue points with, 136–141
    deinterlacing by, 139
    downloading trial version of, 330
    features of, 340, 341
    overview of cue point options, 141
    unable to interpret clip's pixel aspect ratio in, 139
    Video tab for, 140
    XML files used in, 141
On2 VP6 codec
    about, 54
    finding software that modifies settings for, 339
    formula for acceptable bitrates using, 49
    improved image quality with, 52
    strengths and weaknesses, 56–57
    technical requirements for VideoWords, 259
onCaptionDisplay function, 251
onCaptionLoad function, 251
online vs. offline video playback, 70
onVideoDone function, 251
onVideoStart function, 251
open source tools for encoding files, 343
Output Module menu, 38
Output Module Settings dialog (After Effects)
    adjusting alpha channel in, 278, 279
    rendering improved Apollo 13 source files, 301–302

P

Panasonic DVCPro 25 and 50, 14–15, 45
Panasonic DVCPro-HD/ DV 100/ D7-HD, 12, 45
parameters
    AS2 FLVPlayback, 117–121
    AS3 FLVPlayback, 113–117
    specifying for new markers, 134
parameters property, 124
Parameters tab (Component Inspector), 103, 112, 118, 143
path
    indicating to content, 90, 97, 117, 189
    for streaming FLV files, 88
Perian QuickTime Component, 331
permits for filming, 8–9
p-frames (predictive frames), 60–61, 338
phantom power, 19
pixel aspect ratio, 130, 267
pixel dimensions for HD video, 10–11
placing Flash Video on Web pages, 79–110
    building player for authortime-assigned FLV files, 89–92, 96–99, 102–105
    choosing playback controls, 89–90, 97
    FLV Player creation with HTML-assigned FLV files, 93–95, 99–101, 106–108
    gathering files for deployment, 108–110
    integrating SWF file with Dreamweaver, 79–87
    resizing FLVPlayback instance to match frame size, 90–91
    using MediaPlayback component for Flash Players 6 and 7, 102
planning. See also pre-production planning
    selecting codecs, 49, 53–58
    successful Flash Video deployment, 292–295
    video shoots, 7–9
Play and Pause buttons
    adding, 170–175
    behaviors for, 170
    illustrated, 172
playback. See FLVPlayback component; video playback
playback controls, 166–175
    adding Play and Pause buttons, 170–175
    choosing in Select Skin dialog, 89–90, 97
    pausing video on load, 167–170
playing video. See Flash Player; FLVPlayback component; video playback
Playlist class, 224–225, 232
PlaylistExample.as file, 227–230
PlaylistManager class
    adding time values from <ad> nodes as cue points with, 233
    instantiating, 234–237
    using in FLVPlayback component, 231–232
playlists, 223–230
    adding thumbnails to, 230
    custom cell renderers used in List component of, 230
    detecting actions with listeners, 229–230
    determining XML schema for, 223–224
    instantiating PlaylistManager class, 234–237
    loading, 224–230
    specifying child nodes on XML file for, 233
    using XML file for, 223
Porter, Sean, 242

Poster class, 319–320
Poster file, 316
poster SWF file, 294, 316
Prelinger Archives, 224, 332
Premiere Pro CS3
    about, 26
    creating new project, 27–28
    preparing video device for capture in, 26–27
    removing chroma-key background with, 260–261
    starting capture process, 28–30
    using for video capture and editing, 260
pre-production planning
    designing video display, 3–7
    planning user interface for interactive video host, 258–261
    production phases for interactive video host, 260–261
    project checklist, 333–336
    selecting equipment, 9–20
prerecorded playback vs. real-time streaming, 73–74
Preserve Edges option (Interpret Footage dialog), 266
preview parameter, 114
previewing
    Flash Video in browsers, 81
    images in FLVPlayback component, 146–149
    progressive-download video files, 114
processing video, 31–42
    adjusting color temperature, 33, 34–39
    basic effects performed by After Effects, 32–33
    deinterlacing in After Effects, 33, 39–42
    processing interactive footage in After Effects, 265–280
    processor performance while rendering, 31–32
    using rendered or real-time Flash Player effects, 31–32
    working with chroma-keyed video in After Effects, 265–280
producing interactive presentations, 261–280
    creating Web-ready comp, 274–280
    editing video in Final Cut Pro, 264–265
    overview, 261
    processing footage in After Effects, 265–280
    shooting video, 261–264
    using Keylight filter to adjust alpha channel for video, 270–273
    viewing transparency grid, 269–270
production phases. See also pre-production planning
    Apollo 13 documentary, 294–295
    interactive video host, 260–261
profiles
    basing encoding on connection speed, 304–307
    compression, 59–62
    Flash 8 - DV Small, 131
Profiles tab (Flash Video Encoding Settings dialog), 283
progressive enhancement (PE), 293
progressive frames, 10
progressive-download video
    building video player for, 160–162, 163–164
    changing buffer time for, 200
    defined, 66
    delivery of VideoWords presentation as, 259–260
    estimating transfer rate and costs for, 75–76
    previewing, 114
    using with Dreamweaver Flash Video playback, 80
project checklist, 333–336
    client's bitrate requirements, 333

content requiring Digital Rights Management, 334
    delivery of files, 333–334
    determining acceptable quality for client, 335–336
    source video files supplied by client, 334–335
projects. See also Apollo 13 documentary; project checklist;
    VideoWords presentation
    business objectives for VideoWords, 258–259
    delivering as multiple FLV files via HTTP, 280–281
    designating technical requirements for, 259–260
Property Inspector
    changing Flash Video properties in, 81
    modifying Document Class values in, 143–144
    no naming of instance in Var field, 143
props, 9
public-domain video, 224, 332
Publish Settings dialog (Flash CS3), 92, 105

Q
quality
    bitrate choices and content, 182–183
    camcorder lens, 17–18
    determining acceptable content, 335–336
    improving source video file, 297–303
    On2 VP6 codec improvements for image, 52
QuickTime
    format for, 44
    tools, 330–331
QuickTime MPEG2 Playback Component, 46

R
Real Time Messaging Protocol. See RTMP
real-time streaming video
    calculating transfer rate and costs for, 75
    defined, 66
    designing video player for, 162–163, 164–166
    enabling dynamic buffering for, 200–209
    making copies of, 70
    offering multiple bitrates with, 179–180
    optimal requirements for reliable video playback, 293–294
    optimizing with multiple bitrates, 119
    prerecorded playback vs., 73–74
    publishing content for Flash Player 6, 102
    required for banner ads, 240
    requirements for, 72–73
    troubleshooting, 347
    UnhandledAsyncErrorEvent error message while
        playing, 166
reliable deployment. See deploying Flash Video reliably
ReliableVideo class, 317–318
ReliableVideo_AS3.swf file
    goals of, 292
    ReliableVideo class and properties, 317–318
    tasks experienced by user in, 316
ReliableVideoExample document class, 321–323
removing
    chroma-key background, 257, 260–261
    3:2 pulldown, 298–303
Render Queue panel (After Effects)
    illustrated, 37
    rendering Web comp in, 277, 279
    using, 36–39, 42

rendering
  effects in Flash Player and processor, 31–32
  improved Apollo 13 source files, 301–303
  Web comp, 277, 279
Replace Method menu (Keylight filter), 274
resizing
  HDV comp within Web comp, 275
  video displays, 6–7
resolution for HDV format, 13
<root-layout> tag, 184–185, 187
RTMP (Real Time Messaging Protocol)
  duration of video playback and, 70
  estimating bandwidth over, 187–190
  HTTP vs., 65–70, 333–334
  multiple bitrate files delivered via, 296–297
  path for streaming FLV files, 88
  project delivery of FLV file seeked with, 281
  real-time streaming video and, 66
  viewing Flash files over, 66–70
runtime assets, 65

S

sample coding attributes and color, 223
sandbags, 21
Save Captured Clip dialog, 30
saving
  clip list, 26
  cue point settings, 129
scalable videos, 6–7
scaleMode parameter, 114–115
scan modes, 10
scene lists, 26
scouting locations, 8–9
Screen Matte view of Keylight filter, 270–271, 272–273
screen recording codecs, 57–58
Screen Video/Screen Video V2 codecs, 54, 57–58
scriptwriting, 260
search engine optimization (SEO), 82
security. See firewall security
seek/seeked, 67
Select Preview Frame dialog, 114
Select Skin dialog
  choosing modified skin, 153
  choosing player controls in, 89–90, 97
  for FLVPlayback AS2 component, 120
  for FLVPlayback AS3 component, 115
  opening from skin parameter, 115
  selecting FLVPlaybackCaptioning component from, 255
SEO (search engine optimization), 82
Serious Magic Ultra 2, 257, 260–261
server-side scripts
  determining connection speed between FMS application
    and Flash movie with, 188
  FLVPlayback component, 121
shot lists, 7, 8
shotgun microphones, 20
single CCD (charged coupled device), 17
skin parameter, 115–116, 120
skin SWF files, 85
skinAutoHide parameter, 116, 121
skinBackgroundAlpha parameter, 116
skinBackgroundColor parameter, 116

skins
  accommodating extra height for, 116, 121
  choosing AS3 FLVPlayback, 115–116
  choosing for FLV Player, 89–90
  modifying FLVPlayback, 150–156
  options for Flash Player 6 or 7, 102
  uploading skin SWF files, 116, 121
SMIL (Synchronized Multimedia Integration Language) files
  about, 179
  adding dynamic buffering to SMIL-driven FLVPlayback
    component, 201–209
  getting Help for, 187
  preparing, 184–187
  sample file for, 185–186
  unable to select in Content Path dialog, 189
  using FLV files with, 186
<smil> tag, 185
smoothing, dropped frames and, 182
software installation, 329–332
  Adobe FLVCheck tool, 331
  Captionate, 331
  downloading Flash Video encoders, 329–330
  public-domain video, 332
  QuickTime tools, 330–331
  time-limited versions for Adobe software, 329
Sonnati, Fabio, 201
Sony Digital BetaCam format, 14
Sony DVCAM format, 14
Sony HDCAM/HDCAM SR, 12
Sorenson Spark codec
  about, 53
  examples of bitrate with, 50, 51–52
  finding software that modifies settings for, 339
  formula for acceptable bitrates using, 49
  playing real-time streaming video file with, 162
  publishing content for Flash Player 6 or 7, 102
  required for banner ad code, 240
  strengths and weaknesses of, 54–55
Sorenson Squeeze
  converting AIFF to WAV files, 312
  creating Apollo 13 compression presets in, 307–313
  disabling deinterlacing for, 312
  downloading trial version of, 329–330
  features of, 339–340, 341
  Link Audio option in, 310, 311
  unable to export marker data, 136
  updating versions of, 131
  using adjusted video bitrate for, 309
  working with markers in, 131–136
  XML files used in, 135
Sorenson Squish and SquishNet, 343
source parameter, 116–117
source value, 191
source video files
  codecs for, 45–47
  defined, 45
  Flash Player, 74
  Flight of Apollo 11, 160
  ideal formats for, 44–45
  improving Apollo 13 documentary, 297–303
  supplied by client, 334–335
  troubleshooting playback of, 348

spatial compression, 48
standard definition (SD) video, 13–16
    DV formats and, 14
    aspect ratio and frame size for, 13–14
    media for, 14–16
Stearns, Geoff, 64, 82
storyboards, 8
streaming video. *See* real-time streaming video
<styling> node, 253
Super VHS format, 15–16
SWF files. *See also* ReliableVideo_AS3.swf file
    controlling playback of Flash Video content with, 64
    downloading and delivery of, 67
    HTTP protocol for Flash Video embedded in, 65
    inserting in Dreamweaver, 79–87
    locating origin of Dreamweaver, 85
    relationship among FLV, FLA and, 63
    requirements for Flash Video deployment, 293–294
    runtime assets and, 65
    technical requirements for VideoWords, 259–260
    troubleshooting problems playing on Web browser, 348
SWFObject code
    detecting Flash Player with, 82–85
    ExpressInstall feature with, 85–87
    found on companion DVD, 64, 82
    replacing videoContent element with, 325–326
    using progressive enhancement strategy with, 293
symbols, 151–152
Synchronized Multimedia Integration Language. *See* SMIL files

T

talent, 9
technical requirements
    Apollo 13 SWF file, 293–294
    banner ads, 239–240
    VideoWords, 259–260
telecine, 297–298
Telestream Episode, 330, 340, 341
templates for Apollo 13 documentary, 324
temporal compression, 48
3:2 pulldown, 298–303
three CCD (charged coupled device), 17
thumbnails
    adding to playlists, 230
    specifying in HTML document, 295
time property, 123
Timed Text XML, 252–256
Timeline window (After Effects), 276
tools
    Adobe FLVCheck, 331
    caption, 344
    downloading QuickTime, 330–331
    open source encoding, 343
    for removing chroma-key background, 260–261
totalTime parameter, 121
trace() action output, 216
transcribing captions, 254
transparency
    alpha channels and, 257
    viewing transparency grid behind images, 269–270
tripods and stands, 21

troubleshooting, 345–348
tunneled connections, 69
type property, 124

U

UGC (user-generated content), 71
uncompressed audio tracks, 58
UnhandledAsyncErrorEvent error message, 166
Unicode UTF-8 document encoding, 224
updating
    Dreamweaver, 82
    Sorenson Squeeze, 131
uploading
    files for deployment, 108–110
    skin SWF files, 116, 121

V

Var field (Property Inspector), 143
VBR (Variable Bit Rate)
    about, 61–62
    encoding files for HTTP delivery with, 68
    using, 338
version_1_0_1 parameter, 121
versions
    changing Flash CS3 component, 96
    picking Flash Player, 88
    updating Dreamweaver, 82
    updating Sorenson Squeeze, 131
VHS format, 16
video. *See* chroma-keyed video
Video 8 format, 16
video acquisition formats, 27
video bitrates. *See* bitrates
video cameras. *See also* camcorders
    capture sensors for, 16–17
    connecting to computer, 24
    digital cameras as, 16
    exposure controls for, 18
    hard drives and storage for footage, 21–22
    lens quality of, 17–18
    microphones, 18–20
    scouting locations with, 8
    tripods and stands for, 21
video capture. *See* capturing video
video clips
    bitrate of, 47–48
    creating comps from source, 34–35
    creating table of contents with navigation cue points, 122
    effect of maintainAspectRatio parameter on, 120
video codec identifiers, 54
video compression profiles, 59–62
video displays
    chroma-keyed video, 6
    floating, 4–5
    HDV, 13
    masked, 5
    nonfloating, 4
    resizable, 6–7
video encoders, 339–341. *See also* Adobe Flash CS3 Video Encoder
Video Import Wizard, 113

video index, 213–222
    about making, 213
    changing cue point's button color during playback,
        219–222
    creating buttons for each cue point, 216–219
    retrieving cue point data, 213–216
Video object, uses for, 159
video playback. *See also* cue points; deploying Flash Video
    reliably; placing Flash Video on Web pages
        changing video index button color during playback,
            219–222
        controlling behavior in SMIL file, 184–185
        controlling interactive banner ad, 242–248
        duration of content for, 70
        ensuring instant-start, 200
        navigating MediaPlayback component for Flash Players
            6 and 7, 102
        offering users instant start and, 180–181
        pausing video on load, 167–170
        placing FLVPlayback component dynamically on stage,
            144–149
        playing ads during video feature, 231–237
        protocol selection and online vs. offline, 70
        real-time streaming vs. prerecorded, 73–74
        synchronizing with event cue points, 122–123
        turning on captions when volume muted or set to 0, 256
        variations in connection speed and, 52–53
video players. *See* building own video player; Flash Player;
    FLVPlayback component
video production phase, 260
Video Properties dialog, 161
Video tab (Flash Video Encoding Settings dialog), 130, 284
Video tab (On2 Flix Pro), 140
videoContent element, 325–326
VideoPlayer class, 159, 178, 231
videoURL variable, 222
VideoWords class, 288
VideoWords presentation
    about, 258
    business objectives for, 258–259
    deinterlacing footage, 266
    editing video in Final Cut Pro, 264–265
    illustrated, 258
    production phases for, 260–261
    sampling green color from, 268, 269
    shooting video portion of, 261–264
    technical requirements for SWF files of, 259–260
View Options dialog (After Effects), 267
viewing
    all cue points once FLV file loads, 125
    files in AS2 FLVPlayback component, 118
    transparency grid behind images, 269–270

virtual cue points, 123
vixy.net flv2mpeg4, 343–344
VOB (video object) extension, 44
volume parameter, 117, 121

W

wardrobe, 9
WAV files, 312
Web browsers. *See* browsers
Web comp
    exporting to QuickTime video file, 276
    rendering, 277, 279
Web servers
    determining bandwidth from FLVPlayback component
        and, 190–199
    sample files on book's, 292
    uploading skin file with Flash movie SWF file, 121
Web sites, 79–110. *See also* placing Flash Video on Web page
    calculating video transfer rate and costs for, 75–76
    creating interactive comp ready for, 274–280
    delivery of video files via, 71–72
    deploying Flash Video on pages of, 64
    distributable content on high-volume, 71–72
    gathering files for deployment to Web page, 108–110
    HTML file format for, 64
    integrating SWF file with Dreamweaver, 79–87
    progressive enhancement strategy for, 293
    protected or long content on low-volume, 71
    using limited video on low-volume, 71
width specifications in SMIL files, 184–185, 187
Windows computers
    alpha channel color for, 283
    converting AIFF to WAV files on, 312
    Microsoft initialization of browser plug-ins, 83
    using Flash Switcher extension for Firefox on, 87
WordCollection class, 287–288

X

XLR connectors, 19
XML (eXtensible Markup Language)
    controlling captions with Timed Text, 252–256
    defining XML schema for Playlist class, 232
    determining XML schema for playlist, 223–224
    On2 Flix Pro's use of, 141
    specifying child nodes on playlist, 233
    storing cue point information in external files, 123
    used in Sorensen Squeeze, 135
    using for video playlist, 223
    XML schemas for captioned text, 248–249